THE LIFE AND WORK O[

VOLUME

1856–19

THE FORMATIVE YEARS

AND THE GREAT DISCOVERIES

Books by Ernest Jones

DAS PROBLEM DES HAMLET

HAMLET AND OEDIPUS

PAPERS ON PSYCHO-ANALYSIS
(5 volumes)

TREATMENT OF THE NEUROSES

DER ALPTRAUM

PSYCHO-ANALYSIS AND THE WAR NEUROSES
(with Abraham, Ferenczi and Simmel)

ESSAYS IN APPLIED PSYCHO-ANALYSIS
(2 volumes)

HOW THE MIND WORKS
(with Cyril Burt)

ZUR PSYCHOANALYSE DER CHRISTLICHEN RELIGION

ON THE NIGHTMARE

WHAT IS PSYCHO-ANALYSIS

Translations

CONTRIBUTIONS TO PSYCHO-ANALYSIS
by Sandor Ferenczi, M.D.

The Life and Work of

Sigmund

FREUD

volume

1

THE FORMATIVE YEARS
AND THE GREAT DISCOVERIES

1856-1900

ERNEST JONES MD

New York
BASIC BOOKS, INC.
Publishers

Copyright © 1953, by Ernest Jones;
Copyright © 1981 by Mervyn Jones
Manufactured in the United States of America
Library of Congress Catalog Card Number: 53–8700
ISBN: 465–04015–2 (3 vols.)
ISBN: 465–04016–0 (vol. 1)
ISBN: 465–04017–9 (vol. 2)
ISBN: 465–04018–7 (vol. 3)
DESIGNED BY MARSHALL LEE

To Anna Freud,

TRUE DAUGHTER OF AN IMMORTAL SIRE

Contents

Illustrations

Preface

THIS IS NOT INTENDED TO BE A POPULAR BIOGRAPHY OF FREUD: SEVERAL have been written already, containing serious distortions and untruths. Its aims are simply to record the main facts of Freud's life while they are still accessible, and—a more ambitious one—to try to relate his personality and the experiences of his life to the development of his ideas.

It is not a book that would have met with Freud's own approval. He felt he had already in many passages of his writings divulged enough of his personal life—which, indeed, he later regretted having done—and that he had a right to keep private what remained; the world should get on with making use of his contributions to knowledge and forget about his personality. But his repentance of the self-revelations came too late. Ill-natured people were already at work distorting isolated passages with the object of disparaging his character, and this could be rectified only by a still fuller exposition of his inner and outer life. Freud's family understandingly respected his wish for privacy, and indeed shared it. They often sheltered him from a merely inquisitive public. What changed their attitude later was the news of the many false stories invented by people who had never known him, stories which were gradually accumulating into a mendacious legend. They then decided to give me their wholehearted support in my endeavor to present as truthful an account of his life as is in my power.

It is generally agreed that great men by their very eminence forfeit the privilege granted to lesser mortals of having two lives, a public and a private one; often what they have withheld from the world proves to be of equal value to what they have proffered. Freud himself had often expressed regret about the paucity of detail recorded in the lives of great men so worthy of study and emulation. The world would have lost much if nothing were known of his own. What he gave to the world was not a completely rounded-off theory of the mind, a philosophy which could then perhaps be debated without any reference to its author, but a gradually opening vista, one occasionally blurred and then again reclarified. The insight he disclosed kept changing and developing in accord not only with his growing body of knowledge but also with the evolution of his own thought and outlook on life. Psychoanalysis, as is true of any other branch of science, can be profitably studied only as an historical evolution, never as a perfected body of knowledge, and its development was peculiarly and intimately bound up with the personality of its founder.

As we shall see, Freud took elaborate measures to secure his privacy, especially concerning his early life. On two occasions he completely destroyed all his correspondence, notes, diaries, and manuscripts. Both times there were, it is true, external reasons for the clearance: once just before he left his hospital quarters for a homeless existence, and the other time when he was radically altering the arrangements of his domicile. Fortunately the latter occasion, in 1907, was the last; after then he carefully preserved his correspondence. The former one he described in an interesting letter to his betrothed in a passage that follows; he was then twenty-eight years old (April 28, 1885).

"I have just carried out one resolution which one group of people, as yet unborn and fated to misfortune, will feel acutely. Since you can't guess whom I mean I will tell you: they are my biographers. I have destroyed all my diaries of the past fourteen years, with letters, scientific notes and the manuscripts of my publications. Only family letters were spared. Yours, my dear one, were never in danger. All my old friendships and associations passed again before my eyes and mutely met their doom (my thoughts are still with the history of Russia); all my thoughts and feelings about the world in general, and in particular how it concerned me, have been declared unworthy of survival. They must now be thought all over again. And I had jotted down a great deal. But the stuff simply enveloped me, as the sand does the Sphinx, and soon only my nostrils would show above the mass of paper. I cannot leave here and cannot die before ridding myself of the disturbing thought of who might come by the old papers. Besides, everything that fell before the decisive break in my life, before our coming together and my choice of calling, I have put behind me: it has long been dead and it shall not be denied an honorable burial. Let the biographers chafe; we won't make it too easy for them. Let each one of them believe he is right in his 'Conception of the Development of the Hero': even now I enjoy the thought of how they will all go astray."

While appreciating Freud's concluding chuckle in this interesting phantasy we nevertheless dare to hope that the last words may prove to have been exaggerated.

The task of compiling a biography of Freud's life is a dauntingly stupendous one. The data are so extensive that only a selection of them—though it is to be hoped a representative one—can be presented; there will remain ample room for more intensive studies of particular phases in his development. The reasons why I nevertheless yielded to the suggestion that I should undertake it were the considerations pressed on me that I was the only survivor of a small circle of co-workers (the "Committee") in constant intimate contact with Freud, that I had been a close friend for forty years and also during that period had played a central part in what has been called the "psychoanalytical movement." My having passed through the identical disciplines as Freud on the way to psychoanalysis—philosophy, neurology, disorders of speech, psychopathology, in that order—has helped me to follow the work of his pre-analytical period and its transition into the analytical one. Perhaps the fact of my being the only foreigner in that circle gave me an opportunity for some degree of greater objectivity than the others; immeasurably great as was my respect and admiration for both the personality and achievements of Freud, my own hero-worshipping propensities had been worked through before I encountered him. And Freud's extraordinary personal integrity—an outstanding feature of his personality—so impressed itself on those near to him that I can scarcely imagine a greater profanation of one's respect for him than to present an idealized portrait of someone remote from humanity. His claim to greatness, indeed, lies largely in the honesty and courage with which he struggled and overcame his own inner difficulties and emotional conflicts by means which have been of inestimable value to others.

There are several specially important sources of my indebtedness to other people in pursuing this work, without which the book would have been far poorer. First of all the Freud family, all of whom, including his late wife, have given me freely all possible information and literary material. Among the latter are more than 2,500 early family letters, the greater number written by Freud himself, includ-

ing a batch of twenty-five written between 1876 and 1894 to his favorite sister Rosa which were luckily retrieved from Budapest. By
far the most precious were some 1,500 love letters exchanged between
Freud and his future wife during the four years of their engagement.
A "Secret Record" they both wrote in those years had also been preserved.

The Fliess correspondence, which Marie Bonaparte daringly res-
cued from destruction, is a most important source book, the value of
which has been greatly heightened by Ernst Kris's illuminating preface and detailed editorial notes, and I wish to thank the Imago Publishing Press for their generous permission to quote freely from it and
Anna Freud for giving me access to the important unpublished part
of the correspondence.

Contemporary evidence such as has just been mentioned has, of
course, a very special value. Freud's memory, like everyone else's,
could be treacherous at times, and the contemporary data enable one
to render more precise, or even rectify, the accounts of events he
described many decades later.

To Siegfried and Suzanne Cassirer Bernfeld's painstaking researches, aided by their friends in Vienna, every student of Freud's
early life and environment will be permanently indebted. Furthermore, in the course of a regular correspondence they have generously
placed at my disposal all their stores of knowledge; discussion with
them has unravelled many obscure puzzles. I have to thank the Editors of the *Psychoanalytic Quarterly*, the *American Imago*, *Bulletin
of the Menninger Clinic*, and the *International Journal of Psycho-
Analysis* for permission to quote from the Bernfeld writings. Then I
extend my warm thanks to James Strachey, whose unrivalled familiarity with the literary aspects of the Freudian corpus gives him a
unique authority, for reading my manuscripts attentively and making a number of most useful suggestions; his meticulous accuracy has
saved me from many errors of detail. I also wish to thank the
Deuticke Verlag in Vienna for their courtesy in making available
their records of the royalties and sales of the Freud books from
1886 to 1950, and Mrs. Hans Brever, Dr. Brever's daughter-in-law, for
supplying a copy of an etching of him.

Last, and very far from least, I wish to thank my wife for her devoted day-to-day collaboration without which this book would assuredly not have been written.

THE LIFE AND WORK OF SIGMUND FREUD

VOLUME I

1856–1900

THE FORMATIVE YEARS

AND THE GREAT DISCOVERIES

I

Origins

(1 8 5 6 – 1 8 6 0)

SIGMUND FREUD WAS BORN AT 6:30 P.M. ON THE SIXTH OF MAY, 1856, at 117 Schlossergasse, Freiberg, in Moravia, and died on the twenty-third of September, 1939, at 20 Maresfield Gardens, London. That Schlossergasse has since been renamed Freudova ulice in his honor.

In his short autobiography (1925) Freud wrote: "I have reason to believe that my father's family were settled for a long period in the Rhineland (at Cologne), that in the fourteenth or fifteenth century they fled to the east from an anti-Semitic persecution, and that in the course of the nineteenth century they retraced their steps from Lithuania through Galicia to German Austria." [1] When the Nazis promulgated their "racial" doctrines he would, half jestingly, half sorrowfully, complain that the Jews had at least as much right to be on the Rhine as the Germans, having settled there in Roman days when the Germans were still engaged in pressing the Celts westward.

As a young man Freud was interested in his family history, but it is not known now what evidence he had for the Rhineland story, or for the choice of Cologne, beyond the historical knowledge of a Jewish settlement there in Roman times. It appeared to be curiously con-firmed by the discovery in 1910 of a fresco, signed "Freud of Cologne," in the Cathedral of Brixen, now Bressanone, in the South

---

[a] When, in 1931, the citizens of Freiberg, now called Příbor, affixed a memorial tablet on the house where Freud was born, it was discovered that on the local register the date of his birth was entered as March 6. This was probably a clerical error, the explanation of which concerns only the clerk who made it; there was no other entry before October. So, on enter-ing into the world the baby Freud was indirectly the occasion of one of the mental slips which, as Professor Freud forty years later, he was des-tined to elucidate.

1

Tirol. Freud and his brother went there to inspect it, but whether the painter was an ancestor, or indeed a Jew at all, has not been established.

The earliest one knows of the family is at Buczacz, a town a little to the east of Stanislav in Galicia.[2] Here it divided, one part going west to Moravia, the other to Roumania. Some contact was maintained between the two branches, and in his correspondence Freud makes several allusions to Romanian relatives who call on him in Vienna and Paris. One of them, Moritz Freud, married Freud's sister Marie, in March 1886.

Freud's great-grandfather was called Rabbi Ephraim Freud, and his grandfather Rabbi Schlomo Freud.[b] The latter died on February 21, 1856, i.e., shortly before Freud's birth; it was after him that he received his Jewish name of Schlomo.[3]

His father, Jakob Freud, who was born at Tysmenitz in Galicia on December 18, 1815,[c] and whose life extended to October 23, 1896,[4] was a merchant, engaged principally in the sale of wool. He married twice. Of the first marriage, contracted at the age of seventeen, there were two sons, Emanuel, born in 1832 or 1833, and Philipp, born in 1836. When he was forty, on July 29, 1855, he married Amalie Nathansohn in Vienna;[c†, 5] her span of life was even longer, from August 18, 1835, to September 12, 1930. With a father who lived to be eighty-one and a mother who lived to be ninety-five, therefore, Freud would normally be destined to a long life, and he certainly had vitality enough to transcend considerably the eighty-three years allotted to him had it not been for his cancerous affliction. Of Jakob Freud one knows he was slightly taller than his son, that he bore a resemblance to Garibaldi, and that he was of a gentle disposition, well loved by all in his family. Freud remarked that he was the duplicate of his father physically and to some extent mentally.[6] He also described him in rather Micawber-like terms as being "always hopefully expecting something to turn up."[7] At the time of his second marriage he was already a grandfather, his elder son, who lived near by,

[b] The word Rabbi was often only a title of politeness, and does not necessarily imply an ecclesiastical status.

[c] After his marriage he and his wife changed from the Jewish to the Gregorian calendar, and he chose April 1 for his birthday.

[c†] Several writers on Freud have given this date as 1851, evidently misinterpreting a passage in *The Interpretation of Dreams* where that date occurs, but means something else in his life. [5†] It would have been strange if such a fruitful woman had borne no children for the first five years of her marriage.

being by then in the twenties and himself the father of a one-year-old son, John, to be soon followed by a daughter, Pauline. The little Sigmund, therefore, was born an uncle, one of the many paradoxes his young mind had to grapple with.

Of the mother's lively personality the present writer has many recollections, both from Vienna and from Ischl, where she used to spend every summer—and to enjoy card parties at an hour when most old ladies would be in bed. The Mayor of Ischl would greet her birthday (incidentally, the same day as the Emperor's) with a ceremonious gift of flowers, though on her eightieth birthday he jokingly announced that these semiroyal visits of his would in future take place only every ten years. When she was ninety she declined the gift of a beautiful shawl, saying it would "make her look too old." When she was ninety-five, six weeks before she died, her photograph appeared in the newspaper; her comment was: "A bad reproduction; it makes me look a hundred." It was strange to a young visitor to hear her refer to the great Master as *"mein goldener Sigi"* and evidently there was throughout a close attachment between the two. When young she was slender and pretty and she retained to the last her gaiety, alertness, and sharp-witted intelligence. She came from Brody in Northeast Galicia near to the Russian frontier.[d] She spent part of her girlhood in Odessa, where two brothers had settled. Her parents had moved to Vienna when she was still a child, and she had vivid memories of the 1848 revolution there; she had preserved a picture with shot holes dating from that event. Under twenty at her marriage, she bore her first-born, Sigmund, at the age of twenty-one, and subsequently five daughters and two other sons; in order: Julius, who died at the age of eight months; Anna, born when Freud was two and a half years old (on December 31, 1858), Rosa, Marie (Mitzi), Adolfine (Dolfi), Paula, Alexander, the last-named being just ten years younger than Sigmund. All who grew up married, with the exception of one daughter, Adolphine, who stayed with the mother. What with grandchildren and great-grandchildren, the Freud clan became a considerable size, so plainly he came of a prolific stock.

From his father Freud inherited his sense of humor, his shrewd skepticism about the uncertain vicissitudes of life, his custom of

---

d Helen Puner⁵ would trace Amalie's descent from "a famous Talmudic scholar, the eighteenth-century Nathan Halevy Charmatz of Brody," but none of the many Jewish authorities I have consulted have any knowledge of this famous scholar. Apparently he was a rich merchant who was a patron of scholars (Bernfeld).

pointing a moral by quoting a Jewish anecdote, his liberalism and free thinking, and perhaps his uxoriousness. From his mother came, according to him, his "sentimentality." [9] This word, still more ambiguous in German, should probably be taken to mean his temperament, with the passionate emotions of which he was capable. His intellect was his own.

Freud had five uncles. Since Freud attached much importance to neuropathic heredity, much more than we do nowadays, the following details should be mentioned. One of the uncles, a younger brother of his father, who lived in Breslau and whom Freud knew very slightly, had four children. Only one of them was healthy. Of the others one was a hydrocephalic imbecile; another, a promising young man, became insane at the age of nineteen, as did also a sister in the twenties. A son of the Uncle Josef whose conflict with the law turned his brother's hair gray,[e,10] and who lived in Vienna, died of epilepsy. Freud commented on these facts as follows: "So I have to admit to having a regular 'neuropathological taint,' as it is called. Fortunately very little of it has shown itself in our family, except that Rosa and I have a pronounced tendency to neurasthenia." [11]

Uncle Josef was the only one he mentions by name. Incidentally, this was a name that often played a part in his life. His student years (1875-1883) were spent in the Kaiser Josefstrasse in Vienna, Josef Paneth ("my friend Josef" in *The Interpretation of Dreams*) was his friend and colleague in the Institute of Physiology and his successor there, and Josef Breuer was for years an important personage to him—the man who led him along the path to psychoanalysis. It was Joseph Popper-Lynkeus who had come nearest to anticipating him in his theory of dreams. Above all, the biblical Joseph as the famous interpreter of dreams was the figure behind which Freud often disguised himself in his own dreams.[12]

At birth the baby had such an abundance of black ruffled hair that his young mother nicknamed him her "little blackamoor." [13] In adult life his hair and eyes were very dark, but his complexion was not swarthy. He was born in a caul, an event which was believed to ensure him future happiness and fame. And when one day an old woman whom the young mother encountered by chance in a pastry shop fortified this by informing her that she had brought a great man into the world, the proud and happy mother believed firmly in the prediction. Thus the hero's garb was in the weaving at the cradle

e He could only have been fined for this, since the Austrian police archives contain no record of imprisonment.

itself. But Freud, the skeptic, did not wear it lightly. He wrote: "Such prophecies must be made very often; there are so many happy and expectant mothers, and so many old peasant women and other old women who, since their mundane powers have deserted them, turn their eyes towards the future; and the prophetess is not likely to suffer for her prophecies." [14] Nevertheless, the story seems to have been repeated so often that when, at the age of eleven, it was strengthened by a new prophecy, he was willing to be slightly impressed. This he described later as follows.

"One evening, at a restaurant in the Prater, where my parents were accustomed to take me when I was eleven or twelve years of age, we noticed a man who was going from table to table and, for a small sum, improvizing verses upon any subject given to him. I was sent to bring the poet to our table, and he showed his gratitude. Before asking for a subject he threw off a few rhymes about myself, and told us that if he could trust his inspiration I should probably one day become a 'Minister.' I can still distinctly remember the impression produced by this second prophecy. It was in the days of the 'bourgeois Ministry'; my father had recently brought home the portraits of the bourgeois university graduates, Herbst, Giskra, Unger, Berger, and others, and we illuminated the house in their honor. There were even Jews among them; so that every diligent Jewish schoolboy carried a ministerial portfolio in his satchel. The impression of that time must be responsible for the fact that, until shortly before I went to the University, I wanted to study jurisprudence, and changed my mind only at the last moment." [15] In a dream he described years later, he appeared as a Cabinet Minister at a time when that particular ambition must have completely vanished from his waking thoughts; in adult life he had no more than the average interest in politics and modes of government.

Another effect of the mother's pride and love for her first-born left a more intense, indeed indelible, impression on the growing boy. As he wrote later: "A man who has been the indisputable favorite of his mother keeps for life the feeling of a conqueror, that confidence of success that often induces real success." [16] This self-confidence, which was one of Freud's prominent characteristics, was only rarely impaired, and he was doubtless right in tracing it to the security of his mother's love. It is worth mentioning that, as one would expect, he was fed at the breast.

In the household there was also a Nannie, old and ugly, with the nurse's normal mixture of affection for children and severity towards their transgressions; she was capable and efficient. Freud several times refers in his writings to what he called "that prehistoric old woman." [17] He was fond of her and used to give her all his pennies, and he refers to the memory of the latter fact as a screen memory;[f] perhaps it got connected with her dismissal for theft later on when he was two and a half years old. She was a Czech and they conversed in that language, although Freud forgot it afterwards.[18] More important, she was a Catholic and used to take the young boy to attend the church services. She implanted in him the ideas of Heaven and Hell, and probably also those of salvation and resurrection. After returning from church the boy used to preach a sermon at home and expound God's doings.[19]

The half-brother Emanuel's family lived so near and was so intimate that the two families might be regarded as almost one.[g] The psychological complications arising from this are evident. Close by there lived also a family by the name of Fluss, whose importance will appear later. The parents were close friends of Freud's parents. We know of five children, three boys (Alfred, Richard, and Emil) and two girls. One of the latter, Gisela, we shall presently meet. The family weathered the economic storm of 1859, remained in Freiberg, and became affluent. They moved, however, to Vienna in 1878, and the family friendship was unbroken.

Nearly all the data about Freud's childhood are derived from numerous allusions in his writings. Among them is an extremely valuable one which is anonymous. It is the analysis of a screen memory published in 1899 as part of the analysis of a supposed ex-patient who may be called Mr. Y,[21] and Dr. Bernfeld's perspicacity has revealed it as certainly a part of Freud's own analysis which he chose to ascribe to someone else.[22] It was not the only occasion of anonymous writing; his first essay on Moses (1914) was another example;[23] so was the short paper on Börne (1920).[24] The insight displayed by the so-called patient, the way he imparts as fresh information matters that would have been long familiar in his alleged analysis, the highly characteristic expressions and style he employs, and the detailed correspondence of the facts related with the known ones of Freud's earliest surroundings make its provenance quite certain.

Freud had only a few conscious memories of his first three years, as

---

[f] An unimportant memory that is recalled in place of an important one associated with it.

[g] I know of no evidence for Kris's statement that they lived "under one roof";[20] the indications are to the contrary.

indeed of his first six or seven, but in his self-analysis he undoubtedly recovered a great many of the important ones that had been forgotten; he mentions that he was forty-two when he did so. Among the forgotten ones was some knowledge he then had of the Czech language. Among the (consciously) remembered ones are a few, banal enough in themselves, which are of interest only in standing out in the sea of amnesia. One was of penetrating into his parents' bedroom out of (sexual) curiosity and being ordered out by an irate father.[25]

At the age of two he would still wet his bed and it was his father, not his indulgent mother, who reproved him. He recollected saying on one of these occasions: "Don't worry, Papa. I will buy you a beautiful new red bed in Neutitschein" (the chief town of the district).[26] It was from such experiences that was born his conviction that typically it was the father who represented to his son the principles of denial, restraint, restriction, and authority; the father stood for the reality principle, the mother for the pleasure principle. There is no reason to think, however, that his own father was sterner than fathers usually are. On the contrary, all the evidence points to his having been kindly, affectionate, and tolerant, though just and objective. If, however, like other boys at that age he regarded his father as "the most powerful, wisest and wealthiest man," [27] he was soon to be disillusioned in a specially painful manner.

An incident which he could not recollect was of slipping from a stool when he was two years old,[h] and receiving a violent blow on the lower jaw from the edge of the table he was exploring for some delicacy. It was a severe cut which necessitated sewing up, and it bled profusely; he retained the scar throughout life.[i]

A more important occurrence, just before this, was his young brother's death when Freud was nineteen months old and the little Julius only eight months. Before the newcomer's birth the infant Freud had had sole access to his mother's love and milk, and he had to learn from the experience how strong the jealousy of a young child

[h] In one account Freud gives of this he says he was between two and three years of age,[28] in another "not yet two." [29] The former is the more trustworthy.

[i] Helen Puner, in her book on Freud, would connect this injury with his later cancer of the jaw.[30] But she is in error when she adds: "The cancer struck the area of the jaw he had injured as a child," since the former was in the upper jaw on the right side, whereas the scar was on the lower jaw on the left side (personal observation when Freud was shaved for an operation).

can be. In a letter to Fliess (1897) he admits the evil wishes he had against his rival and adds that their fulfilment in his death had aroused self-reproaches, a tendency which had remained ever since.[j, 31] In the same letter he relates how his libido had been aroused towards his mother, between the ages of two years and two and a half, on the occasion of seeing her naked. So we see that the infant Freud was early assailed by the great problems of birth, love, and death.

There is every reason to think that the most important person in Freud's early childhood was, next to his parents, his nephew John, a boy only a year older than himself. They were constant companions, and there are indications that their mutual play was not always entirely innocent. Affection and hostility between them alternated, as one would expect, but it is certain that, at least on Sigmund's side, the feelings aroused were much more intense than is usual. He wrote later, when speaking of his boyhood ideals, Hannibal and Marshal Masséna: "Perhaps the development of this martial ideal may be traced yet farther back, to the first three years of my childhood, to wishes which my alternately friendly and hostile relations with a boy a year older than myself must have evoked in the weaker of the two playmates." [33] John was naturally the stronger of the two, but little Sigmund stood up well to him and gave as good as he got. He was certainly endowed with a fair amount of pugnacity, though this became quite subdued with maturity; one could know him pretty well without suspecting what fires burned, or had burned, below his contained demeanor.

When Freud came to review his childhood he repeatedly indicated how his ambivalence towards John had conditioned the development of his character. "Until the end of my third year we had been inseparable; we had loved each other and fought each other, and, as I have already hinted, this childish relation has determined all my later feelings in my intercourse with persons of my own age. My nephew John has since then had many incarnations, which have revivified first one and then another aspect of a character that is ineradicably fixed in my unconscious memory. At times he must have treated me very badly, and I must have opposed my tyrant courageously. . . ." [34] Furthermore: "An intimate friend and a hated enemy have always been indispensable to my emotional life; I have always been able to create them anew, and not infrequently my child-

[j] In the light of this confession it is astonishing that Freud should write twenty years later how almost impossible it is for a child to be jealous of a newcomer if he is *only* fifteen months old when the latter arrives.[32]

ish ideal has been so closely approached that friend and enemy have coincided in the same person; but not simultaneously, of course, as was the case in my early childhood." [35]

He soon learnt that this companion, of nearly his own age, was his nephew, the son of his brother Emanuel, and that he addressed father Jakob as grandfather. The older and stronger boy should surely have been the uncle, not he. Freud's mental endowment was doubtless native to him, but the complexity of the family relationships must have afforded a powerful incentive to his budding intelligence, to his curiosity and interest. From earliest days he was called upon to solve puzzling problems, and problems of the greatest import to him emotionally. For that reason it is worth while laying further stress on that complexity and trying to imagine what it must have signified to the growing child's mind.

When in later life (probably at nineteen) his half-brother Emanuel remarked to him that the family had really consisted of three generations—that is, that Jakob should be Sigmund's grandfather—Freud found the remark illuminating.[36] It evidently accorded with his own early feelings. The problem of the family relationships came to a head with the birth of the first sister, Anna, when he was just two and a half years old. How and why had this usurper appeared, with whom he would have once again to share his mother's warm and previously exclusive love? The changes in her figure[37] told the observant child the source of the baby, but not how it had all come about. And at the same moment, when his mother was in bed with the new baby, his Nannie disappeared. As he learnt later, she had been caught stealing his money and toys, and Philipp had insisted on her being apprehended;[k] she was sent to jail for ten months.[38] Having reason to suspect Philipp's implication in the disappearance, he asked him what had become of her and received the jokingly ambiguous answer: *"Sie ist eingekastelt."* An adult would have understood

---

[k] Most people, including even Dr. Bernfeld, have assumed that this anecdote, related in *The Interpretation of Dreams*, referred to the elder brother, Emanuel. Emanuel was twenty-three years older than Freud, and Philipp just twenty. In a letter to Fliess, however, he says twice over that the half-brother in question, twenty years older than himself, was Philipp.

One would remark on the coincidence (?) that the boy from whom Freud derived early sexual knowledge in the Freiberg period was also called Philipp. It seems odd that he should have remembered, and also troubled to record, this name, but it was from his brother Philipp that he had learned something about pregnancy.[38†]

this as meaning: "She has been locked up in prison," but the child's mind took it more literally as "she has been put in a chest." This connects with a fascinating analysis Freud made forty years later of an apparently unintelligible memory from his childhood.[39] He saw himself standing before a chest and tearfully demanding something of his half-brother, Philipp, who is holding it open. Then his mother, notably slender (i.e., not pregnant), comes into the room, presumably from the street. At first he supposed the memory must refer to some teasing on the brother's part, interrupted by his mother's appearance. The psychoanalysis of the memory, however, gave a very different picture of the episode. He had missed his mother, who had probably gone out for a walk, and so had anxiously turned to the naughty brother who had put his Nannie in a chest, and begged him to release his mother from the same fate. The brother obligingly opened the chest to reassure him that there was no mother there, whereupon he began to cry. Further analysis revealed that the chest was a womb symbol and that the anxious request to the brother concerned not merely the mother's momentary absence but the more agitating question whether another unwelcome little brother had been put into that all-important locality. Philipp was the one who had to do with putting people in "chests" and the boy had formed the phantasy that his half-brother and his mother, who were of the same age, had cooperated in producing the usurping Anna.

The experience seems to have had a lasting effect, since Freud never liked that sister. But he evidently reconciled himself to such occurrences, and the next one drew out the affectionate side of his nature; Rosa became his favorite sister, with Adolfine (Dolfi) a good second.

As seen through a child's eyes it was not unnatural that he should pair off Jakob and Nannie, the two forbidding authorities. Then came Emanuel with his wife, and there remained Philipp and Amalie who were just of an age.[39]† All this appeared very tidy and logical, but still there was the awkward fact that Jakob, not Philipp, slept in the same bed as Amalie. It was all very puzzling.

What we have called the logical pairing off would have a deeper psychological advantage and motivation. By removing his father to a more remote order in the household he would absolve him from rivalry about the mother and from the mischief of creating unwelcome children. There is every reason to think that Freud's conscious attitude to his father consistently remained, despite the latter's representing authority and frustration, one of affection, admiration, and respect. Any hostile component was thoroughly displaced on to the figures of Philipp and John.[40] It therefore came as a great shock to Freud when forty years later he discovered his own Oedipus complex, and had to admit to himself that his unconscious had taken a very different attitude towards his father from that of his consciousness. It was no chance that this insight came about only a year or two after his father's death.

In tracing, as best we can, the genesis of Freud's original discoveries, we may therefore legitimately consider that the greatest of them—namely, the universality of the Oedipus complex—was potently facilitated by his own unusual family constellation, the spur it gave to his curiosity, and the opportunity it afforded of a complete repression.

Freud never alluded in his writings to Emanuel's wife.[1] Pauline, his niece, was on the other hand of some emotional significance. In the screen memory that Dr. Bernfeld unraveled, an amorous attachment to her is manifest, and beyond that an unconscious phantasy of her being raped by John and himself together. Freud himself related how he and his nephew used to treat the little girl cruelly,[42] and one may assume that this included some erotic component—whether manifest or not. The latter feature is the first sign that Freud's sexual constitution was not exclusively masculine after all, to "hunt in couples" means sharing one's gratification with someone of one's own sex.

This memory was part of a rural scene. From it and other ones it is evident that the boy Sigmund was already affected by the beauty of nature. The impressions of country scenes made at this early age were lasting. Throughout life his appreciation of landscape afforded one of his keenest aesthetic enjoyments. He was brought up close to meadows; and the forest itself, where he used to toddle with his beloved father, was but half a mile away.

Freiberg is a quiet little town in the southeast of Moravia, near the borders of Silesia, and 150 miles northeast of Vienna. Příbor, to give it its Czech name since it was of Czech origin, was founded in 1215 by the Earl Yaroslav of Sternberk—the man who was to defeat the Tartars in the year 1241; King Vladislav II had proclaimed it a free town in 1493. It was one of a trio, with Breisach and Brünn, that were proud of the stand they had made against the Swedes in the Thirty Years' War. Czech was the predominant language, but

[1] Except when she was an old lady.[41]

the Jews would speak German (or Yiddish) among themselves.

The town was dominated by the steeple, 200 feet high, of St. Mary's Church, which boasted the best chimes of the province. The population, which at the time of Freud's birth was about five thousand, was almost all Roman Catholic, only 2 per cent being Protestants and an equal number of Jews. A child would soon observe that his family did not belong to the majority and never attended the church, so that the chimes rang out not brotherly love but hostility to the little circle of non-believers. Perhaps there was an echo of these chimes in that night long after when his sleep was disturbed by church bells so that, to put an end to the annoyance, he dreamed that the Pope was dead.

For the man responsible for the welfare of this little family group the times were more than anxious. Jakob Freud was a wool merchant and, for the past twenty years, textile manufacture, the town's staple source of income, had been on the downgrade. As elsewhere in Central Europe, the introduction of machines had increasingly threatened handwork. In the forties the new Northern Railway from Vienna had by-passed Freiberg, dislocating trade there and leading to considerable unemployment. The inflation following the Restoration of 1851 increased the poverty of the town further and by 1859, the year of the Austro-Italian war, it was pretty well ruined.

Jakob's business was directly affected. But there were still more sinister portents to add to his anxiety. One result of the 1848-1849 revolution had been to establish Czech nationalism as a power in Austrian politics and consequently to fan Czech hatred against the German-Austrians, the ruling class in Bohemia and Moravia. This easily turned against the Jews, who were German in language and education; in fact, the revolution in Prague had started with Czech riots against Jewish textile manufacturers. The economic distress combined with the rising nationalism to turn against the hereditary scapegoats, the Jews. Even in little Freiberg the grumbling clothmakers, Czech to a man, began to hold the Jewish textile merchants responsible for their plight. No actual attack appears to have been made on them or their property, but in a small and backward community one could never feel sure.

Even had all this not been so, the educational facilities in a small and remote decaying town did not hold much prospect of a peasant woman's prediction of young Sigmund's future greatness being fulfilled. Jakob had every reason to think that there was no future for him and his in Freiberg. So in 1859, when Sigmund was just three years old, the ancient march of the family—Palestine, Rome, Cologne, Lithuania, Galicia, Moravia—was resumed, as he himself had to resume it once more nearly eighty years later. He remembered the long ride in the horse-drawn vehicle and his first sight of a railway. This took him from his beautifully rolling country with its meadows, hills, and forests to the town of Leipzig. Jakob spent a year there, doubtless sounding the chances of trade, and then they moved on to Vienna.

On the way to Leipzig the train passed through Breslau, where Freud saw gas jets for the first time; they made him think of souls burning in hell! [43] From this journey also dated the beginning of a "phobia" of traveling by train,[44] from which he suffered a good deal for about a dozen years (1887-1899), before he was able to dispel it by analysis. It turned out to be connected with the fear of losing his home (and ultimately his mother's breast)—a panic of starvation which must have been in its turn a reaction to some infantile greed. Traces of it remained in later life in the form of slightly undue anxiety about catching trains.

On the journey from Leipzig to Vienna, a year later, Freud had occasion to see his mother naked: an awesome fact which forty years later he related in a letter to Fliess[45]—but in Latin! Curiously enough he gives his age then as between two and two and a half, whereas he was in fact four years old on that journey. One must surmise that the memories of two such experiences had got telescoped.

Emanuel, with his wife and two children and his brother Philipp, went to Manchester, England, where his knowledge of cloth manufacture stood him in good stead and brought him some success. His half-brother never ceased to envy him for this migration,[46] and England remained to him for life his country of preference. It is good to think that his last days were spent there, cheered by the warm reception and comfort that awaited him.

Freud has taught us that the essential foundations of character are laid down by the age of three and that later events can modify but not alter the traits then established. This was the age when he was taken away or, when one thinks of the circumstances, one might almost say torn away from the happy home of his early childhood, and one is drawn at this moment to review what little we know of that period, to ponder on its influence on his later development.

Speculation is out of place here. We gather that he appears to have been a normal sturdy child, and we can only note the few features that distinguish his circumstances from those of the average run of children. They are few, but important.

He was the eldest child, at least of his mother, and for a time therefore the center of what may be called the inner family. This is in itself a fact of significance, since an eldest child differs, for better or worse, from other children. It may give such a child a special sense of importance and responsibility or it may imbue him with a feeling of inferiority as being—until another child appears—the feeblest member of his little community. There is no doubt that the former was true in Freud's case; responsibility for all his relatives and friends became a central feature of his character. This favorable turn was evidently secured by his mother's love and, indeed, adoration. Self-confidence was built up to a degree that was very seldom shaken.

On the other hand, this precious possession could not be altogether taken for granted. It was challenged, and he had to cope with the challenge. Although he was the only child, there was his nephew John who by rights should take a second place, but paradoxically was older and stronger. It needed all his vigor to contend with him and to maintain his position of primacy.

Darker problems arose when it dawned on him that some man was even more intimate with his mother than he was. Before he was two years old, for the second time another baby was on the way, and soon visibly so. Jealousy of the intruder, and anger for whoever had seduced his mother into such an unfaithful proceeding, were inevitable. Discarding his knowledge of the sleeping conditions in the house, he rejected the unbearable thought that the nefarious person could be his beloved and perfect father. To preserve his affection for him he substituted his half-brother Philipp, against whom there was, besides, the other grudge of having robbed him of his Nannie. All this seemed more likely and certainly less unpleasant. It was early days to grapple with the inevitable problem of reality. And when the world that mattered was one where phantasy seemed more rational than fact, and appearance more congruent than actuality, then indeed it called for every effort.

It was an emotional solution he had found, not an intellectual one, and from the very beginning of his life to the end Freud was never satisfied with emotional solutions only. He had a veritable passion to *understand*. At the outset this need to understand was stimulated in a way from which there was no escape. His intelligence was given a task from which he never flinched till, forty years later, he found the solution in a fashion that made his name immortal.

II

Boyhood and Adolescence

(1 8 6 0 – 1 8 7 3)

WE KNOW LESS OF THIS PERIOD OF FREUD'S LIFE THAN OF HIS CHILD-
hood. He had not the same motive to investigate it or write about it
as he had with his early development when he embarked on it at the
age of forty-one.[a] What little we know comes from his mother and
sister[b] and from occasional remarks of his in later life. From these
impressions one gets a picture of him as having been a "good" boy,
not an unruly one, and one much given to reading and study. His
mother's favorite, he possessed the self-confidence that told him he
would achieve something worth while in life, and the ambition to do
so, though for long the direction this would take remained uncertain.

The early years in Vienna were evidently very unpleasant. Freud
said later that he remembered very little of the early period between
the ages of three and seven: "They were hard times and not worth
remembering." He greatly missed the freedom and enjoyments of
the countryside, which he was not to see again for thirteen years.
There were the parks in Vienna, and later on occasional visits to a
spa, Roznau, in Moravia, necessitated by his mother's tuberculosis,
but all that was very different from the open country where he had
once been so happy. It gave a good reason for his dislike of Vienna,
to which two further powerful motives were added later.[c]

Freud's continuous memories began at the age of seven. There are
only five incidents in the years between three and seven of which we

---

[a] From memory Freud gives forty-two,[1] but the contemporary evidence is
decisive (see Chap. XIV).
[b] But one dare not attribute absolute accuracy to all of her memories, and
many of her dates are demonstrably incorrect.[2]
[c] Anti-Semitism and the reception of his work.

have any record. The first, related by his mother, was of his soiling a chair with his dirty hands, but consoling her with the promise that he would grow up a great man and then buy her another[d]—another example of what is nowadays called a restituting tendency, akin to the earlier promise to his father to buy him a red bed. It is an indication that love was stronger than aggression. The next, and more interesting one, he related himself.[3] It was almost his sole recollection from this time. When he was five years old his father handed him and his little sister a book (a narrative of a journey through Persia) with the mischievous suggestion that they amuse themselves by tearing out its colored plates: certainly not an austere father. It was a queer form of education, but it had an effect. Freud subsequently traced to this episode the earliest passion of his life—that of collecting and possessing books—but he also calls it a "screen memory" for something more primitive. Another memory was of his mother assuring him at the age of six that we were made of earth and therefore must return to earth.[4] When he expressed his doubts of this unwelcome statement she rubbed her hands together and showed him the dark fragments of epidermis that came there as a specimen of the earth we are made of. His astonishment was unbounded and for the first time he captured some sense of the inevitable. As he put it: "I slowly acquiesced in the idea I was later to hear expressed in the words 'Thou owest nature a death.'" This misquotation from Shakespeare's *Henry IV* (Part I, Act V, Sc. 1, and Part II, Act III, Sc. 2) is not because "nature" occurs in place of "God" with Goethe and several classical authors, since Freud ascribes it to Shakespeare in a letter to Fliess.[5] It may have been influenced by *Tristram Shandy*, of which Freud was particularly fond, since Sterne there makes the same substitution (Book V, Ch. 3).[e]

Another incident refers to the conscious recollection of having urinated (deliberately) in his parents' bedroom at the age of seven or eight, and being reprimanded by his father, who testily permitted himself the exclamation: "That boy will never amount to anything,"[7] an estimate alien to his father's usual pride in his son. He wrote about it: "This must have been a terrible affront to my ambi-

[d] According to Anna Bernays. It is probably a distortion of the bed story (see p. 7).

[e] An example of an *unconscious* mistake in quotation is that from the Emperor Josef's monument cited in the *Non vixit* dream in *The Interpretation of Dreams*. Wittels offered an ingenious interpretation of it which Freud accepted.[6]

tion, for allusions to this scene occur again and again in my dreams, and are constantly coupled with enumerations of my accomplishments and successes, as if I wanted to say: 'You see, I have amounted to something after all.' " The last memory was an anxiety dream, at the age of six or seven, which Freud analyzed many years later and traced to a repressed incestuous wish. It seems to have been the last severe anxiety dream he ever experienced.[8]

The first abode in Vienna was in the Pfeffergasse, a small street in the quarter (largely Jewish) called the Leopoldstadt, near to fields and woods that adjoined the Prater. The rapid growth of the family led to a move to a larger flat in the Kaiser Josefstrasse, where they lived from 1875 to 1885. It consisted of living room, a dining room, three bedrooms, and a "cabinet." [f] The sister says: "We had many rooms and were fairly prosperous." But the accommodation does not seem excessive for eight persons. Furthermore, one knows that the father often received financial assistance from his wife's family, so that the word "prosperous" is doubtless a euphemistic expression. There was no bathroom, but once a fortnight a couple of strong carriers brought a large wooden tub, with several kegs of hot and cold water, into the kitchen and fetched them away the next day. When the children were old enough, however, their mother would take them to one of the many public baths. The "cabinet," a long and narrow room separated from the rest of the flat, with a window looking on to the street, was allotted to Sigmund; it contained a bed, chairs, shelf, and writing desk. There he lived and worked until he became an interne at the hospital; all through the years of his school and university life the only thing that changed in it was an increasing number of crowded bookcases. In his teens he would even eat his evening meal there so as to lose no time from his studies. He had an oil lamp to himself, while the other bedrooms had only candles.

An illustration of the esteem in which he and his studies were held in the family is a sad story related by his sister. When she was eight years old their mother, who was very musical, got her to practise the piano, but, though it was at a certain distance from the "cabinet," the sound disturbed the young student so much that he insisted on the piano being removed; and removed it was. So none of the family received any musical education, any more than Freud's children did later. Freud's aversion to music was one of his well-

f This account of the accommodation comes from his sister Anna and apparently applies to the second flat, though she does not make this quite explicit.

known characteristics. One well remembers the pained expression on his face on entering a restaurant or beer garden where there was a band and how quickly his hands would go over his ears to drown the sound. Yet, as we shall see, this is not the full story.

After the first lessons with his mother, Freud's father took charge of his education before sending him to a private school.[9] Though self-taught, he was evidently a man of parts, above the average in intelligence and outlook. If the account is true, then the good progress of the boy would be evidence of the satisfactory relationship between him and his father. He related that from the age of twelve he used to accompany his father in walks in the neighborhood of Vienna.[10] In that time there was not the interest in sport and athletics that has since become so general in Central Europe, and doubtless the main exercise he indulged in was that of walking, especially on mountains. He remarked later that going for walks alone had been his chief pleasure in his student days.[11] He also said he was fond of skating,[12] but in those days this was a very primitive art. He was a good swimmer and never missed an opportunity of bathing in lake or sea. He mentioned that he only once sat on a horse and did not feel comfortable in the situation.[13] But he was assuredly a good walker. When he was sixty-five he took part in a walking tour in the Harz Mountains with half a dozen colleagues who were a quarter of a century younger, and he excelled all of us both in speed and in endurance.

The only difference between father and son seems to have been on an occasion when Freud, then seventeen years old, indulged his propensity for buying books to such an extent that he was unable to pay for them.[14] His father was not at all the strict paternal type then so common, and he used to consult the children over various decisions to be made. These discussions took place in what was called the "Family Council." An example was the choice of a name for the younger son. It was Sigmund's vote for the name of Alexander that was accepted, his selection being based on Alexander the Great's generosity and military prowess; to support his choice he recited the whole story of the Macedonian's triumphs.[15]

On the other hand, the father was after all a Jewish patriarch and so demanded corresponding respect. Moritz Rosenthal, the pianist, tells a story of how one day he was having an argument with his father in the street when they encountered Jakob Freud, who laughingly reproved him thus: "What, are you contradicting your father?

My Sigmund's little toe is cleverer than my head, but he would never dare to contradict me!" [16]

Of Freud's religious background not a great deal is known. There was, of course, the Catholic Nannie,[i] and perhaps her terrifying influence contributed to his later dislike of Christian beliefs and ceremonies. His father must have been brought up as an orthodox Jew, and Freud himself was certainly conversant with all Jewish customs and festivals. His children have assured me that their grandfather had become a complete freethinker, but there is some evidence to the contrary. He was undoubtedly a liberal-minded man of progressive views and it is not likely that he kept up orthodox Jewish customs after migrating to Vienna. On the other hand, Ernst Freud possesses a Bible which his grandfather presented to his father (Freud) on the latter's thirty-fifth birthday when Jakob was seventy-five years old. The inscription, in Hebrew, runs as follows:

"My dear Son,

"It was in the seventh year of your age that the spirit of God began to move you to learning. I would say the spirit of God speaketh to you: 'Read in My book; there will be opened to thee sources of knowledge and of the intellect.' It is the Book of Books; it is the well that wise men have digged and from which lawgivers have drawn the waters of their knowledge.

"Thou hast seen in this Book the vision of the Almighty, thou hast heard willingly, thou hast done and hast tried to fly high upon the wings of the Holy Spirit. Since then I have preserved the same Bible. Now, on your thirty-fifth birthday I have brought it out from its retirement and I send it to you as a token of love from your old father."

Freud's mother too preserved some belief in the Deity. Thus when he was about to set up in practice as a family man she called down the blessing of Almighty God on his endeavors.[17]

When Freud spoke of his having been greatly influenced by his early reading of the Bible he can only have meant in an ethical sense, in addition to his historical interest. He grew up devoid of any belief in a God or Immortality, and does not appear ever to have felt the need of it. The emotional needs that usually manifest themselves in adolescence found expression first in rather vague philosophical cogi-

[i] See pp. 5-6.

tations and, soon after, in an earnest adherence to the principles of science.

When he was nine years old he passed an examination that enabled him to attend high school (Sperl Gymnasium) ʲ a year earlier than the normal age.¹⁸ He had a brilliant career there. For the last six of the eight years he stood at the head of his class.ᵏ He occupied a privileged position and was hardly ever questioned in class.

When, at the age of seventeen, he was graduated with the distinction *summa cum laude,* his father rewarded him with a promise of a visit to England, which was fulfilled two years later. From a contemporary letter to a friend, Emil Fluss, we happen to know some details of the examination. In the German-Latin translation he obtained pass marks; in Latin-German, a passage from Vergil which he had read for his own pleasure, in Greek-German, a passage of twenty-three verses from—appropriately enough—Sophocles' *Oedipus,* and in mathematics (to his great surprise), credit marks; and in the German essay on "Considerations on the Choice of a Profession," distinction marks.ˡ The examiner informed him that he had what the poet Herder termed an "idiotic" ᵐ style, i.e., one both correct and distinctive. He added half jokingly to his friend: "You didn't know you were exchanging letters with a German stylist. You had better keep them carefully—one never knows." ¹⁹ However, unfortunately only one of these letters survived. It should be noted that these examination results relate only to the written examination, since the letter was written before the viva-voce ones. He must have done especially well in the latter, if his sister is right in saying that he passed *summa cum laude.*

He repaid his father's instruction by in his turn helping his sisters with their studies. He even exercised some censorship over their reading, telling them that they were too young to read; when his sister Anna was fifteen, for instance, she was warned off Balzac and Dumas.²⁰ He was altogether the big brother. In a letter of July 1876, to

---

ʲ The Leopoldstäder Kommunalreal- and Obergymnasium. It acquired the colloquial name of Sperlgymnasium after 1870 when it expanded from the Taborgasse into the Sperlgasse.

ᵏ When his sister says he was head of his class for eight years, and matriculated at eighteen, she makes two slips of memory. Dr. Bernfeld has retrieved from the school records Freud's place in every semester!

ˡ I use the current English expressions. The German words are, respectively, *befriedigend, lobenswert,* and *ausgezeichnet.*

ᵐ Reverting to an earlier use of the word, meaning "personal," "separate"; cf. "idiomatic."

his sister Rosa, four years younger than himself, who was staying at Bozen with their mother, he warned her against having her head turned by a slight social success. She had given a performance on the zither, an instrument with which she was only a little familiar. The letter is full of worldly wisdom on the theme of how unscrupulous people are in overpraising young girls, to the detriment of their later character. Such experiences can end in the trinity of their becoming vain, coquettish, and insufferable! The advice was illustrated, as was always so characteristic of Freud, by a legendary anecdote.

An earlier opportunity for his helpfulness had occurred during the Austro-Prussian War when he was only ten years old. His father would take him to see the wounded soldiers being transferred from the train to hay carts on their way to the hospital. The plight of the wounded impressed him deeply and he begged his mother to let him have her old linen so that he could make what was called *"Charpie"* for them, the predecessor of medicated cotton. The girls made this in their schools, and Sigmund asked his teachers to organize *"Charpie"* groups in the boys' schools as well.[21]

There is no doubt that young Sigmund was engrossed in his studies and was a hard worker. Reading and studying seem to have filled the greater part of his life. Even the friends who visited him, both in school years and later, were at once closeted in the "cabinet" for the purpose of serious discussion, much to the pique of his sisters who had to watch the youths pass them by. A notable feature was his preference for comprehensive monographs on each subject over the condensed accounts given in the textbooks,[22] a preference which was also prominent in later years in his archaeological reading. He read widely outside the studies proper, although he mentions that he was thirteen before he read his first novel.[n, 23]

He had a very considerable gift for languages, of which his becoming later a recognized master of German prose was only one example. Besides being completely at home in Latin and Greek, he acquired a thorough knowledge of French and English; in addition he taught himself Italian and Spanish. He had of course been taught Hebrew. He was especially fond of English and he told me once that for ten years he read nothing but English books.

Shakespeare in particular, whom he started reading at the age of eight,[24] he read over and over again and was always ready with an apt quotation from his plays. He admired his superb power of

n Probably this means a modern novel. He had already read the German classics.

expression and, even more, his extensive understanding of human nature. Yet I can recall some faddist ideas he had about his personality. He insisted that his countenance could not be that of an Anglo-Saxon but must be French, and he suggested that the name was a corruption of Jacques Pierre.[o] He wanted me to make a study of the Baconian interpretations and contrast them with psychoanalytic interpretations. Not that he was an adherent of Baconianism, as was his teacher Meynert,[25] but he thought it worth while to disprove it. At the time he had pooh-poohed Meynert's enthusiasm for the idea with the sage remark, "In that event Bacon would then have been the most powerful brain the world has ever borne, and it seems to me that there is more need to share Shakespeare's achievement among several rivals than to burden another important man with it." [26] But in later life he was greatly taken with the idea of the Earl of Oxford being the real author of the plays and was rather disappointed at my skepticism.

A Gentile would have said that Freud had few overt Jewish characteristics, a fondness for relating Jewish jokes and anecdotes being perhaps the most prominent one.[p] But he felt himself to be Jewish to the core, and it evidently meant a great deal to him. He had the common Jewish sensitiveness to the slightest hint of anti-Semitism and he made very few friends who were not Jews. He objected strongly to the idea of their being unpopular or in any way inferior,[q] and had evidently suffered much from school days onward, and especially at the University, from the anti-Semitism that pervaded Vienna. It put an end forever to the phase of German nationalistic enthusiasm through which he passed in early years.[28]

Submission was not in his nature, and his father never regained the place he had held in his esteem after the painful occasion when he told his twelve-year-old boy how a Gentile had knocked off his new fur cap into the mud and shouted at him: "Jew, get off the pavement." [29] To the indignant boy's question: "And what did you do?" he calmly replied: "I stepped into the gutter and picked up my cap." This lack of heroism on the part of his model man shocked the youngster who at once contrasted it in his mind with the behavior of Hamilcar when he made his son Hannibal swear on the

[o] He told me later that he had got this notion from Professor Gentilli of Nervi.

[p] In 1897 he told a friend he was making a collection of wise Jewish anecdotes.[27]

[q] Miss Puner's statement that he resented *being* a Jew is quite unfounded.

household altar to take vengeance on the Romans. Freud evidently identified himself with Hannibal, for he said that ever since then Hannibal had a place in his phantasies.

During his development Freud went through an unmistakable militaristic phase, which he traced ultimately to the battles with his nephew in early childhood. One of the first books that fell into his childish hands after he had learned to read was Thiers' *Consulate and Empire*. He tells us how he pasted onto the backs of his wooden soldiers little labels bearing the names of Napoleon's marshals.[30] His favorite one was Masséna, usually believed to be a Jew; he was aided in his hero worship by the circumstance that they were both born on the same date, a hundred years apart.[r] The Franco-Prussian War, which broke out when he was fourteen, aroused his keen interest. His sister relates how he kept a large map on his writing desk and followed the campaign in detail by means of small flags. He would discourse to his sisters about the war in general and the importance of the various moves of the combatants. His dreams of becoming a great general himself, however, gradually faded, and any remaining military interest must have received a final quietus from the boring experience of spending a year in the army when he was twenty-three and in the midst of absorbing scientific research.

His nephew John visited the family in 1870, and the boys took part together in a duologue[s] before an audience of children, Sigmund's role being that of Brutus.[31]

In 1873 there was an International Exhibition in Vienna, and Mrs. Bernays has a story about her brother being much taken by specimens of Lincoln's letters and by the copy of the Gettysburg address, which he committed to memory and declaimed before his sisters. In the catalogue of the American pavilion, however, which is still extant, there is no mention of any such documents, so possibly the story has got touched up in the course of years. In any event, her date of 1879 is incorrect.[t]

[r] This is by no means exact. It is a date that has been disputed, but Princess Joachim Murat was good enough to examine the birth certificate in the possession of her brother, the Duc de Rivoli, Masséna's great-grandson, and that gives September 6, 1759.
[s] This was taken from a duet in an early version of Schiller's *Die Räuber* (Act IV, Sc. 5), the pronouncedly parricidal content of which Freud did not mention in the allusion he makes to the incident.
[t] My suspicions were confirmed by finding a remark in a letter to Martha Bernays (July 1, 1882). His future brother-in-law Eli Bernays had just made him a present of a copy of the Declaration of Independence (see

Freud was nineteen before he first visited the land of his dreams, England. He had never ceased to envy his half-brother for being able to live in England and bring up his children far from the daily persecutions Jews were subject to in Austria.[32] All we know about the visit was his story of his embarrassment at introducing genders where they did not belong in English,[33] his sister's account of an extremely enthusiastic letter Emanuel wrote to his father lauding his young brother's development and character, that the visit had heightened his long-standing admiration for Oliver Cromwell [u, 34] (after whom he named his second son), and that a talk with his half-brother had the effect of softening the criticism of his father over the cap-in the-gutter episode. He confessed later that he used to indulge in the phantasy of having been born Emanuel's son, when his path in life would have been much easier.[35] His sister adds that it was on that visit that he decided to adopt a medical career, but she puts the decision two years late. His father thought he was too soft-hearted for such work—he also had a considerable horror of blood—but he persisted, saying, according to his sister, "I want to help people who suffer." Whether this be true or not—it almost certainly is not—the motive adduced was assuredly not the only one, or the main one. The reasons Freud himself gave for the choice were, as we shall see, very different.

Of his sexual development during these years we know of only one incident. From what we know of his balanced maturity, and from the evidently successful sublimations of his adolescence, one would suppose that he went through a calmer development than the majority of youths.

The incident in question, however, is of considerable interest. It is the one Bernfeld unraveled from the anonymous description Freud published under the disguise of a supposed patient whom Bernfeld labels Mr. Y.[36] In 1899, when it was written,[v] nothing was known of Freud's early personal life, but he did not reprint the essay where it would naturally belong, in either the *Sammlung kleiner Schriften* (Collection of Small Papers) or the *Psychopathology of Everyday Life*. Ten years later he inserted into the second edition of *The Interpretation of Dreams*, which contains so many personal allusions, a remark (concerning his facial scar) which would reveal the

---

illustration, page 67), but there is no mention of the story related by his sister Anna.

[u] Cromwell's reintroduction of the Jews into England must have been a considerable factor in this.

[v] It was sent to the publishers in the middle of May.[37]

personality of the so-called patient. When the *Gesammelte Schriften* (Collected Writings) were being arranged in 1925, Freud could not refuse the editors permission to include the beautiful little essay in question, "*Screen Memories.*" It would have been too pointed and would certainly have aroused their suspicion of a mystery. But at the same time he took care to erase from *The Interpretation of Dreams,* which was also being reprinted for the *Collected Writings,* the revealing passage—even at the cost of making the context there unintelligible.[38] It is therefore plain that Freud regarded the story in the screen memory, or rather the deep personal feelings connected with it, as something especially intimate, though the grounds for this are far from evident to anyone else. Nor could all the precautions he took prevent its being pretty clear to several of us that the "patient" must have been himself.

The story relates his first love experience at the age of sixteen when—for the only time in his life—he revisited his birthplace. He stayed there with the Fluss family who were friends of his parents and who were in the same textile business as his father. With their daughter, Gisela, a year or two younger than himself, a companion of his early childhood, he fell in love on the spot. He was too shy to communicate his feelings or even to address a single word to her, and she went away to her school after a few days. The disconsolate youth had to content himself with wandering in the woods with the phantasy of how pleasant his life would have been had his parents not left that happy spot where he could have grown up a stout country lad, like the girl's brothers, and married the maiden. So it was all his father's fault. As might be expected, the phantasy was accompanied, though quite unconsciously, by a deeper, plainly erotic one. The whole episode got associated later in his mind with the discovery that his father and his half-brother Emanuel had the plan of weaning him from his intellectual pursuits and replacing them by more practical ones, after which he would settle in Manchester and marry his half-brother's daughter, Pauline, another playmate of early childhood. Gisela Fluss and Pauline were thus identified with each other. The love episode with the former, and the unconscious erotic phantasy that accompanied it, must have reanimated the infantile rape phantasy concerning Pauline (and, doubtless, ultimately his mother also). We have here the reason why Freud was so secretive about it; it contained both halves of the Oedipus complex.

When faced with the difficulty of finding a livelihood in Vienna, he often reflected on this second, lost opportunity of an easier life and thought that there had been much to be said for his father's plan. But it was not to be. That the young lady left him cold[w] when he saw her on his visit to Manchester[x] at the age of nineteen may well be one of the factors in his decision to persist in a scientific career. Had her charms equaled those of the country lass, much might have been different in our world.

[w] On the other hand he found her sister Bertha, who was two years younger, very attractive, and several times mentions her in his letters to Martha Bernays.

[x] A cynic must not say it was the glimpse of Manchester, for even this did not weaken his Anglophilism.

III

The Choice of Profession

(1 8 7 3)

ON LEAVING SCHOOL FREUD HAD TO FACE THE ANXIOUS PROBLEM OF choosing a career. He had not yet come to any decision, and his father had left him entirely free in the matter. The boyhood dreams of becoming a great general or a Minister of State had long vanished in the face of reality. For a Viennese Jew the choice lay between industry or business, law, and medicine. The first of these was quickly discarded by someone of Freud's intellectual type of mind, in spite of his occasional regrets for a more assured existence. There seems to have been a temporary hesitation over the study of jurisprudence with the idea of taking up some social work—an echo of the early political ambitions—but deep impulses were driving him in another direction; incidentally, it is a curious fact that the only examination in his life at which he failed was in medical jurisprudence.[1]

To medicine itself he felt no direct attraction. He did not conceal in later years that he never felt at home in the medical profession, and that he did not seem to himself to be a regular member of it. I can recall as far back as in 1910 his expressing the wish with a sigh that he could retire from medical practice and devote himself to the unraveling of cultural and historical problems—ultimately the great problem of how man came to be what he is. And yet the world has rightly greeted him as, among other things, a great physician!

Here is his own account: "Although we lived in very limited circumstances, my father insisted that in my choice of a profession I

27

should follow my own inclinations.[a] Neither at that time, nor indeed in my later life, did I feel any particular predilection for the career of a physician. I was moved, rather, by a sort of curiosity, which was, however, directed more towards human concerns than towards natural objects; nor had I grasped the importance of observation as one of the best means of gratifying it. My early familiarity with the Bible story (at a time almost before I had learnt the art of reading) had, as I recognized much later, an enduring effect upon the direction of my interest. Under the powerful influence of a school friendship with a boy rather my senior who grew up to be a well-known politician I developed a wish to study law like him and to engage in social activities. At the same time, the theories of Darwin, which were then of topical interest, strongly attracted me, for they held out hopes of an extraordinary advance in our understanding of the world; and it was hearing Goethe's beautiful essay on Nature read aloud at a popular lecture by Professor Carl Brühl[b] just before I left school[c] that decided me to become a medical student." [2]

Here is another version: "After forty-one years of medical activity, my self-knowledge tells me that I have never really been a doctor in the proper sense. I became a doctor through being compelled to deviate from my original purpose; and the triumph of my life lies in my having, after a long and roundabout journey, found my way back to my earliest path. I have no knowledge of having had in my early years any craving to help suffering humanity. My innate sadistic disposition was not a very strong one, so that I had no need to develop this one of its derivatives. Nor did I ever play the 'doctor game'; my infantile curiosity evidently chose other paths. In my youth I felt an overpowering need to understand something of the riddles of the world in which we live and perhaps even to contribute something to their solution. The most hopeful means of achieving this end seemed to be to enroll myself in the medical faculty; but even then I experimented—unsuccessfully—with zoology and chemistry, till at last, under the influence of Brücke, the greatest authority who

[a] Miss Puner says that Freud was convinced of his father's coercion in the choice, but I know of no evidence in support of this.
[b] Dr. Bernfeld tells me that, according to Fritz Eckstein, an old friend of Freud's, Freud wrote a review of this lecture for a daily newspaper, which, however, has not yet been traced. The lecture itself was on Comparative Anatomy!
[c] Elsewhere he says that he listened to this critical lecture *after* leaving school and while he was still undecided about his future profession.

affected me more than any other in my whole life, I settled down to physiology, though in those days it was too narrowly restricted to histology. By that time I had already passed all my medical examinations; but I took no interest in anything to do with medicine till the teacher whom I so deeply respected warned me that in view of my restricted material circumstances I could not possibly take up a theoretical career. Thus I passed from the histology of the nervous system to neuropathology and then, prompted by fresh influences, I began to be concerned with the neuroses. I scarcely think, however, that my lack of genuine medical temperament has done much damage to my patients. For it is not greatly to the advantage of patients if their physician's therapeutic interest has too marked an emotional emphasis. They are best helped if he carries out his task coolly and, so far as possible, with precision." [3]

Divine curiosity of this order may focus on the riddles of human existence and origin or extend to the nature of the whole universe; with Freud the former was evidently true. Again, such curiosity may seek satisfaction in one of two ways, through philosophical speculation or through scientific investigation. We know which path Freud in fact followed, but Wittels has made the shrewd suggestion that Freud was perhaps one of those whose bent towards speculative abstractions is so powerful that he is afraid of being mastered by it and feels it necessary to counter it by studying concrete scientific data. [4] This is confirmed by a reply Freud once made to my question of how much philosophy he had read. The answer was: "Very little. As a young man I felt a strong attraction towards speculation and ruthlessly checked it." We know from the last chapter of *The Interpretation of Dreams* and other of his writings that he possessed a remarkable capacity for abstract thought, but he used it in the interests of reality.

Goethe's dithyrambic essay is a romantic picture of Nature as a beautiful and bountiful mother who allows her favorite children the privilege of exploring her secrets. This imagery attracted the youthful Freud more than the prosaic prospect of marrying a relative in Manchester. His outlook was the reverse of materialistic. He chose an ideal career, irrespective of poverty or wealth, rather than worldly comfort.

Wittels thinks that what attracted Freud in the Goethe essay was not only the sense of beauty in nature but that of meaning and purpose. [5] There is no reason to think that Freud ever cudgeled his brains about the purpose of the universe—he was always an unrepentant atheist—but that mankind was moved by various purposes, motives, aims, many of which need not be evident ones, was a conception he must always have had in his mind, long before he developed it so brilliantly by solving the riddle of the Sphinx. It is reasonable to suppose that this restless search into the meaning of humanity and human relations was first generated in connection with the puzzling problems of his early family life; there again his dictum that the first two or three years of life are decisive for the formation of character and personality would seem to be well illustrated.

An interesting passage from Bernfeld may well be quoted at this point: "The childhood phantasies and the adolescent day dreams of Freud, as far as we know them, do not foretell the future originator of psychoanalysis. They fit a general, a reformer, or a business executive rather than the patient, full-time listener to petty complaints, humdrum stories, and the recounting of irrational sufferings. It was a long way from the child who devoured Thiers' story of Napoleon's power and who identified himself with the Marshal Masséna, Duke of Rivoli and Prince of Essling, to the psychoanalyst who cheerfully admits that he has, in fact, very little control even over those symptoms and disturbances which he has learned to understand so well. Twelve years old, ne still thinks of himself as a candidate for cabinet rank and, as an adolescent, he plans to become a lawyer, and to go into politics. Then, at seventeen, shortly after his graduation from High School, Freud suddenly retreats from his search for power over men. He turns to the more sublime power over nature, through science, and he decides to study 'natural history'—biology to us today. Power, prestige, and wealth should come to him only contingent to his being a great scientist." [6]

Bernfeld here adumbrates the important topic of the "search for power over man." It is commonly supposed that this attitude is characteristic only of men of an aggressively domineering type, of which unfortunately we have of late witnessed many notorious examples. Psychoanalysis has, on the contrary, revealed that it is a universal human characteristic; one, however, which may assume many diverse forms, some evident and some non-recognizable. Furthermore, it is incorrect to regard it as a purely aggressive tendency. A great part of its motivation is more truly an expression of deep fears in infancy. The sense of badness within—whether primordial or the results of introjections—is commonly projected outwards on to other human beings in the endeavor to get rid of it. The advantage of this expulsion. however. is counterbalanced by the fear that, now the badness is outside one, it is no longer under one's control. Hence the need to make efforts to influence, to control, or in extreme cases to dominate, one's fellow beings.

This apparently irrelevant disquisition on psychoanalytical theory is interpolated here so as to avoid creating a false impression when one speaks of Freud's "search for power over men." The most obvious form of such a desire is the military one—force and conquest being apparently so decisive—frequent enough among boys before they discover that the civil (political) arm is more potent than the military arm, and this was the early development we observe with Freud. But at the critical period of his life we are now considering, the great change was beginning in which the primacy of the intellect was recognized. He perceived that the ultimate secret of power was not force, but understanding, a fact to which the great achievements of science in the past three centuries bear ample witness. Before this truth could be applied to man's behavior it was necessary, so he thought, to learn something about nature, man's place in nature, and man's physical constitution. Here it was Darwin who pointed the way, and the excitement caused by Darwin's work was at its height in the seventies in every country in Europe.

In a conversation I once had with him on the balanced nature of the Greek ideal, supremacy in both intellectual and physical achievements—the word "aesthetic" perhaps forming a link between the two —Freud remarked: "Yes, that combination is certainly preferable. For various reasons the Jews have undergone a one-sided development and admire brains more than bodies, but if I had to choose between the two I should also put the intellect first."

This transformation from force to understanding, ultimately from the body to the intellect, was extremely thorough and far-reaching. In spite of extensive provocation Freud hardly ever indulged in controversy: it was distasteful to his nature. Like Darwin, and unlike most men of science, he responded to criticism, sensitive as he was to it, simply by continuing his researches and producing more and more evidence. He had little desire to influence his fellow men. He offered them something of value, but without any wish to force it on them. He disliked debates or even public scientific discussions, the object of which he knew was mainly controversial, and it was in deference to this attitude that papers read at psychoanalytical congresses have never been followed by discussion of them. And, although wildly untrue statements have been made to the contrary, I can firmly assert—and no one could be in a better position to judge it at first hand—that his attitude towards his colleagues and pupils was never domineering. Any dominating position he achieved was solely the indirect result of the respect which is the meet due of any great man.

One may legitimately wonder whether this revolutionary change was furthered by the intense love experience described in the anonymous autobiographical fragment to which reference has already been made. Since the episode was a significant one in Freud's life, and indeed may have had a bearing on the choice of career, it is a matter of interest whether it took place at the moment of that choice or a year earlier, and the arguments in favor of each date may be mentioned. The subject of the story, Mr. Y, is said to have visited his old home, where the episode occurred, at the age of seventeen, i.e., in the vacation following the final school examination when Freud was debating the choice of a career and when a special holiday was very much in place. According to his sister, their father was so pleased with the result of the Matura (University entrance examination) that he rewarded his son with the promise of a trip to England. She says further that this took place "soon after," but it is possible that she here confounds it with the Freiberg holiday, since Freud himself gives nineteen, not seventeen, as his age on the English visit and there seems no reason to doubt this.[d] The summer of 1873 was when the Stock Exchange in Vienna crashed, not a very propitious moment for embarking on an expensive holiday, which apparently had to be postponed for two years. It seems plausible that, to console the youth for his disappointment in not visiting his English brothers, the father arranged the minor trip to Freiberg in the meantime.

On the other hand, in his letter to the Mayor of Freiberg, on the occasion of the tablet (1931), Freud says he last visited his birthplace at the age of sixteen "when still a schoolboy" [7] (which he would no longer be in the vacation at the age of seventeen), and it would require evidence, not speculation, to rebut such a definite statement. The accuracy of his memory is supported by two other data: (1) In The Interpretation of Dreams he remarks that he committed a Czech nursery rhyme to memory—which would almost certainly have been at Freiberg—in his seventeenth year;[8] (2) Mr. Y, in the story of the screen memory, mentions that he went to visit his relations

---

[d] He gave seventeen as his age in the first edition of The Interpretation of Dreams (p. 304) but nineteen in all the subsequent ones.

abroad three years later than the episode related. Freud was nine-teen when he traveled to England.

So we may take it that when Freud gives Mr. Y's age at thirty-eight (in the screen memory story), when his actual age was forty-three, he also changed the age at the love episode from sixteen to seven teen.[e] It is known that Freud took very complicated measures in later years, when his own self-disclosures had greatly heightened the risk of discovery, to conceal the identity of the supposed patient, so that it was vastly important to him to preserve the secrecy. One must ascribe that to the links between the experience itself and the deeply repressed forbidden impulses of infancy, a link he himself mentions. It would seem reasonable to suppose that there was a painful reaction to the discovery that he could be carried away by a surge from the depth and, further, to the pain of finding that the experience itself had been so fruitless. Was this increased wave of sexual repression a contributory factor in his turning so sharply from the chances of worldly ambition and ease towards the cold flame of idealism that the intellect promised? It was ten years before he ventured to fall in love again, but that time it was more successful.

To return to the choice itself, Freud had a very orderly mind (and also orderly habits), and his power of organizing a mass of facts into a systematic grouping was truly remarkable; his command of the literature on the subject of childhood paralyses, or on that of dreams, is one example alone of this. But on the other hand he rather spurned exactitude and precise definition as being either wearisome or pedantic; he could never have been a mathematician or physicist or even an expert solver of chess problems. He wrote easily, fluently, and spontaneously, and would have found much rewriting irksome. His translators will bear me out when I remark

[e] This conclusion was subsequently confirmed by finding a letter (October 28, 1883) to Martha Bernays describing the incident in full and mentioning that he was then sixteen years old. On looking back he attributed his infatuation to Gisela's black hair and eyes and to the deeply moved state of mind that this visit to his birthplace had induced. It was evidently not the girl's charms themselves, since he commented on his lack of taste; he also said that he never exchanged a single word with her. So it was love of some internal image of his own plainly derived from far deeper sources but associated with his early home.

The girl herself married a Herr Popper in Vienna, an acquaintance of Freud's. It was not the famous Popper-Lynkeus on whom Freud was so reluctant to call in later years (see p. 359); this Popper married only on his deathbed.

that minor obscurities and ambiguities, of a kind that more scrupulous circumspection could have readily avoided, are not the least of their trials. He was of course aware of this. I remember once asking him why he used a certain phrase, the meaning of which was not clear, and with a grimace he answered: *"Pure Schlamperei."* [f] We touch here on one of his main characteristics—his dislike of being hampered or fettered. He loved to give himself up to his thoughts freely, to see where they would take him, leaving aside for the moment any question of precise delineation; that could be left for further consideration.

We have already noted his early tendency to speculative rumination, one which he sternly checked. The motive for this checking was perhaps only in part the intellectual perception of its dangers in leading him astray from objectivity; had it not taken place there was also the danger of releasing unconscious thoughts for which the time was as yet far from ripe. It needed the courage and motives of a man of forty to pursue his self-examination to its last conclusion.

Such considerations made him feel the need of intellectual discipline, and everything pointed to science as the supreme opportunity. Science then meant, as it still does to many people, not only objectivity, but above all exactitude, measurement, precision, all the qualities in which Freud knew he was lacking. Moreover, in the nineteenth century the belief in scientific knowledge as the prime solvent of the world's ills—a belief that Freud retained to the end—was beginning to displace the hopes that had previously been built on religion, political action, and philosophy in turn. This high esteem for science reached Vienna late from the West, particularly from Germany, and was at its height in the seventies, the time in question. Freud was certainly imbued with it, and so, despite his native talent for exploring the unknown and introducing some sort of order into chaos, he must have felt that strictness and accuracy had an important place—visibly so in the "exact sciences."

The conflict between giving himself up unrestrainedly to thinking—and doubtless also to the play of phantasy—and the need for the curb of a scientific discipline ended in a decided victory for the latter. The contrast might be expressed in his later terminology of pleasure-principle versus reality-principle, although the latter soon became also invested with great pleasure. Perhaps it corresponds also with the contrast between the belief in free will and that in de-

[f] Pure sloppiness.

terminism, an ancient antinomy he was so brilliantly to resolve a quarter of a century later. As often occurs in such situations, the restraining power seems to have been not only thorough, but perhaps excessive. For, as we shall see later, a freer and bolder use of his imagination would have brought him world fame more than once in the course of his laboratory researches had he not cautiously refrained from pursuing the inferences of his work to their logical conclusion.

That Freud was ambitious in his pursuit of knowledge as the secret of achievement, success, and power is shown by a passage in the letter to Emil Fluss cited earlier, where he bemoans his dread of mediocrity and refuses to be reassured by his friend. Throughout his life he was modest concerning his achievements and he displayed the stern self-criticism that one finds with those who have set themselves lofty goals and had great expectations. I told him once the story of a surgeon who said that if he ever reached the Eternal Throne he would come armed with a cancerous bone and ask the Almighty what he had to say about it. Freud's reply was: "If I were to find myself in a similar situation, my chief reproach to the Almighty would be that he had not given me a better brain." It was the remark of a man not easily satisfied.

Freud's development during the next few years can well be understood when one considers the state of mind we have endeavored to depict. He would be a laborious and painstaking student, but one not likely to excel in the "exact" sciences. Biology offered him some understanding of the evolution of life and man's relationship to nature. Later on physiology and anatomy would teach him something of man's physical constitution. But would this arid path ever bring him nearer to his ultimate goal, the secrets of man's inner nature, towards which the deepest urges impelled him? We know that the medical study of man's physical afflictions brought him no nearer, and perhaps even impeded his progress. That, however, he finally attained his goal, though by an extraordinarily circuitous route, he rightly came to regard as the triumph of his life.[9]

IV

The Medical Student

(1 8 7 3 – 1 8 8 1)

IT IS NOT SURPRISING THAT MEDICAL STUDIES ENTERED UPON IN SUCH an unorthodox fashion should pursue an irregular and protracted course. Freud did in fact spend over them three years longer than necessary. In later years he talked of his colleagues having twitted him over his dilatoriness, as if he were a backward student, but there were very good reasons for the delay. It was just in the fields he was supposed to traverse rapidly that he would have liked to spend his life.

Freud entered the University of Vienna in the autumn of 1873, at the early age of seventeen. Professor Victor Kraft's researches in the Archives of the University, undertaken at Dr. Bernfeld's instigation, have resuscitated a complete list of the lectures he attended throughout the course of his studies, so that we can now follow them closely step by step.[1] He admitted himself that he pursued in only a negligent fashion the studies proper to the medical career itself and seized every opportunity to dally in those that interested him as well as to forage in neighboring fields.

In his first semester, October 1873 to March 1874, Freud signed up for twenty-three hours a week: twelve lectures in anatomy and six in chemistry together with practical work in both. During his first summer semester, which ran from the end of April till late July, he spent twenty-eight hours weekly in anatomy, botany, chemistry, microscopy, and mineralogy. With a characteristic overflow of interest he also followed a course on "Biology and Darwinism" given by the zoologist Claus, and one by Brücke on "The Physiology of Voice and Speech." It was his first sight of the famous Brücke, who became so important to him later. So passed the first year.

36

In the following winter semester (1874-1875) he continued as a regular medical student with twenty-eight hours weekly spent on anatomical dissection, physics, physiology (by Brücke), and zoology for medical students (by Claus). Once a week, however, he took a glance at philosophy in Brentano's reading seminar. Attendance at a three years' course in philosophy had been obligatory for medical students in Vienna since 1804, but was so no longer after 1872.

In his fourth semester, in the summer of 1875, we find Freud striking out on a more independent line. He attended the lectures on zoology proper (fifteen hours a week), not those on "zoology for medical students." He took two physics classes, one more than was required in the medical curriculum. He continued with the seminars on philosophy and added another course of Brentano's, on Aristotle's logic. Eleven hours a week were given to Brücke's physiology lectures.

This leaning to biology became more pronounced in the following summer semester, when he spent ten hours a week on practical zoology in Claus's laboratory. Anatomy and physiology took up the rest of his time, but he still attended Brentano's reading once a week.

At the end of the semester in March 1876, after having been a University student for two and a half years, he began the first of his numerous original researches. It was suggested to him by Professor Claus. Carl Claus, the head of the Institute of Comparative Anatomy, had come from Göttingen to Vienna two years before, with the task of bringing the zoology department to a more modern level. He was especially interested in marine zoology, and in 1875 he was allowed to found the Zoological Experimental Station at Trieste, one of the first of its kind in the world. Funds were placed at his disposal to send a few students to Trieste for several weeks of study and research twice a year. One of the first to be given this grant, in March 1876, was the young Freud; so evidently his teacher thought well of him.[2] A scientific excursion to the shores of the Adriatic must have been sought after, so the grant was valued as a distinction. It was Freud's first sight of a southern civilization, as well as his first effort in scientific research, and his sister recalls the visit as an important episode in his life.

In the summer term between the two visits to Trieste he concentrated on biology. He attended fifteen lectures a week on zoology and only eleven on other subjects; in addition, there were three of Brentano's on Aristotle. In physiology for the first time he encountered Exner and Fleischl, important figures later, and there were a few lectures on spectrum analysis and the physiology of plants.

The task assigned to him concerned what had remained a puzzling problem since the days of Aristotle. The gonadic structure of eels had never been settled. As he wrote in his paper: "No one has ever found a mature male eel—no one has yet seen the testes of the eel, in spite of innumerable efforts through the centuries." The difficulty was evidently bound up with their extraordinary migration before the mating period. In 1874 Syrski at Trieste had described a small lobed organ and considered that it represented the missing testes. It was a finding that obviously had to be checked, and this is what Freud set out to do. Claus was plainly satisfied with his beginning, since he renewed the grant for another visit in September of the same year. Later, between October and January, he was able to supply his student with rather more mature animals. In all, Freud dissected some four hundred eels and he found the Syrski organ in many of them. On microscopic examination he found its histological structure to be such that it might well be an immature testicular organ, though there was no definite evidence that it was so. Nevertheless, his paper, which Claus presented to the Academy of Sciences (March 15, 1877, published in the April number of its *Bulletin*), was the first of a series that confirmed Syrski's suggestion.

In the circumstances no one could well have done better, but Freud was much more dissatisfied with his inconclusive results than was his chief. An ambitious youth must have hoped for a task where some brilliant and original discovery would be made.[a] In the abstract of his scientific writings which he presented to the University some twenty years later, on the occasion of his applying for the title of Professor, he gave such a disparaging version of this piece of work as almost to insinuate that it had been a futile and pointless one.[3] It was the only occasion in this list of researches that he mentioned the name of the teacher who suggested the work, and one cannot help detecting a note of resentment against him.

We come here to the end of his third year, a date concerning which Freud later (1925) made the following comment: "During my first three years at the University I was compelled to make the discovery that the peculiarities and limitations of my gifts denied me all success in many of the departments of science into which my youthful

[a] One is tempted to make the perhaps irrelevant remark that the future discoverer of the castration complex was disappointed at not being able to find the testes of the eel.

eagerness had plunged me. Thus is learned the truth of Mephistopheles' warning: 'It is in vain that you range round from science to science; each man learns only what he can.' At length in Ernst Brücke's Physiology Laboratory I found rest and satisfaction—and men, too, whom I could respect and take as my models; the great Brücke himself and his assistants Sigmund Exner and Ernst von Fleischl-Marxow." [4]

There was clearly a contrast in Freud's mind between his former chief, Claus, and the later one, Brücke: dissatisfaction with the former—although he was a man of the highest scientific repute—and admiration for the latter. Since both men were, objectively speaking, of the same type, it is likely that some personal feeling entered into the matter. Bernfeld has pointed out that Claus was twenty years older than Freud, while Brücke was forty years his senior.[5] These differences in age correspond exactly with on the one hand that between Freud and his half-brother, the imagined rival with his mother in early childhood, and on the other hand that between Freud and his omniscient and beloved father. At all events the irritation and frustration of the zoological laboratory were replaced by a sense of inner peace and satisfaction in the physiological laboratory, despite the similarity of the researches he carried out in both. The young student accepted guidance and criticism from the old Brücke—"the greatest authority I ever met" [6]—as he had admiringly looked up to his father in early childhood. He patiently settled down to the regular medical studies and, for the next five semesters, he attended no courses outside these, not even on philosophy, which now disappeared from his interests. His researches had to be carried out in overtime work added to this full curriculum, or, as is more probable, by cutting out some of the latter.

Freud always spoke later of his respect and admiration for this unchallenged authority, sentiments which were also tinged with awe. A reprimand by Brücke for being late one day, when the student was "overwhelmed by the terrible gaze of his eyes," [7] was recalled years afterwards, and the image of those steel-blue eyes would throughout his life appear at any moment when he might be tempted to any remissness in duty or to any imperfection in executing it scrupulously.

What manner of man was this who left such an indelible impression on the young Freud, and who, as he says, influenced him more than any other man in his life? [8] When someone makes a remark about another man such as the one just cited, one may be sure that there is a significant affinity between their natures. It does not necessarily mean that their personalities closely resemble each other, but it does mean that the admired man incorporates some ideal towards which the "influenced" man is striving. In the present instance it is not hard to discern that ideal. It can only be that of scientific integrity combined with a whole-hearted faith in its ethical value. The word faith is used advisedly, since the analogy between this attitude and that of religious or political ideals is not altogether remote. Like most adolescents Freud had the need to "believe in something" and in his case the something was Science with a capital.

Freud was to remain throughout his life unswervingly loyal to the aspect of science that represents the ideal of intellectual integrity, to the truth as he could best see it. But another aspect of science, tedious exactitude, did not fare so well. To be tied down to exactitude and precise measurement was not in his nature. On the contrary, it conflicted with certain revolutionary tendencies that would burst the bonds of conventions and accepted definitions, and one day they did. For the next ten years, however, such tendencies were sternly kept in abeyance, and he made every effort to enlist "scientific discipline" to curb what he vaguely felt was in him. He was a good student, conducted useful researches, but the discipline was won at the expense, for some years, of his native boldness and imagination.

Brücke himself was an excellent example of the disciplined scientist that Freud felt he should aim at becoming. To begin with, he was German, not Austrian, and his qualities were the very opposite to the Viennese *Schlamperei*, with which Freud must already have been only too familiar, and for which he felt a good-natured contempt perhaps mingled with a slight, sneaking sympathy.

Brücke's Institute was an important part indeed of that far-reaching scientific movement best known as Helmholtz's School of Medicine. The amazing story of this scientific school started in the early forties with the friendship of Emil Du Bois-Reymond (1818-1896) and Ernst Brücke (1819-1892), soon joined by Hermann Helmholtz (1821-1894) and Carl Ludwig (1816-1895). From its very beginning this group was driven forward by a veritable crusading spirit. In 1842 Du Bois wrote: "Brücke and I pledged a solemn oath to put into effect this truth: 'No other forces than the common physical-chemical ones are active within the organism. In those cases which cannot at the time be explained by these forces one has either to find the specific way or form of their action by means of the physical-mathematical method or to assume new forces equal in dignity to the chemical-physical forces inherent in matter, reducible to the force of attraction and repulsion.' " [b]

These men formed a small private club which in 1845 they enlarged to the *Berliner Physikalische Gesellschaft* (Berlin Society of Physicists). Most of its members were young students of Johannes Müller; physicists and physiologists banded together to destroy, once and for all, vitalism, the fundamental belief of their admired master. Du Bois-Reymond, Brücke, Helmholtz, and Ludwig remained lifelong friends. Within twenty-five or thirty years they achieved complete domination over the thinking of the German physiologists and medical teachers, gave intensive stimulus to science everywhere, and solved some of the old problems for ever.

Of this group of important men Helmholtz was certainly the preeminent member. Several years later he paid a short visit to Vienna, and Freud regretted not having had the chance of catching sight of him. He added, "He is one of my idols." [10]

Brücke, whom in Berlin they jocularly called "Our Ambassador in the Far East," published in 1874 his *Lectures on Physiology*. The following account of the physical physiology that captivated the student Freud is abstracted from the introductory pages: Physiology is the science of organisms as such. Organisms differ from dead material entities in action—machines—in possessing the faculty of assimilation, but they are all phenomena of the physical world; systems of atoms, moved by forces, according to the principle of the conservation of energy discovered by Robert Mayer in 1842, neglected for twenty years, and then popularized by Helmholtz. The sum of forces (motive forces and potential forces) remains constant in every isolated system. The real causes are symbolized in science by the word "force." The less we know about them, the more kinds of forces do we have to distinguish: mechanical, electrical, magnetic forces, light, heat. Progress in knowledge reduces them to two—attraction and repulsion. All this applies as well to the organism man.

Brücke then gives an elaborate presentation in his two volumes of what was at the time known about the transformation and interplay of physical forces in the living organism. The spirit and content of these lectures correspond closely with the words Freud used

[b] This and some of the following paragraphs are, with his kind permission, paraphrased from two valuable essays of Dr. Bernfeld's [9] The whole chapter owes a great deal to his researches.

in 1926 to characterize psychoanalysis in its dynamic aspect: "The forces assist or inhibit one another, combine with one another, enter into compromises with one another, etc." [11]

Very closely connected with this *dynamic* aspect of Brücke's physiology was his evolutionary orientation. Not only is the organism a part of the physical universe but the world of organisms itself is one family. Its apparent diversity is the result of divergent developments which started with the microscopic unicellular "elementary organisms." It includes plants, lower and higher animals, as well as man, from the hordes of the anthropoids to the peak of his contemporary Western civilization. In this evolution of life, no spirits, essences, or entelechies, no superior plans or ultimate purposes are at work. The physical energies alone cause effects—somehow. Darwin had shown that there was hope of achieving in a near future some concrete insight into the "How" of evolution. The enthusiasts were convinced that Darwin had shown more than that—in fact had already told the full story. While the skeptics and the enthusiasts fought with each other, the active researchers were busy and happy putting together the family trees of the organisms, closing gaps, rearranging the taxonomic systems of plants and animals according to genetic relationships, discovering transformation series, finding behind the manifest diversities the homologous identities.

This physiology was a part of the general trend of Western civilization. Slowly, continuously, it had risen and grown everywhere through the preceding two or three hundred years, steadily gaining momentum from the end of the eighteenth century and increasing rapidly in velocity and expansion after the 1830's. This trend, weaker in Germany than in England and France, was interrupted there from about 1794 to 1830 by the period of *Naturphilosophie* (philosophy of nature).

Naturphilosophie is the name of the pantheistic monism, close to mysticism, which, professed by Schelling—repeated, developed, and varied by a host of writers—was eagerly accepted by the average educated man and literary lady. The Universe, Nature, is one vast organism, ultimately consisting of forces, of activities, of creations, of emergings—organized in eternal basic conflicts, in polarity; reason, conscious life, mind being only the reflection, the emanation, of this unconscious turmoil. These ideas have been expressed before and since and contain the seeds of some of the scientific theories of the nineteenth century and of our time. But it is not the ideas that were characteristic of the movement nor even the romantic temper enveloping them. That was a general European trend. What characterized the German *Naturphilosophie* is the aspiration expressed in the name "speculative physics" (which Schelling himself gave to his endeavors) and the unbalanced megalomanic emotionalism of the phantasy and style of these writers. An English philosopher puts it thus: "They exhibit tendencies that seem foreign to the course of European thought; they recall the vague spaciousness of the East and its reflection in the semi-oriental Alexandria." [12]

Physical physiology—although not by itself—overthrew this philosophy and took its place. As has happened before, the conqueror introjected the emotionalism of the victim. "Unity of science," "science," "physical forces" were not merely directing ideas or hypotheses of scientific endeavor: they became almost objects of worship. They were more than methods of research—they became a *Weltanschauung*. The intensity of this temper varied from scientist to scientist; from place to place. In Berlin with Du Bois-Reymond it was at its maximum, strangely mixed with Prussian nationalism. In Austria, *Naturphilosophie* never had much power, therefore the fanaticism in physiology was at a minimum in Vienna and with Brücke. Yet it was there.

Freud himself, inspired by Goethe, who was one of the first pioneers, passed through a brief period of the pantheistic *Naturphilosophie*. Then, in his enthusiasm for the rival physical physiology, he swung to the opposite extreme and became for a while a radical materialist. That this was a highly emotional reversal of attitude was demonstrated in a discussion in a students' society where he behaved very rudely to his philosophical opponent[c] and obstinately refused to apologize; there was even for the moment some talk of a duel.[13]

So much for the ideas of the Brücke Institute where Freud was "stuck," as he termed it, for six years. But they were good and fruit-ful years, which he later described in unrestrained superlatives as "the happiest years of my youth." It was there that he developed the particular physiological framework into which he tried later to cast his discoveries in psychology.

Brücke's personality was well suited to the uncompromising idealistic and almost ascetic outlook characteristic of the school of Helmholtz. He was a small man with a large and impressive head, a balanced gait, and quiet, controlled movements; small-lipped, with the famous "terrifying blue eyes," rather shy, but stern and exceedingly silent. A Protestant, with his Prussian speech, he must have

[c] The redoubtable Viktor Adler, the future Social Democratic leader.

seemed out of place in easygoing Catholic Vienna, an emissary from another and more austere world—as indeed he was. A conscientious and indefatigable worker himself, he exacted the same standard from his assistants and students. Here is a typical anecdote. A student who in one of his papers had written: "Superficial observation reveals . . ." had his paper returned with the objectionable line violently crossed out and Brücke's comment on the margin: "One is not to observe superficially." He was one of the most dreaded of examiners. If the candidate muffed the answer to his first question, Brücke sat out the remaining ten or twelve minutes of the prescribed examination period, stiff and silent, deaf to the pleas of the candidate and the Dean who had also to be present. The general opinion had him labeled as a cold, purely rational man. What degree of violent force against himself and his emotions he needed to build up this front is revealed by his reaction to the death of his beloved son in 1873. He forbade his family and friends to mention his son's name, put all pictures of him out of sight, and worked even harder than before. But this man was completely free of vanity, intrigue, and lust for power. To the student who proved his ability he was a most benevolent father, extending counsel and protection far beyond scientific matters. He respected the student's own ideas, encouraged original work, and sponsored talents even if they deviated considerably from his own opinions. It is said that no pupil or friend ever became unfaithful to him.

Ernst von Fleischl-Marxow (1846-1891), whose friendship meant much to Freud and whose untimely death he deeply deplored, was a physicist as well as a physiologist. In many respects he was quite the opposite of Brücke. He was young, handsome, enthusiastic, a brilliant speaker, and an attractive teacher. He had the charming and amiable manners of old Viennese society, ever ready to discuss scientific and literary problems with a flow of challenging ideas. These qualities were in strange contrast to his pathetic part as hero and martyr of physiology. At twenty-five while conducting research in pathological anatomy he contracted an infection. An amputation of the right thumb saved him from death. But continued growth of neuromas required repeated operations. His life became an unending torture of pain and of slowly approaching death. This mutilated and aching hand performed experimental work of technical perfection. His sleepless nights he used for studying physics and mathematics. When with his growing skill in the sciences this drug became ineffective he began the study of Sanskrit.

Brücke's other assistant, Sigmund Exner (1846-1926), who later succeeded him in the Chair of Physiology, made up the trio: professors and assistant professors. It was they whom Freud recalled as "men whom I could respect and take as my models." His life's endeavor was to apply their principles to the study, first of the nervous system, and then of the mind. When he was nearly seventy he said on a solemn occasion: "My life has been aimed at one goal only: to infer or to guess how the mental apparatus is constructed and what forces interplay and counteract in it."

Exner was the one of the three who least appealed to Freud. He was an excellent scientist, but a very ambitious man; vain and dictatorial, although he had a jovial manner.

We have dwelt on the background of the Brücke Institute at some length for the following reason. It has often been assumed that Freud's psychological theories date from his contact with Charcot or Breuer or even later. On the contrary, it can be shown that the principles on which he constructed his theories were those he had acquired as a medical student under Brücke's influence. The emancipation from this influence consisted not in renouncing the principles, but in becoming able to apply them empirically to mental phenomena while dispensing with any anatomical basis. This cost him a severe struggle, but then his true genius consisted throughout in emerging successfully from severe struggles.

Yet Brücke would have been astonished, to put it mildly, had he known that one of his favorite pupils, one apparently a convert to the strict faith, was later, in his famous wish theory of the mind, to bring back into science the ideas of "purpose," "intention," and "aim" which had just been abolished from the universe. We know, however, that when Freud did bring them back he was able to reconcile them with the principles in which he had been brought up; he never abandoned determinism for teleology.

In the autumn of 1876, after his second return from Trieste and while still occupied with his zoological research, he was accepted in the Institute of Physiology at the age of twenty as what was called a *famulus*, a sort of research scholar. The abode itself of the famous Institute was far from being commensurate with its high aspirations and admirable scientific achievements. The Institute was miserably housed in the ground floor and basement of a dark and smelly old gun factory. It consisted of a large room where the students kept their microscopes and listened to lectures, and two smaller ones, one of which was Brücke's sanctum. There were also on both floors a few small cubicles, some without windows, that served as chemical, electrophysiological, and optical laboratories. There was no water supply, no gas, and of course no electricity. All heating had to be done over a spirit lamp, and the water was brought up from a well in the yard where also a shed housed the animals experimented on. Nevertheless this Institute was the pride of the medical school on account of the number and distinction of its foreign visitors and students.

Although Brücke preferred students to present their own project for research, he was quite ready to formulate a problem for those beginners who were too timid or too vague to do so themselves. He set Freud behind the microscope on work connected with the histology of the nerve cells. In a paper read some six years later Freud described in the following words the general situation as he found it: "Very soon after the recognition of the nerve cells and of the nerve fibers as the fundamental parts of the nervous system there began the efforts to clarify the finer structure of these two elements, motivated by the hope of using the knowledge of their structure for the understanding of their function. As is well known, up to now neither sufficient insight nor agreement has been reached in either of these two directions. One author thinks of the nerve cell as granulated, the other as fibrillose; one thinks of the nerve fiber as a bunch of fibrils but another as a liquid column. Consequently, while one elevates the nerve cell to the basic source of nervous activity another degrades it to a mere nucleus of the Schwann sheaths."

Together with this problem of the intimate structure of the nervous elements goes the interesting question of whether the nervous system of the higher animals is composed of elements different from those of the lower animals, or whether both are built of the same units. This topic was highly controversial at that time. The philosophical and religious implications seemed to be very disturbing. Are the differences in the mind of lower and higher animals only a matter of degree in complication? Does the human mind differ from that of some mollusc—not basically, but correlative to the number of nerve cells in both and the complication of their respective fibers? Scientists were searching for the answers to such questions in the hope of gaining definite decisions—in one way or another—on the nature of man, the existence of God, and the aim of life.

To this vast and exciting field of research belonged the very modest problem which Brücke put before Freud. In the spinal cord of the Amoecetes (Petromyzon), a genus of fish belonging to the primitive Cyclostomatae, Reissner had discovered a peculiar kind of large cell. The nature of these cells and their connection with the spinal system elicited a number of unsuccessful investigations. Brücke wished to see the histology of these cells clarified. After a few weeks Freud came to him with the quite unexpected discovery that nonmyelinated fibers of the posterior (sensory) nerves originated in some of the Reissner cells. Other fibers, probably also sensory, coming from these cells pass behind the central canal to the opposite side of the spinal cord. Although this finding did not explain the nature of the cells, it did promise a simple solution and eliminated various hypotheses current in the literature. Brücke, it seems, thought this was good enough for a beginner, and pressed for publication. Freud obliged by hurriedly putting together a report. His dissatisfaction with the unfinished work, however, is noticeable in many places in the paper. In style and organization it was far below the paper on the eels and the succeeding publications of his student years. Brücke presented the study at the Academy of Sciences at its meeting of January 4, 1877. It appeared in the January Bulletin of the Academy. It was the first paper of Freud's to be actually published, since the one on his first piece of research, on the eel, did not appear until three months later.

Freud continued in his thorough investigation on the Reissner cells, and published a second report on the Petromyzon in July of the following year (1878). Here he assembled an amazingly complete bibliography—eighteen pages of his report deal with the literature. This historical conscientiousness was not quite favorable to the young scientist's ambitions: "I must accuse myself of having falsely thought that I was the first one to describe—based on direct and certain observations—the origin of the posterior nerve roots in certain cells of the Petromyzon. Only shortly after the publication of my paper did I find in Stieda's abstracts of the Russian literature an abstract of a paper by Kutschin which contains important information on the origin of the posterior root. Due to the friendliness of Professor Stieda in Dorpat, who had sent me the Russian paper, I could examine the pictures by Kutschin and satisfy myself that Kutschin had seen in his preparations, as long ago as 1863, convincing proof of the origin of the posterior roots in the posterior cells. By way of apology I can only say that Kutschin's statements—perhaps because his pictures were not available to the German histologists—were quite generally overlooked."

Aided by an improvement in the technique of the preparation,

Freud established definitely that the Reissner cells "are nothing else than spinal ganglion cells which, in those low vertebrates, where the migration of the embryonic neural tube to the periphery is not yet completed, remain within the spinal cord. These scattered cells mark the way which the spinal ganglion cells have made throughout their evolution." This solution of the problem of the Reissner cells was a triumph of precise observation and genetic interpretation—one of the thousands of such small achievements which have finally established among scientists the conviction of the evolutionary unity of all organisms.

But what was really new was the genetic tracing of the unipolar cells from the bipolar ones. This meant that the cells of the nervous system of lower animals showed a continuity with those of higher animals, and that the sharp distinction previously accepted no longer existed.

Freud had made a major discovery with Petromyzon: "The spinal ganglion cells of the fish have long been known to be bipolar (possessing two processes), while those of the higher vertebrata are unipolar." This gap between lower and higher animals Freud closed. "The nerve cells of the Petromyzon show all transitions from uni- to bipolarity including bipolars with T-branching." This paper, in content, presentation, and implication was without any doubt well above the beginner's level: any zoologist would have been proud to have made these discoveries. Brücke presented it at the Academy on July 18, 1878, and it appeared in its *Bulletin*, eighty-six pages long, the next month.

The same general problem was the aim of Freud's next investigation which he conducted by his own choice in the summer months of 1879 and 1881. This time the objects were the nerve cells of the crayfish. Here he examined the live tissues microscopically, using a Harnack No. 8 lens—a technique which, at that time, was very little known, undeveloped, and difficult—and he reached the definite conclusion that the axis cylinders of nerve fibers are without exception fibrillary in structure. He was the first to demonstrate this fundamental feature. He recognized that the ganglion consists of two substances, of which one is netlike and the origin of the nerve process. This study, which Freud himself got presented at the Academy of Sciences at the meeting of December 15, 1881, and which appeared in the *Bulletin* of the Academy in January 1882, excels in the choice of its method, the exacting care given to its development, the caution shown in the argumentation, the direct approach to the key problem as well as its precise, definite, and significant results.

With this paper and the two preceding ones Freud had done his share to pave the way for the neurone theory. One might safely go even a little further and claim, as have Brun[14] and Jelliffe,[15] that Freud had early and clearly conceived the nerve cells and fibrils to be one morphological and physiological unit—the later neurone. In his research papers he confined himself strictly to the anatomical point of view, although he made it clear that his investigations were conducted with the hope of gaining insight into the mystery of nerve action. Only once, in a lecture on "The structure of the elements of the nervous system" which summarizes his work, did he venture into this land beyond histology with the one paragraph: "If we assume that the fibrils of the nerve have the significance of isolated paths of conduction, then we should have to say that *the pathways which in the nerve are separate are confluent in the nerve cell:* then the nerve cell becomes the 'beginning' of all those nerve fibers anatomically connected with it. I should transgress the limitations I have imposed on this paper were I to assemble the facts supporting the validity of that assumption: I do not know if the existing material suffices to decide the problem, so important for physiology. If this assumption could be established it would take us a good step further in the physiology of the nerve elements: we could imagine that a stimulus of a certain strength might break down the isolation of the fibrils so that the nerve as a unit conducts the excitation, and so on.'

This lecture Freud delivered at the Psychiatric Society[d]—within a year after he left the Brücke Institute—in 1882 or 1883.[e] It was published in the *Jahrbücher für Psychiatrie* early in 1884. There he

[d] In various bibliographies of Freud's writings this society is listed under several different titles, creating confusion and suggesting there were different societies. Dr. Solms, the present Secretary, has kindly sent me an authentic account of it. In 1868 the *Verein für Psychiatrie und forensische Psychologie* was founded, and on May 9, 1895, changed its name to the *Verein für Psychiatrie und Neurologie;* in references this is often abbreviated to *Psychiatrischer Verein.*

Its official organ was called, from 1868-1869 the *Vierteljahrschrift für Psychiatrie,* from 1871-1878 the *Psychiatrische Centralblatt,* from 1879-1891 the *Jahrbücher für Psychiatrie,* and since then the *Jahrbücher für Psychiatrie und Neurologie.*

[e] In his bibliography (1897) Freud gives 1882 as the date, but he was by no means infallible in such matters. The reports of the Society in the medical periodicals for 1882 are complete and do not mention his lecture. Those for 1883 do not either, but they are incomplete, so the point must be left open.

gave an account of the whole situation in which his highly specialized investigation originated. He detailed his methods and findings and in a few sentences intimated the far-reaching vistas opened by his results. We find here the same caution and boldness, the same style of argumentation which characterizes the many accounts of his findings in psychoanalysis which Freud later gave to audiences unfamiliar with the aims, methods, and experiences of the specialist. The first lecture of this kind shares with its successors the condensation of complex networks of facts and of complicated chains of thought into a few simple and lucid sentences.

This unitary conception of the nerve cell and processes—the essence of the future neurone theory—seems to have been Freud's own and quite independent of his teachers at the Institute. There is certainly in his few sentences both a boldness of thought and a cautiousness in presentation; he makes no real claim. But two comments seem in place. The lecture containing those remarks was delivered four or five years after he had conducted the researches on which they were based, so that the period of rumination was a long one. Then, after so much time for reflection, one would have thought that a little of the free and bold imagination he was so often to display in later years would have carried him the small step further, for he was trembling on the very brink of the important neurone theory, the basis of modern neurology. In the endeavor to acquire "discipline" he had not yet perceived that in original scientific work there is an equally important place for imagination.

Actually no notice was taken of these precious sentences, so that Freud's name is not mentioned among the pioneers of the neurone theory. There were many such pioneers, the chief being Wilhelm His with his embryological studies on the genesis of nerve cells, August Forel with his observations on the Wallerian degeneration following injury or section of nerve fibers, and Ramon y Cajal with his beautiful preparations made by the use of Golgi's silver impregnation. The final establishment of the neurone theory is usually dated from Waldeyer's comprehensive monograph in 1891, in which the word "neurone" was first employed. It was not the only time that Freud narrowly missed world fame in early life through not daring to pursue his thoughts to their logical—and not far-off—conclusion.

Another characteristic of the original scientist, however, he did display. Scientific progress typically proceeds from the invention of some new method or instrument which reveals a new body of fact. Astronomy, for instance, had come to a dead end before the invention of the telescope, and then bounded forward once more. Now, the histological researches just recorded were made possible, or at all events greatly facilitated, by an improvement in technique which Freud devised in 1877, soon after entering the Institute. It was a modification of the Reichert formula, a mixture of nitric acid and glycerine, for preparing nervous tissue for microscopical examination. Freud used it first when studying the spinal cells of the Petromyzon, but the following quotation from his published account of the method in 1879 illustrates the wide range of his investigations.

"I use Reichert's mixture as I have modified it for the purpose of preparing in a guaranteed and easy way the central and peripheral nervous system of the higher vertebratae (mice, rabbits, cattle). . . . I have tried the method with the cerebral nerves of infants— Professor Dr. E. Zukerkandl kindly participating. We have found that it considerably facilitates the preparation of nerves situated in the bone channels and in the preparation and disentanglement of anastomoses and nerve networks. . . . Furthermore, I have used it successfully for the preparation of mucous and sweat glands, Pacini bodies, hair roots, etc." [16] This mixture destroys the connective tissues and makes it easier to remove the muscles and bones, so that both the central nervous system and its peripheral branches are laid bare for separate examination.

A few years later he made a more important technical invention— the gold chloride method of staining nervous tissue—but neither method was much used outside the Vienna Institute. He must have been an expert technician, for in his researches on the nervous tissue of crayfish he speaks of special studies of his material *in vivo,* a delicate enough operation; it was a method he had learned from Stricker. Incidentally one may mention that he drew himself the illustrations for his publications on the Petromyzon, one in the first and four in the second.

Evidently, therefore, Freud had early grasped the fact that further progress in knowledge requires new or improved methods. Then come the new facts thus discovered, followed by the organization of the new and old knowledge in a theory of them. The theory may then lead to speculation, a glancing and guessing at questions and answers beyond existing means of observation. It is extremely rare for one and the same man to be equally successful in all these phases of development. Freud's work in psychoanalysis was to prove an example of this rarest case. He devised the instrument, used it to discover a great number of new facts, provided the organizing theory, and ventured on stimulating speculations beyond the actually known.

In the lecture previously alluded to (1882) he described a new technique, the new findings, the theory adequate to them, with some glances beyond. It was on a small scale, it was hampered by an over-curbing of the imagination, but it was the future Freud in embryo.

One notable feature in Freud's neurological researches was his ad-herence to anatomy. The microscope was his one and only tool. Physiology seemed to mean histology to him, and not experimenta-tion: statics, not dynamics. This might at first sight seem strange in a man of Freud's active mind, but reflection shows that it corre-sponded to something highly significant in his nature.

In later years he was to complain—not quite fairly—that there had been too much histology in Brücke's Institute and that he had been condemned to a subordinate part of physiology, but it was certainly something in himself that attached him to it or else kept him away from experimentation. It is true that Brücke did not share the con-tempt some of his fellow physiologists felt for the mere microscopist. In his mind there was no opposition between anatomy and physi-ology, between the microscope and experimentation; his first work on the structure of cells (1847), which made him famous, had combined both approaches. Nevertheless, in Freud's time Brücke and his two assistants, Exner and Fleischl, used animal experimenta-tion extensively. It is also true that to understand the active forces of the organism one has to have a good knowledge of its structure, the material on which those forces work. Still that is no reason why some-one whose deepest urge was to understand those forces should for so long confine himself to the problems of structure alone.

There was certainly no lack of opportunity. He was free to choose whatever problem or method interested him. Moreover, in 1882, when he exchanged Brücke's laboratories for Meynert's and was again free to choose, it was once more the microscope to which he turned.

When he first, as an eager beginner, asked Brücke for a problem to work on he was given a histological one. Did some docility or feel-ing of inferiority interpret this, as Dr. Bernfeld suggests, as being relegated to an inferior sphere, where it was his duty to remain ever-more, leaving the higher experimental activities to the three profes-sors, to "grown-ups?" [17] Possibly so, but in his attitude one senses something deeper and highly characteristic of his personality.

There are two sides to this preference of the eye over the hand, of passively seeing over actively doing; an attraction to the one, an aversion to the other. Both were present. Of the former something will be said presently. The latter is plainly indicated in a letter he wrote in 1878, the year we have reached, to a friend, Wilhelm Knöpfmacher, in which he wrote: "I have moved to another laboratory[f] and am preparing myself for my proper profession—mutilating animals or tormenting human beings—and I decide more and more in favor of the former alternative." [18] He was the last man who could ever permit himself to be brutal or cruel, and he was even extremely averse to interfering with other people or striving to influence them. When later on it fell to his lot to treat neurotic patients he soon abandoned the method—customary then and recently revived in another form—of stimulating them by means of electricity. And it was not long before he gave up the use of hypnosis, which he found "a coarsely interfering method." He chose instead to look and listen, confident that if he could perceive the structure of a neurosis he would truly understand and have power over the forces that had brought it about. Pierre Janet, who has erroneously been regarded as a predecessor of Freud's, adopted in the eighties the alternative method of approach. He devised some beautiful and very ingenious experiments which led to some vivid descriptive conclusions, but they brought him not one step nearer to the forces at work. It was the passive method that succeeded, not the active one.

That there was a pronounced passive side to Freud's nature is a conclusion for which there is ample evidence. He showed little aggressiveness in his life and only on two exceptional occasions did he deign to reply to his opponents. An active role in life would not have suited him. He once remarked that there were three things to which he felt unequal: governing, curing,[g] and educating. But what is significant is the extraordinary change that must have set in at about the age of sixteen or seventeen. Gone is the pugnacious child who fought vigorously with his playfellow, the boy full of military ardor, the youth who dreamed of becoming a Cabinet Minister and ruling the nation. Was, after all, the two days' encounter with a country girl so very fateful?

Whatever the reason, we observe the profundity of the change in the direction of power. Dominating fellow beings is entirely replaced by understanding them. Only knowledge will give power. And that in the long run—how long!—this proved true, that Freud can be said

[f] I.e., Stricker's.
[g] Evidently in the sense of active intervention.

to be the first ever to effect radical changes in human personality, was surely the greatest triumph for the method he was unconsciously moved to select: statics had led to dynamics. What a daemonic intuition must have been at work! Perhaps we are nearing a clue to the mysterious problem of how it was that just this man was destined to discover psychoanalysis and reveal the unconscious mind of man.

Three times he essayed the experimental method, and each time unsuccessfully. When this happens to someone with at least average intelligence there must be some inner resistance at work; his heart cannot be in it. The first attempt was in 1878 when he worked in the summer term and a portion of the summer vacation in Stricker's laboratory. Solomon Stricker, a vain man of uncertain temper, who was a contemporary of Claus, was a full Professor and had been the head of the Pathological Institute for five years. He is credited with transforming pathology from an anatomical into an experimental physiological discipline. This was presumably what impelled Freud to work under him. All we know about the result is that at a meeting of the *Gesellschaft der Ärzte* (Society of Physicians) on October 17, 1879, Stricker introduced a paper on acinous glands with the statement that his student Freud had, at his suggestion, conducted experiments on this topic for six months, but had accomplished nothing.[19] That was the end of this first attempt. After Freud's failure Stricker tackled the problem himself, on the basis of some new ideas supplied by Spina, and obtained with him some interesting results. Freud himself returned to the Brücke Institute and to the microscope, beginning his research on the nerve cells of the crayfish, where, incidentally, he paid high tribute to T. H. Huxley's book on that animal.

Six years later, in 1884, after he had left Brücke, he made another attempt. He returned to Stricker's laboratory and participated, together with Wagner-Jauregg, Gaertner, Spina, and Koller, in some animal experiments as part of an investigation into the function of glands in relation to the circulatory system.[20] Again he accomplished nothing, and he confined himself from then on to brain anatomy.

The third short attempt, in 1885, was a small part of his examination of the coca plant. In studying its effect on the body he had the idea, so as to find out whether the characteristic euphoria was justified or illusory, of testing the effect of the drug on muscular strength as measured by the dynamometer, a rather crude instrument. He ascertained, working together with Koller, that the strength was actually increased, but the study was a poor effort. The technique was over-simplified and the exposition uncertain and uncritical, the work of an ordinary beginner, on quite another plane from his valuable histological researches of years before.

When in later years Freud bemoaned the lack of success in his first three years as a medical student, meaning in zoology, where he was unduly hard on himself, it would have been more to the point if he had said (experimental) physiology rather than zoology.

In the summer or autumn of 1879 Freud was called up for his year's military service. That was far less strenuous in those days than now. Medical students continued to live at home and had no duties except to stand about in the hospitals. The hardship was the terrible boredom, perhaps the reason why a few years later it was decreed that they had to spend half their time undergoing military training proper. Freud spent his twenty-fourth birthday under arrest (May 6, 1880) for being absent without leave.[21] He was interested to meet at dinner five years later the General Podratzsky who had sentenced him, but he bore him no grudge since he admitted that he had failed to attend eight visits in succession.[22]

In the first part of the year Freud was able to cope with the boredom by devoting himself to translating a book by John Stuart Mill, the first of five large books he translated. It was congenial work, since he was specially gifted as a translator. Instead of laboriously transcribing from the foreign language, idioms and all, he would read a passage, close the book, and consider how a German writer would have clothed the same thoughts—a method not very common among translators. His translating work was both brilliant and rapid. This was the only work, original or translation, he ever published that had no connection with his scientific interests,[h] and, although the contents of the book probably appealed to him, his main motive was undoubtedly to kill time and, incidentally, earn a little money.

The editor of Mill's collected writings in German was Theodor Gomperz, a philosopher and historian of high standing in Vienna. When fifty years later his son Heinrich was preparing a biography of his father, he asked Freud how he came to be the translator of the twelfth volume. Freud replied, in a letter dated June 9, 1932, that Gomperz had inquired at a party for someone to replace Eduard Wessel, the young translator of the twelfth volume who had died sud-

[h] Exceptions to this statement are the section on Samuel Butler in Israel Levine's "*Das Unbewusste*" (The Unconscious)[23] and Marie Bonaparte's book *Topsy*, on which he and Anna Freud spent their time while waiting for Nazi permission to leave Austria in 1938.

denly, and that Brentano had given him Freud's name. Freud had for a couple of years attended Brentano's lectures, as indeed had half Vienna, since he was a very gifted lecturer, but whether Brentano remembered him from his seminars or whether Freud's name was passed on to him by one of their mutual friends—Breuer, for instance, was Brentano's family physician—is not known, nor does it seem of any importance.

Three of Mill's essays were concerned with social problems: the labor question, the enfranchisement of women, and socialism. In the preface Mill said that the greatest part of these was the work of his wife. The fourth, by Mill himself, was on Grote's Plato. Freud remarked many years later (in 1933) that his knowledge of Plato's philosophy was very fragmentary, so perhaps what there was of it had been derived from this essay of Mill's. He added, however, that he had been greatly impressed by Plato's theory of reminiscence, one which Mill treats sympathetically, and had at one time given it a great deal of thought. Many years later he wove some suggestions of Plato's into his book, *Beyond the Pleasure Principle*.

The researches we have described took up, after all, only the smaller part of his time, which was mostly devoted to medical studies, pathology, surgery, and so on. Here he had many distinguished and inspiring teachers. Some—such as Billroth, the surgeon, Hebra, the dermatologist, and Arlt, the ophthalmologist—were world-famous men and attracted crowds of enthusiastic students. They gave more than the routine knowledge of contemporary medicine; they were brilliant innovators in their several fields and instilled in their students the spirit of scientific medicine. Yet Freud remained cool towards their work. For Billroth, it is true, he retained a great admiration. The only lectures he found at all interesting were Meynert's on psychiatry, a field that must have seemed very novel to him, the devotee of laboratories. As his letter to Knöpfmacher shows, he doubted seriously whether he would ever want to become a physician.

He knew, however, that all the leading physiologists, such as Helmholtz, Du Bois-Reymond, and Brücke himself, had qualified for the degree of M.D. and some had even practiced medicine. So at long last he suddenly decided to follow in their footsteps and take the necessary examinations, called in Vienna *rigorosa*. What we term the preliminary scientific examination is nowadays (also in Vienna) taken at the end of the first year of study, or even in school before entering any medical institution. In those days, however, it could be postponed until all the studies were completed, and Freud did not miss availing himself of the opportunity for delay. So he had hurriedly to furbish up what he had learned years ago. With what he called a well-justified fear he faced his friend, Professor Fleischl, on June 9, 1880, for his first *rigorosum* in chemistry, botany, and zoology. He said: "I escaped disaster only through the clemency of fate or of that of the examiners." He was interested in chemistry, or admired its exactitude, but he had no aptitude for it. He remarked that his interest in botany was never very great; at the examination he failed to identify a crucifer and was saved only by his theoretical knowledge. This is rather surprising when one thinks of his fondness for the country and his unusual familiarity with flowers. Nevertheless, his grading in the examination, conducted by Fleischl, was "excellent."

On the same day, in the second *rigorosum*, on general medicine, Hoffman passed him as "satisfactory" only, because Freud had failed in forensic medicine. Freud worked in Brücke's laboratory for another ten months before he went up for the third *rigorosum* on the several medical specialities. Hoffman was again the examiner and passed him, on March 30, 1881, with the grading "excellent." This result, according to Freud, was due only to the photographic memory that he had enjoyed all through his childhood and adolescence, although it was gradually becoming unreliable. He had not used the long interval for preparation for the examination, but "in the tension before the final examination I must have made use of the remnant of this ability, for in certain subjects I gave the examiners apparently automatic answers which proved to be exact reproductions of the textbook which I had skimmed through but once, and then in greatest haste." Thus his M.D. degree is dated March 31, 1881. The graduation ceremonies took place in the beautiful aula of the baroque building of the old University. Freud's family were present, and Richard Fluss with his parents, old friends of his early childhood years in Freiberg, Moravia.

The obtaining of this medical qualification was in no sense a turning point in Freud's life, and not even in itself an event of much importance. It was a thing that had to be done in the course of events, and he could no longer be teased as a loafer.[24] But he went straight on working in the Brücke Institute following the course that would perhaps in due time lead to a Chair in Physiology. Any fond dream of that sort was, however, to be shattered in hardly more than a year's time.

V

Medical Career

(1 8 8 1 – 1 8 8 5)

ONE MAY WONDER ABOUT FREUD'S STATE OF MIND DURING THE YEARS
he spent in Brücke's laboratory. They were incompatible with any
plans for a future livelihood, which his poor economic situation
would obviously make necessary. He could not have been oblivious
of such a staring fact, and even of the high probability that it would
mean some form of medical practice. But he pushed it aside as long
as he could and must have had strong reasons for doing so. Two such
reasons are readily to be discerned. One was his aversion to the practice of medicine, a matter that is a problem in itself. The other was
his great liking for his laboratory work. This had more than one
source. He presumably found the work itself interesting, but more
important was his consistent preference for research over mere practice. To discover something new and thus add to our stock of knowledge was perhaps the strongest motive in his nature. Furthermore,
there was the need to discipline himself in scientific method and
thus counteract his wilder and more speculative propensities, which
dear as they might be could lead him far astray if not controlled.

So he determined to continue with the congenial and disciplinary
research work as long as he decently could, depending first on hi~
father's willing support and, when this began to fail, on being helped
by friends. At the same time, however, he also continued his regular
medical studies and finally decided, in March 1881, to pass the quali-
fying examinations. This no doubt alleviated the self-reproaches his
three years' delay had been causing him, but, as we shall presently see,
it brought him face to face with graver problems.

The medical qualification appeared outwardly to make no difference. Freud continued for another fifteen months to work as before

in the Physiological Institute, now devoting his whole time to it. Some two months later he was promoted to the position of Demonstrator, one with some teaching responsibility; he held this position from May 1881 to July 1882. We have no record of any further researches in the Institute during the latter part of his period as Demonstrator, the duties of which were probably engrossing. He finished those on the crayfish in the autumn of 1881, and his paper on it was presented at a meeting of the Academy of Sciences in that December.

Simultaneously with this activity he worked for a year on advanced investigations in the analysis of gases in Ludwig's Chemical Institute, where his friend Lustgarten was an Assistant. Although he rather liked chemistry he had no success in it, and he later spoke of this wasted year as an unfruitful one, the recollection of which was humiliating.[1] Indeed, he afterwards termed 1882 "the gloomiest and least successful year of my professional life." [2]

Freud held the position of Demonstrator for three semesters. In the natural course of events, however prolonged, it would lead on[a] to that of Assistant, then Assistant Professor, and finally Professor of Physiology in the beloved Institute, this being the logical goal. At the end of the third semester, however, in June 1882, an event took place which may truly be called one of the great turning points in his life, one that before many years had passed resulted in his finding himself, unwittingly at first, in his permanent career.

This event was the decision to earn his livelihood as a physician and resign his position in Brücke's Institute. His own account of it, in his *Autobiography* (1923), runs as follows: "The turning point came in 1882 when my teacher, for whom I had the highest possible esteem, corrected my father's generous improvidence by strongly advising me, in view of my bad financial position, to abandon my theoretical career. I followed his advice, left the physiology laboratory and entered the General Hospital." [3] One year later, he gave substantially the same presentation in another place: ". . . till the teacher, whom I so deeply respected, warned me that in view of my restricted material circumstances I could not possibly take up a theoretical career." [4]

When some people, e.g., Wittels, assumed that there had been a break between him and Brücke, Freud definitely contradicted this and repeated that he had left on Brücke's advice.[5] Brücke certainly retained a warm interest in Freud's career. He was his chief sponsor

[a] Provided one was a Gentile!

in his application for the rank of *Privatdocent*, being merely seconded by Meynert and Nothnagel, and it was his influence that procured for Freud against strong opposition the invaluable traveling grant for the study in Paris. They remained on entirely friendly terms; Brücke was one of the first people he visited on his return from Paris four years later.[6]

The economic prospects were certainly dark enough. Both the Assistants were only ten years older than Freud himself and so would not be likely to vacate such a position for him for years to come. As for the distant Chair, Freud was sixty-nine when Exner, Brücke's successor, died, so in the most favorable circumstances it would have been a very long wait. Furthermore, the salary paid to an Assistant was so exiguous that he could hardly support himself without private means, and certainly could not found a family.

With those prospects, and with Freud's own poor financial background, how long could he expect to continue in his present course? He had at first been quite dependent on his father's support; a few small honorariums for his publications and in 1879 a University grant of 100 gulden ($40) [7] were the only contributions of his own. The father, then aged sixty-seven and burdened with a family of seven children, was in poor and very uncertain financial circumstances, and at times had to be helped out by loans and gifts from his wife's family. His small capital had been lost in the financial crash of 1873. The time had already come, moreover, when he had ceased to earn, and he and his family were for years in very sore straits. It is true that he had supported his young doctor son generously and willingly with the improvidence that characterized him. Earlier he had hoped his son would enter business, but with perhaps a sigh he resigned himself to the intellectual career and without doubt he was proud of his son's successes and achievements. He was content that Freud should continue on the path he had chosen and glad to be able to make it possible as long as he could. It is also true that Sigmund's needs were very modest. Apart from peace and quiet for reading, and the company of like-minded friends, he wanted little else than books. These certainly made some demands on his pocket money. There were times when he had to borrow money from friends, but he repaid it conscientiously, even sooner than had been expected; one such episode is mentioned in a letter that has survived from the correspondence with his friend Knöpfmacher. About this time, however, he found a philanthropic patron in the person of Breuer, who made him almost regularly a "loan."

By 1884 this debt reached the considerable sum of 1,500 gulden ($580).[9]

All in all, the picture was not a bright one. One can only wonder what Freud's state of mind was on the subject. He was twenty-six. He did not want to be a physician. Yet he was in a blind alley, with practically no future prospects of ever earning a livelihood. The lack of foresight, and indeed of a sense of reality, seem so foreign to the Freud we knew later, who was always alive to the practical issues of life. From his subsequent accounts of the happenings one could even get the impression that it was only Brücke's homiletic intervention that suddenly woke him out of a dream, the dream of idealistically serving the cause of science irrespective of mundane considerations. Not at all the independent Freud we knew.

It is not the only time that Freud preferred to give an unfavorable impression of himself rather than disclose something of his private life. What he revealed of his life was far more carefully selected and censored than is generally supposed. The contemporary evidence gives, as it often does, a very different picture.

One would not know from the *Autobiography* whether Brücke went out of his way to offer his weighty advice or whether Freud had approached him for his opinion; further, why that important talk took place just when it did. Nor does one see what Brücke had to contribute to what Freud must already have known. That his future was most uncertain and that his financial basis was precarious were evident enough facts.

In truth Freud had not at all been blind to the realities of his situation, nor was the decision an unexpected one. From the moment of acquiring the degree of M.D. he had contemplated "with an increasingly heavy heart" the unescapable decision facing him of leaving his laboratory work for the practice of medicine.[10] But what brought the matter to a head at a particular moment was something new in his life. He had fallen head over ears in love! More than that: in a garden in Mödling, on the fateful day of Saturday, June 10, he had received intimations from the lady, Martha Bernays, that made him dare hope for his suit. On the next day he thought matters over, came to a definite decision, and on the following morning he informed Brücke of it. It was no news to him to hear that Brücke had no intention of parting with either of his two valuable Assistants, Fleischl and Exner, so that the Institute offered no prospects whatsoever. The die was cast.

Now, although Freud never mentioned this motive in forming his

resolution, it was evidently the decisive one. It was like him to suppress it. Bernfeld remarks, in calling attention to it, that in the self-
confessions scattered throughout his writings Freud figures at times
as a villain, a parricide, ambitious, petty, revengeful, but never as a
lover (save for a few very superficial allusions to his wife).[11]

It would be natural if he felt some resentment against fate at this
break in his chosen career. If he felt any against Brücke, which
would have been quite unreasonable, he never displayed it. But later
in the year there was a curious outburst that perhaps makes the topic
not altogether impertinent. In the Address to the Psychiatric Society to which allusion has already been made,[b] there was the usual
criticism of those who were opposed to the conclusions he was expounding. A particularly sharp one, however, was directed against
Fleischl, who was his friend, but who was also his immediate superior
in the Institute, to whose position he might have hoped to succeed.
He took to pieces very thoroughly a study of his on the structure of
nerve fibers, rejecting the conclusions unreservedly. More than this,
he resorted even to the method of personal psychological interpretation, one he firmly deprecated in later years, and pointed out
what the motives of the observer might be. Since this was so alien to
his usual contained attitude, it is hard not to associate it, as Bernfeld does,[12] with the dissatisfaction and frustration at having to leave
the Institute. It is an example of the ambivalent changes between
friendliness and hostility on which he had himself commented in connection with the lasting influence of his childhood experience with
his nephew John.

Freud confessed in later years how he had secretly cherished the
thought that his advancement would be favored by Fleischl's death,
but afterwards he was shocked at hearing his successor in the Institute, Paneth, openly voicing the same wish.[13] As it turned out,
Fleischl and Paneth died within a year of each other.

The decision had undoubtedly been a very painful one, but Freud
accepted it resolutely. In admitting to Martha what a wrench the
"separation from science" had been, he cheerfully added "but perhaps it is not a final one." [14] The first step he took was an unavoida-
ble one. There was evidently no alternative to earning a living by private practice, and to do so—unless one would remain in the lowest
ranks of the profession—meant acquiring some clinical experience in
a hospital, something in which he was as yet quite deficient; medical
students in those days, at least on the Continent, learned through

b See p. 150.

lectures and demonstrations only, and had no experience in personal care of patients. So Freud planned to spend two years living and studying in the hospital and thus acquire a more thorough and first-hand knowledge of all branches. As things turned out he stayed there fully three years. If he could attain the position there as *Sekundararzt*, a combination of our (resident) House Physician and Registrar, he would be at least in the middle class of the profession, and with luck might rise still higher. So this step he took without delay, and on the thirty-first day of July he inscribed himself in the General Hospital of Vienna.

He chose to begin with surgery, giving as his reasons that the work was so responsible that it would compel his serious attention and further that he was already accustomed to using his hands. He found the work physically tiring and only remained a little over two months in the surgical wards. The visits lasted from 8:00 to 10:00 o'clock and again from 4:00 to 6:00; from 10:00 to 12:00 he had to spend reading the literature on the cases just examined. Presumably the chief, Professor Billroth, was on holiday, since some time later Freud mentioned that they had not met.

On October 4 he called on the great Nothnagel, bearing an introductory letter from Meynert. Nothnagel had just arrived in Vienna from Germany to occupy the Chair of Medicine, which he retained until his death twenty-three years later. The influence of a man in that position was very great, and Freud rightly surmised that his career, especially in his future practice, would depend very much on Nothnagel's grace. In a long letter he gave a full description of the house, of Nothnagel's personal appearance and manner, together with a verbatim account of the interview. Nothnagel had two Assistants. There was a vacancy, but it was already promised. So Freud asked him if he might function in his department as an "*Aspirant*," roughly the position of our Clinical Assistant, until he could be appointed a *Sekundararzt*. Meynert spoke again to Nothnagel in his favor, and Freud thus entered his Clinic as *Aspirant* on October 12, 1882.[15] He was then given a nominal salary.

The branch of the hospital where Freud was now working was Nothnagel's Division of Internal Medicine. Nothnagel was a great physician, if not so original as his predecessor Rokitansky. He came to Vienna from Germany in 1882, and died in 1905. His conception of medical duties was extremely strict. He said to his students: "Whoever needs more than five hours of sleep should not study medicine. The medical student must attend lectures from eight in the morning until six in the evening. Then he must go home and read until late at night." He had, moreover, a generous and noble character and was idolized by his students and patients alike. Freud admired and respected him, but he could not emulate his enthusiasm for medicine. He found no more interest in treating the sick patients in the wards than in studying their diseases. By now he must have been more convinced than ever that he was not born to be a doctor.

What this aversion really signified is hard to determine. It was assuredly no lack of respect for the profession of medicine, as might perhaps be thought. On the contrary, there are signs that he regarded it as a Promised Land—or, to be more accurate, a Forbidden Land—into which for some reason he was not destined to enter. Only a few years later, in August 1888, in reply to a friend's advice to become a regular physician, he wrote: "I entirely agree with you, but nevertheless I cannot do what you recommend. . . . I have not learnt enough to be a physician. In my medical development there is a rift which was later painstakingly bridged. I could only learn enough to become a neuropathologist.c And now I lack, not youth, but time and independence to make up for what I missed. Last winter I was pretty busy; so I could just make ends meet with my big family and had no time left for study." [16] In other words, there was some sense of inferiority in the matter, which he ascribes—not at all plausibly—to insufficient knowledge or even an incapacity to learn: he who could acquire knowledge so swiftly and easily. Plainly it was a matter of inhibition rather than incapacity. Perhaps from his remark, quoted earlier, about tormenting human beings, one should infer some inhibition in dealing with physical suffering and, as a doctor, sometimes even having to add to it.

Freud served under Nothnagel for six and a half months, till the end of April,d and on May 1, 1883, transferred to Meynert's Psychiatric Clinic, where he was at once appointed *Sekundararzt*.[18]

He now moved into the hospital,e the first time he had left home except for short holidays. He was then twenty-seven years old. He never again slept at home.

c One senses a slightly bitter note here.
d Dr. Bernfeld was misinformed when he wrote that Freud was not in the hospital in the first four months of 1883.[17]
e In one of the books on Freud his position is called that of an "internee," which reminds one of a favorite anecdote of Freud's concerning an erratic doctor who was given a medical post in an asylum; it was said to be the most considerate way of getting him there.

His new chief, Theodor Meynert (1833-1892), was at least as distinguished in his sphere as Brücke was in his, so Freud could look up to him with the same respect, if not quite the same awe. Meynert's lectures had been the only medical ones that had aroused his interest as a student. In his writings we hear of "the great Meynert in whose footsteps I followed with such veneration," [19] and in spite of bitter personal disappointments in later years he always recalled him as the most brilliant genius he had ever encountered.

Freud agreed with the general opinion that Meynert was the greatest brain anatomist of his time, but he had only a moderate opinion of him as a psychiatrist.[20] Nevertheless it was from the study of the disorder called "Meynert's Amentia" (acute hallucinatory psychosis) that he obtained the vivid impression of the wish-fulfillment mechanism he was to apply so extensively in his later investigations of the unconscious.

Meynert's only possible rival of that period was Flechsig of Leipzig, a matter that, as Bernfeld suggests, probably had a fateful effect on his later relationship with Freud.[21]

Freud served in Meynert's Clinic for five months, two months in the male wards and then three in the female. This constituted his main purely psychiatric experience. In his letters of the time he was enthusiastic about what a stimulating teacher Meynert was—"a more stimulating person than a host of friends." It was hard work, and the seven hours daily in the wards were barely sufficient to cover the ground. He was determined to master the subject and read assiduously in it—Esquirol, Morel, etc.; he remarked how little psychiatrists seemed to understand of it. The month's holiday due to him in August he spent also at work in the hospital, acting then as Senior *Sekundararzt* in place of his friend Holländer who was on leave. He obtained, however, two weeks' leave from work in September, but only went away for a couple of days to Baden, just outside Vienna.

These months in the Psychiatric Clinic were satisfactory in more than one respect. Freud mentioned that he had made many good friends among the resident physicians, and added, "So I can't be a quite unbearable person." When the united *Sekundarärzte* made a protest to the authorities about the accommodation in the Pathological Institute, it was Freud they chose to be their spokesman, so he was evidently already beginning to stand out among the rest.

On October 1, 1883, Freud moved to Von Zeissl's Department of Dermatology.[22] Von Zeissl had retired the year before, and his place had not yet been filled. In Freud's time Dr. Anscherlik functioned temporarily as Superintendent.[23] Freud's junior colleague was Maximilian Zeissl, son of the late Superintendent, and Freud learned a good deal from him. There were two such departments in the hospital: one for ordinary skin diseases, the other for syphilitic and other infectious ones. It was the latter Freud wanted experience in, because of the important connection between syphilis and various diseases of the nervous system. He regretted, however, that he worked only in the male ward, and so did not see the same disorders in women. It was very light work, the ward visits finishing at ten in the morning and taking place only twice a week. He thus had plenty of time for the laboratory.

During the three months in which Freud was thus engaged he also attended special courses in naso-laryngology, where he found himself clumsy in the use of the instruments when doing the practical work in the Policlinic. He applied to work under Urbantschitsch, but that course was full, so he joined Ultzmann's.

Before she left for Wandsbek Martha used to visit Freud in his hospital lodging. In the October after leaving Meynert's service he had to move to a different room, and in order to keep Martha in touch with the details of his daily life he described the new room and drew a diagram of it which is reproduced here. To brighten the room that had never been graced by Martha's presence he asked her to embroider two "Votive panels" he could hang over his desk. He chose two inscriptions for the purpose: one, adapted from *Candide*, was

Travailler sans raisonner; [f]

the other, which Fleischl told him came from St. Augustine, was

En cas de doute abstiens toi.[g]

Three years later, when he was setting up in private practice, he got her to embroider a third one, this time a favorite saying of Charcot's:

Il faut avoir la foi.[h]

At the end of 1883 he advanced to the status of having two rooms in the hospital.

In October his friend Holländer told him there was a prospect of

[f] Let us work without philosophizing.
[g] When in doubt, abstain.
[h] One must have faith.

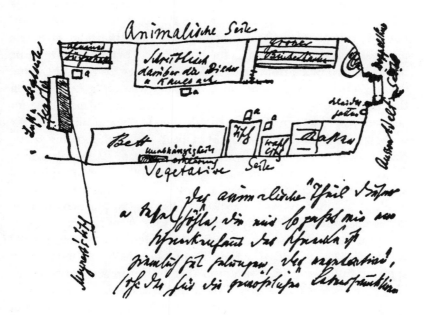

A DIAGRAM OF SIGMUND FREUD'S ROOM IN THE GENERAL HOSPITAL OF
VIENNA, DRAWN BY HIM FOR MARTHA BERNAYS (1883).

A clearer copy prepared by the author is shown below.

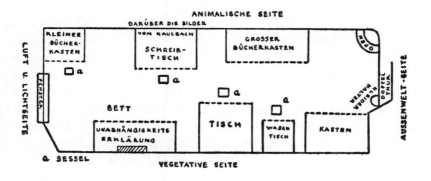

Meynert's being given a neurological department, and he at once envisaged the possibility of his getting the post of Assistant there. Meynert, however, did not get his neurological department until June 1886, when Freud was already in private practice. Its only importance to him then was that it would have been the most favorable place to find clinical material for his lectures, but by that time he had fallen too much from grace in Meynert's eyes for this. In the following January, 1884, there was a rumor of Meynert's Assistant (in the psychiatric wards) leaving—though actually he did not leave for another year—and Freud debated whether he should apply for the post. It would mean a position of respect, a doubling of his salary, the certainty of becoming a Docent, and command of the laboratory. On the other hand it meant wasting time with the "unfruitful psychiatry," the absence of any neurological cases, the study of which would help him towards his goal of a neurological practice—and going against Breuer's contrary advice. He soon decided not to apply.

A year later there was more talk about Meynert's getting a ward for nervous cases, and this time Freud thought more seriously of applying to become his Assistant in that event; Breuer also approved of the idea. He would marry, live on his salary and courses, receive any private patients in the hospital, and so be able to live in modest circumstances in a home of his own outside. But the question never really arose.

On January 1, 1884, Freud entered on his longest spell of work in the hospital. The department was given the name of *Nervenabtheilung* (Nervous Diseases), but as often as not there were no nerve cases there. When they arrived, the Superintendent, Franz Scholz, who was no longer interested in such cases, turned them out as soon as he could,[24] but there was a conspiracy among the doctors in charge of admittance to bring more in. The Superintendent seems to have been interested in nothing but keeping down the costs, so the patients went hungry and only the cheapest medicines could be prescribed; new drugs could not be tested since they were more expensive. With that one proviso, however, the younger doctors had a free hand, and Scholz even encouraged any research they might undertake. Freud was revolted by the condition of the wards. They were not kept clean, so that the occasional sweeping meant an intolerable cloud of dust. No gas was installed anywhere in the hospital, and after dusk the patients had to lie in complete darkness. The doctors would make their rounds, and even perform any urgent operations, with the aid of a lantern. Freud resolved to expose this state of affairs in the public press as soon as he left the hospital, but there is no evidence that he ever did so.

Fleischl had told him it was desirable to publish some clinical contributions before applying for his docentship, and in the first week of entering the department he was lucky enough to come across a suitable case. It was the first of three he published in 1884.

Freud worked on steadily for the next six months, spending two hours a day, between ward visits, in the laboratory. But in July something very exciting happened. Three days before he had arranged to leave for his month's holiday in Wandsbek, news came that the Montenegrin Government had sent an urgent request for some Austrian doctors to help them control the frontier across which an epidemic of cholera was threatening to spread. To Freud's dismay both Moritz Ullmann, the other junior *Sekundararzt*—there were two of them—and the senior one, Josef Pollak, volunteered for this adventure, and he was left alone, the only doctor in the department. His chief, Scholz, had already left on his two months' holiday. Freud's first impulse was to resign altogether from the hospital, proceed to Wandsbek, and then take his chance as a general practitioner somewhere. But cooler reflections, aided by the calming influence of his friends Fleischl and Breuer, prevailed, and he consented to stay.

Two new junior doctors were placed under him, and Freud himself had the responsible position of Superintendent, a jump of two grades in rank. When Martha asked him to explain its significance, he tersely replied: "It means the Hospital Director invites you to sit down in his presence." He entered on his new position on July 15 and occupied it for six weeks, for the last month of which his salary was raised to 45 gulden ($18). He had made it a condition that he should be given the rank of Senior *Sekundararzt* when normal arrangements were re-established, but this promise was only partly kept; he was given the rank for three months after his return from leave, until January 1.[25]

He now had full charge of 106 patients, with ten nurses, two *Sekundarärzte*, and one *Aspirant* under him. The *Aspirant* was a Dr. Steigenberger, a devoted admirer of Martha's who regarded the victorious Freud with awe. Freud enjoyed the experience, although he groaned, "Ruling is so difficult." He also profited by it professionally: "In these weeks I have really become a doctor." [26] On September 1 he left for his well-earned holiday in Wandsbek.[27]

On his return Scholz reproached him for not having been economical enough, but seemed to be mollified when Freud gave him a satisfactory account of the medical work. Relations between them, however, were evidently strained. Meanness was a trait Freud abhorred and he did not always conceal his opinion. As we shall see, matters came to a head in the following February.

Freud said that in the spring of 1885 he was appointed Lecturer in Neuropathology "on the ground of my histological and clinical publications." [28] He was evidently referring to his attaining the position of *Privatdozent*. This rank, so important in Austria and Germany, has no exact counterpart in American or British Medical Schools; perhaps the nearest equivalent is that of an Oxford or Cambridge Don. A *Privatdozent* has not the right to attend faculty meetings, nor does he receive any salary, but he is permitted to hold a certain number of classes—usually on topics outside the regular curriculum. The position is highly prized. It is a necessary condition for any university advancement, and it enjoys high prestige with the general public, since it is an assurance of special competence. Very few such positions are granted, so that the small group is an élite. The requirements for the appointment are very high, and evidence is demanded of independent, original, and valuable achievements as documented by a considerable number of publications.

From the beginning of his medical career he had had this goal well in mind. What was important to him was not only the professional standing it brought, but the greatly improved prospects of securing a medical practice that would enable him to marry. In 1883 he hoped that the staining method he had devised would be successful enough to win him the desired prize, but a year later it had become evident that his thesis would have to be based on the researches he was then carrying out on the anatomy of the medulla. By May of this year he was hoping to be able to apply by the following Christmas. In June, however, he was tempted to deviate from the plan by receiving an offer to travel in charge of a psychotic patient whose expectation of life was estimated at ten months (probably a case of general paralysis). In that time he would earn 3,000 gulden ($1,150), which would mean being able to marry a whole year earlier than he had expected. It would also mean, however, leaving the hospital for good and dropping out of the running for the chance of the higher rank. He did not hesitate in his choice, in spite of his impatience at the long engagement, and he continued his work. He had been earning money by giving a course without the legal right to do so and a senior colleague displaced him in it. So he wondered if he had ˎ

chance of becoming a Docent at once without waiting to finish the anatomical work on which he had counted for this purpose. Breuer agreed and when he approached Nothnagel for his opinion the great man was most gracious and emphatic in his confidence that Freud would succeed. He assured him that he would be present at the deciding meeting and that he was man enough to get the matter through, whatever the opposition.[29] Thus emboldened, Freud sent in his application on January 21, 1885. The present writer is amused to read in a letter that he designated the *curriculum vitae* which had to accompany the application as "a preliminary work for my biography." [30]

Freud's application, signed January 2, 1885, contained a *curriculum vitae*, the bibliography of his published works, and his proposed program of teaching, *Lehrplan*. "If the Honorable College of Professors will grant me the lectureship (*Dozentur*) on Diseases of the Nervous System, then it is my intention to promote in two ways the instruction of this branch of human pathology; first, through lectures and classes on the anatomy and physiology of the nervous system, as far as knowledge of this kind is the necessary preparation for the understanding of the neuropathological facts; secondly, through classes and lectures, in which nerve patients will be presented, the necessary methods of examination will be shown, and the present knowledge concerning the pathology of the nervous system will be taught. For this latter purpose *Herr Primarius* Dr. F. Scholz has very kindly put at my disposal the material of the Fourth Division in the General Hospital in which I am serving as *Sekundararzt*." Dr. Scholz confirmed this promise with his signature.

In the Faculty meeting of January 24 a committee was elected, consisting of Meynert, Brücke, and Nothnagel, for the purpose of discussing the application and of reporting their findings to the Faculty. On February 1 Brücke communicated his opinion briefly to the committee: "The microscopic-anatomical papers by Dr. Freud were accepted with general recognition of his results. In so far as they have been checked up to now they have been confirmed. I know his work well and I am ready to sign any report that recommends the acceptance of the applicant. I am willing to appear at a committee meeting, if such a meeting should become necessary." On February 5 Nothnagel agreed with Brücke's opinion and on February 28 Brücke presented to the Faculty meeting the report of the committee, written by himself and countersigned by Meynert and Nothnagel.

In his report Brücke analyzed carefully and extensively Freud's three histological papers on "The Posterior Roots in Petromyzon" (1877-1878) and "The Nerve Cells in Crayfish" (1882), calling the latter work "very important." He gave shorter, appreciative abstracts of "A New Method for Anatomical Preparations of the Central Nervous System" (1879), "A Histological Method for the Study of Brain Tracts" (1884), "A Case of Cerebral Hemorrhage" (1884), and "On Coca" (1884). He mentioned the zoological paper on the eels (1877) and Freud's summary of his neurohistological studies, "Structure of the Elements of the Nervous System" (1884). He closed with the following recommendation: "Dr. Freud is a man with a good general education, of quiet and serious character, an excellent worker in the field of neuro-anatomy, of fine dexterity, clear vision, comprehensive knowledge, and a cautious method of deduction, with the gift for well-organized written expression. His findings enjoy recognition and confirmation, his style of lecturing is transparent and secure. In him the qualities of a scientific researcher and of a well-qualified teacher are so well united that the Committee submits the suggestion that the Honorable College resolve on his admission to the further habilitation tests." The Faculty meeting accepted this recommendation immediately by twenty-one to one.ht

This was the decisive phase and the good news was telegraphed at once to the betrothed. Three months later he received the invitation to attend the oral examination on June 13, and that brought up the anxious matter of costume. A silk hat and white gloves were bought, but it was hard to know whether to borrow the full evening suit that was expected or get one made with no prospect of being able to pay for it; he decided on the latter. The chief anxiety over the examination itself was whether Meynert would be so annoyed at Freud's acting as a *locum tenens* with Leidesdorf, whom he hated, that he would search for weak points in Freud's knowledge and thus embarrass him. However, all went well. There were two other candidates, Lumpe and Ehrendorfer. Freud was the first to be ushered into the room where seven or eight of the great ones were seated. He was questioned, first by Brücke and then by Meynert, on the anatomy and pathology of the spinal cord, a subject on which he felt quite at home. He did so well that Brücke followed him out of the room to tell him how excellent his speeches had been and to convey compliments from others present. A full account of the proceedings was dispatched to Martha immediately after.

ht These details, taken from Dr. Bernfeld's paper,⁸¹ were unearthed from the University Archives at his suggestion by Prof. Viktor Kraft.

On June 20 the Faculty decided, but this time only by nineteen votes to three, to allow him to give his trial lecture. This was a public performance and was duly announced in the newspapers. It took place in the lecture theater of Brücke's Institute, "where I had done my first work with an unequaled enthusiasm and where I had hoped to become my chief's Assistant. Should this be an omen that after all I may be allowed to come back to scientific work and theory? Do you believe in omens?" [32] He had chosen as his topic, "The Medullary Tracts of the Brain," and the official report states that the lecture was accepted with unanimous satisfaction.

The Faculty decided on July 18 to recommend Freud's being appointed a *Privatdocent* in Neuropathology, but even then the formalities were not quite at an end. On August 8 he was requested to report to the Police Headquarters to ascertain if his character was worthy of the honor and whether his past conduct had been irreproachable; announcing this he jokingly added: "I was resolved to divulge nothing." Then a month later, on September 5, 1885, after due consideration the Ministry decided to ratify the appointment, and Freud really became a *Privatdocent*.

Freud worked in Scholz's so-called *Nervenabtheilung* for only fourteen months, not twenty, as other writers have said. Towards the end of February 1885 the Hospital Director informed him that his chief, Scholz, wished him transferred to another department. Freud protested to Scholz, but in vain; they had some words about their different outlook on the running of a hospital.[33] So on March 1 he entered the Ophthalmological Department, although he retained his former room. This meant bringing his courses to an end; the last one finished on March 6.[34] He regretted this, since he said he had enjoyed both the learning and the teaching in them. At this time the Director suggested he might apply for the higher position of Senior *Sekundararzt*. Knowing that Scholz would not consider him for this post, he applied to a new Superintendent, Hein, but was defeated by a more senior applicant;[35] actually the latter was subsequently disqualified on the ground of his being a Hungarian, but Freud decided then not to reapply for the vacancy. So he continued in the Ophthalmological Department. He worked there for three months, and on June 1 transferred to the Dermatological Department under Kaposy, whose Assistant was Freud's friend Lustgarten; Freud had cooperated with Kaposy two years before in investigating the electrical resistance of the skin.[36] The day before this, however, he was invited by Obersteiner to act as *locum tenens* in a private mental hospital he maintained in Oberdöbling, just outside Vienna. He got permission from his chief, Kaposy, to do so, and took up his work there on June 7.[37] He was to receive board and lodging, with 100 gulden ($40). The resident head of the sanatorium was Professor Leidesdorf, who took to Freud and helped him later in various ways. It was a socially superior institution and Freud had to wear a silk hat and white gloves so as to function properly. Among the sixty patients there was a son of Marie Louise, Napoleon's Empress; he was a hopeless dement. Freud liked the life there and asked Martha how she would like to live there if their more ambitious plans went awry. But while there, great news arrived. To explain this we have to go back a little.

On March 3, 1885, Freud mentioned in a letter that he intended to apply for a postgraduate *Stipendium* (traveling grant) which the Ministry was offering to the successful candidate among the junior *Sekundarärzte*. The amount was the munificent sum of 600 gulden ($240), and it was understood that six months leave of absence would accompany it. The latter point did not concern Freud, since his intention was to resign from the hospital before setting out, but he planned to be away from Vienna for six months. It was not explained how even in those days anyone could travel to any distance and sustain life for six months on the sum in question, especially since a half of it was paid only a couple of months after the leave expired! But Freud was never deterred by obstacles of that nature and he immediately formed the resolution to get to Charcot in Paris if it was at all possible. Knowing, however, the cardinal part played by favoritism in Vienna, he had no hope whatever of being the lucky candidate.

The final date of entry was May 1, and the meeting to make the decision was to be a month later. That gave the applicants some weeks in which to pursue their search for support. Freud at once set about canvassing hard, and between this activity and his preoccupation with the uncertain chances he got very little work done in the next two months. His friend Lustgarten won over Professor Ludwin, the new *Primarius* of the *Abteilung* (Superintendent of the Department) in which Freud was working. Nothnagel and Meynert promised their support and Breuer got hold of the famous surgeon Billroth. Professor Leidesdorf, at whose private psychiatric institution Freud had just spent three weeks acting as *locum tenens,* joined in and secured the support of Pollitzer, the famous otologist, and others. This, however, somewhat alarmed Freud, since he knew that Meynert hated Leidesdorf and might on that account weaken in his support. Still more serious was the fact that Brücke, one of the strongest supporters, was taken ill a few weeks before the meeting, though fortunately he recovered in time.

His betrothed, convinced of his superiority, rather derided all these efforts to obtain influential support, whereupon Freud, more realistically minded, made the spirited reply: "Just wait, and you will see that I will have only myself to thank for any success I may achieve."

Neither of them could guess what a critical moment this was to prove in Freud's life. It was assuredly the experience with Charcot in Paris that aroused Freud's interest in hysteria, then in psychopathology in general, and so paved the way for resuscitating Breuer's observation and developing psychoanalysis. At the moment all that mattered to him was to secure a standing in the medical profession that would hold out some prospect of earning enough to marry. But he mournfully wrote, "It is no good thinking of it. I must find some other way of winning you as my wife." And he decided in any event to leave the hospital at the end of that summer, to travel to Wandsbek to spend a month with Martha, and then—if it was not to be Paris—to return to Vienna and try his luck in private practice.

As the time approached for the choice Freud reckoned that he could count on eight votes out of twenty-one. There were two other applicants and when he heard that one of them was a nephew of the influential Professor Braun he considered his case as good as lost. There was, it is true, still the off-chance that a divided poll might enable him to slip in between the other two, but even this vanished when the dangerous nephew was advised to withdraw on the score of youth. On the day, May 30, when the professional Faculty met in full array, Freud wrote sadly, "This is the day when someone else will get the grant." On the next day, however, he learned that no decision had been reached and that the matter had been referred to a subcommittee of three consisting of a supporter of each applicant (the withdrawal of the third took place later). He was annoyed at this "postponement of an empty hope."

Three more weeks passed in argument and counter-argument. Then on the night before the really final decision, Freud dreamed that his representative, who was none other than Brücke, told him he had no chance because there were *seven* other applicants with more favorable prospects. Since there had been seven brothers and sisters besides himself in the family it is not hard to perceive the reassurance in this simple little dream. He had certainly been, not only the most promising, but the most favored, and any compunction he may have felt on this score was well represented in the dream by the stern Brücke, whom nevertheless he knew he could trust implicitly.

On the next day, June 20, he dispatched a dithyrambic letter to the woman he now felt so much nearer winning. He had won by thirteen votes to eight. "Oh, how wonderful it is going to be. I am coming with money and am staying a long while with you and am bringing something lovely for you and shall then go to Paris and become a great *savant* and return to Vienna with a great, great nimbus. Then we will marry soon and I will cure all the incurable nervous patients and you will keep me well and I will kiss you till you are merry and happy—and they lived happily ever after." [i]

A couple of days later Fleischl told him that what had brought him the success had been "Brücke's passionate intercession, which had caused a general sensation." [38]

Another interruption to Freud's medical course threatened while he was still at the sanatorium: a suggestion that he accompany Fleischl, who was in very bad health, on his vacation.[j] This came to nothing, so he returned to his work under Kaposy on June 30. He also took an otological course. He seems to have found difficulties in the use of the ophthalmoscope, laryngoscope, and otoscope, and it is not likely that he ever had enough practice to become expert with them.

On the last day of August 1885 Freud left the General Hospital for good, after having lived and worked there for just a month over three years. It was nearly the end of his general medical experience. The nineteen weeks he spent in Paris were devoted exclusively to neurology. Then for three weeks he studied children's diseases under Baginsky in Berlin, a topic he had missed in his Vienna training. The other reason for doing so was the offer he had received to take charge of the neurological department of Kassowitz's Childrens' Clinic. The important work he did there on infantile paralyses belongs to his neurological productions.

To become a good general practitioner Freud would have needed more experience in midwifery and surgery, but on the medical side he was fully equipped. Three years' residence in a hospital as a doc-

---

[i] *Und wenn sie nicht gestorben sind, so leben sie heute noch.*
[j] See p. 192.

tor was very different from merely obtaining a medical qualification. That during these years he had carried out important researches as well, and also been recognized as a Docent in Neurology, shows that they were very well spent. He was twenty-nine years old when they came to an end.

Eighteen eight-five was thus a year of success. He had finished his important researches on the medulla, which would presently be published, he had won his way to Charcot and Paris, and he could present himself there as a *Privatdozent* in Neuropathology.

VI

The Cocaine Episode

(1 8 8 4 – 1 8 8 7)

DURING THE THREE HOSPITAL YEARS FREUD WAS CONSTANTLY OCCUPIED with the endeavor to make a name for himself by discovering something important in either clinical or pathological medicine. His motive was not, as might be supposed, simply professional ambition, but far more the hope of a success that would yield enough prospect of private practice to justify his marrying a year, or possibly two years, earlier than he dared expect in the ordinary course. He must have been very prolific of ideas in his search and in his letters he repeatedly hints at a new discovery which may lead to the desired goal; in the event, none of them did. Unfortunately he gives for the most part only tantalizing glimpses of what the ideas were. The only two he dilates on are the ones that brought him nearest to success: the gold chloride method of staining nervous tissue and the clinical use of cocaine.

As we shall see, the latter case was more than one of the routine efforts and the problems it raises merit the description of it as an episode.

Freud's own account of it runs as follows: "I may here go back a little and explain how it was the fault of my fiancée that I was not already famous at that early age. A side interest, though it was a deep one, had led me in 1884 to obtain from Merck some of what was then the little-known alkaloid cocaine and to study its physiological action. While I was in the middle of this work, an opportunity arose for making a journey to visit my fiancée, from whom I had been parted for two years. I hastily wound up my investigation of cocaine and contented myself in my book on the subject with prophesying that further uses for it would soon be found. I suggested, however, to my friend Königstein, the ophthalmologist, that he should investigate the question of how far the anesthetizing properties of cocaine were applicable in diseases of the eye. When I returned from my holiday I found that not he, but another of my friends, Carl Koller (now in New York), to whom I had also spoken about cocaine, had made the decisive experiments upon animals' eyes and had demonstrated them at the Ophthalmological Congress at Heidelberg. Koller is therefore rightly regarded as the discoverer of local anesthesia by cocaine, which has become so important in minor surgery; but I bore my fiancée no grudge for her interruption of my work." [1]

The rather unnecessary initial and concluding remarks suggest that someone ought to be blamed, and there is plenty of evidence that it was himself that Freud really blamed. In another context he wrote: "I had hinted in my essay that the alkaloid might be employed as an anesthetic, but I was not thorough enough to pursue the matter further." [2] In conversation he would ascribe the omission to his "laziness."

So for the second time Freud had missed fame by a hair's breadth. He might have consoled himself with the reflection that his revered master, Brücke, had suffered a similar fate. In 1849 he recognized that the red reflex from the eye came from the retina, but had not the wit to put a lens in front of it so as to focus its vessels. In the following year his friend, Helmholtz, did so, and so was hailed as the discoverer of the ophthalmoscope.

The somewhat disingenuous excuse Freud gave for the failure when writing his *Autobiography* must cover a deeper explanation, since it does not tally very closely with the facts. To begin with, the parting had lasted not two years, but one.[a] The cocaine essay was finished on June 18, 1884,[4] and Martha Bernays had left Vienna for Wandsbek only on June 14, 1883.[5] Nor was there any sudden opportunity for visiting her, as his passage rather suggests. From the very time of her departure he planned to do so in the summer holiday of the following year,[6] and there are many references in the correspondence to his difficulty in saving up, gulden by gulden, the sum necessary to cover the cost of the journey. As the time approached he planned to leave in the third week of July, and, since he delivered his manuscript to the editor on the date he had promised, June 20, he was hard put to it to find some other distraction to allay his impatience during the five weeks that remained before he could depart for

[a] In a letter to Wittels Freud even said "several years." [b] So in retrospect, as well as at the time, the waiting had seemed terribly long.

his holiday. As things turned out he was not able to go before September.

The first we hear of the cocaine topic is in a letter of April 21, 1884, in which he gives news of "a therapeutic project and a hope." "I have been reading about cocaine, the essential constituent of coca leaves which some Indian tribes chew to enable them to resist privations and hardships. A German[b] has been employing it with soldiers and has in fact reported that it increases their energy and capacity to endure. I am procuring some myself and will try it with cases of heart disease and also of nervous exhaustion, particularly in the miserable condition after the withdrawal of morphium (Dr. Fleischl). Perhaps others are working at it; perhaps nothing will come of it. But I shall certainly try it, and you know that when one perseveres, sooner or later one succeeds. We do not need more than one such lucky hit to be able to think of setting up house. But don't be too sure that it must succeed this time. You know, the temperament of an investigator needs two fundamental qualities: he must be sanguine in the attempt, but critical in the work."

At first he did not expect much would come of the matter: "I dare say it will turn out like the method; [c] less than I imagined, but still something quite respectable." The first obstacle proved to be the cost of the cocaine he had ordered from Merck of Darmstadt; instead of a gram costing, as he had expected, 33 kreuzer (13 cents) he was dismayed to find it cost 3 gulden 33 kreuzer ($1.27). At first he thought this meant the end of his research, but after getting over the shock he boldly ordered a gram in the hope of being able to pay for it sometime. He immediately tried the effect of a twentieth of a gram; he found it turned the bad mood he was in into cheerfulness and gave him the feeling of having dined well "so that there is nothing at all one need bother about," but without robbing him of any energy for exercise or work. It occurred to him that since the drug evidently acted as a gastric anesthetic, taking away all sense of hunger, it might be useful for checking vomiting from any cause.[8]

At the same time he decided to offer the drug to his friend Fleischl, who was in the throes of distress in his endeavor to free himself from an addiction to morphia which he had been using to excess because of intolerable nerve pain. It was a decision he bitterly regretted in

[b] This was an Army doctor, Theodor Aschenbrandt, who had made the observations in question on some Bavarian soldiers during the preceding autumn maneuvers.[7]

[c] I.e., the gold chloride method he invented.

years to come. The occasion of it was a report he had read in the *Detroit Medical Gazette* of its use for this purpose. Fleischl clutched at the new drug "like a drowning man" [9] and within a few days was taking it continually. The rest of the Fleischl story will be told presently.

Freud was now becoming more and more enthusiastic. Cocaine was "a magical drug." He had a dazzling success with a case of gastric catarrh where it immediately put an end to the pain.[10] "If it goes well I will write an essay on it and I expect it will win its place in therapeutics, by the side of morphium and superior to it. I have other hopes and intentions about it. I take very small doses of it regularly against depression and against indigestion, and with the most brilliant success. I hope it will be able to abolish the most intractable vomiting, even when this is due to severe pain; in short it is only now that I feel I am a doctor, since I have helped one patient and hope to help more. If things go on in this way we need have no concern about being able to come together and to stay in Vienna." He sent some to Martha "to make her strong and give her cheeks a red color," he pressed it on his friends and colleagues, both for themselves and their patients, he gave it to his sisters. In short, looked at from the vantage point of our present knowledge, he was rapidly becoming a public menace. Naturally he had no reason at all to think there was any danger in such proceedings, and when he said he could detect no signs of craving for it in himself, however often he took it, he was telling the strict truth: as we know now, it needs a special disposition to develop a drug addiction, and fortunately Freud did not possess that.

Some of his colleagues reported success in the use of the drug, others were more doubtful. Breuer, with his characteristic caution, was one of those who was not impressed.

Freud had difficulty in obtaining the literature on this out-of-the-way subject, but Fleischl gave him an introduction to the library of the *Gesellschaft der Ärzte* (Society of Physicians) where he came across the recently published volume of the Surgeon General's catalogue that contained a complete account of it. He was now (June 5) reckoning on finishing the essay in another fortnight and then working on his electrical researches to occupy the remaining four or five weeks before he would be free to go to Wandsbek. He finished it on the eighteenth, and half of it was in print the next day. It appeared in the July number of Heitler's *Centralblatt für die gesammte Therapie.*

The essay, although a comprehensive review of the whole subject—far the best that had yet appeared—might well be ranked higher as a literary production than as an original scientific contribution. It was couched in Freud's best style, with his characteristic liveliness, simplicity, and distinction, features for which he had found little scope when describing the nerves of the crayfish or the fibers of the medulla. It was many years before he again had the opportunity of exercising his literary gifts. There is, moreover, in this essay a tone that never recurred in Freud's writings, a remarkable combination of objectivity with a personal warmth as if he were in love with the content itself. He used expressions uncommon in a scientific paper, such as "the most gorgeous excitement" that animals display after an injection of cocaine, and administering an "offering" of it rather than a "dose"; he heatedly rebuffed the "slander" that had been published about this precious drug. This artistic presentation must have contributed much to the interest the essay aroused in Viennese and other medical circles.

He began the essay by going at length into the early history of the coca plant and its use by the South American Indians, then describing it botanically and reciting the various methods of preparing the leaves. He even gave an account of the religious observances connected with its use, and mentioned the mythical saga of how Manco Capac, the Royal Son of the Sun-God, had sent it as "a gift from the gods to satisfy the hungry, fortify the weary, and make the unfortunate forget their sorrows." We learn that the news of the wonderful plant reached Spain in 1569 and England in 1596, how Dr. Scherzer, the Austrian explorer, brought home from Peru in 1859 coca leaves that were sent to Niemann, the assistant of Woehler—the chemist infamous for daring to synthetize urea. It was Niemann who isolated the alkaloid cocaine from the plant.

He then narrated a number of self-observations in which he had studied the effects on hunger, sleep, and fatigue. He wrote of the "exhilaration and lasting euphoria, which in no way differs from the normal euphoria of the healthy person. . . . You perceive an increase of self-control and possess more vitality and capacity for work. . . . In other words, you are simply normal, and it is soon hard to believe that you are under the influence of any drug. . . . Long intensive mental or physical work is performed without any fatigue. . . . This result is enjoyed without any of the unpleasant after-effects that follow exhilaration brought about by alcohol. . . . Absolutely no craving for the further use of cocaine appears after the first, or even repeated, taking of the drug; one feels rather a certain curious aversion to it." Freud confirmed Mantegazza's conclusions about the therapeutic value of the drug, its stimulant and yet numbing action on the stomach, its usefulness in melancholia, and so on. He described a case of his own (Fleischl's) where he had employed cocaine in the process of weaning a morphia addict. The total value of the drug was summed up as applicable in "those functional states comprised under the name of neurasthenia," in the treatment of indigestion, and during the withdrawal of morphine.

As to the theory of its action Freud made the suggestion, since confirmed, that cocaine acts not through direct stimulation of the brain but through abolishing the effect of agencies that depress one's bodily feelings.[d]

In his final paragraph, written hurriedly, he said: "The capacity of cocaine and its salts, when applied in concentrated solutions, to anesthetize cutaneous and mucous membranes suggests a possible future use, especially in cases of local infections. . . . Some additional uses of cocaine based on this anesthetic property are likely to be developed in the near future." This is the aspect that he subsequently reproached himself with not pursuing, but the view taken here is that this self-reproach was somewhat misplaced. It is not altogether likely that Freud, even with more time at his disposal, would have thought of the surgical application, one foreign to his interests. The local uses he had in mind were concerned only with deadening the pain of cutaneous infections, and when he suggested to his ophthalmological friend Königstein that cocaine could be applied to the eye both of them thought of this in terms of alleviating the pain of trachoma and similar conditions. For Freud cocaine was an analgesic, not an anesthetic, and anyhow he was far more interested in its internal use than in any external application.

The psychology of the self-reproach would seem to be more complex. It is true that Freud hoped to achieve some measure of fame through his study of cocaine, but he could not know that a much greater measure of fame than he had imagined was within the grasp of whoever would apply cocaine in a certain way. When he realized this, which he was slow to do, he blamed himself, but also inculpated his fiancée. The latter irrational feature is, as is usually so, a hint of some unconscious process. There are two further ones. In a letter to Wittels forty years later he wrote: "I know very well how it happened to me. The study on coca was an allotrion which I was

[d] *Gemeingefühl* (coenesthesia).

eager to conclude." The word "allotrion," with its punitive connotation, was one familiar to Freud from his schoolteachers' use of it to signify anything, such as a hobby, that detracted from the serious fulfillment of a duty. Freud's interest in cocaine, which he termed a "side interest," was of just this nature, taking him far from his serious "scientific" work in neuropathology. A hobby, if intensely pursued, always indicates a very personal interest, often one divorced from a man's main vocation, and the deep sources in the personality from which the interest arises are commonly associated with some sense of guilt.[e] Now what evidently fascinated Freud in the coca plant was its extraordinary repute of being able to heighten mental and physical vigor without apparently having any harmful subsequent effect. After all, that had been the whole point of the article by Aschenbrandt which had fired Freud's imagination. But cocaine heightens vigor only when this has been previously lowered; a really normal person does not need the fillip. Freud was not in the latter fortunate position. For many years he suffered from periodic depressions and fatigue or apathy, neurotic symptoms which later took the form of anxiety attacks before being dispelled by his own analysis. These neurotic reactions were exacerbated by the turmoil of his love affair, with its lengthy privation and other difficulties. In the summer of 1884 in particular he was in a state of great agitation before the approaching visit to his betrothed, and by no means only because of the uncertainty about its being possible. Cocaine calmed the agitation and dispelled the depression. Moreover, it gave him an unwonted sense of energy and vigor.

Depression, like any other neurotic manifestation, lowers the sense of energy and virility: cocaine restores it. Any doubt about this being the essence of the matter is dispelled by the following passage from a letter of June 2, 1884, written on hearing that Martha did not look well and had no appetite. "Woe to you, my Princess, when I come. I will kiss you quite red and feed you till you are plump. And if you are froward you shall see who is the stronger, a gentle little girl who doesn't eat enough or a big wild man *who has cocaine in his body*.[f] In my last severe depression I took coca again and a small dose lifted me to the heights in a wonderful fashion. I am just now busy collecting the literature for a song of praise to this magical substance."

[e] In Freud's dreams this theme of guilt about his hobbies appears together with a vigorous self-defense.[11]
[f] Here italicized.

To achieve virility and enjoy the bliss of union with the beloved, he had forsaken the straight and narrow path of sober "scientific" work on brain anatomy and seized a surreptitious short cut: one that was to bring him suffering in place of success. Within a couple of months another was to attain world fame through cocaine. But that was through a use beneficial to humanity, whereas two years later Freud was to be contemned for having through his indiscriminate advocacy of a "harmless" and wonderful drug introduced what his detractors called the "third scourge of humanity." [g] Last of all he was to reproach himself for having hastened the death of a dear friend and benefactor by inculcating in him a severe cocaine addiction.

It would be hard not to suffer all these blows without feeling them to be just punishments. For what? The answer to this question we must leave to the psychoanalysts, but at least we can understand why Freud had to associate his self-reproach with the thought of his wife-to-be, and that the excuse he gave of "not being thorough enough" was only a thin hint of what was behind.

All this, however, lay in the future, and Freud, innocent of any inkling of it, went off at the beginning of September to enjoy a happy holiday in Wandsbek. On his return four weeks later he learned that something big had happened.

At this point a new figure enters on the scene: Carl Koller, a man eighteen months younger than Freud, who won the distinction of inaugurating local anesthesia. Koller was at the time an interne in the Department of Ophthalmology, where he aspired to become an Assistant. His thoughts ran so exclusively on the subject of eye diseases that, according to Freud, his monomania became rather tiresome to his colleagues. Rightly perceiving the need for it, he was particularly set on finding some drug that would anesthetize the sensitive surface of the eye; he had already tried various drugs, such as morphine and chloral bromide, but so far in vain. In one of his later lectures, desiring to point a moral, Freud related the following incident.

"One day I was standing in the courtyard with a group of colleagues of whom this man was one, when another interne passed us showing signs of intense pain. [Here Freud told what the localization of the pain was, but I have forgotten this detail.] I said to him: 'I think I can help you,' and we all went to my room, where I applied a few drops of a medicine which made the pain disappear in-

[g] The other two being alcohol and morphium.

stantly. I explained to my friends that this drug was the extract of a South American plant, the coca, which seemed to have powerful qualities for relieving pain and about which I was preparing a publication. The man with the permanent interest in the eye, whose name was Koller, did not say anything, but a few months later I learned that he had begun to revolutionize eye surgery by the use of cocaine, making operations easy which till then had been impossible. This is the only way to make important discoveries: have one's ideas exclusively focused on one central interest." [12]

Freud had begun some tests with a dynamometer to ascertain whether the apparent increase of muscular strength obtained by the use of cocaine was a subjective illusion or was objectively verifiable, and in these he cooperated with Koller. They both swallowed some cocaine and, like everyone else, noticed the numbing of the mouth and lips. This meant more to Koller than to Freud.

Koller read Freud's essay when it appeared in July, pondered over it, and early in September, after Freud had left Vienna for Hamburg, appeared in Stricker's Institute of Pathological Anatomy carrying a bottle containing a white powder. He announced to the Assistant there, Dr. Gaertner,[h] that he had reason to think it would act as a local anesthetic in the eye. The matter was at once easily put to the test. They tried it first on the eyes of a frog, a rabbit, and a dog, and then on their own—with complete success. Koller wrote a "Preliminary Communication" dated early in September, and got Dr. Brettauer to read it and make practical demonstrations at the Ophthalmological Congress that took place at Heidelberg on September 15. On October 17 he read a paper in Vienna before the Gesellschaft der Ärzte, which he published shortly afterwards. It contained the sentence: "Cocaine has been prominently brought to the notice of Viennese physicians by the thorough compilation and interesting therapeutic paper of my hospital colleague Dr. Sigmund Freud."

Freud had also called the attention of a closer ophthalmological friend, Leopold Königstein, a man six years older than himself and a Docent of three years' standing, to the numbing powers of cocaine and had suggested that he use it to alleviate the pain of certain eye complaints, such as trachoma and iritis. This Königstein faithfully did, with success, and it was only some weeks later, early in October, that he extended its use to the field of surgery by enucleating a

[h] The Professor Gaertner who in a dream of Freud's, the night after Stricker's Festschrift appeared, disturbed his discussion with Königstein.[14]

dog's eye with Freud's assistance. He was just a little too late. At the meeting on October 17 he also read a paper describing his experiences with cocaine, but without mentioning Koller's name. It looked like an ugly fight for priority, but Freud and Wagner-Jauregg managed to persuade him, reluctantly, to insert in his published paper a reference to Koller's "Preliminary Communication" of the previous month and thus to renounce his own claim. As we shall see, Koller did not reciprocate Freud's chivalrous behavior.

On April 5, 1885, Freud's father called on him with the news that there was something wrong with the sight of one of his eyes. Freud was inclined to make light of it and regard it as something temporary, but Koller, who happened to be there, examined it and made the diagnosis of glaucoma.[13] They called in their senior, Königstein, who operated, and very successfully, the next day, Koller, who administered the local anesthetic with Freud's assistance, gracefully remarked that the three people concerned with the introduction of cocaine were all present together.[14] Freud must have been proud to have helped his father and to prove to him that he had after all amounted to something.[i]

Freud remained on the friendliest terms with Koller. He was one of the most enthusiastic of the friends who congratulated him on the successful outcome of his duel with an anti-Semitic colleague, and he was greatly concerned about his serious illness later in the year. The last mention of him is of Freud's writing to congratulate him on an appointment in Utrecht, with the hope of visiting him there from Paris.

Koller later emigrated to New York, where, as Freud had predicted, he had a successful career. But even at the beginning of his achievement he committed a "symptomatic error" which indicated some disturbance in his personality that came to open expression in later years. When publishing the paper he had read in Vienna in October 1884, he quoted Freud's monograph as dating from August instead of July, giving thus the impression that his work was simultaneous with Freud's and not after it. Both Freud and Obersteiner noticed the "slip" and corrected it in subsequent publications. As time went on Koller presented the discrepancy in still grosser terms, even asserting that Freud's monograph appeared a whole year *after* his own discovery, which was therefore made quite independently of anything Freud had ever done.[15]

Perhaps we may correlate this curious behavior with the fact that

[i] See p. 16.

in hospital days Freud had treated him privately for a neurotic affection;[16] "negative transferences," as they are called, often endure.

It has generally been assumed that Freud must have been very disappointed and also angry with himself on hearing of Koller's discovery. Interestingly enough, this was not at all so. This is how he reported it. "My second piece of news is pleasanter. A colleague has found a striking application for coca in ophthalmology and communicated it to the Heidelberg Congress, where it caused great excitement. I had advised Königstein a fortnight before I left Vienna to try something similar. He really discovered something and now there is a dispute between them. They decided to lay their findings before me and ask me to judge which of them should publish first. I have advised Königstein to read a paper simultaneously with the other in the *Gesellschaft der Ärzte*. In any event it is to the credit of coca, and my work retains its reputation of having successfully recommended it to the Viennese." [17]

Evidently at this time Freud still regarded the province of cocaine as, so to speak, his private property. Its value when taken internally was the main thing, and he kept on experimenting with a variety of diseases he hoped it would cure. So far from being disconcerted by Koller's discovery, he viewed it as one more of the outlying applications of which his beloved drug was capable. It took a long time before he could assimilate the bitter truth that Koller's use of it was to prove practically the only one of value and all the rest dust and ashes.

On the day after hearing of Koller's work, the chemical firm of Merck invited Freud to investigate a new alkaloid, ecgnonin, which had been isolated from cocaine, and sent him 100 grams. Together with Fleischl, whose appearance was very irregular, he experimented with frogs, rabbits, and other animals, and also with himself. It proved to be very toxic with lower animals, but he could take very large doses himself without perceiving much effect.

When the Physiological Club re-opened for the fall session Freud received many congratulations on his cocaine monograph. Professor Reuss, the Director of the Eye Clinic, told him that it had "brought about a revolution." Professor Nothnagel, handing him some of his reprints, reproached him for not having published the monograph in his journal. In the meantime he was experimenting with diabetes, which he hoped to cure with cocaine. If it succeeded he could marry a year earlier and they would be rich and famous people. But nothing came of it. Then his sister Rosa and a friend of his, a ship's surgeon, had favorable experiences in the use of cocaine for averting seasickness, and Freud hoped this was another future for it. He expressed his intention of trying the effect of cocaine after making himself giddy on the swing boats in the Prater, but we hear nothing more of the experiment.

And just then came the discussion between Koller and Königstein at the *Gesellschaft der Ärzte* which opened his eyes somewhat to the importance of what had happened. In describing the meeting he says he got only 5 per cent of the credit and so came off poorly. If only, instead of advising Königstein to carry out the experiments on the eye, he had believed more in them himself, and had not shrunk from the trouble of carrying them out, he would not have missed the "fundamental fact" (i.e., of anesthesia) as Königstein did.[18] "But I was led astray by so much incredulity on all sides." It was the first self-reproach. And a little later he wrote to his future sister-in-law: "Cocaine has brought me a great deal of credit, but the lion's share has gone elsewhere." [19] He had to note that Koller's discovery had produced an "enormous sensation" throughout the world.

To return to the story of Fleischl, which was of immense importance to Freud, not only in connection with cocaine. Something has been said of his personality in an earlier chapter.[j] Freud first admired him from a distance, but after leaving the Brücke Institute he had come to know him more personally. In February 1884, for instance, he speaks of his "intimate friendship" with Fleischl. Earlier than this, in the month of his engagement, he wrote of him as follows: "Yesterday I was with my friend Ernst v. Fleischl, whom I have hitherto, before I knew Martha, envied in all respects. Now I have the advantage over him. He has been engaged for ten or twelve years to someone of his own age, who was willing to wait for him indefinitely and from whom he has now for some unknown reason parted. He is a most distinguished man, for whom both nature and upbringing have done their best. Rich, trained in all physical exercises, with the stamp of genius in his energetic features, handsome, with fine feelings, gifted with all the talents, and able to form an original judgment on most matters; he has always been my ideal and I could not rest till we became friends and I could experience a pure joy in his ability and reputation." He had promised Fleischl not to betray his "secret" that he was learning Sanskrit. Then followed a long phantasy how happy such a man with all these advantages could make Martha, but he broke off to assert his own claim to

j See p. 44.

her. "Why shouldn't I for once have more than I deserve? Martha remains my own!" [20]

On another occasion he wrote: "I admire and love him with an intellectual passion, if you will allow such a phrase. His destruction[k] will move me as the destruction of a sacred and famous temple would have affected an ancient Greek. I love him not so much as a human being, but as one of Creation's precious achievements. And you needn't be at all jealous."

But this wonderful man suffered on a grand scale. The quite unbearable nerve pain which had already tormented him for ten years gradually wore him down. His mind became periodically affected. He took large doses of morphia, with the usual consequences. Freud got his first insight into his condition on a short visit in October 1883. "I asked him quite disconsolately where all this was going to lead to. He said that his parents regarded him as a great *savant* and he would try to keep at his work as long as they lived. Once they were dead he would shoot himself, for he thought it was quite impossible to hold out for long. It would be senseless to try to console a man who sees his situation so clearly." A fortnight later he had another affecting interview. "He is not the sort of man you can approach with empty words of consolation. His state is precisely as desperate as he says, and one cannot contradict him. . . . 'I can't bear,' he said, 'to have to do everything with three times the effort others use, when I was so accustomed to doing things more easily than they. No one else would endure what I do,' he added, and I know him well enough to believe him."

As was mentioned above, it was early in May 1884 that Freud first administered cocaine in the hope that thereby Fleischl would be able to dispense with the morphia, and for a short time this was very successful. From then on Freud visited him regularly, helped him to arrange his library, and so on. But only a week later, in spite of the cocaine weaning him from morphia, Fleischl's condition was pitiable. After several vain attempts to get an answer to his knockings Freud procured help and he, Obersteiner, and Exner burst into the room to find Fleischl lying almost senseless with pain. Breuer, his doctor, then arranged that Obersteiner should get into his room every day with a master key. A couple of days later, Billroth, having had no success with several operations on the stump of the hand, tried the effect of electrical stimulation under narcosis; as one might expect, the result was disastrous and Fleischl's state worse than ever.

Fleischl shared Freud's optimistic view about the value of cocaine,

[k] Referring to his terrible disease and approaching death.

and when a shortened translation of the monograph was published in the *St. Louis Medical and Surgical Journal*, in December 1884, he added a note describing his own good experiences with it in connection with the withdrawal of morphia. He considered the two drugs were antithetical.

In January 1885 Freud, who had now been trying to relieve the pain of trigeminal neuralgia by injecting cocaine into the nerve, hoped to do the same for Fleischl's neuromata, but no good seems to have come of it. On an occasion in April Freud had sat up all night with him, Fleischl spending the whole time in a warm bath by his side. He wrote that it was quite impossible to describe this, since he had never experienced anything like it; "every note of the profoundest despair was sounded." It was the first of many such nights he passed in the following couple of months. By this time Fleischl was taking enormous doses of cocaine; Freud noted that he had spent no less than 1,800 marks ($428) on it in the past three months, which meant a full gram a day—a hundred times the quantity Freud was accustomed to take, and then only on occasion. On June 8 Freud wrote that the frightful doses had harmed Fleischl greatly and, although he kept sending Martha cocaine, he warned her against acquiring the habit. He noted Brücke's endless kindness to Fleischl, who was, it will be remembered, his Assistant at the Institute.

Even before this, however, Freud had lived through a good deal. "Every time I ask myself if I shall ever in my life experience anything so agitating or exciting as these nights. . . . His talk, his explanations of all possible obscure things, his judgments on the persons in our circle, his manifold activity interrupted by states of the completest exhaustion relieved by morphia and cocaine: all that makes an *ensemble* that cannot be described." But the stimulation emanating from Fleischl was such that it even compensated for the horrors.

Among Fleischl's symptoms were attacks of fainting (often with convulsions), severe insomnia, and lack of control over a variety of eccentric behavior. The cocaine had for some time helped in all these respects, but the huge doses needed led to a chronic intoxication, and finally to a delirium tremens with white snakes creeping over his skin. This came to a crisis on June 4. On calling in the evening Freud found him in such a state—Brücke and Schenk were also there—that he went to fetch Breuer and then spent the night there. It was the most frightful night he had ever spent.

Towards the end of June Breuer told him that Fleischl's relatives wanted Freud to spend the month of August in St. Gilgen looking after him. It would have meant leaving the hospital prematurely, missing some courses, and also breaking off the anatomical researches in the middle, but Freud for personal reasons was inclined to consent. In the end Fleischl insisted on being alone. Freud thought he could not go on for more than another six months, but Fleischl lived six painful years longer.

Freud had throughout been puzzled by the irregular action of cocaine in different subjects, one which greatly impeded its clinical employment. In order to have a means of testing its action objectively and, if possible, ascertaining on what these variations depended, he decided to make observations on muscular capacity and on swiftness of reactions under cocaine. For the former purpose he used a dynamometer, a not very accurate instrument, and in November 1884 he resumed with various colleagues the observations he had started with it in July with Koller. Incidentally, it seemed to have been an instrument with a special interest for him, since he bought one when he was in Paris so as to observe his own "nervous states." [21] For the second purpose he worked with Herzig, using Exner's neuro-amoebimeter. The results were published in the *Wiener medizinische Wochenschrift*, January 31, 1885. The paper is of interest as being the only experimental study Freud ever published, and its rather dilettante presentation shows that this was not his real field. The ideas are all good, but the facts are recorded in a somewhat irregular and uncontrolled fashion that would make them hard to correlate with anyone else's observations.

A few definite conclusions emerged from the work. One was that muscular strength, as thus tested, has considerable intrinsic variations, e.g., at different times of the day and on different days even in the same person. The increase produced by cocaine is very slight in perfect health and is pronounced only when the subject is fatigued or depressed. Freud concluded that cocaine has no direct action on the neuromuscular system, but only through improving, in certain circumstances, the general state of well-being.

At the turn of the year a popular article on Freud's monograph appeared in the *Neue Freie Presse*, which was copied in the American press.[22] It was his old school friend, Franceschini, who wrote it. For some time afterwards Freud was plagued by having to answer letters demanding further information or help. He decided to reprint his essay in pamphlet form in an issue of 500 copies, and to take the opportunity to make various additions to it. This was published in the middle of February 1885 under the same title of "On Coca."

In March he reported that after giving two more lectures on the subject he hoped to have done with it. It was probably the same lecture and was delivered on March 3 at the Physiological Club and on March 5 at the *Psychiatrische Verein* (Psychiatric Society); it was published in the *Medico-Chirurgische Centralblatt*, August 7, 1885. It seems to have met with considerable success. Freud was gratified at *The Lancet* abstracting it.

The lecture was a general review of the topic. He pointed out that, while psychopathology is rich in methods that reduce overstimulated nervous action (bromides, etc.), it was poor in those that can raise any lowered activity, e.g., with weakness or depression of the nervous system. What the use of cocaine in certain cases proved was that an interfering agent of an unknown nature acting centrally could sometimes be removed by chemical means. He admitted that in some cases of morphia addiction it was not helpful, whereas in others it was of great value. He had seen no cases of cocaine addiction. (This was before Fleischl had suffered from cocaine intoxication.) So he could say that in such cases: "I should unhesitatingly advise cocaine being administered in subcutaneous injections of 0.03-0.05 grams per dose and without minding an accumulation of the drug."

But Freud was far from having done with the episode. Too much general interest, both pro and contra, had been aroused for that. In April an American firm offered him 60 gulden ($24) to test their cocaine in comparison with Merck's, and it proved to be as good. In the same month he was conducting "coca experiments" with Königstein, but he did not say what they were. In the next month we hear that there were always new uses being found for cocaine; the latest was that patients with hydrophobia could swallow after their throats had been painted with it.[23]

The tide, however, was beginning to turn. In July appeared the first of Erlenmeyer's pointed criticisms in the *Centralblatt für Nervenheilkunde*, which he edited. Freud's comment was: "It has the advantage of mentioning that it was I who recommended the use of cocaine in cases of morphium addiction, which the people who have confirmed its value there never do. Thus one can always be grateful to one's enemies."[24] It contrasted with an overextravagant praise which Wallé had expressed earlier in the year.[25] At a medical congress held in Copenhagen in the summer, Obersteiner, in a paper entitled "On the Employment of Cocaine in Neuroses and Psychoses," warmly defended Freud, as did some others; he sent a reprint of it to Freud in Paris together with a friendly letter. He confirmed the value of cocaine during the withdrawal of morphia, which he had tested in a number of cases in his private sanatorium at Oberdöbling. But in January of the following year, in a paper on intoxication psychoses, he had to admit that the continued use of cocaine could lead to a delirium tremens very similar to that produced by alcohol.

Early in 1886 Freud had the experience of meeting in Paris Dr. Knapp, then America's leading ophthalmologist. In a company of acquaintances Knapp greeted him as the man who had introduced cocaine to the world, and congratulated him on the achievement. It was a welcome balm.

In the same year, 1886, however, cases of cocaine addiction and intoxication were being reported from all over the world, and in Germany there was a general alarm. Erlenmeyer, in a second attack in May, doubtless written as a protest against Wallé's enthusiasm, voiced it in no uncertain terms: This was the occasion when he coined the phrase "the third scourge of humanity." [26] Erlenmeyer had written a book entitled *Ueber Morphiumsucht* (On Morphia Addiction) in 1884, and in its third edition, 1887, he incorporated what he had written about cocaine addiction in his first article.[27] At the end of the book he has a sentence praising the literary qualities of Freud's essay on coca, but adding without comment, "He recommends unreservedly the employment of cocaine in the treatment of morphinism." The third edition was reviewed by no less a person than Arthur Schnitzler, who broke a lance for Freud in the course of it.[28]

The man who had tried to benefit humanity or, at all events, to create a reputation by curing "neurasthenia" was now accused of unleashing evil on the world. Many must at least have regarded him as a man of reckless judgment. And if his sensitive conscience passed the same sentence, it could only have been confirmed by a sad experience a little later when, assuming it was a harmless drug, he ordered a large dose of it to a patient who succumbed as the result.[29] How much the whole episode affected Freud's reputation in Vienna is hard to say: all he said himself about it later was that it had led to "grave reproaches." It could not have improved matters when a little later in the year he enthusiastically supported Charcot's strange ideas on hysteria and hypnotism. It was a poor background from which to shock Viennese medical circles a few years later with his theories on the sexual etiology of the neuroses.

In a paper published in the *Wiener medizinische Wochenschrift* of July 9, 1887, Freud made a rather belated reply to all the criticisms.[30] It was occasioned by an article written by W. A. Hammond, which Freud quotes extensively in his support. He had two lines of defense. One was that no case of cocaine addiction was (then) known except in cases of morphia addictions, suggesting that no one else could fall a victim to it. Any habit formation was not, as was so commonly believed, the direct result of imbibing a noxious drug, but was due to some peculiarity in the patient. In this he was, of course, perfectly right, but the argument carried no conviction at the time.

The second line was more equivocal. The variable factor accounting for the uncertain effect of cocaine in different people he attributed to the lability of the cerebral blood vessels: if the pressure in them is stable, cocaine has no effect; in other cases it produces a favorable hyperemia, but in still others a toxic effect. Since this could not be determined beforehand, it was essential to refrain from giving subcutaneous injections of cocaine in any internal or nervous maladies. By the mouth cocaine was harmless, under the skin sometimes dangerous. He again claimed the Fleischl case (without naming him) as the first one of morphia addiction to have been cured by the use of cocaine.

In this second line of defense, which could only have been unconsciously determined, Freud had made a particularly bad shot. In January 1885 he had, very logically, tried to relieve trigeminal neuralgia by injections of cocaine into the nerve.[31] It was not successful, perhaps from lack of surgical skill. But in the same year W. H. Halsted, America's greatest surgeon and one of the founders of modern surgery, injected it into nerves with success, and thus laid the basis of nerve blocking for surgical purposes. He paid dearly, however, for his success, for he acquired a severe addiction to cocaine, and it took a long course of hospital treatment to free him from it. He was thus one of the first new drug addicts.

In seeking to avert from his magic substance the stigma of being a dangerous drug Freud could appeal to general prejudice in implicating hypodermic injections as the real peril. This prejudice against the hypodermic needle existed for many years, and indeed is only now dying away; analysis of patients who have an unwonted dread of it leaves no doubt about its symbolic meaning to the unconscious mind.

When Fleischl was offered cocaine he immediately administered it to himself in the form of subcutaneous injections. Years afterwards Freud asserted he had never intended this, but only oral administration.[32] There is, however, no evidence of any protest on his part at the time, and some months later he was himself advocating subcutaneous *injections* of large doses for just such cases as Fleischl's, i.e., withdrawal of morphine, and he presumably used them. It was his then chief, Professor Scholz, who had recently perfected the technique of the hypodermic needle, and doubtless Freud acquired it from him. He employed it a good deal in the next ten years for various purposes,[33, 1] and at one place in his writings he mentions his pride at never having caused an infection thereby. On the other hand, in his dreams (e.g, the Irma one), the theme of injections occurs more than once in association with that of guilt.

In the references to his previous writings Freud gave in his apologia in 1887, in which he implicated the hypodermic needle as the source of the danger in the employment of cocaine, he omitted any reference to the 1885 paper in which he had strongly advocated the evil injections. Nor is the latter paper included in the 1897 list of his writings he had to prepare when applying for the title of Professor. No copy of it is to be found in the collection he kept of his reprints. It seems to have been completely suppressed. If that were due to an unconscious repression, one would not be surprised to come across a similarly unconscious self-betrayal, since the two things so often go together. It was Wittels who first noticed that in *The Interpretation of Dreams* Freud referred to his recommendation of cocaine in 1885;[36] actually this mistake occurs in all the eight editions (including the *Collected Papers* and the *Collected Works*). Freud was so completely unaware of the trick his unconscious had played on him that he asked Wittels where he had written 1885 and added, "I suspect a mistake on your part." [37] Wittels did not himself perceive any significance in the slip, but the more alert Bernfeld did.[38] It was of course in 1884 when he recommended the use of cocaine, but it was in 1885 that he recommended the use of the (dangerous) injections.[39] That was the little scar remaining.

What is instructive in the cocaine episode is the light it throws on Freud's characteristic way of working. His great strength, though sometimes also his weakness, was the quite extraordinary respect he had for the *singular fact*. This is surely a very rare quality. In scientific work people continually dismiss a single observation when it does not appear to have any connection with other data or general knowledge. Not so Freud. The single fact would fascinate him, and

---

[1] He mentions having cured a case of sciatica in this way.[34]

he could not dismiss it from his mind until he had found some explanation of it. The practical value of this mental quality depends on another one: judgment. The fact in question may be really insignificant and the explanation of it of no interest; that way lies crankiness. But it may be a previously hidden jewel or a speck of gold that indicates a vein of ore. Psychology cannot yet explain on what the flair or intuition depends that guides the observer to follow up something his feelings tell him is important, not as a thing in itself, but as an example of some wide law of nature.

When, for example, Freud found in himself previously unknown attitudes towards his parents, he felt immediately that they were not peculiar to himself and that he had discovered something about human nature in general: Oedipus, Hamlet, and the rest soon flashed across his mind.

That is the way Freud's mind worked. When he got hold of a simple but significant fact he would feel, and know, that it was an example of something general or universal, and the idea of collecting statistics on the matter was quite alien to him. It is one of the things for which other, more humdrum, workers have reproached him, but nevertheless that is the way the mind of a genius works.

I said that this quality could also be a weakness. That happens when the critical faculty fails in its duty of deciding whether the singular fact is really important or not. Such a failure is most often caused by some interference from another idea or emotion that has got associated with the theme. In the cocaine episode we have examples of both success and failure; hence its interest. Freud observed on his own person that cocaine could paralyze some disturbing element and thus release his full normal vitality. He generalized from this single observation and was puzzled why in other people it led to addiction, and ultimately to intoxication. His conclusion was right that they had within them some morbid element of which he was free, although it was many years before he was able to determine what precisely that was.

On the other hand, when he made the single observation of Fleischl's addiction to cocaine, he wrongly connected this with the unimportant fact that he used injections. He did not do so at first, when he was himself recommending the use of them. When, however, his later misfortunes concerning the use of cocaine came about, his reaction of self-reproach and sense of guilt had to be focused. It was focused on the heinous needle, his recommendation of which had then to be obliterated. That the choice accords well with the explanation given earlier of his self-reproach few would deny.

VII

Betrothal

(1 8 8 2 – 1 8 8 6)

NO MAN'S INNER LIFE, THE CORE OF HIS PERSONALITY, CAN BE COMPRE-
hended without some knowledge of his attitude towards the basic
emotion of love. Nothing reveals the essence of his personality so
piercingly and completely as the gross, and subtle, variations of the
emotional responses in this sphere, since few situations in life test so
severely his mental harmony.

This was a side of his nature that Freud kept strictly reserved for
his private life: his capacity for love and tenderness. His children
were, of course, well aware of it in his relation to them, but of his
emotional experiences with his wife—or future wife—he never spoke
or wrote. The old lady herself, when the early days of their engagement were mentioned, would respond with a beatific smile that recalled her great happiness, but any information she would vouch-
safe was naturally factual rather than emotional. Her lover had been
wonderful, in her eyes quite perfect; that was the essence of what she
had to convey. Only after her death, at the end of 1951, was it possible to inspect the voluminous love letters she had preserved, and I
am privileged to have been the only person to do so.

It was not only in later years that the letters narrowly escaped
destruction. After her husband's death Mrs. Freud several times
threatened to burn them and desisted only on her daughters' request.
During part of the engagement itself the couple maintained a joint
"Chronicle" and the intention was to preserve this, with its record of
that exciting period, and to destroy all the letters on the day they got
married. When the time came, however, she had not the heart to sacrifice all that evidence of devotion, and in the event both survived. So
did also a diary Freud wrote of his wooing.

98

Freud's first savor, at the age of sixteen, of what love could mean we have already mentioned.[a] It was clearly a pure phantasy, since there was no relationship at all with Gisela Fluss herself. It is pretty certain that the emotion did not touch him again till ten years later, when he met his future wife. In a letter to her he wrote that he had never paid attention to girls and was now paying heavily for his neglect. Even any physical experiences were probably few and far between. In a letter to Dr. Putnam on the subject of greater freedom in this sphere in youth, he added, "although I myself availed myself but little of it." [1] This is not surprising when one considers Freud's preoccupation with work and his extensive sublimations resulting from considerable repression.

Those who were familiar with Freud's domestic environment in later years could easily have formed the impression that his marriage had been a simple affair of two people suited to each other being drawn together and deciding to marry. In his writings nothing is said about the matter beyond the fact that they were separated during a long engagement. And the only other data available, e.g., from his sister Anna, is merely misleading.

How different was the truth, as revealed in the love letters! There we are confronted with a tremendous and complicated passion, one in which the whole gamut of emotion was evoked in turn, from the heights of bliss to the depths of despair with every grade of happiness and misery being felt with unsparing intensity. It may be said with all circumspection that, quite apart from the special interest attaching to Freud's personality, the set of letters would be a not unworthy contribution to the great love literature of the world. The style is at times reminiscent of Goethe, but the delicacy of feeling, the exquisite tenderness, the precision of phrasing, the range of vocabulary, the wealth of allusion, and, above all, the distinction, the profundity and nobility of thought they display, are Freud's own. And, withal, in the lighter moments how amusing, though the task of conveying the special type of humor to a different audience and in a different language is beyond the present writer.[b]

Freud wrote more than nine hundred letters to his betrothed. In the four and a quarter years of their engagement they were separated for fully three years. Their custom was to write daily, and an occasional gap of two or three days was a distressing event that

[a] See p. 25.
[b] For instance: *Meine geliebte Braut. Soweit das Schreiben. Was nun folgt ist Umschreibung.*

needed a great deal of explanation; on a day when there was no letter Freud's friends would chaff him and express their disbelief in his
really being engaged. On the other hand there were very many occasions when two or even three letters had to be composed on the same
day. Nor were the letters brief, or only very exceptionally so. Four
pages would count as a very short one, and there were times when
they ran to twelve closely written pages; there was even one of
twenty-two pages. Early in the correspondence he asked Martha
whether she would prefer him to write in Latin or Gothic characters,
and to his biographer's distress she chose the latter.

Although such correspondence is commonly given the name of
"love letters," it will not be supposed that they contain nothing but
emotional declarations. These they assuredly did not lack, but in
calmer moods Freud would write at length on all sorts of topics.
They thus constitute a diary of his day-to-day doings and interests.
His clinical and laboratory activities are described, with his hopes
and disappointments in his work. There is news about his friends
and superiors, often with vivid descriptions of their appearance
and personality. Freud was very adept at describing people. Among
those of whom there are graphic pen pictures in the letters are Baginsky, Benedikt, Charcot, Daudet, Fleischl, Hering, Mendel, Nordau,
Nothnagel, Sir William Siemens, and Weigert.

Martha was fully informed about his social life, and of course
there is constant discussion of the members of their respective families. There are frequent literary discussions about their reading, and
above all there are many casual reflections on the problems of life
and the general philosophy of living. From such a rich treasure
house only abstracts can be presented in a book dealing with the
life of Freud as a whole, but there is scarcely a chapter, at least in
this first volume, that is not indebted to the data contained in these
letters. Moreover, and this is a matter of the greatest interest, ideas
are from time to time expressed which foreshadow later developments of Freud's thought—in some instances coming to fruition only
half a century later.

Before discussing the relationship it will be well to introduce
the bride-to-be. Martha Bernays, born on July 26, 1861, and
therefore five years younger than Freud, came of a family distinguished in Jewish culture. Her grandfather, Isaac Bernays, had
been Chief Rabbi of Hamburg during the reform movement that
swept through orthodox Judaism in the revolutionary years around
1848, and he had fought hard to stem it. He was related to Heine

and his name is mentioned repeatedly in Heine's letters, where he is called a *geistreicher Mann*—a man of high intelligence. It was his brother who first printed one of Heine's poems—in the liberal Jewish newspaper *Vorwärts* which he edited in Paris—and to whom the poet sent greetings in a letter to no less a person than Karl Marx. One of the sons, Michael, became a Professor of German at the University of Munich, a position achieved at the cost of renouncing his faith, and later became *Lehr-Konsul*, a sort of official reader, to King Ludwig of Bavaria; he wrote a massive book on Goethe. Another brother, Jacob, who following the Jewish custom went into mourning for his brother's apostasy, taught Latin and Greek at the University of Heidelberg, but refused his brother's price for a professorship. The third brother, Berman, Martha's father, was a merchant, and he too was true to his faith.

Berman Bernays and his family had come to Vienna from Hamburg in 1869, so that Martha had been there for thirteen years, from the tender age of eight, before she met Freud. She retained a memory of her mother's tears sizzling on the cooking stove in her distress at having to leave her beloved Hamburg; we shall see that the mother was never satisfied until she returned to her old home. Martha's father became secretary to a well-known Viennese economist, Lorenz von Stein; hence his presence in Vienna. On a cold night on December 9, 1879, he was stricken with heart failure and died in the street. After his death his son Eli occupied for some years his old position.

Freud had made an admirable choice of mate and few marriages could ever have been so happy and satisfactory as his. But until this haven was reached many stormy seas had to be traversed.

Martha Bernays was slim, pale, and rather petite. That her winning ways made her very attractive to men is evident from the many allusions to the ardor of her admirers and suitors, a matter that gave Freud some ground for his jealousy. Although it was never mentioned in the letters, we know from Frau Professor Freud herself that before she met her future husband she had nearly been engaged to be married to a businessman much older than herself, Hugo Kadisch. It was her brother Eli who dissuaded her from the match, insisting it was foolish to marry unless one was really in love. This was one of the sources of her gratitude to her brother which made her situation so difficult later when Freud wanted her to share in his quarrel with him.

On the delicate question of her good looks Freud expressed himself with his usual candor in reply to a self-depreciatory remark of hers: "I know you are not beautiful in a painter's or sculptor's sense; if you insist on strict correctness in the use of words then I must confess you are not beautiful. But I was not flattering you in what I said; I cannot flatter; I can, it is true, be mistaken. What I meant to convey was how much the magic of your being expresses itself in your countenance and your body, how much there is visible in your appearance that reveals how sweet, generous, and reasonable you are. I myself have always been rather insensitive to formal beauty. But if there is any vanity left in your little head I will not conceal from you that some people declare you to be beautiful, even strikingly so. I have no opinion on the matter." [2] Nor were his remarks in the next letter much more encouraging to a girl of twenty-two. "Don't forget that 'beauty' only stays a few years, and that we have to spend a long life together. Once the smoothness and freshness of youth is gone then the only beauty lies where goodness and understanding transfigure the features, and that is where you excel." A couple of years later there is a more detailed description referring to a photograph she sent him: "In your face it is the pure noble beauty of your brow and your eyes that shows in almost every picture. Then as if nature wanted to preserve you from the danger of being merely beautiful she shaped your nose and mouth more characteristically than beautifully, with an almost masculine expression, so unmaidenly in its decisiveness."

She still retained at the age of ninety[c] her exceptionally attractive manner and grace. The three words that would best describe her disposition are "sweet," "gracious," and "devoted." But, as Freud was painfully to discover, she was not at heart docile and she had a firmness of character that did not readily lend itself to being molded. Her personality was fully developed and well integrated: it would well deserve the psychoanalysts' highest compliment of being "normal."

Martha was well educated and intelligent, though she would not be called an intellectual. In later years the affairs of everyday life were rich enough to absorb her attention.

Freud was throughout unnecessarily concerned about her health, and would often say that she had only two duties in life, to keep well and to love him. For the first couple of years of their engagement he used to insist on her taking Blaud's pills and drinking wine, from which one would surmise that, like so many girls in that period,

[c] She died at this age, after twelve years of widowhood, on November 2, 1951.

she suffered from chlorosis. She accepted the recipe without enthusiasm, and Freud commented: "What prophet counts with his own wife? She loves him, but she doesn't believe him. If I stay in Vienna I shall of course get a family doctor for you, preferably Breuer."

Eli Bernays married Freud's eldest sister, Anna, on October 14, 1883. It has generally been supposed that their engagement preceded Freud's and that in fact it was through their engagement that Freud met Eli's sister Martha. The truth was quite otherwise. Actually Freud's engagement, on June 17, 1882, preceded Eli's at Christmas 1882 by nearly six months. We do not even know whether Martha's acquaintanceship with Freud's sisters, which was the beginning of it all, came about through Eli, who was a friend of Freud's, or in some other way. The latter seems more likely, since there is evidence that the Freud and Bernays families were acquainted with each other.

In her obituary notice of her brother Anna told a story of how the two engaged couples had taken tickets for the Ringtheater on the night of the tragic fire, December 8, 1881, when over six hundred of the audience lost their lives; but fortunately they had decided to spend the evening elsewhere. To judge from the biographies of the time, however, the sale of tickets on that fateful evening must have been enormous, since half Vienna claimed to have had the same lucky escape. Freud had at that time not even met his future bride.

On an evening in April 1882 Martha and probably her sister Minna were visiting the Freud family. Freud himself on returning from work usually rushed straight to his room to resume his studies, irrespective of visitors. But on this occasion he was arrested by the sight of a merry maiden peeling an apple and chatting gaily at the family table; to the general surprise he joined the family. That very first glimpse was a fatal one. For several weeks, however, he found it easier to present an unsociable and rather eccentric exterior than to court her straightforwardly, but as soon as he apprehended the seriousness of his feelings he hurried to bind her to himself "because any suggestion of artificiality towards such a girl would have been unbearable." He sent her a red rose every day, not a Viennese Rosenkavalier silver one, but one with the same significance; each was accompanied by a visiting card with a motto, in Latin, Spanish, English, or German. His first compliment, which he afterwards recalled, was to liken her to the fairy princess from whose lips fell roses and pearls, with, however, the doubt whether kindness or good sense came more often from Martha's lips. From this came his favorite name for her, "Princess." He was, however, very careful about compliments. Once, some time later, when thanking her for two charming letters, he added: "There are people who have the art of combining with a fresh compliment an older rudeness that they haven't expressed. You can hear them saying, for instance, 'You look so well, really intelligent and mature.' From which one is to infer that formerly one had looked like a young moron and should be obliged to them for the considerate way in which they had refrained then from saying so. I should be just as unfair were I to say how your letters stimulate and refresh me: it would be unfair to your previous ones."

On the last day of May they had their first private talk together as they walked down from the Kahlenberg arm in arm. In his diary that day he wondered whether he could mean remotely as much to her as she did to him, but, alas, it was also the day when he interpreted her declining a little gift of oak leaves on the walk as coolness; it made him hate oak trees. On the following day he strolled with her and her mother in the Prater and asked her so many questions about herself that when she got home she told her young sister Minna about it all and added: "What do you make of it?" She got the rather damping answer: "It is very kind of Herr Doctor to take so much interest in *us*."

On June 8 he found her making a portfolio for her cousin Max Mayer and concluded he had come on the scene too late. But only two days later she was charming to him and in a garden in Mödling they came across a double almond, which the Viennese call a *Vielliebchen*, and which exacts a forfeit from each in the form of a present. By now the attraction was evidently mutual, and for the first time Freud dared to hope. The next day she sent him a cake of her own baking for him to "dissect," signing the note "Martha Bernays." Before sending it off, however, a copy of *David Copperfield* arrived from him, so she added a few warm lines of thanks, signed "Martha." Again two days later, June 13, she was dining with his family, and he took possession of her name card as a souvenir; in appreciation of the gesture she pressed his hand under the table. It was not unobserved by his sisters, who no doubt drew their own conclusions. The next day, Wednesday, she again wrote him a few lines, which, however, he did not receive until Saturday, the day of the engagement. On the following day they both went for a stroll accompanied by her brother and she told him she had plucked for him in Baden a sprig of lime blossom, which she gave to him on the Saturday. Emboldened by this news, Freud, who already had permission to write to her in Hamburg and the privilege of calling her by her first name, sought to extend it to the intimacy of "Du." So he went home and wrote his first letter to her, which is here reproduced in full.

"My sweet darling girl,[d]

"I do not yet know how I shall bring these lines to the eyes of the dear girl: I think I shall get my sisters to arrange with Eli to assure our meeting on Sunday and smuggle in this audacious letter. But I know that I cannot put off writing to you that in the few minutes we shall have together I shall not find the leisure and perhaps the courage to talk over everything with you: the little intrigues and plans your absence in Hamburg calls for. Dear Martha, how you have changed my life. It was so wonderful today in your home, near to you, but I could not bring myself to use in my own interests the few moments Eli left us alone; it would have seemed to me to be a violation of the hospitality so warmly accorded, and I would not do anything base when near you. I could have wished that the evening and the stroll had had no end. I dare not write what moved me. I could not believe that I should not see your dear features for months, nor can I believe I am running no danger when fresh impressions affect Martha. So much of hope, doubt, happiness and privation have been condensed into the narrow space of two weeks. But there is no longer mistrust on my side: had I doubted ever so little I should never have revealed my feelings in these days. Martha, I am to get the letter you spoke of, am I not?

"You are leaving and you must put up with my writing to you. How shall we arrange that no one knows about it? In the first place for my dear girl's sake, and then because as a poor man I should have to be ashamed of what everyone would reproach me with as injudicious thoughtlessness. Only Martha not, I hope. And I know I can do no other: I have experienced Martha's magic. A little plan has occurred to me. If a man's handwriting would appear strange in your uncle's house, Martha could address a number of envelopes with her own tender hand, and I would then fill the precious shell with a beggarly content. I cannot do without Martha's answers; what seemed to us strange yesterday is today a vital need painfully missed. I am not yet clear about my own address.

"It won't come. I cannot say here to Martha what I still have to say. I lack the confidence to finish the sentence, the line that the girl's glance and gesture forbids or allows. I will only allow myself to say

[d] In English, the rest in German.

one thing: the last time that we see each other I should like to address the loved one, the adored one, as 'Du,' and be assured of a relationship which perhaps will have for long to be veiled in secrecy.

"How much I venture in writing that! If Martha's mood does not respond to mine when she reads these lines released from all restraint she will laugh at me or withdraw in annoyance. And I have to wait a long and fateful day until I read in her eyes the dispersal of my fears.

"But I venture, and I am not writing to a stranger, but to the girl whom I may call my dearest friend—it is true, only since a few days, but nevertheless through countless threads of thought.

"For the friend's consideration of this letter begs

"her

"Dr. Sigmund Freud"

Freud related subsequently that the answer to this rather unusual letter was "a tender handshake under the table," [3] but in the diary written the week after the events the story runs as related above. Martha's response to the letter when he saw her in his home on the Saturday was to present him with a ring of her father's which her mother had given her—perhaps for such a purpose. It was, of course, too large for her, and Freud wore it on his little finger. He then had it copied on a smaller scale for her, since the family knew of her owning it, and remarked that, after all, hers must be the original one, since everyone loves her.[e] Only a month later the following accident happened to his: "Now I have a tragically serious question for you. Answer me on your honor and conscience whether at eleven o'clock last Thursday you happened to be less fond of me, or more than usually annoyed with me, or perhaps even 'untrue' to me—as the song has it.[f] Why this tasteless ceremonious conjuration? Because I have a good opportunity to put an end to a superstition. At the moment in question my ring broke where the pearl is set in. I have to admit that my heart did not sink, I was not seized with forebodings that our engagement would come to no good end, no dark suspicion that you were just at the moment occupied in tearing my image from your heart. A sensitive man would have felt all that, but my only thought was that the ring would have to be repaired and that such accidents are hardly to be avoided." [4] What had happened was that a surgeon had just stuck a knife in Freud's throat to relieve

[e] An allusion to the ring story in Lessing's *Nathan der Weise*.
[f] Eichendorff: *Das zerbrochene Ringlein*.

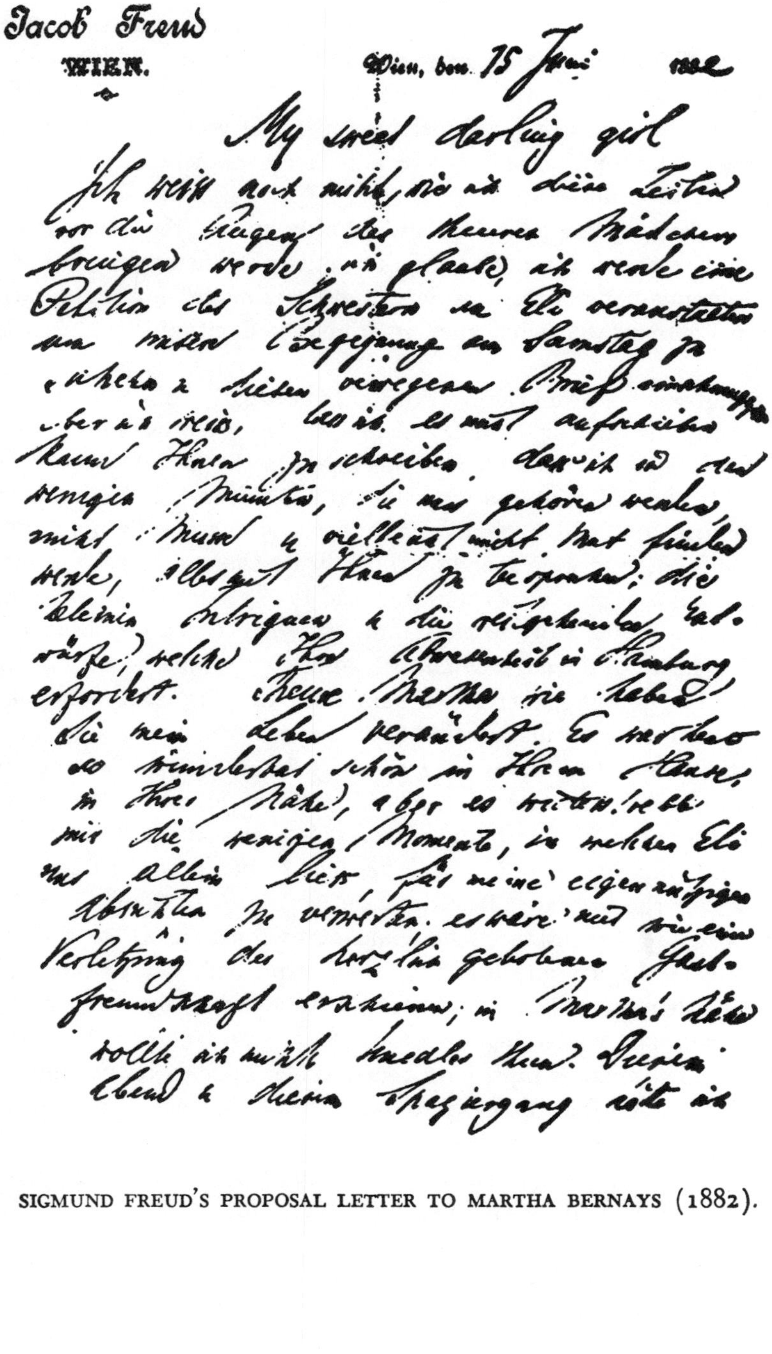
Jacob Freud
WIEN.

Wien, den 15 Juni 1882

My sweet darling girl

Ich weiss noch nicht, wie ich diese Zeilen
vor die Augen des theuren Mädchens
bringen werde, ich glaube, ich werde eine
Petition der Schwestern an Eli veranstalten
um mittels [illegible] am Samstag zu
sichern u. diesen verwegenen Brief [illegible]
[illegible] [illegible] es nicht aufschieben
kann Ihnen zu schreiben, denn ich [illegible] den
wenigen Minuten, die uns gehören werden,
nicht Muth u. vielleicht nicht Fassung finden
werde, selbst Ihnen zu besprechen: die
kleinen Intriguen u. die rücksichtslosen Ent-
würfe, welche Ihre Abwesenheit in Hamburg
erfordert. Theure Martha wie haben
Sie mein Leben verändert. Es war heute
so wunderbar schön in Ihrem Hause,
in Ihrer Nähe, aber es [illegible]
mir die wenigen Momente, in welchen Eli
uns allein liess, fast meine eigennützigen
Absichten zu [illegible] es wäre mir wie eine
Verletzung der herzlich gebotenen Gast-
freundschaft erschienen; in Martha's Nähe
wollte ich mich [illegible]. Diesen
Abend u. diesen Spaziergang [illegible]

SIGMUND FREUD'S PROPOSAL LETTER TO MARTHA BERNAYS (1882).

an anginal swelling, and in his pain he had banged his hand on the table. And Martha at the same moment was occupied in nothing more baleful than eating a piece of cake. Sure enough, a year later, and again during an anginal attack (though a mild one) the ring broke again, and this time the pearl was lost. A year later still she gave him a new ring, also bearing a pearl. It was December 1883 before Freud could afford to give her an engagement ring, a plain one with a garnet.

The date of the fateful Saturday, after which they considered themselves engaged, was June 17, one which they never forgot. They even commemorated the seventeenth of every month for some years; it was February 1885 when they first forgot to mention it in their letters.

Freud saw her again the next day only fleetingly, but evidently did not waste his time, since he noted that he had given her more kisses in those two days than he had to his sisters in the twenty-six years of his life. The following morning she left for Wandsbek, a suburb of Hamburg, to spend a holiday with her uncle, Elias Philipps; her mother and sister were spending theirs in Reichenau. It was the first of half a dozen painful partings they had to experience.

The traditional story in the family was that as soon as Martha's mother heard of the engagement she immediately whisked her daughter off to Hamburg, there to remain until the marriage could take place, with the explanation that if an engagement had to be a long one the couple had better be apart. Mrs. Freud herself described it to me rather in those terms, and with an ill-disguised air of admiration at her mother's resolute behavior. She was altogether very attached to her mother and much influenced by her, a matter that presently gave rise to great difficulties with her lover. To the very end of her long life, for instance, she could never bring herself to do any reading in the daytime because, as she explained, her mother had brought her up to know that was the time for work, and reading was a relaxation to be reserved for the evening. Yet in the present instance her memory must have deceived her, since it was not until a whole year later that the move to Wandsbek took place, and then for reasons quite unconnected with the engagement.

In the meantime this had to remain a terrible secret, and elaborate precautions had to be taken. An old friend of hers, Fritz Wahle, whose letters to her would presumably arouse no suspicion since he was himself engaged, addressed a number of envelopes, but on the right upper corner on the back there would be the letter M to indicate from whom they really were. Her letters to Freud were to reach him, not at home, but through the laboratory assistant at Brücke's Institute.

From the beginning of their acquaintance Freud's personality must have impressed Martha, the more so since, to Freud's pleasure, she found he resembled her father. From her letters from then on it is evident that she truly and deeply loved him. Yet for long Freud was given to doubting her love, and to the end of their engagement reproached her for what he called the *primum falsum* of their relationship—that he had fallen in love with her nine months earlier than she with him, that she had accepted him against her inclinations, and that he had gone through a terrible time while she was trying to love him but couldn't. The only truth in all this seems to have been that her love naturally took longer to assume the passionate form into which his had instantly flared, but it was always hard to get ideas out of Freud's head once they had found a foothold. In a letter of April 9, 1884, he refers to it as the only wrong she had committed, but two years later he admitted that most girls say yes without being really in love; that usually developed afterwards.

Naturally the secret was hard to keep from those near. A couple of days after the parting Freud joined a group of friends in a café and was on tenterhooks lest the five who knew (Fritz, Schönberg, and the three Fluss brothers) betray it to the four who didn't. His sister Rosa asked him if he was writing to Martha, but he denied it "like a statesman grown gray in lying." A few days later, however, three of the sisters had somehow learned the truth, and a fortnight later Anna, the eldest, did also.

It looks as if Martha's mother also had some suspicion, although she did not learn the truth until months later. For in a letter in July Freud remarked: "Your Mamma will not be very pleased with my visits. She told Minna she did not like our being together so often, since we seem to get on too well. My admiration for her perspicacity: but the precaution comes too late, doesn't it, my dear."

Freud's attitude towards the loved one was very far from being one of simple attraction. It was a veritable *grande passion*. He was to experience in his own person the full force of the terrible power of love with all its raptures, fears, and torments. It aroused all the passions of which his intense nature was capable. If ever a fiery apprenticeship qualified a man to discourse authoritatively on love, that man was Freud.

The day after parting he was afraid to wake from what had perhaps been a deceptive dream of bliss, and he could not believe in his good fortune. But a week later he asks why he should not for once get more than he deserved. Never had he imagined such happiness.

Freud's characteristic aversion to compromises, to evasions, and palliations of the full truth displayed itself to the full in this greatest emotional experience of his life. Their relationship must be quite perfect; the slightest blur was not to be tolerated. At times it seemed as if his goal was fusion rather than union. This aim, humanly impossible in any case, was bound to encounter thwartings when confronted with a steadfast personality, since Martha, with all her sweetness, was not a pattern of yielding docility. Only a week after the parting there was the first faint hint of his intention, never to be fulfilled, to mold her into his perfect image. Rebuking him for sending her an extravagant present she said firmly: You mustn't do that. This brought an immediate reproof, followed by his usual self-reproach for conveying one. "Martha must give up saying so categorically, 'You mustn't do that.' She is no longer the eldest daughter, the superior sister: she has become quite young, a sweetheart only a week old, who will quickly lose every trace of tartness. . . . How detestable of me that was. I dare scold a dear girl and can't show her what ardent tenderness burns with it at the same moment."

Much more serious trouble, however, soon descended. A certain Max Mayer in Hamburg, a cousin of Martha's, had, before she met Freud, been her first predilection. That was enough for the first stirrings of jealousy. It was fed by one of his sisters rather maliciously telling him how enthusiastic Martha had been over some songs Max had composed and sung to her. Then Max infuriated Freud by remarking that Martha was in need of love so that she would readily find a husband! As if she was the sort of girl to go searching for a husband! No, she would hold it better to throw a pearl back into the sea if it could find no owner worthy of it. There came a time when Martha was forbidden to refer to him as Max, only as Herr Mayer.

Freud always tormented himself far more than anyone else. Even after this first mild episode he had to write that he had quite got over the mood in which he had written and felt ashamed. "Can there be anything crazier, I said to myself. You have won the dearest girl quite without any merit of your own, and you know no better than only a week later to reproach her with being tart and to torment her with jealousy. The loved one is not to become a toy doll, but a good comrade who still has a sensible word left when the strict master has come to the end of his wisdom. And 1 have been trying to smash her frankness so that she should reserve her opinion until she is sure of mine. This reproach of tartness seems to me almost more unjustified than the next one I made. When a girl like Martha is fond of me how can I fear a Max Mayer or a legion of Max Mayers? . . . It was the expression of my clumsy, self-tormenting kind of deeply rooted love. . . . Now I have shaken it off like a disease. . . . The feeling I had about Max Mayer came from a distrust of myself, not of you." This clear wisdom, however, did not last, and got clouded over again and again.

Max was soon put in the shade by a more disturbing figure, this time not a stranger to Freud, but a close friend, Fritz Wahle. Max was a musician and Fritz an artist, disquieting facts in themselves. Freud had views about their capacity to please ladies, and indeed had once been told that Fritz in particular had the reputation of being able to coax any woman away from another man. "I think there is a general enmity between artists and those engaged in the details of scientific work. We know that they possess in their art a master key to open with ease all female hearts, whereas we stand helpless at the strange design of the lock and have first to torment ourselves to discover a suitable key to it."

Fritz was engaged to a cousin of Martha's, Elise, but he had long been a brotherly friend to Martha, bringing her out and encouraging her in various ways. It was an intimate friendship, although apparently with no serious *arrière-pensée*, but—*terribile dictu*—there had been at least one occasion when she had allowed him to give her a kiss. Moreover, this had happened on the very day when Freud and Martha had walked hand in hand down from the Kahlenberg and, not divining his feelings, she had withdrawn herself. This disturbing piece of knowledge was communicated later to Freud by his friend Schönberg, whom he had pressed to tell him the worst, but long before then there had been tribulation enough. It began through Fritz's assuming that his old footing with Martha would undergo little change, an assumption she apparently did not contradict. It is certain that neither of them recognized any serious undercurrent. Nor did Freud at first, although he found the tone of their correspondence unseemly and incomprehensible. Then Schönberg observed that Fritz's behavior was queer. He had burst into tears on hearing of his friend's engagement, and since then, however affectionate her letters, he had gone about complaining that Martha was neglecting him and that her letters were cold.

Schönberg called his two friends to a colloquy in a café so as to thrash matters out and re-cement their friendship. Fritz was surly and certainly queer. He threatened to shoot Freud and then himself if Freud did not make Martha happy. Freud, still innocent, laughed aloud, whereupon Fritz impudently said that if he wrote to Martha instructing her to dismiss Freud, he was sure she would obey him. Still Freud did not take it very seriously. Then Fritz called for pen and paper and wrote a letter to her on the spot. Freud insisted on reading it, and it made the blood rush to his head; Schönberg, who also read it, was equally shocked. It contained the same "Beloved Martha" and "undying love" as before. Freud tore the letter in pieces, at which Fritz left in mortification. They followed him and tried to bring him to his senses, but he only broke down in tears. This softened Freud, whose own eyes became moist; he seized his friend's arm and escorted him home. But the next morning a harder mood supervened, and he felt ashamed of his weakness. "The man who brings tears to my eyes must do a great deal before I forgive him. He is no longer my friend, and woe to him if he becomes my enemy. I am made of harder stuff than he is, and when we match each other he will find he is not my equal." As for interfering between him and Martha " 'Guai a chi la tocca.' [†] I can be ruthless."

Freud at last understood the situation, although Martha would not accept his view of it and protested that Fritz was nothing but an old friend. But it was clear to him now that Fritz was really in love with her without knowing it consciously. "The solution of the puzzle is this: only in logic are contradictions unable to coexist; in feelings they quite happily continue alongside each other. To argue like Fritz is to deny one half of life. Least of all must one deny the possibility of such contradictions in feeling with artists, people who have no occasion to submit their inner life to the strict control of reason." [5] There spoke the future psychologist. Furthermore, he remembered that Martha had been Fritz's pupil, so that what looked like weakness of character on his part was merely a peculiarity of teachers. "One has to consider the past, since without understanding it one cannot enjoy the present; nor can one understand the present without knowing the past." In that sentence is an essential part of psychoanalysis.

Martha, however, would have none of his explanations. It was nothing but a simple friendship, as indeed Fritz himself assured

[†] "Woe to him who touches it (or her)." The cry of the King of Lombardy when assuming the Iron Crown.

Freud when they met a few days later. Possibly her unconscious knew better, since she displayed the characteristic response of a kind woman to an unlucky lover: great pity for him. Freud decided the only thing to do was by hook or by crook to borrow enough money to enable him to travel to Wandsbek and there re-establish the troubled harmony. This he did, arriving there on July 17, their "engagement day" and staying ten days, his first of half a dozen visits there. In the letter announcing his coming he added:

> Journeys end in lovers meeting
> Every wise man's son doth know

Before leaving, however, he went through some terrible moments. Fritz's threat to order Martha to give him up because he tormented her raised his doubts about his hold on her, which perhaps he had overestimated. This aroused an appalling dread.[g] Then her letter assuring Fritz that their friendship was quite unchanged drove him into a frantic state in which he wandered through the streets for hours in the night.

The week before he managed to get to Wandsbek passed in a better mood, but a far from calm one. A letter of August 7 opens with the following very characteristic passage. "Astronomers tell us that there are stars whose gleaming we now see which began to burn hundreds of thousands of years ago and perhaps are already in the process of extinction. So far away are they from us, and even for the rays of light which travel 40,000 miles a second without becoming tired. I always found that hard to imagine, but now it seems easier when I think how you are smiling over my affectionate letters while my feelings are torn by doubts and care, and how you are being hurt by my hardness and my distrust just when I am full of tenderness that struggles in vain for expression. There are two ways of avoiding this incongruity. One would be not to report any mood that presumably will not last for a week. The other is nevertheless to do so and to retain one's cheerfulness, superior to the tricks that life plays with us. We have scorned the first way, that of sparing each other's feelings, because it can lead to estrangement, and so we have to follow the second. Just think, half the time that passes between my question and your answer—more than that, sixty-four out of those ninety-six hours—are so drawn out by harrowing thoughts about you that in the end a poor man can't distinguish an hour from a month or a

[g] *Entsetzliche Angst.*

year. Just think how empty, and therefore short, millenniums of which we are not aware must appear; and then you must admit that the delay in the events that interest astronomers is not greater than that forced on us by your summer holiday in Wandsbek."

In the plan to travel to Wandsbek the need for secrecy presented considerable difficulty. He planned to deceive Eli by making out he was going for a tramp in what is euphemistically called Saxon Switzerland; but there was a likelihood of rain, which would deprive the story of its plausibility. In Wandsbek itself, where he stayed at the Post Hotel, there was the problem of meeting Martha without her relatives finding out he was there. He called on a friend of Martha's, having a false name ready in the event of her appearing unfriendly, and doubtless would have worn a false beard had he not had his own. Days of despair passed before Martha managed to arrange a rendez-vous, in the market place in Hamburg. As he said, "Women are much cleverer at such things than men." The few meetings were very happy and on his return to Vienna he wrote that he was refreshed for a hundred years.

It was probably at this time that he proposed to Martha that they should regard themselves as engaged for a probationary period of a year; she dismissed the idea in a single word "nonsense." It was evidently a device for testing her, and he said later that had they been so cool and reasonable they would certainly have parted forever after a week.[6]

The restored happiness, however, did not last long. A little more than a week after his return he had to confess that his reprimand to Martha had not been so entirely objective as he had thought—he had deceived himself at the time—and that he was really jealous. How jealous! He learned all the tortures in which jealousy is supreme. In lucid moments he knew that his distrust in Martha's love sprang from a distrust of his own lovableness, but that only made it worse. He had none of the magic for women that Max and other artists had. He would give his right hand not to be haunted by the thought that Max and Fritz had been dear to her and that he could never be a substitute for them. It was a penance to expiate for his indifference to women in his youth. The suffering was so great that it would cost him nothing to drop his pen and sink into eternal sleep. The day after this, despair was replaced by fury. "When the memory of your letter to Fritz and our day on the Kahlenberg comes back to me I lose all control of myself, and had I the power to destroy the whole world, ourselves included, to let it start all over again—even at the risk that it might not create Martha and myself—I would do so without hesitation."

A couple of weeks later he wrote about his hatred of Fritz, whom in other circumstances he could have loved. But she must never try to bring them together; the memory would always be too painful. On her return to Vienna, on September 11, there were signs that Fritz even yet was not prepared to resign himself to the altered state of affairs. Schönberg intervened and in a letter to Martha tried to deal frankly with the whole situation. Freud also informed her that unless she rejected the slightest approach on Fritz's part he would settle the affair finally with him. The first talks were not satisfactory. Martha was evasive and silent; it was a pity to spoil the few beautiful moments together. But Freud was adamant, and she finally agreed with him about Fritz. If she had not then, as he told her more than once later, they would have parted.[7] Fritz himself gave no further trouble, but the wound was long in healing. Even three years later Freud called the painful memory "unforgettable."

Fritz's place was taken by two still more troublesome rivals, in Martha's own family: her brother and her mother. They must be introduced. Eli Bernays, a year older than his sister, was an open-hearted friend of Freud's, of a generous nature and a talent for giving appropriate presents. Freud treasured the copy of the American Declaration of Independence he gave him and hung it up over his bed in the hospital. Freud was very fond of him before the rupture, and he said later it had cost him "the greatest effort" to effect it. Eli was much better off than anyone else in the two families: he edited a journal on economics and was a shrewd businessman. He entirely supported his mother and two sisters after his father's death in 1879 and also helped the Freud family after his marriage with the eldest sister, Anna. He took a less serious view of life than did Freud, who regarded him as somewhat of a spoilt child—the eldest child and the only surviving son in his family—just his own position for his first ten years. This judgment of Freud's, however, was certainly mistaken.

The brother, Isaac, who had died at the age of seventeen when Eli was twelve years old, had been the mother's favorite, and she used to treat Eli rather harshly; there seems to have been a certain rivalry about which was the head of the family after the father's death. But Eli always did his duty by his mother very scrupulously. He loved his two sisters, particularly Martha, and did all he could for them. When Martha was due to return to Vienna in September 1882, Eli went to Hamburg to escort her home. Freud was alarmed lest he stay in the same hotel in Wandsbek as Freud had stayed in just before, and so discover his name in the register; fortunately Eli preferred a more comfortable hotel in Hamburg itself.

Martha's mother, Emmeline Bernays, née Philipp (May 13, 1830-October 26, 1910), was an intelligent and well-educated woman: her family had come from Scandinavia and she could still speak Swedish. Like her husband she adhered to the strict rules of orthodox Judaism, and her children were brought up to do the same. This was in itself a serious source of friction, since Freud would have no truck with it and despised what to him was pure superstition. Out of consideration for her mother's feelings Martha would on the Sabbath, when writing was forbidden, compose a letter in pencil in the garden rather than use the pen and ink in her mother's presence. That sort of thing greatly annoyed Freud and he would call her "weak" for not standing up to her mother. "Eli little knows what a heathen I am going to make of you," was a remark he made early on, and on the whole—in the practical affairs of life—he succeeded. In Freud's first allusion to the mother he said: "She is fascinating, but alien, and will always remain so to me. I seek for similarities with you, but find hardly any. Her very warm-heartedness has an air of condescension, and she exacts admiration. I can foresee more than one opportunity of making myself disagreeable to her and I don't intend to avoid them. One is that she is beginning to treat my young brother, of whom I am very fond, badly; another is my determination that my Martha's health shall not suffer by yielding to a crazy piety and fasting." The two things he most complained of in her were first her complacency and love of comfort, in contrast with his passion for threshing matters out, however painful might be the proceeding, then her refusal to resign herself to her age and put the children's interest first as his own mother would always do. She remained the head of the family, in the father's place, and according to Freud this was too masculine an attitude, to which he evidently reacted in a negative fashion. Schönberg regarded it as pure selfishness, as did Freud.

Freud was evidently looking for trouble, and he found it or made it. There was to be no other male than himself in Martha's life, at all events in her affection. This postulate seems also to have included her mother. Martha's own attitude to her mother was one of devotion and strict obedience; her mother's resolute will was to her not selfishness but something to be admired, and not questioned. Her sister Minna, on the other hand, was quite frank in her criticisms of her mother; it was the first bond between her and Freud. He neatly characterized the contrast with psychological acumen: "You don't love her very much and are as considerate as possible to her; Minna loves her, but doesn't spare her."

At the moment, in July 1882, Eli was staying with the Freuds, another sign of the close relationship between the two families.[h] He was so friendly and charming that Freud was rather ashamed of the great secret he was hiding from him. But he remarked even then, only a fortnight after the engagement, that Eli was going to be his "most dangerous rival." And a few weeks later, Eli, towards whom he used to feel so friendly, had become "unbearable" to him.

The "opportunity" in question soon presented itself. Alexander, then only sixteen years old, had been taken on by Eli to learn something of what proved to be his subsequent sphere of work, and, as was customary in those days, was at first paid nothing. After nine weeks Freud, who had other reasons for doing so, instructed his brother to ask for a salary and to leave in the event of a refusal or even delay. Eli promised to start paying him in January, two months later, and Alexander dutifully left. Eli was perturbed and complained to Freud, to which Freud replied in his characteristic uncompromising fashion. The former reported Freud's rudeness to his mother, who naturally sided with her son. Martha, with whom Freud discussed all the aspects fully, took his side, though she regretted the sharpness in his behavior. Freud said later that had she not done so he would have broken with her, so strongly did he feel he was in the right. Martha was, however, very distressed at the thought of a split between him and her family, and begged him to make some move towards remedying the situation. At evidently some cost to his feelings he made the effort. He sent Frau Bernays an exposition of his attitude in a letter (October 25) which has been preserved, although torn in pieces—presumably by the angry mother. After some stilted compliments he worked laboriously through every aspect of the matter, regardless of her feelings. It was a most unfortunate effort in diplomacy, an art in which Freud never achieved much eminence.

This affair, however, seems to have blown over for the time being. Eli, who was an eligible *parti* and in a better social and financial position than anyone in the Freud family, was courting the eldest

[h] Frau Bernays herself was staying with them in the spring of 1883, while Freud's brother Alexander lived with the Bernays family in the autumn of 1882.

sister and became engaged to her just after the turn of the year. Freud was very pleased about it and became more friendly with Eli, recognizing that he must be a good fellow to marry a penniless girl when he could have done much better. The news, combined with the family atmosphere of Christmastime, was perhaps the reason why the young couple decided to divulge their secret to Mamma, which they did on December 26, at the same time making her a present of Schiller's *Glocke*. We do not know how she took the news, but there are indications that it was long before she reconciled herself to Martha's choice of a suitor with neither means nor prospects, and moreover one obviously out of sympathy with her religious views.

In a letter to Minna on January 22 Freud wrote: "We freely confess that we were very unjust to Eli. In all important matters he shows himself to be high-minded and understanding."

In the previous October Frau Bernays had announced her intention to go back to live in her old home town, Wandsbek, just outside Hamburg. She had never liked Vienna, and she was not on the best of terms with her son. The decision, therefore, had nothing to do with parting the engaged couple. Martha thought of telling her of the engagement as a reason for changing her mind, but she reflected that her mother already knew of Minna's engagement to a Viennese, which had had no influence on her decision; so she refrained and kept the secret a while longer. The young couple do not seem to have taken Mamma's intention very seriously, however—it was too terrible to contemplate. For in January they started writing an account of their engagement—to be read in far-off days—in what they termed a *Geheime Chronik* (Secret Record), on the score that, being in the same town, there would be few letters to remind them in the future of those exciting days.

They wrote alternately; it was a combination of diary and self-confession. Freud's first entry contained the following: "There is some courage and boldness locked up in me that is not easily driven away or extinguished. When I examine myself strictly, more strictly than my loved one would, I perceive that Nature has denied me many talents and has granted me not much, indeed very little, of the kind of talent that compels recognition. But she endowed me with a dauntless love of truth, the keen eye of an investigator, a rightful sense of the values of life, and the gift of working hard and finding pleasure in doing so. Enough of the best attributes for me to find endurable my beggarliness in other respects. . . . We will hold together through this life, so easily apprehensible in its immediate aims but so incomprehensible in its final purpose." They would study history and poetry together "not to beautify life, but in order to live it." [8]

In March 1883 Freud's hostility to Eli revived and was stronger than before. Freud's disapproval of him at this time, the reasons for which cannot be given here, persisted until after Freud's marriage, and Martha came somewhat to share them. His displeasure was heightened by Eli's support of Mamma's decision to move to Hamburg. For years the two old friends did not speak. Freud did not go to Eli's wedding with his sister Anna in October 1883, though this was partly because of his dislike of formal occasions. It was a full-dress affair and accompanied by ceremonies which Freud described (from hearsay) as "simply loathsome"; he did not think then that his time would come to submit to the same ceremonies.

Eighteen months later he was just leaving his home when Eli entered to pay a visit; they bowed to each other without a word. Then Freud, taking advantage of Eli's absence, went to call on his sister to congratulate her on the birth of her first child. He made it clear to her, however, that she was not to regard this gesture as indicating any reconciliation with her husband.

In 1892 Eli visited the United States to ascertain the prospects there, and the year following he fetched his wife to settle in New York. By that time Freud's antipathy had lost all its former intensity. He not only helped his brother-in-law over the financial difficulties of emigrating, but kept one of the two children, Lucie, with his own family for a year until matters could be arranged in the new country. For the rest of their lives the two men remained on fairly friendly terms. The family feeling persisted, and years later Freud accepted the offer of his brilliant nephew, Edward L. Bernays, to translate and arrange for American publication of *The Introductory Lectures.*

In the meantime, as the result of this rupture, Freud no longer cared to visit Martha's home, and for two months they met only in the street or in the crowded flat of the Freud family. These disagreeable circumstances changed only when he had a room of his own in the hospital, from May 1, where she used then to visit him. More serious were the stern demands he made on her. She had to change her fondness for being on good terms with everybody, and always to take his side in his quarrel with her brother and mother. In fact, she must recognize that she no longer belonged to them, but only to him. She must give them up and also her "religious prejudices" into the bargain. Martha could do nothing but stonewall and hope for more peaceful times. But this very attitude of silence and "evasion" was the thing most calculated to annoy Freud: he much preferred having things out in an open conflict.

Mamma's Hamburg plan began to ripen. Schönberg protested vehemently against his betrothed (Minna) being taken away, but all in vain; calling her a selfish old woman had no effect. Eli encouraged his mother's idea, doubtless thinking he would have more peace in her absence. Martha's entreaties and protests were not so vigorous as Freud wished—another source of disagreement—but to her Mamma's wish was law. In the end the departure took place, and Freud was separated from Martha for the second time, on June 17, 1883, and now for a quite unforeseeable future. Mamma had tried to pacify him by saying they were only going to Hamburg to see how they liked it and would decide later about settling there. Later on Freud often referred to this "deception."

Freud had been disturbed lest Martha's poor health, with pale cheeks and blue rings under her eyes, might have proceeded from his ardent embraces in the unsatisfactory circumstances of their occasional meetings.[9] It was the first hint of what he was later to describe as the anxiety neurosis of engaged couples. But the total separation that her departure for Hamburg meant affected him much more severely than her. His situation was certainly bleak at that time. He had not yet started on any research work that might further his professional and marriage prospects, the family cares were crushing,[i] and now he was even deprived of the only consolation—sharing his troubles in talks with Martha—that had sustained him. His distress was accompanied by resentment against her mother and brother who had not taken his interests into account, and against Martha herself for not fighting harder. The month that followed was filled with bitterness on his side, bewilderment on hers, and mutual misunderstandings of a kind frequent enough in such circumstances, but which Freud's intense nature deepened to a level of pure tragedy. It is just this tragic tone so characteristic of his emotions in this period of his life that is hard to present here in this brief summary without reproducing a considerable number of long letters—which for more reasons than one is not feasible.

It would be very misleading to convey the impression that disagreements and bitterness filled the greater part of his correspond-

[i] See pp. 157-8.

ence. On the contrary, it should be stated with the greatest emphasis that, apart of course from the diary contents of the letters, passages expressing the utmost devotion, exquisite tenderness, and deep mutual understanding constitute the main feature and far outweigh the painful ones. They are passages on which it would not be seemly to dilate here: furthermore, as in any study of a personality, it is the conflicts that most engage one's attention as revelations of it.

We have now enumerated all the external sources of disagreement. Allusion to them, it is true, recurs from time to time, but we have next to be concerned with the more important internal sources: both, as is usually so, became interrelated. As much of the attraction in love comes from the differences in temperament between two persons as from the similarities between them—probably even more in the cases where the attraction, as here, assumes a specially intense and passionate form. With Freud and Martha great temperamental differences existed, and it was a remarkable triumph on both sides that a successful *modus vivendi* between them was ultimately achieved.

Martha's temperament, being the more normal of the two, is the easier to describe. She felt sure of his love and therefore made few demands for reassurance. Nor had she any reason, inner or outer, to be jealous. She recognized the necessity for mutual adjustment and that up to a point it was the man's place to direct it. The slow pace at which she could make the desired changes in various attitudes perturbed her, and maddened the impatient Freud; it produced in her at times doubts about her being worthy to be his mate. Much more disturbing, however, were the occasions where his criticisms seemed to her to be unjustified and his demands either unreasonable or at least of a nature she could not fulfill. This led to many bewildering and perplexing situations which taxed her diplomacy to the utmost. In the issue she emerged successfully, but only after passing through several crises where she felt tried to the limit. Her first instinctive reponse to those demands was on the lines of what Freud called her mother's typical weakness, a quality he heartily despised: namely, by appeasement. Her mother always took the easy way, at whatever cost of evasion or even lack of candor. This could not be said to be at all true of Martha, but nevertheless she had enough of her mother in her to prefer harmony whenever possible and, when not, to agree politely to differ with the opponent. But she had in addition something very tough and spirited in her personality and when forced to an issue, an art in which Freud was accomplished, she could stand up for herself with even greater tenacity than he could maintain.

The upshot of all this was that, although Martha allowed herself to be extensively influenced in many respects—including that of orthodox religious customs—in all major personal issues she proved stronger than Freud and held her ground. Her inner steadfastness and firmness combined with her unfaltering love carried her through to a successful goal. With Freud, on the other hand, his bark always proved worse than his bite. Or, if I may continue with metaphors, his was a velvet hand in an iron glove. After an outburst of cold, hard, and apparently unrelenting anger with unassuageable bitterness the moment always came after a few days of misery when he would soften—the thought of her tears would immediately do that—and he would then see matters in a truer proportion. His innate gentleness always conquered.

Apart from the greater intensity of his emotions, Freud's temperament differed from Martha's in several respects. She had the woman's natural desire to be loved, but she was sure it was being fulfilled. He, on the other hand, had not only this desire or need more strongly than is customary with men, but perpetual uncertainty about whether it was being fulfilled. He was tortured, therefore, by periodical attacks of doubt about Martha's love for him and craved for repeated reassurances of it. As commonly happens then, special tests were devised to put the matter to the proof, and some of them were inappropriate or even unreasonable. The chief one was complete identification with himself, his opinions, his feelings and his intentions. She was not really his unless he could perceive his "stamp" on her; without this there was no way of telling to whom she might be engaged. Yet a little more than a year later he expressed his gladness over the resistance she had offered, in spite of the pain it had caused him, since his appreciation of her "compact" personality only made her more precious than ever.

Insofar as their interests were identical Martha passed the test very well, but when it was a matter of submerging or denying her own standards in life she held her own. Possessiveness, exclusiveness in affection, absolute fusion of attitudes towards various people: all this beat in vain against Martha's "compact" personality. And the time came when he was glad he had failed. After all, the last thing he wanted was a doll, although he dearly wanted someone to share in his fights.

The demand that gave rise to the most trouble was that she should not simply be able to criticize her mother and brother objectively and abandon their "foolish superstitions," all of which she did, but she had also to withdraw all affection from them—this on the grounds that they were his enemies, so that she should share his hatred of them. If she did not do this she did not really love him. It is all rather reminiscent of the classical situation in childhood where a boy hopes, or perhaps demands, that his mother should share his opposition to his father. And, of course, Freud had some reason to regard them as his opponents. They had torn his betrothed from him, and he probably sensed that her mother cherished the hope of weaning her daughter in that way from her attachment to an ineligible and undesirable young man. He was not far out when he termed her "the enemy of our love." A year later he sent Mamma a tart letter that relieved his feelings somewhat, but he wrote to Martha: "I have put a good deal more of my wrath in cold storage which will be dished up some day. I am young, tenacious, and active: I shall pay all my debts, including this one." That again was a bark, for only a month later, when he visited Wandsbek, he got on good terms with Mamma and remained so ever after; at the next Christmas he was even sending her a present.

It was asking too much of a devoted daughter to repudiate her mother entirely, and Martha never consented to do so. And although she cooled towards Eli she never forgot he was her brother and that she owed much to him. She held her ground in spite of Freud's insistent demands, alternating with passionate pleas. Few women would have kept their head in such painful circumstances or have succeeded as she did in retaining her lover's affection.

As a rule engaged, and also married, couples go through the process of mutual adjustment automatically, guided by the events of the moment, and without reflecting on what exactly is happening to them. Freud, on the contrary, was aware from the very outset that they had a definite "task" in front of them, and there was something almost systematic in his planning of it. "Sparing each other can only lead to estrangement. It doesn't help at all: if there are difficulties they have to be overcome." His hatred of half measures, and his determination to probe the truth to the bitter end, however bitter, must have become interwoven with the aggressive side of his nature, leading to a combination that was very hard to counter. He even admitted that it was boring if one could find nothing wrong in the

other person to put right. The path Martha followed of avoiding unpleasantness could only result in parting them. All these remarks
come from the first month or two of the engagement.

Everything points to a remarkable concealment in Freud's love
life; perhaps we may say that it was something that had to be carefully protected. It could be set free and displayed only under very
favorable conditions. Even in his relations with the woman he loved
so much one has the impression that he often needed to express some
hardness or adverse criticism before he could trust himself to release
his feelings of affection. The deep gentleness and love in him were
often covered with a harder layer, one which might mislead observ-
ers into forming a false impression of his nature. Towards the end
of his engagement he told Martha that he had never really shown
her his best side; perhaps it was never fully revealed in all its
strength. But Martha divined enough to give her an unshakable confidence that with him love would always be the victor in any complicated emotional situation, and this was a sure support in the trials
she had to endure.

Naturally the most difficult part of the mutual adjustment was in
the early part of the engagement. Most of it had been accomplished
after eighteen months or so, though even after that there were at
times severe enough relapses. The nine months they were together
in Vienna before the great separation were, in spite of many wonderful moments, not very happy ones. In these months before she felt
free with him Martha was probably a little afraid of her masterful
lover, and she would commonly take refuge in silence. This Freud
always found very trying to cope with. He would become hard or
even bitter in turn, and it was long before he acquired the freedom
to overcome her resistances by demonstrations of love. Throughout
Freud's life everything he achieved came the hard way, and this was
also true of his happiness.

A further reason why Freud was so insistent on the perfection of
their mutual adjustment was that he had endowed Martha with his
own best attributes—or rather had perceived them in her—and
hoped to fortify them in himself through close contact with her. She
had a truly noble character and he felt one could not have a mean or
common thought in her presence. On the lines of William James's
distinction between the "once-born" and the "twice-born," Freud
recognized that there are rare people, of whom Martha was one, who
seem to be good and kind by nature in contrast with those, such as
himself, who attain that level only after considerable inner struggle.

He thus felt that he had much to gain from her apart from human happiness. When he said he would be in her debt when he died he had more than one reason for his gratitude. She protected him from any kind of meanness, and he would do nothing improper or unworthy even in order to gain her in marriage—better wait for years than that. Near the end of the engagement Martha astonished him by saying she had some bad thoughts she had to suppress. He replied: "I had believed you didn't know such things. There are people who are good because nothing evil occurs to them, and others who are good because they conquer their evil thoughts. I had reckoned you to the former class. No doubt it is my fault that you have lost your guilelessness. It doesn't matter greatly; whoever has much contact with life must lose it, and in place of it build up a character." [10]

Plainly, however, there was a certain incompatibility between his desire to acquire goodness from Martha and his almost equally strong desire to get her to share his feelings of hatred and hostility. When she was loath to do so it could be ascribed to weakness and cowardice or else to her innate goodness and gentleness. Freud oscillated at different times between these two explanations, but in the long run he came to subscribe to the latter. It was of course over her relations with her mother that Freud found it hard to decide between the two views. When she showed respect and consideration for her mother, despite the latter's unfriendliness to their engagement, Freud thought it impossible that anyone in the world could be so good and noble as all that; it was easier to think that she didn't love him. And when she would not consent to eating ham or breaking away from her mother's customs in other ways, Freud became almost self-righteous: "It was not pleasant to think I am better than the girl I was trying to win." All this, however, changed when he himself became reconciled to the mother, only a month after making this remark.

That is all that needs to be said here about the first critical year of the engagement. Before leaving it I may relate a passage from that period in which Freud depicts imaginatively a memorable moment. The letter (June 30, 1882) begins: "In a simple village at the foot of the Kahlenberg which bears the name Grinzing after its wine stands a plain low house, one like all the others around it. But whether it was that a great Master had long ago dwelt in it who knew how to lure its secrets from the human heart and to express in word or sound what seemed unutterable, perhaps a Beethoven or a Lenau, or whether in that spot something had happened to scorn all barriers and set free all passions, there is a magic in this poor little dwelling and 1 should rarely care to pass close to it. I cannot give the reason for it, but I have seen it myself: when two people shy of each other have come up to the windows of the uncanny little house, talking of things that do not matter, their thoughts imperceptibly master them and break down all bars; then one of the two utters a word, a sentence, one beyond his control, and the other wonders and muses, and there comes a sudden silence. And who can tell what changes between them that silence has wrought."

"What a pity that the day has to end just when one is fully enjoying it."

"And when someone has become dear, just then that someone has to go far away."

"Really far away?"

But Martha was silent; they both were, as they passed by the uncanny little house. Isn't that the style of Dickens?

"Who was that unknown person who left Martha just when they had got fond of each other? How one regretted knowing so little of the attractive girl, so sure of herself, so reticent, so gently decided in her opinions and inclinations. Perhaps she had given her affection to the friend who had left her and repented having betrayed herself to a stranger. Was it one of her cousins about whom rumor had spoken, or a serious man, a friend of her father's, one of the many such who visited her home? There is only one of whom such questions could be asked,[it] and he would say: 'It was a girl from whom Martha has just parted. A man may still win the high prize of Martha's love, and no other than you deserves it.' It seemed unbelievable, but nevertheless it was true; it became a ravishingly beautiful reality. Was the other part of the interpretation true as well?"

The two weeks after her departure for Wandsbek in June 1883, were among the worst they lived through. Martha, in very sweet and patient letters, consented to become his "comrade in arms,"[j] as he desired, but made it clear she did not propose to join him in an assault on her family. One bitter letter comes after another accusing her of weakness, cowardice, and of choosing easy paths instead of bravely facing painful situations. They culminated in one on the last day of the month where he said that unless she admitted how justified were his demands he must recognize he had failed. He is too exhausted to fight any further. "Then we break off our correspondence. I shall

[it] I.e., Schönberg.
[j] *Kampfgenosse.*

have nothing more to demand. My stormy longing heart will then be dead. There will be nothing left for me but to do my duty at a forlorn post, and when the time of success comes you will find in me an unassuming and considerate partner in life. . . . If you are not what I took you for it is my fault for wooing you without knowing you." She especially resented this idea of her influence weakening his spirit: "A woman should soften but not weaken a man." Her letters had the desired effect. On July 1 he wrote: "I renounce what I demanded. I do not need a comrade in arms, such as I hoped to make you into; I am strong enough to fight alone. You shall not hear another harsh word. I observe that I do not gain what I wanted in you, and I shall lose my loved one if I continue. I have asked of you what is not in your nature, and I have offered you nothing in return. . . . You have certainly given up the least valuable thing: the indispensable part, on which I hang with all my feelings and thoughts, you remain for me, a precious sweet loved one."

Resignation, however, never suited Freud. He often expressed his satisfaction that they had been through such a terrible time. "Such memories bring people closer than hours lived together. Blood and sufferings in common make the firmest bonds." [11]

Freud was already displaying the gift for divining the thoughts of others for which he became so famous later. As he said: "I have a talent for interpreting." [k] He was constantly reading between the lines of Martha's letters, so that she found no escape in reticence. He divided them into two groups: "open" ones, where everything was expressed, and "hidden" ones, where something was concealed; and he showed a really uncanny intuition in sensing the slightest hints. He also discovered, what he commented on in later life, that an unrestrained use of such a gift does not make for easy relationships. Could he have restrained himself it would have saved both him and her much tormenting, but that was contrary to his single-minded aim. On occasion, however, the effect was tragi-comical. Thus once when he asked her what she was keeping back she did not bother to answer the question for a couple of letters, and he got very wrought up about all sorts of possibilities—serious ill-health and even unfaithfulness on her part. She then confessed that she had had a slight stomach upset! But he had been right; there was something. And Freud's emotions at any such uncertainties were very desperate. On the day after getting that news he wrote: "I know now how dear you are to me. I have no other wish than to kiss you once more and then

[k] *Deuterei.*

die with you. After we have lived so long in happy intimacy I have a horrror of living alone even another day."

Of the distressing part that Freud's poverty played in these years we shall learn something in a subsequent chapter.[1] It was of course the one and only obstacle to his union with his betrothed, and also an important reason for her family's objection to him as a suitor. It galled him that only very seldom could he give her even a meager present. He counted such occasions as among the "greatest moments" in his bleak life. But even on the dismal topic of finance he did his best to look for a bright side. Quite early he wrote: "I am reconciled to our being so poor. Think, if success were exactly proportionate to the deserts of the individual, should we not miss the fervor of affection? I should not know whether you loved me or the recognition I had received, and were I unfortunate the lady might say: 'I don't love you any more; you have proved to be valueless.' It would be as hateful as the uniforms one sees about where the man's worth is written on his collar and on his breast." [12] Or again: "When we can share—that is the poetry in the prose of life." [13]

Freud partook in much of the prudishness of his time, when allusions to lower limbs were improper. Eighteen months after a shocking occurrence he wrote: "You don't seem to know how observant I am. Do you remember how in our walk with Minna along the *Beethovengang* you kept going aside to pull up your stockings? It is bold of me to mention it, but I hope you don't mind." There had to be an apology for even a milder allusion. Contrasting her with the robust woman of two thousand years ago he remarked that the foot of the Venus di Milo would cover two of hers. "Forgive the comparison, but the antique lady has no hands." In the middle of 1885 Martha announced her wish to stay with an old friend, recently married, who, as she delicately put it, "had married before her wedding." Contact with such a source of moral contamination, however, was sternly forbidden, though it is only fair to say that he also had other objections to the lady concerned.

We may now once more view the story chronologically. After the two or three very painful weeks that followed the separation matters were quieter for a while. Towards the end of the next month Freud still believed it likely that the family would come back to Vienna, and now he was not at all sure he would welcome it. There would be the former difficulty of making fleeting appointments, in the hospital

[1] See Chap. IX.

or in the streets, he would be distracted from his work, his ardent embraces might again impair Martha's health. All very reasonable; but he little knew then how terribly he was to suffer in the coming years from loneliness, privation, and longing. Naturally Frau Bernays had no idea whatever of returning. The "adjustment" proceeded, and the second year saw it pretty well established, although difficulties still arose later. By May of the following year he optimistically thought it was no longer possible for them to quarrel, but only a couple of weeks later severe reproaches were once more revived about Martha's consent to the separation. They were accompanied by a violent revolt against what he called his dependence, meaning financially.

Before that, however, towards the end of February there was a severe storm that lasted several days. Just prior to it he had remarked how the eight months since the parting had gone like a week; his absorption in his new anatomical work had no doubt helped. Now it was the old trouble again, her attachment to her mother. There was no special occasion for it, unless one connects it with a painful sciatica he was suffering from at the time, but anyhow his emotions could arise spontaneously and periodically did so. It was soon over and his "evil passions" died down, to be replaced by exceptionally strong expressions of love and tenderness. He admitted: "My loved one, you are waiting for a not very agreeable man, but I hope for one who will give you no cause for regret."

The sciatica brought out one of Freud's characteristics that was to become prominent in old age—his great dislike of helplessness and his love of independence. He could do nothing against the stream of relatives and friends who poured into his room, but it irked him greatly. "I seem like a woman in her lying-in, and I curse at times over the unrestrained love.[m] I would rather listen to hard words and be healthy and work; then I would show the people how fond I am of them."

In April the year began to "creep," and the summer was passed between his joyful expectation of his month's holiday in Wandsbek and his excitement over his cocaine discoveries.[n] His state of tension kept mounting through those months, and then on July 12, only three days before his departure, came the intervention of the Montenegrin Government which stopped it.[o] He was furious, and

[m] *Entfesselte Liebe.*
[n] See p. 78
[o] See p. 69.

for a moment thought of throwing up everything, his hospital prospects, the docentship itself, and his future career rather than miss the longed-for reunion. "I was so miserable, as if my whole life had been destroyed." Better thoughts soon supervened, and the postponement proved very profitable in giving him an unequalled opportunity for medical experience.

Some of his warmest love passages date from this time, and yet only a fortnight later more trouble arose, perhaps as an aftermath of his disappointment. He told Martha he considered it urgent that she leave her mother's home (and influence), and that he would ask Fleischl if he could procure her a suitable position—of course in Vienna. The obstacle that had prevented this at the time of the separation, namely, her insistence on being in a Jewish house for dietary reasons, no longer existed. But Martha made a double *faux pas* in her response. First she suggested that she stay with her brother in Vienna while they were searching for the situation; this idea she promptly dropped on getting Freud's acid comment. Then she incautiously added that the plan was a good one because it would lessen the burden on her mother. As if that were the idea behind it! Freud said sarcastically, "according to that, it would be the same if you went to Hungary." The remark had left him quite "uprooted," and he wrote two of his most furious letters. She had thought first of her mother, not of him. "If that is so, you are my enemy: if we don't get over this obstacle we shall founder. You have only an Either—Or. If you can't be fond enough of me to renounce for my sake your family, then you must lose me, wreck my life, and not get much yourself out of your family." Once more Martha's tact and sweetness succeeded in smoothing things over, and then they could look forward happily to the time together.

Happily, but very impatiently. The last month of waiting, August, was an "eternal" one. Halfway through Freud was trying to listen to a patient's heart, but could hear nothing but the rushing of a railway train. By the end of it he wrote: "While it is the privilege of the Lord that in his sight a thousand years are but yesterday, we poor humans have to delight in the opposite; for us a day can be a thousand years. It is an invention of the devil that suffering lengthens time and joy shortens it."

The month of September in Wandsbek seems to have been one of unalloyed happiness, to judge from the subsequent allusions to it. Martha had met him at the station at six in the morning, and he greeted her "as in a dream." And, although only a couple of months before Freud had sworn he would not even speak to her mother, when it came to the point he for the first time got on good terms with her, which from then on were permanent. Evidently Martha had at last persuaded him that he came first in her love, although some consideration for her mother still remained. And a couple of months later he observed that their relationship was far lovelier than before the reunion.

This happy experience, however, intensified Freud's longing for the permanent union, and until that happened two years of suffering from the privation had to elapse. It is true he felt more secure in her affections, and his research work that was to bring them together was going well, but the grim fact of the privation remained.

Freud's attitude towards the parting and the privation it entailed changed fundamentally after the month in Wandsbek in 1884. Before that there had been bitter resentment, chiefly against her mother but in part also against Martha, for their having been torn apart so much against his will. The happy time there was a turning point in their relationship. From now on he was confident of her love, except for rare relapses in mood, and he had also discovered that Mama was a human being, not an ogre. The resentment at the separation changed into longing, which grew more and more intense as the hope of fulfillment grew nearer.

Moreover, he came to look on it in a different light. By the spring of 1885 he had realized that the suffering would have been even more painful, and perhaps unendurable, had Martha been able to remain in Vienna, so near and yet so far. In the March of that year he wrote: "In one thing I was in the wrong, and I think I can now admit it. That is, I can no longer reproach anyone that you had to be away from Vienna in these years. I know I should have borne it still more badly had you been here and not belonged to me. My thoughts would have been always with you, and I should have had no peace in my work. I should always have been expecting you or wanting to go to you; and the worse things were going with me, the farther off happiness seemed, the more unbearable and disconsolate I should have become. In a whole year we should not have had half so many wonderful days as we had last September, and I don't know if you would have kept your fondness for me for long. As bad as it is at present it is still the best in all the circumstances possible for us." A fortnight later he recurred to the theme: "I cannot get away from the thought that had you been here I should have persuaded you to get married without knowing what we should live on, or that we should have been the kind of unhappy couple that end in a sensation for the newspapers, or that finally you would have ceased to be fond of me. I am able to be so reasonable, to work and to bear deprivation, only because I don't see you."

The combination of passion and resentment characteristic of the earlier part of the engagement had now been changed into deep love. This had a purer intensity than before, but naturally it had not begun to pass into the calmer love he was to experience after marriage. He himself was well aware of the concentration and also the egoism of love. When the news came that his best friend, Schönberg, was dying,[p] he confessed that the blue rings under Martha's eyes agitated him more than his friend's sad state.

Freud was always very anxious about the health and safety of his precious betrothed. In the summer of 1885 there was news that she was not quite well. "I really get quite beside myself when I am disturbed about you. I lose at once all sense of values, and at moments a frightful dread comes over me lest you fall ill. I am so wild that I can't write much more." The next day after getting a card from her he wrote: "So I was quite wrong in imagining you to be ill. I was very crazy[q]. . . . One is very crazy when one is in love." [14] Thirty years later Freud was to discuss the pathological nature of the state of being in love,[15] and he had some personal experience to instruct him.

When Martha was on a holiday in Lübeck and played with a phantasy of being drowned while bathing, he replied: "There must be a point of view from which even the loss of the loved one would seem a trivial occurrence in the thousands of years of human history. But I must confess I take the extreme opposite one in which the event would be absolutely equivalent to the end of the world, at least the world so far as I am concerned; when my eyes can see no more it can continue—what is Hecuba to me!" A month or two later, à propos his friend Schönberg's approaching decease, he wrote: "I have long since resolved on a decision, the thought of which is in no way painful, in the event of my losing you. That we should lose each other by parting is quite out of the question: you would have to become a different person, and of myself I am quite sure. You have no idea how fond I am of you, and I hope I shall never have to show it." [r] Even the slightest ill-health was disturbing.

[p] See p. 165.
[q] Närrisch.
[r] I.e., through suicide.

In the summer she had a cold in the head, and he warned her that if she was ill when he left Vienna he would go straight to Paris instead of first spending the few weeks in Wandsbek they had planned; but on second thoughts he threatened in that event to spend all his six months there and give up the journey to Paris.

Eighteen eighty-five was a far happier year than the preceding ones, not merely because of his professional successes in that year, but above all because since the Wandsbek visit in the autumn before, he felt confident he had succeeded in completely winning Martha's love. He felt sure, however, he could not have won it without the hard fight they had had with each other. In January of that year he answered a remark of Martha's on how wise they now were and how foolishly they had behaved towards each other in earlier times: "I admit we are now very wise to have no doubts about our love, but we couldn't be if all that had not gone before. If in those many painful hours you caused me two years ago and later, the depth of my misery then had not made me aware of the strength of my love in an indubitable fashion, I should not have gained the conviction I now have. Do not let us despise the times when only a letter from you made life worth living and when a decision from you was awaited as a decision over life and death. I don't know how I could have done otherwise; they were hard times of fight and final victory, and it was only after them that I could find peace to work in order to win you. Then I had to fight for your love as I now have to for you, and I had to earn the one just as I now have to earn the other."

Whether this was so or not, it is characteristic of Freud's belief that he could not expect anything good to come to him by itself; he would have to strive hard for anything he got in life. His experience of life seemed to confirm this view, but he himself did not always choose the easiest way.

In that year he could assure her that he loved her far more than three years ago when he hardly knew her: what had been an image was now a personality. So the world seemed as if enchanted. "In the early days my love for you was mingled with bitter pain, then later came the cheerful confidence of lasting loyalty and friendship, and now I love you with a kind of passionate enchantment which is the only feeling left and which has exceeded my expectations."

We may now descend from these heights and relax the tension by relating two less serious stories. The first one was when in that winter Martha asked his permission to skate. Freud sternly refused, not as one might suppose from fear of her breaking her leg but because it might necessitate her being arm in arm with another man than himself. He was, however, not quite sure on the point, so he asked his friend Paneth for a ruling. Three days later he granted permission, but on condition that she was to skate unaccompanied.

Then six months later came another problem. "We have just now such a heat wave as might be the cause of the most affectionate lovers parting. I picture the process thus. The girl is sitting in a corner as far as she can from the burning windows. He, whose love is even hotter than the thermometer, suddenly comes across to her and implants a warm kiss on her lips. She gets up, pushes him away, and cries out peevishly: 'Go away, I am too hot.' He stands there for a moment bewildered, his features betray one emotion after another, and finally he turns round and leaves her. That bitter, unimaginably bitter, feeling he takes with him, against which he is quite helpless, I know myself. What she may be thinking is hidden from me, but I believe she rails at him and comes to the conclusion, 'If he is so petty as to feel hurt at that, he can't love me.'—That is what comes of the heat."

In the six weeks Freud spent at Wandsbek in the autumn of 1885 he established permanently good relations with Mamma; after that he sent cordial greetings to her in his letters to Martha. There remained only Eli, and that obstacle took longer to overcome. Not that the rest of Martha's family much approved of her marriage to a heathen. "They would have preferred you to marry an old Rabbi or Schochet.* We are both glad that didn't happen, and the relatives may behave as they like about it. An advantage of your family not liking me is that I get you without any family appendages, which is what I most wish." Uncle Elias in particular, as head of the family, was offended that Freud had not asked his permission to woo Martha, where the answer would certainly have been in the negative. Perhaps to make up for this remissness, but evidently more in a facetious mood, Freud ceremoniously proposed for Martha's hand to her mother (June 1886); her answer, if there was one, is not recorded.

Freud was rightly proud of his independent behavior in the whole affair. "Such perseverance as we have shown should melt a heart of stone, and you will see that when we marry the whole family will wish us luck. Then we shall serve as a model for future generations of lovers, and only because we had the courage to get fond of each other without asking anyone's permission. For people are secretly quite content when something extraordinary happens; they only

* The Jewish butcher who follows Kosher rules.

make difficulties before they accept it, and they are not willing to experience it themselves or let their dear ones do so. So we are like the people who walk on a tight rope or climb poles whom any audience applauds, although the same audience would be very unhappy to see their own sons and daughters doing the same thing instead of using a convenient ladder or staying comfortably below." [16]

On October 11, 1885, Freud left Wandsbek for Paris. Martha was left alone, since on the same day her mother departed for Vienna to inspect her new granddaughter and her sister left for Geldern where she was paying a visit. His life and experiences in Paris are described elsewhere.[t] The memory of the happy time in Wandsbek combined with his feeling of strangeness in a foreign land to give him an aching loneliness from which he suffered greatly during his sojourn there. So on December 20 he left there to spend a week at Wandsbek, the first Christmas union. The pain of his longing for Martha he described as "a punishment for not having fallen in love when I was nineteen instead of twenty-nine."

He passed a couple of days at Wandsbek again on his way from Paris to Berlin, and from Berlin itself he dashed back there for a week-end. Then came Vienna and the great struggle to establish himself. Something of this struggle and the plans for marrying will be related in the next chapter, but before concluding the story of the relationship during the betrothal time we have to consider a startling episode that took place in June of that year, three months before the wedding. We have learned how the mutual adjustment had progressed so favorably in the previous couple of years as apparently to be as nearly perfect as such human matters can be: all the previous doubts, fears, dissatisfactions, suspicions, and jealousies had one by one been laid to rest. So what could be more unexpected than to learn that the most bitter quarrel of the whole engagement time broke out in that June in question and was within an ace of destroying forever their hopes of marriage.

To understand it we have to picture Freud's state of mind at the time. On top of the disappointment at not achieving fame from his work on cocaine, he was learning of the growing attacks at his having provoked the danger of a new drug addiction. This must have been disconcerting, but much more important was his deep doubt about the possibility of earning a living from practice in Vienna; in May he had thought this very unlikely. Even the patients who came he felt curiously, and no doubt unjustifiably, incompetent to cope with.

[t] See Chaps. IX and X.

Most important of all, however, was the mounting tension at the thought of his long-deferred hopes at last approaching fulfillment. The possibility of some new obstacle appearing at the last minute must have haunted him, the more so since he still had not been able to solve the financial arrangements on which everything depended.

It would have taken several years to save from his practice enough to make marriage possible; thus it depended almost entirely on the money Martha had. Even so, the problem of furnishing was not yet solved, and all his attempts to borrow money for the purpose had so far been unsuccessful. Then in June came the news of his having to attend military maneuvers in August, with its accompanying expense and loss of earning. The whole situation was thus as tense as it well could be.

At this moment the fresh obstacle he feared presented itself. Martha had entrusted half of her *dot* to her brother Eli. Freud's idea of such a trust was that the notes would be locked up in a safe, or at most placed in a bank account and not touched. He does not seem to have been able to distinguish between investment and speculation, and in fact never invested a penny of his money until late in life. To a business man like Eli, on the other hand, the idea of "idle money" was completely abhorrent, so he invested Martha's money. He had heavy commitments and at that juncture, some investments not having proved successful, he was not finding it easy to lay his hand on ready money. This situation, so familiar to businessmen, had for Freud an equivocal meaning. The distinction between capital and currency was one he was not familiar with; either money was there or it was not. So, hearing that Eli was having difficulties, he put the worst construction on the news, and told Martha to ask for her money back. After a fortnight—Eli seems always to have been a dilatory letter writer—there came an evasive postcard which aroused Freud's darkest suspicions and reanimated all his old mistrust and hostility. He sent a number of frantic letters to Martha, insisting that she use the strongest pressure on Eli to release the money, which evidently it was not very convenient for him to do. He told Martha of his suspicions that Eli had used the money for himself, which she denounced as a calumny. She was quite sure Eli would pay, he had never let her down in his life, and her loyalty to her brother to whom she owed so much made her resent the strong language Freud was using about him.

Then the old emotions that had long lain dormant and which seemed to have been dissipated burst forth with a greater violence than ever before. His loved one was siding, not with him, but with his hated rival, the villain who was thwarting the union with her; and at the last moment after all the years of waiting and deprivation. It was quite unendurable. It was truly unbelievable that the confidence he had at last come to repose in her love should after all prove to be misplaced, that it should now be betrayed at this critical moment, and that they were face to face with an irreparable rupture.

The crisis came when Eli, hearing from Martha that the money was needed to furnish their home, offered to arrange this by the installment purchase of the furniture on his own surety. Instead of rejecting this solution out of hand Martha toyed with it, much as she disliked the idea of installment purchase, and that for Freud was the breaking point. To be beholden to someone whose promises he did not trust, to be exposed to the risk of his home being distrained at any moment and his practice scattered: if Martha could not see the madness of accepting such a proposal that really would be the end. He addressed an ultimatum to her with four points, the first of which was that she was to write an angry letter to her brother calling him a scoundrel. Martha got no further than that point.

Then there were threats of letting Eli feel the weight of his wrath and denouncing him to his chief. On second thoughts, however, and without a word more to Martha, Freud himself wrote a forcible letter to Eli and got Moritz, a future brother-in-law, to deliver it by hand and explain how serious the situation was. Eli got the money together somehow and sent it to Martha the next day. With an air of injured innocence he declared he had had no idea she wanted it so very urgently, that he hadn't even known the wedding was to take place so soon, and that he deplored the "brutal" manners of her future husband. Martha rebuked Freud for his unmannerly behavior and expressed her amazement that he should be so wrought up over "a few shabby gulden." He explained to her that it was not the money as such that mattered, but that their hope of married happiness had been at stake. She was not to write to him again until she promised to break off all relations with Eli. They were by now on the edge of an abyss.

But Martha's tact and firmness again won. The crisis was over, though it left both of them shattered. Martha even admitted that for the first and only time she had felt herself destitute of any love. What sustained her was the memory of how her lover had turned back to her in the Alserstrasse years ago after having angrily left her.[17] She knew his tenderness would in the last resort overcome everything else. But she was utterly exhausted. Freud, on the other hand, although he said he had nearly perished, was rather triumphant at having single-handed defeated his enemy without any help from her, and the hurricane blew itself out. How the remaining difficulties in the way of the marriage were overcome will be related presently.

In reading through the tremendous story I have outlined here one apprehends above all how mighty were the passions that animated Freud and how unlike he was in reality to the calm scientist he is often depicted. He was beyond doubt someone whose instincts were far more powerful than those of the average man, but whose repressions were even more potent. The combination brought about an inner intensity of a degree that is perhaps the essential feature of any great genius. He had been torn by love and hate before, and was to be again more than once, but this was the only time in his life—when such emotions centered on a woman—that the volcano within was near to erupting with destructive force.

VIII

Marriage

(1 8 8 6)

FREUD WAS NOT ONLY MONOGAMIC IN A VERY UNUSUAL DEGREE, BUT FOR a time seemed to be well on the way to becoming uxorious. But just as after a time he recognized that his love "was passing from its lyric phase into an epic one," [1] so he was realist enough to know that a happy marriage would be less tempestuous than the emotional period that preceded it. "Society and the law cannot in my eyes bestow on our love more gravity and benediction than it already possesses. . . . And when you are my dear wife before all the world and bear my name we will pass our life in calm happiness for ourselves and earnest work for mankind until we have to close our eyes in eternal sleep and leave to those near us a memory every one will be glad of." [2] A wish that was wholly fulfilled, but a rather unusual one to express in the first weeks of an engagement.

He had already informed her that she must expect to belong entirely to his family and no longer to her own. So the statement he quoted from Meynert a year later that "the first condition in every marriage should be the right to expel one's in-laws" seems to have been a one-sided one.

Mostly, however, his picture of their future was drawn in a lighter vein. "All we need is two or three little rooms where we can live and eat and receive a guest and a hearth where the fire for cooking does not go out. And what things there will have to be: tables and chairs, beds, a mirror, a clock to remind the happy ones of the passage of time, an armchair for an hour of agreeable day-dreaming, carpets so that the *Hausfrau* can easily keep the floor clean, linen tied up in fancy ribbons and stored on their shelves, clothes of the newest cut and hats with artificial flowers, pictures on the wall, glasses for the daily water and for wine on festive occasions, plates and dishes, a larder when we are suddenly overcome with hunger or a guest arrives unexpectedly, a large bunch of keys which must rattle noisily. There is so much we can enjoy: the bookcase and the sewing basket and the friendly lamp. And everything must be kept in good order, else the *Hausfrau*, who has divided up her heart in little bits, one for each piece of furniture, will object. And this thing must be a witness to the serious work that keeps the house together, and that thing of one's love for beauty, of dear friends of whom one is glad to be reminded, of towns one has seen, of hours one likes to recall. All of it a little world of happiness, of silent friends and emblems of honorable humanity." [3]

Children do not come into this picture, at the beginning of the engagement; Freud's great fondness for children had not yet become manifest. A couple of years later second thoughts appear. "It is a happy time for our love now. I always think that once one is married one no longer—in most cases—lives for each other as one used to. One lives rather with each other for some third thing, and for the husband dangerous rivals soon appear: household and nursery. Then, despite all love and unity, the help each person had found in the other ceases. The husband looks again for friends, frequents an inn, finds general outside interests. But that need not be so."

For some time the question of ceremonial at the wedding was a burning one. The thought of it was anathema to Freud; he detested all ceremonies, especially religious ones. He hoped his own wedding would be as quiet and secret as possible. When there was talk of his sister Anna's approaching marriage to Eli Bernays in 1883 he asked Martha: "Will you willingly do without the ring, the presents, congratulations, the being stared at and criticized, even the wedding dress and the carriage that everyone gazes at and even the 'Ah' of admiration when you appear? You must of course have your own way in the matter: I dare not even show what I dislike, but I trust that our intentions will coincide." That looks as if she was to have her own way provided it was his, but when it came to the point he usually deferred to her.

He once went to a Jewish wedding, when his friend Paneth married Sophie Schwab. He gazed at the scene with a fascinated horror and then wrote a letter of sixteen pages describing all the odious detail in a spirit of malign mockery. [4]

There could hardly have been a moment in the long engagement when the predominant thought in Freud's mind was not of how soon he could bring it to a close. All his endeavors were bent to that sole aim. He tried one idea after another, devised one invention after another, in the hope of achieving some reputation that would give him enough prospect of a livelihood by practice to enable him to marry. As it happened, nothing helped but his solid histological investigations. He seemed to know that, and so pursued them with ardor, but there could never have been the exclusive concentration on research for its own sake that he had previously been capable of, and was again to be. His prospects were, as he put it at the beginning, "utterly bleak." There was no sign even of being able to live without borrowing, let alone repaying his mounting debts. But he struggled on, never doubting that one day the tide would turn. It was a very long time before it did, even after he married, and there were many years of hard economic struggle ahead of him.

Freud estimated at various times that it would not be safe to marry without 2,500 gulden ($1,000) as a backing to carry him over the first precarious year. When the time came he had only the 1,000 that remained from the donation Paneth had made him a couple of years before. But in the meantime Martha's well-to-do Aunt Lea Löwbeer had come to the rescue, and they could count on a dowry of three times this amount.

In all these circumstances it was of course for long impossible to predict when marriage would be feasible, and at times there were gloomy talks of ten or fifteen years, with reference to friends who had had to wait such periods; Martha's own mother had been engaged for nine years. But after the first year had passed Freud began to hope that another three years might suffice, which they did to a month. Six months later, however, he despondently thought it would take another five years. This thought was unbearable and a month later he wrote asking why they should lose the best years of their youth and suggesting that they marry in poverty, being content with two rooms and some dry bread in the evening. In another year's time he impatiently suggested they should marry in the coming August, as soon as his docentship was ratified; then they would not need to write to each other for ten years. In the next month he made a more serious proposal. Instead of guessing dates it was high time they decided on a definite one and he suggested June 17, 1887, five years to a day from the moment of their engagement. Martha assented to this, which gave Freud nearly as much pleasure as her original "yes." A couple of months later, when he knew he had the traveling grant for Paris, he advanced the date to December 1886, but in the spring of the following year, writing from Berlin, all he could be sure of was that the date would not be later than the one first fixed for June 1887. However, as soon as he got back to Vienna in April 1886 and knew that his post at the Kassowitz Institute was assured, his hopes again rose and he now counted on November of that year. The long awaited goal was almost within sight. But Freud had first to see whether he could establish himself in Vienna.

He left Berlin on the morning of April 3 and arrived in Vienna on the following day. He went first to a hotel, but since his room there was too small to write in he got his mother to find him a room at 29 Novaragasse, two doors from where the family now lived, and spent a week there while he was looking for somewhere permanent where he could start practice.

There were many visits to pay after such a long absence, and the general situation had to be explored. Breuer kissed and embraced him warmly, but in an interview a fortnight later he expressed himself pessimistically about Freud's professional chances. In his opinion Freud's best plan would be to take low fees, treat a good many people gratis, and count on earning only 5 gulden ($2) a day for the first two years. Since there was nothing to live on for such a stretch of time, Freud concluded he would have to emigrate after six months, but Breuer thought there was no hope in that either unless he went as a waiter. After a day or two, however, Freud got over his discouragement, though he thought Breuer's advice to accept low fees was probably sound. His friend Holländer had a more promising idea. He was negotiating to found a sanatorium for nervous and mental cases. Freud would be installed there, would marry in six months' time, and employ Minna and Dolfi in the domestic sphere; in time some cured patients would marry them. Freud seems to have been quite agreeable to the plan, but nothing came of it. Another friend, Heitler, immediately engaged him to cooperate with him in the *Centralblatt für Therapie* which he edited. The arrangement with Kassowitz held, and Freud's department opened at once. He was to work there from three to four on Tuesdays, Thursdays, and Saturdays. Meynert was friendly and invited him to his laboratory.[5] Nothnagel was less warm and could not promise much, but he proved to be a man better than his word; apparently he had a noncommittal nature.

Freud observed that all these men had a certain characteristic "manner," so that he had better decide to adopt one also. He chose to exploit his native tendency to uprightness and honesty: he would make a "mannerism" of that, and the various people would have to get used to it. If it didn't succeed, at least he would not have lowered himself.

On April 15 he moved to a suite he had taken at 7 Rathausstrasse, just behind the magnificent Town Hall, the best professional quarter in Vienna. He paid 80 gulden ($32) a month for it with service included. It had a hall and two large rooms. One of them was divided by a curtain, so that the far half could be used as a bedroom. There was also a small room which would serve for ophthalmoscopic work. The flat was elegantly furnished, and all he had to buy was a medical couch; books and bookcases he already had. There was a glass professional plate, with gold letters on a black background, for the street, and a porcelain one for his door; Breuer's wife insisted on fixing them herself.

Before this, however, Freud had already had his first consultation, at Pollitzer's house. The fee went at once to Wandsbek, to buy a feather for Martha and some wine to be merry on. A week later there was another consultation with Pollitzer, which brought in 15 gulden. But then Pollitzer was shocked to hear through Fleischl that Freud, with no means of his own, was planning to marry a penniless girl. Since Freud had the opportunity of marrying someone with a dowry of 100,000 gulden ($40,000), his opinion of his common sense went down badly.

Freud made known his start in private practice by the following announcement in the daily newspapers and medical periodicals: "Dr. Sigmund Freud, Docent in Neuropathology in the University of Vienna, has returned from spending six months in Paris and now resides at Rathausstrasse 7." That in the *Neue Freie Presse* cost him 20 gulden ($8). He also sent out 200 cards to various doctors. The date of this fateful venture was Easter Sunday, April 25, 1886, a curious day to choose, since everything in Vienna was closed or suspended on that holy day. In a letter of April 12, 1936, he wrote: "Easter Sunday signifies to me the fiftieth anniversary of taking up my medical practice." [6] It has been suggested that Easter had an emotional significance for him, dating from the Catholic Nanny who used to take him to the church services in Freiberg, but to begin work on such a day seems like an act of defiance.

For the next few months he recounted his daily earnings and for the most part gave also a description of the patients. The greater number of the paying ones came from Breuer, those who came direct being mostly gratis ones. "Breuer is doing everything possible." In July Nothnagel sent him the Portuguese Ambassador. Shortly afterwards Freud had occasion to meet Nothnagel in a consultation and to his surprise and gratification learned that Nothnagel had sent him several patients previously, although for various reasons none of them had turned up. So he felt surer of support from the great man. Although there were naturally fluctuations in the practice, days with nothing at all, on the whole his success was greater than he had expected; once his waiting room was full from twelve to three. In the month of June alone he earned 387 gulden ($155), a very satisfactory sum for a beginner and more than the 10 gulden ($4) daily he needed to live on.

Freud, however, felt little confidence in his medical abilities, and he repeatedly complained of his sense of inadequacy when dealing with patients. After all, sole responsibility in private practice was different from the communal work in a hospital to which he had got so accustomed. His confidence was further impaired when things went wrong. Once, for instance, he performed a slight operation on a well-known actor, Hugo Thimig, but unsuccessfully. The patient wrote him a courteous letter of thanks, but did not come back. Freud returned the fee he had sent him. He wrote to his bride-to-be that he needed a good sense of humor to save him from getting "ashamed of his ignorance, embarrassment, and helplessness."

He had plenty to occupy him that summer. Every morning he worked in Meynert's laboratory pursuing his anatomical researches.[7] Besides writing the paper on them that was published in August he continued with the Charcot translation, composed his traveling report, prepared the address for the Medical Society, the one that was postponed till October, and gave two lectures on hypnotism. Then there was the work in the Kassowitz Institute and his own practice.

In those circumstances he decided to give no courses of university lectures that summer. Wagner had all the hospital material, and the only other source was the Policlinic, where Benedikt was the chief. There, however, permission was granted only by a vote of the staff, and Holländer had prior claims. Besides, one had to pay the very considerable sum of 400 gulden ($160) for the permission. Meynert asked Freud what topic he was choosing for his autumn lectures and on being told they were to be anatomical said that in that case he need not give his.[a]

a See p. 207.

Before long, however, all these activities were dwarfed in importance by the baffling problems surrounding the great marriage question. He was still quite uncertain whether he could find a living in Vienna and early in May wrote that his hope of doing so was small. Towards the end of April he possessed only 400 gulden, enough to maintain himself for six weeks or so. It was not before July that he could feel confident he had a good footing.

One evening at the Breuers' Freud spoke of his approaching marriage, but when Matilde Breuer entered into the theme with interest, Breuer started up crying, "For God's sake, don't egg him on to get married," and he advised Freud not to think of it for another two years.[8] It was the first sign of some change in Breuer's attitude towards Freud, one that proved fateful to their friendship in years to come. His former encouragement was being replaced by an attitude of dampening any enthusiasm of Freud's, both in his personal life and his later work in psychopathology. His attitude had been most satisfactory so long as Freud was a young son in need of help, but he seemed to grudge his growing independence as many fathers do with their children. However, it was some years yet before this change became evident.

Throughout the long engagement the one obstacle had been the financial one, and this became really acute as the hopeful moment approached. Most complicated calculations fill the letters for the next couple of months, but by working them over it becomes possible to describe the essential situation pretty concisely. In addition to what Freud still had as the remains of the Paneth donation, Martha had 1,800 gulden ($720) saved from her legacy and her aunt's gift. Of this she needed 1,200 for her trousseau and all the house linen, which it was customary for the bride to bring with her. She had placed 800 gulden ($320) in her brother's keeping, and, as was recounted in the preceding chapter, her delicacy in demanding them from her brother led to the gravest quarrel. In the end, after Freud had sternly intervened, Eli sent her the money towards the end of June.

Freud had undertaken to give his own family 500 gulden ($200) a year for their urgent needs; he estimated that the wedding, honeymoon, and traveling expenses would cost the same amount; he proposed to insure his life for 1,000 gulden a year, payable quarterly; and then there was the furnishing, rent, and some reserve for living expenses to be calculated. It was evident that the margin was more than narrow. The first thing to go was the insurance, Freud promising not to leave her a widow for at least a year. If the rent was not too high they might possibly manage, but without any furniture whatever. He wanted to obtain this on the installment purchase system, but the thrifty Martha was averse to the extra expense this would in the long run entail and no doubt did not like the idea of beginning married life on such a basis. There was so much talk about furniture that Freud commented: "I have the impression that the dearest woman in the world is mortal on that point and regards a husband as a supplement—a necessary one, it is true—to a beautiful home."

Freud tried in vain to borrow more money from his friends, and then wrote to his future mother-in-law begging her to raise a loan with her wealthy sister. At first he thought 1,000 gulden would do, but presently he had to double this. The request, however, was an awkward one, which might make a bad impression on the only relative from whom Martha still had expectations, and it fell through.

In the middle of June Freud began to get concerned, without any reason, about Martha's health and very anxious that it should be perfect when they got married. So he sent her a sum of money with strict injunctions that she was to spend it only on a holiday. "If I find you have spent it on a garment I will tear it up when I come, and if I don't know which it is I will tear them all up." This joking remark was the first sign of the anger that presently burst out over her attitude towards her brother.[b]

The next day his letter betrayed the impatience his long privation, now approaching its end, had induced. Raising the matter of the marriage formalities, he continued: "Then I shall breathe again, my darling, and willingly let myself be once more harassed and economize, and if we sometimes have to rack our brains to know where this or that is coming from, what will it matter? After all, we shall be two together and far removed from the direst poverty which doesn't prevent so many people from loving each other, instead of consoling ourselves with the thought of a future which could never be so beautiful as what had been sacrificed for it. How long does one stay young, how long healthy, how long does one stay pliable enough to adapt oneself to the changing mood of the other? You would be an old maid if I let you wait until I can save up to pay for everything, and you would have forgotten how to laugh. I miss you so much since I am back, so that I hardly live like a decent human being. I miss you in every way, because I have taken you to myself in every respect, as sweetheart, as wife, as comrade, as working companion, and I have to live in the most painful privation. I cannot employ my time,

b See pp. 136-7.

I do not enjoy anything, for weeks I haven't borne a cheerful expression, and in short I am so unhappy."

At this moment another blow fell on the sorely tried couple. Freud was called up for a month's army maneuvers, something he had not expected until the following year. This meant not only certain expenses in outfit, etc., but also the loss of a whole month's earnings on which they had counted in their calculations. Freud faced the situation stoically and was resolved not to allow it to interfere with their plans. Frau Bernays, on the other hand, was horrified at the idea of going forward in such circumstances, and the following letter is an expression of her feelings at the moment and also of her masterful temperament in general.

"Dear Sigi:

"Your letter astonished me *not a little,* and the *only* sensible passage in it was, 'I am once more prepared to give up our wedding plans.' That you could for a *single* moment in the present circumstances, when you have to interrrupt your practice for almost two months, think of marrying in September is in my opinion an abysmally irresponsible piece of *recklessness. Another* word would be more fitting, but I will not use it. I shall *not* give my consent to such an idea. As you know from my letter of the twenty-third, I had already taken steps to obtain money for your marriage and had this unhappy military business not come in between I should certainly have been in favor of not postponing the wedding any longer. But since through this calamity your livelihood is completely endangered, the plan has become in a word *impossible* and impracticable.

"When a man without means or prospect gets engaged to a poor girl he tacitly shoulders a heavy burden for years to come, but he cannot make anyone else responsible for it. He cannot, however, increase this burden by in the end marrying out of despair, which is just what you are doing. If one has waited for four years, then a few months more or less hardly matter, and on calm reflection you must certainly admit that.

"To take a flat in August, just before you are going away for five or six weeks, is literally to throw money (which unfortunately is rare enough) out of the window. So what I think is this. You keep your present flat till November, or if you think it is a pity for the money you can give it up and rent another one on your return. You then begin your practice over again, and if it turns out to be possible you can arrange for the wedding at the end of the year. That makes a difference of three months, which is surely unimportant. Don't think that I can't imagine how uncomfortable your present life is, but to run a household without the means for it is a *curse*. It is one I have myself borne for years, so I can judge. I beg and implore you not to do it. Do not let my warning go unheeded, and wait quietly until you have a settled means of existence.

"First regain some calmness and peace of mind which at present is so entirely wrecked. You have no reason whatever for your ill-humor and despondency, which borders on the pathological. Dismiss all these calculations, and first of all become once more a sensible *man*. At the moment you are like a spoilt *child* who can't get his own way and cries, in the belief that in that way he can get everything.

"Don't mind this last sentence, but it is really true. Take to heart these truly well-meant words and don't think badly of

"Your faithful
"Mother" [9]

We do not know whether Freud answered this pronunciamento, but it certainly did not affect his decision.

All that remained was to find a suitable home for the young couple and to furnish it, but both were extremely difficult problems. Without somewhere to practice Freud could not earn, nor could they live in completely unfurnished rooms. A telegram early in July from Martha conveyed the joyful news of a solution: "Hurrah, 1,250 gulden ($500) Löwbeer!" This was a wedding present from Aunt Lea in Brünn. Freud in writing back remarked that the postal authorities must have been misled by the "Hurrah" into regarding the telegram as of military import, since it finished "*Lorbeer.*" ᶜ In addition there was another present of 800 marks ($190) from her Uncle Louis Bernays, in London, which she valued even more because it meant a greater sacrifice on his part. So now the cost of furniture was covered and they could go ahead with the preparations. The subsequent correspondence discussed in detail matters of furnishing, of interest only to the young people concerned. Freud missed her help in these delicate problems of color schemes and curtains, but he had recourse to his sister Rosa, so between one thing and another everything was managed in time before he left.

Apart from natural impatience, the main reason for the change of date from November to September was a purely practical one. In Vienna suites were let by the quarter, either August 1 or Novem-

ᶜ Laurels.

ber 1. Despite all his efforts and advertising Freud found that suitable ones were extremely scarce. He could only search in the evenings. It was a harassing problem, since he was bent on having a home to bring his bride to and his time before leaving for the military maneuvers was limited. The most suitable suite he found was one in the Ferstelgasse, but it had the great drawback of being vacant only in November and that would mean losing practice in the best month of the year, October, which he could not afford to contemplate. Then he might retain his present flat with the two extra rooms now occupied by the tenants from whom he had been renting, but that would cost the sum of 1,400 gulden ($560), which again was out of the question. But he learned that it was easy to get a suite in the newly built *Kaiserliches Stiftungshaus*, commonly known as the *Sühnhaus*, the "House of Atonement" which the Emperor had erected on the site of the ill-fated Ringtheater.[d] Few were willing to occupy a building with such dismal associations, and he asked Martha whether she shared the prevailing superstition. She telegraphed her agreement to take the flat in the middle of July and Freud secured it on the spot. She had had well-grounded misgivings on another score, the high rental. This was 1,600 gulden ($640) a year, payable quarterly, a sum which was certainly more than they had counted on. But Freud's customary optimism and boldness brushed aside her doubts.

There were four large rooms in the flat. The address was 5 Maria Theresienstrasse, their entrance to the block being there, on the side opposite to the *Schottenring*. The Freuds' eldest child, Mathilde, was the first to be born in the new building, on October 16, 1887, and the Emperor sent an aide-de-camp with a gracious letter of congratulation on the new life arising on the spot where so many lives had been lost. Anna Bernays speaks in her memoir of its being accompanied by a handsome vase from the Imperial porcelain workshops, but unfortunately no one else in the family ever knew of its existence.

One last blow was to fall on Freud before the consummation of his hopes. All along he had comforted himself with the thought that in Germany, where he would marry, a civil ceremony was all that was necessary, so he was spared the painful dilemma of either changing his "Confession," which he could never have seriously intended, or going through the complicated ceremonies of a Jewish wedding, which he abhorred. Now, early in July, Martha had to inform him that although a civil marriage was valid in Germany, Austria would

d See p. 103.

not recognize it, so that on reaching Vienna they would find themselves unmarried. There was nothing for it, therefore, but to go through a Jewish ceremony. But she made this as easy as possible for him. It was arranged on a week day, when very few friends could attend, and so could take place in her mother's home; a silk hat and frock coat could thus replace the more formal and customary evening dress. And so it was arranged.

The military maneuvers in Olmütz, of which something will be said in the next chapter, lasted from August 9 to September 10. Freud then returned to Vienna to change from his uniform and left there for Wandsbek the following day. He found that the military pay had been only one half of what he had been led to expect, so he had to write privately to his future sister-in-law, Minna Bernays, to borrow money for the fare to Wandsbek. He had managed, however, to buy a wedding present for his bride, a beautiful gold watch. There was to have been a coral necklace for Minna, but since the Portuguese Ambassador had not yet paid his fees this had to be forgone.

The civil marriage took place on September 13 in the Town Hall of Wandsbek. Sixty-five years later the bride still vividly recollected how the official at the ceremony had commented on her signing her new name in the marriage register without the least hesitation. Freud spent the nights of the twelfth and thirteenth at the house of Uncle Elias Philipp, who was charged with the task of coaching him in the Hebrew *Broche* (prayers) he would have to recite at the wedding proper that would take place the following day. He probably bit his lip when he stepped under the *Chuppe*,ᵉ but everything went off well. Only eight relatives were present besides the immediate family, and the couple then departed for Lübeck.

From Lübeck they wrote a joint letter to Mamma in Wandsbek, in alternating sentences. Freud's concluding one was: "Given at our present residence at Lübeck on the first day of what we hope will prove a Thirty Years' War between Sigmund and Martha." The war never arrived, but the thirty years reached to fifty-three. The only sign of "war" recorded in all the ensuing years was a temporary difference of opinion over the weighty question whether mushrooms should be cooked with or without their stalks. His joking promise of two years previously that they would have a quarrel once a week was quite forgotten. There was ample opportunity in the outer world

ᵉ The baldachin, representing the Temple, under which a Jewish couple stands during the wedding ceremony.

for the expression of any remaining need of emotional disputation, so the domestic harmony was unimpaired.

After a couple of days they moved on to Travemünde in Holstein on the Baltic where the main part of the honeymoon was spent. On the journey homewards they stayed a while in Berlin, in Dresden, and in Brünn, where they had to thank the Aunt Lea who had made the marriage possible, and so to Vienna, which they reached on October 1. Here the bride was warmly welcomed by Freud's friends and was soon made to feel at home.

The bride was then just twenty-five and her husband thirty. They must have been a good-looking couple. Freud was a handsome man, slender but sturdy, with his well-shaped head, regular features, and dark flashing eyes. He was five feet seven inches tall and weighed just over 126 pounds. His wife later was fond of extolling the beautiful tan with which he had returned from his military exercises.

In the most Churchillian fashion Freud had been able to prepare his wife only for a hard time before the better future he fully expected would arrive. At first this prospect was fully borne out. In his first month, the October from which he had hoped so much, practice was extremely poor. It was a fine month and all the doctors complained that people preferred to enjoy the warm weather rather than come for any treatment. Freud wrote to Minna that he had the choice of thinking his professional success in the summer was exceptional or its present failure was so; naturally he preferred to believe the latter. He earned only 112 gulden ($45) in the whole month and needed 300 ($120) a month for current expenses alone. So matters were more than trying, although they both made a joke of it all. He had already pawned the gold watch Emanuel had given him, and now his wedding present to Martha, her gold watch, had to go too unless Minna would help them—which of course she did. But in the next month the tide began to turn, so the venture had not been so reckless after all.

The consultation hour was at noon, and for some time patients were referred to as "negroes." This strange appellation came from a cartoon in the *Fliegende Blätter* depicting a yawning lion muttering "Twelve o'clock and no negro."

Freud had at last reached the haven of happiness he had yearned for. There can have been few more successful marriages. Martha certainly made an excellent wife and mother. She was an admirable manager—the rare kind of woman who could keep servants indefinitely—but she was never the kind of *Hausfrau* who put things before people. Her husband's comfort and convenience always ranked first. In the early years he used to discuss his cases with her in the evening, but later on it was not to be expected that she should follow the roaming flights of his imagination any more than most of the world could.

Frau Professor, as she became a few years later, never became a real Viennese. She retained her rather precise Hamburg speech, and never adopted the easygoing Viennese ways. She had been as much German as Jewish and that had certain advantages in broadening the family atmosphere. Freud had weaned her from the Jewish orthodoxy in which she had been brought up, and religion played no part in the household. But when she was very old, after her husband's death, she would find interest in discussing Jewish customs and festivals with anyone of a similar cast of thought.[10]

Presently children began to arrive and complete their happiness. In a letter two years later Freud wrote: "We live pretty happily in steadily increasing unassumingness. When we hear the baby laugh we imagine it is the loveliest thing that can happen to us. I am not ambitious and do not work very hard." Three children, a daughter and two sons (October 16, 1887; December 6, 1889; and February 19, 1891) were born in the first domicile. The sons were named Jean Martin after Charcot (not after Luther, as has been said) and Oliver after Cromwell, Freud's early hero. More room was needed for the growing family, so in August 1891 they moved to the well-known address of 19 Berggasse which had the added advantage of being less expensive. A year later more room was gained by renting three rooms on the ground floor, which served as Freud's study, waiting and consulting rooms. Freud lived there for forty-seven years. Three more children were born there, a son and two daughters (April 6, 1892; April 12, 1893; and December 3, 1895). The son was named Ernst after Brücke.

Freud was not only a loving but also an indulgent father, as one might expect from his general principles. The numerous illnesses of the children naturally caused him much concern. When his eldest daughter was five or six years old she nearly died of diphtheria, the "dangerous illness" to which Freud refers in his writings. At the crisis the distracted father asked her what she would like best in the world and got the answer "a strawberry." They were out of season, but a renowned shop produced some. The first attempt to swallow one induced a fit of coughing that completely removed the obstructive membrane and the next day the child was well on the way to recovery, her life saved by a strawberry—and a loving father.

When there were six children his sister-in-law, Minna Bernays (June 18, 1865-February 13, 1941), joined the family late in 1896, and remained with them until her death. Previous to this, after the death of Schönberg, to whom she was engaged, she had been a lady's companion, an occupation she never found congenial. As a girl she had gone about her housework with a duster in one hand and a book in the other, so it is not surprising that intellectual, and particularly literary, interests absorbed her life. She was remarkably skillful with her hands also, and her embroidery productions were works of art. She was one of those people who have a special gift for devising suitable presents, and I once heard her say that if the time ever came when she couldn't think of one it would be time to die. *Tante* Minna was witty, interesting, and amusing, but she had a pungent tongue that contributed to a store of family epigrams. She and Freud got on excellently together. There was no sexual attraction on either side, but he found her a stimulating and amusing companion and would occasionally make short holiday excursions with her when his wife was not free to travel. All this has given rise to the malicious and entirely untrue legend that she displaced his wife in his affections. Freud always enjoyed the society of intellectual and rather masculine women, of whom there was a series in his acquaintanceship. It is perhaps surprising that "Tante Minna" never helped Freud in his literary work, for instance by learning shorthand[f] and typing. But Freud could never be parted from his pen, which he used for both his private correspondence and his scientific writings: he evidently thought best when he had it in his hand.

In the next few years the family spent their summer holidays in the Semmeringgebiet, alternating between Mariazell and Reichenau. There is no record of Freud's going farther afield until his journey to Nancy and Paris in 1889.[g]

[f] Freud himself knew shorthand and employed it for his hospital case-taking, but he never used it later.

[g] See p. 238.

IX

Personal Life

(1 8 8 0 – 1 8 9 0)

FROM HIS CORRESPONDENCE ONE RECEIVES TWO OUTSTANDING IMPRES-
sions of Freud's life in this period: his terrible poverty, and the high
quality of his friends. Of the latter we shall speak presently.

Freud's attitude towards money seems always to have been unusually normal and objective. It had no interest in itself; it was there to
be used, and he was always very generous whenever he had the opportunity. He might even be said to have been somewhat casual about it
except when he needed it desperately for a particular purpose;
whether he gave it away or accepted it from a friend, whether he lent
it or borrowed it, was all much the same. In his early student days his
needs were so modest that it could not have been of very much importance; books were the chief thing money could buy.

At the same time he was quite realistic about money and was far
from despising it. It could obviously bring so much, and the lack of
it entailed privation. He therefore minded very much being thwarted
in his wishes, to travel or whatever else, for the lack of money. And
few people have suffered more thwarting for this reason than Freud
in his early manhood, since his wishes never lacked intensity.

After his engagement this matter of being thwarted by poverty became really serious. He had to announce that he was a poor man,
without a penny, with no prospects, since even a country practitioner needed a modicum of capital to start a practice. This appears
to have been the main reason for keeping the engagement secret as
long as possible. The family he wished to marry into would have
found him totally ineligible, and his friends simply reckless.

The first thing he did, a fortnight after his engagement, was to put himself "under curatel," because of his extravagance, by making his betrothed his banker. He instructed her to insert a silver coin in the box: "Metal has a magical power and attracts more; paper flies in the wind. You know, I have become superstitious. Reason is frightfully serious and gloomy. A little superstition is rather charming." [1] But he really did have a vein of superstition, of which many examples are mentioned in the correspondence. For instance, he related how as a boy he had chosen the number seventeen for a lottery that told one's character and what came out was the word "constancy," which he now connected with the number of their betrothal day, seventeen. He sent Martha all the money he could spare and she took charge of the common fund; from this he borrowed and paid back according to his financial situation. There were times when she seemed shy at accepting the money, but he rallied her by asking her whether they belonged together or not, or whether she wished to return to the relationship of Fräulein and Herr Doktor.

Moreover, he engaged himself to send her a weekly day-to-day account of his expenses, and a few of these have been preserved. From the first one, in the middle of September 1882, we learn that the only two meals he took in the day cost him 1 gulden 11 kreuzers (45 cents) altogether.[a] Twenty-six kreuzers (10 cents) went for cigars, on which he comments, "a scandalous amount." One day 10 kreuzers went in chocolate, but the excuse is added, "I was so hungry in the street as I was going to Breuer's." One day 10 gulden were missing because he had lent them to Königstein, but the next day a missing gulden can only be entered as "? lent." Then he had to confess to losing the sum of 80 kreuzers at a game of cards.

This dire poverty continued for years, and even in the nineties there are many references in the Fliess correspondence to his anxiety about making ends meet. In the summer of 1883 he mentions the occasion of a friend's urgently needing to borrow a gulden for a few days. Freud's worldly balance, however, was reduced to the total sum of 4 kreuzers, so he beat about until he could borrow the desired gulden—unfortunately too late for the contingency. He commented, "Don't we lead a wonderful Bohemian life? Or perhaps you are not receptive to that kind of humor, and pity my miserable state?" No wonder he laughed when Fleischl predicted that one day he would earn 4,000 gulden ($1,600) a year. It was not always so amusing.

[a] At that time a gulden was equal to 40 cents, a kreuzer to two fifths of a cent; money was of course worth perhaps four times as much as now, but it seems to have been correspondingly scarce.

On another occasion, a year later, he did not have even 4 kreuzers and had no prospect of getting anything to eat for three days before his monthly pittance from the hospital became due; fortunately a pupil he was coaching paid him 3 gulden and that saved the situation. It hurt him when for the first time in ten years he was unable to buy his sister Rosa even a small birthday present; this was after his stay in Paris. How irksome must the pettinesses inseparable from poverty have been to a man of Freud's large-mindedness and large-heartedness. I can remember in later years his bursting out at a waiter in a restaurant who was making minute inquiries into how many pieces of bread we had eaten; "You make us ashamed in front of foreigners."

Clothes were naturally a very difficult problem, especially since Freud all his life set store on a neat appearance, and, indeed, pointed out its close connection with self-respect. He had, it is true, an extremely accommodating tailor, apparently a friend of the family, but after all he had at times to be paid at least an installment. When his tailor was told that Freud was one of the cleverest men in the hospital Freud commented, "the good opinion of my tailor matters to me as much as that of my professor." Every expense had to be thought over; he would beforehand discuss with Martha the desirability of using some of their small capital for a new suit, or even a new necktie; on one occasion Martha presented him with one, so for the first time he had two good ties. There were times when he could not go out of doors because of the holes in his coat being too large, and he twice mentions having to borrow a coat from Fleischl in order to call on a respectable friend.

The two spheres, however, where Freud felt the privation most acutely were, first, his inability to give his betrothed more than the most trifling of presents or even comforts, she also being equally poor, still less to visit her; then his concern about the urgent needs of his family. He was astonished to hear Martha was drinking a glass of beer a day for her health, and asked "wherever do you get the money from?" A dream of his that never came true was one day to be able to give her a gold snake bangle (*eine goldene Schlange*). This began as early as 1882, and there are many allusions to it. At the beginning of 1885, when he was applying for his docentship, he was really hopeful, and he assured her that all Docents' wives wore gold snake bangles to distinguish them from the wives of other doctors. But his hopes were dashed again and again. It was only after three and a half years, at Christmas 1885, that he managed to procure her a *silver* one in Hamburg. As for visiting her, the cost seemed prohibitive. He could, with considerable trouble, get a free ticket as far as the Austrian frontier, which meant traveling in his officer's uniform, but how to get through Germany? Once his half-brothers Emanuel and Philipp had to go to Leipzig on business, and Freud managed to meet them there: Emanuel was the only person he ever showed "almost the whole of a letter of Martha's." He had two motives for the journey in addition to his unwavering fondness for Emanuel, whom he had not seen since the latter visited Vienna in 1878. One was to enlist his help for the family, the other the wild hope that Emanuel might be able to pay his fare on to Hamburg, a hope that proved illusory. The cost of that fare was a constant preoccupation in the year after Martha left Vienna: he reckoned such a visit would mean the expenditure of 224 gulden ($90), which was a formidable sum indeed. When he ultimately got to Hamburg (after the cocaine episode) he had only 8 marks ($1.90) a day to pay for both their expenses, and of course no gold bangle. Similarly, on the next visit to Hamburg after he had left the hospital he had only 40 gulden to keep him for a whole month there. Later on, the stay in Paris would have been impossible on the official traveling grant, but various friends helped him financially. His expenses, with clothes and laboratory material, came to 300 francs ($58) a month.[b] He saved up there 50 francs to buy a Christmas present for Martha.

Then there was his own family, a constant anxiety and burden. His father, never a very enterprising or successful man, was now nigh on seventy and was relapsing into a state of fatalistic helplessness and even childishness. It was some time since he had earned anything, and it is hard to say what the family lived on. There was, it is true, a momentary hope in July 1883 when a Roumanian cousin got the old man to travel to Odessa, with the prospect of some business transaction that might bring in a few hundred gulden; he went there, but without any success. The six women seem to have conducted, if not a shiftless, at least a very muddled menage, and when late in 1884 Emanuel endeavored to bring some order into it Freud was skeptical about its being maintained for long. Curiously enough, Freud mentions his mother in only two connections; that she was very given to complaining, and that she suffered from a serious tu-

[b] His memory must have betrayed him when half a century later he told Marie Bonaparte that he lived there on 100 francs (about $19) a month. This was approximately what the traveling grant would have yielded, hence perhaps the misunderstanding.[2]

berculosis of the lung. The latter was naturally a grave anxiety, and it was Freud's care to see to it that she left Vienna in its hot season for the country. In 1884, for instance, he wrote that they were all trying to keep her alive a little longer; he would have been relieved, and very surprised, to know that she was to survive for nearly a half century longer into a hale old age. What saved the situation at that particular moment was Fleischl's sending Freud a pupil. He did what he could, but often and often he had to admit he had nothing at all to send to his mother, or to the family. At such times he could not bring himself to visit his home and witness their miserable condition. He repeatedly grieved over the sight of his sisters' state of emaciation, and once, when he was invited out to lunch, he related how hard he found it to eat roast meat with the knowledge of how hungry his sisters were.[3] There was a time when the father, younger son, and three sisters were somehow subsisting on 1 gulden a day.

Nowadays the solution would have been found in the sisters going out to work, but at that time it was not so easy. The opportunities for suitable work were very limited, and menial work would have impaired the chances of marriage. The eldest daughter had got married in October 1883, and her husband, Eli Bernays, who had a good position, helped very considerably. The second one had a sharp disappointment in this respect. The third one went to Paris for a year as a *bonne*, and actually managed to send her mother 200 francs ($39); incidentally, she learnt no French at all in the time. In October 1884 there was an overhaul of the situation, the expenses necessary for the household calculated and divided up. Emanuel, who was never well off, undertook to contribute £50 ($243) a year, and Freud's share was put down at 10 gulden ($4) a month. Emanuel also invited Rosa to stay with him in Manchester, which she did from November 1884 to August 1885. A room was let to a lodger, and two of the girls went out to work. Even then the alleviation was only temporary, and Freud did his best to exceed his quota. In addition he paid 10 gulden a month for his brother's training. There were two occasions when his contribution got lost in the post: once it was 13 gulden, the other time (from Paris), 10 gulden. On neither occasion could he afford to replace the sum. As late as May 1885 Freud was writing, "The same yearly and daily problems, no money at home, no fire in the stove, mother ill and in need of country air." To attend to these urgent needs he was prepared to give up his month at Wandsbek to which he was looking forward on his way to Paris. When in Paris he tried to send them 30 gulden ($12) a month; "then at least they cannot starve." It is little wonder that Freud came to abhor poverty.

Freud's own income in these years was exiguous, uncertain, and derived from several sources, all of which he faithfully chronicled. There was, to begin with, the hospital allowance from April 1883. He was given a room and fire with, as Bernfeld drily remarks, the same pittance as the lamplighter.[4] Afterwards this rose to 30 gulden a month, less than half of what his meals cost him. For long his midday meal consisted of a plate of veal, which cost 60 kreuzers (12 cents), the evening one of corned beef and cheese for 36 kreuzers; sweets could be dispensed with. At one time he tried to save time and money by cooking for himself, or rather, not cooking. He bought a coffee machine, together with a store of cold ham, cheese, and bread. Martha didn't think much of this regime, and it probably did not last long.

Abstracting for a medical periodical yielded 20 gulden a quarter. On one occasion he was paid 15 gulden for setting up some scientific apparatus. Throughout his four years of hospital life Freud had private patients, which in those days was allowed; at the end of 1884 he even had a plate on his door for this purpose. In the first couple of years they were sent by friends, mostly by Breuer, but in July 1884 he proudly announced that he had seen the first patient to come to him from outside, someone who had heard of his cocaine discovery; he paid Freud 2 gulden. His usual fee was 3 gulden ($1.20), but for this he sometimes had to journey across Vienna to administer an electrical treatment. Once, after treating a patient for some months, he was paid the sum of 55 gulden. He said he owed it all, but was not so foolish as to pay his debts with it; there were more urgent needs. In March 1885 he was excited at being called to his first consultation, in Budweis, which, however, did not come off.

Then there were pupils, mostly sent by Fleischl. This source of income started in the summer of 1884, pupils usually paying 3 gulden an hour. For a period he rose at five in the morning to give a lesson before breakfast and so have more time for his work. More lucrative were the courses of lecture-demonstrations he began arranging in November 1884, usually to American doctors studying in Vienna; several were given in English, the first being on February 3, 1885. He gave several of these courses, the greater part being on clinical neurology, but one on the medical uses of electricity. The number attending varied from six to ten, which was the limit he allowed. A course consisted of twenty-five lectures and lasted five weeks; it brought him in the considerable sum of 200 gulden ($80). Unfortunately this profitable source of income lasted only three months, there being difficulties over material. Lastly there was the translation of the Charcot book in 1886, for which he received 290 gulden.[c]

Still all this was far from balancing his budget, and he had regularly to rely on borrowing from friends. He spoke of a friend Weiss as his banker, but he could only have borrowed trivial sums from him. The earliest helper was his old schoolteacher, Hammerschlag, a man who was himself very poor and subsisted on a small pension. "During my student years he often, and without even being asked, helped me out when I was desperately hard up. I was to begin with very ashamed, but then, when he and Breuer were of the same mind, I gave in and agreed to owe to such good friends without any personal obligation." On one occasion Hammerschlag was given 50 gulden to use where he thought it most deserving; he passed it to Freud, who in turn gave most of it to his family.

Breuer, however, was the principal donor. For a considerable period he used to lend, or give, Freud a certain sum every month. This would seem to have started in Freud's last year at the Brücke Institute, not long before he got engaged. In *The Interpretation of Dreams* there is an allusion to a friend, unmistakably Breuer, who had helped him for four or five years;[5] the last payment he made to Freud was in February 1886.[6] At all events, by May 1884 his debt had reached the sum of 1,000 gulden ($400), on which fact Freud commented, "It increases my self-respect to see how much I am worth to anyone." By November it had grown to 1,300 gulden,[7] and by the following July to 1,500,[8] a very considerable sum. It went on increasing, since the amount he quoted many years later was 2,300 gulden.[9] As long as he was on good terms with Breuer—and for years their relationship was excellent—this indebtedness was bearable, but we know that it greatly irked Freud after the break in the nineties.[d] Breuer always made it easy for him. Freud mentioned having more than once expressed to Breuer the feeling of lowered self-respect at accepting money, but Breuer insisted, not merely that he could afford such amounts, but that Freud should recognize his own value in the world. Nevertheless, a sensitive nature like Freud's could not help feeling some painfulness in the situation. He wrote once, "Breuer seems to regard these loans as a regular institution,

[c] Instead of the 400 on which he had counted.
[d] See p. 255.

but I always mind them." His longing for independence, economic and otherwise, was constant and indeed vehement.

Fleischl became another stand-by. In the summer of 1884 he told Freud he should without any bashfulness borrow whatever he needed, and asked him why he borrowed only from Breuer and not from himself. "Within a small and select circle of men who are in accord over the most important things it would be just as wrong for one of them not to share his opinions with the others as for one of them to be unwilling to accept any help." After that Freud borrowed sums from him on several occasions, and when he left for Paris Fleischl told him to be sure to write if he was in need. He died before he could be repaid.

Joseph Paneth, like Fleischl, had private means, and had the same attitude towards helping others less fortunate. With him it took another form. In April 1884 he apprised Freud of his intention to set aside the sum of 1,500 gulden ($600) for him as a donation that would shorten the time of his waiting to marry. The interest of 84 gulden he could use for visiting Martha, and the capital was always at his disposal. Freud was naturally very happy over this, and wrote to Martha that they seemed to be entering on the second volume of their interesting romance, one he entitled "Riches" after "Little Dorrit." In fact, the whole thing sounded like a chapter out of Dickens.[10] "Isn't it splendid that a rich man should seek to ameliorate the injustice of our birth and the illegitimacy of his own favored position?"

In any event Freud was not able to keep this capital intact. He had to break into it more than once to defray his expenses in Paris and Berlin, and at the end of that visit a third of it had gone.

Martha on her side too came across a fairy godparent. In November 1883 her Uncle Louis Bernays promised her and her sister 50 marks ($12) each every quarter, but, since it was intended as an indirect way of helping her mother, most of it went to the mother. In March of the next year, however, she announced prospects of a much larger gift. Freud seized the opportunity to jest romantically. "Since your Highness has now such better prospects and is justified in entertaining higher pretensions I consider myself obliged to give back to you the promise you made to me in quite other circumstances. True love is that which before everything is unwilling to stand in the way of the loved one, etc. Then three days later you would come to my room in your familiar frock and hat, would pay all my debts, and say, 'Take care to be on good terms with me; you are now dependent, not on Professor X or Dr. Y or on the public, but solely on me.'

Whereupon I should kiss your hand." In the spring of 1885 the news became more definite. There were in fact two strokes of luck close together. A relative of her mother's mother had died, leaving her the sum of 1,500 marks ($357). Then, a couple of weeks later, came the still better news. Her mother's sister, Lea Löwbeer, was to give Martha and Minna 2,500 gulden ($1,000) each. Freud alluded to his earlier phantasy "taken from the worst kind of novel," and added, "You know, it is only poor people who are embarrassed at being given anything: the rich never are." A few days later came the statement: "I solemnly promise to take you even if you don't get those 1,500 marks. In the worst case I will take you together with 150,000,000 marks."

Several times in his writings Freud mentioned his need for a loved friend and a hated enemy. That dramatic utterance had this much of truth in it that he could both love and hate passionately, and also that the one was apt to evoke the other, but the inference sometimes drawn that such emotions occupied much of Freud's life or were a prominent feature of his personality is untrue; I know of only five or six examples of them. Although most quarrels have of course two sides to them, some are more one-sided than others. If my personal opinion is of any interest, I should say that the disagreements with Eli Bernays and, later, with Breuer were more of Freud's making; those with Meynert and Jung (also Adler) were of the opposite kind. In those with Fliess and Ferenczi both sides seem to have been so involved as to make it harder to pass an opinion. I trust that my numerical impartiality will not go unnoticed.

Nor would it be true to say that he was a difficult person to get on with or to be friends with. He was not at all a man who set himself out to charm or please with social graces anyone he met; on the contrary, his initial approach might even be rather brusque. But on the other hand he was the kind of man of whom it would be said that the better you knew him the more you liked him. At all events there is no doubt at all about both the number and the strength of his friendships, at every period of his life, and that fact should speak for itself.

Freud himself knew that he had not the capacity of showing himself off to the best advantage at the first contact with a new acquaintance. "I regard it as a serious misfortune that Nature did not give me that indefinite something which attracts people. If I think back on my life it is what I have most lacked to make my existence rosy. It has always taken me a long time to win a friend, and every time I meet someone I notice that to begin with some impulse, which he does not need to analyze, leads him to underestimate me. It is a matter of a glance or a feeling or some other secret of nature, but it affects one very unfortunately. What compensates me for it is the thought of how closely all those who have become my friends keep to me." [11]

At the beginning of this decade Freud was still a medical student and also a research student at the Physiological Institute. This, together with omnivorous reading, occupied most of his time, but he had a good deal of social life as well. There were family friends as well as personal ones.

Of the older generation Professor Hammerschlag, who had taught Freud the Scriptures and Hebrew in school, was the most important. Freud said of him, "He has been touchingly fond of me for years: there is such a secret sympathy between us that we can talk intimately together. He always regards me as his son." He had the highest opinion also of Hammerschlag's wife: "I do not know any better or more humane people, or so free from any ignoble motives." Years later Freud named his youngest daughter after a daughter of Hammerschlag's who in 1885 was married to Rudolf Lichtheim of Breslau, a man who died within a year; and another daughter after his niece, Sophie Schwab, whose wedding with Josef Paneth Freud attended.

There were two quite distinct groups of strictly personal friends: those he got to know in his medical and scientific work, mostly older than himself; and a little group of about his own age. The latter, fifteen or twenty in number, constituted what they called the *Bund* (Union). They used to forgather regularly once a week in the Café Kurzweil for conversation and games of cards and chess. They would also at times make little expeditions in the Prater or the surroundings of Vienna, accompanied by girl friends—often sisters. But Freud took little notice of the opposite sex, a fact that avenged itself when he came to fall in love.

Among the *Bund* companions were Eli Bernays, Ignaz Schönberg, the three brothers, Fritz, Richard, and Emil Wahle, as well as Gisela Fluss's three brothers, Richard, Emil, and Alfred. The last three dated from Freiberg days, having come to Vienna in 1878 long after the Freud family. The first three named were to play an important part in Freud's life in the next couple of years. Schönberg was in the early eighties his best friend; with the other two there were quarrels that led to lasting estrangements.

Freud spoke of his *Bund* companions as school friends, but it does not follow that they had all gone to the same school as he had. The only ones dating from school time were Herzig, now a colleague in the hospital; Robert Franceschini, the only other one from Freud's class to become a medical student but who had to give up for reasons of health; Knöpfmacher, to whom Freud wrote some letters that have been preserved from that and an earlier time; Richard Wahle; Silberstein; Braun; and Wagner. Then there were Rosanes; Brust, who was for a time engaged to Rosa Freud; Bettelheim, an army doctor; Lustgarten, a biochemist who subsequently settled in New York, all from a later period.

No one in Freud's family knew how he came to have such a good knowledge of Spanish. The mystery was disclosed in a letter he wrote to Martha on the occasion of his coming across an old school friend, Silberstein, whom he had not seen for three years. He was Freud's bosom friend in school days and they spent together every hour they were not in school. They learnt Spanish together and developed their own mythology and private words, mostly derived from Cervantes. In another book they found a philosophical dialogue between two dogs who lay before the door of a hospital, and they appropriated their names for themselves. Silberstein was Berganza, Freud was Cipion, and used to sign the letters to his friend, *"Tu fidel Cipion, pero en el Hospital de Sevilla."* One cannot resist imagining his astonishment had someone suddenly addressed him as Cipion half a century later! They constituted a learned society to which they gave the name of *Academia Cartellane*, and in connection with it wrote an immense quantity of belles-lettres composed in a humorous vein. As they grew up their interests diverged and the past was buried; the friend became a banker.

The story of Fritz Wahle has already been related,[c] but we may say something here about the other two friends who played an active part in Freud's current life. Ignaz Schönberg was already (1881-1882) engaged to Martha Bernays' younger sister Minna, then a girl of sixteen; had things gone well, therefore, he would have become Freud's brother-in-law. They looked forward to being a happy quartet together. Freud once remarked that two of them were thoroughly good people, Martha and Schönberg, and two were wild passionate people, not so good, Minna and himself: two who were adaptable and two who wanted their own way. "That is why we get on better in a criss-cross arrangement; why two similar people like

• See pp. 112-5.

Minna and myself don't suit each other specially; why the two good-natured ones don't attract each other." As to his own type of woman he wrote once: "A robust woman who in case of need can single-handed throw her husband and servants out of doors was never my ideal, however much there is to be said for the value of a woman being in perfect health. What I have always found attractive is someone delicate whom I could take care of."

Schönberg was already infected with pulmonary tuberculosis, a common enough complaint in Vienna. Since most people recovered from it, the condition was not at first taken very seriously. He was a gifted and serious person, but rather humorless and also unde-cided. In the summer of 1883 the state of his lungs worsened. He retired to Gleichenberg in Styria, and in June Freud went there to escort him to Steinamanger, a spa in Hungary. Freud strongly, though in vain, urged the family to send him south for the winter; he thought there was a good chance of recovery if this were done, and warned them against the danger of his wintering in Vienna.

In the spring of 1884 Freud treated Schönberg's mother, who had heart disease, for a couple of months, with a satisfactory outcome. He was desperately in need of money then and it was some months before he could get the family to pay his fee of 60 gulden ($24). His friend naturally felt the meanness of his brother, who was responsible for the debt.

In April 1884 Schönberg, who had no income, secured a position with Professor Monier Williams in Oxford to assist in the preparation of a Sanskrit Dictionary; he was to receive £150 ($729) a year. He left in May, just after obtaining his university degree, and offended Freud by not saying good-by, possibly feeling awkward at the nonpayment of Freud's fees for the long and successful treatment of his mother.

In Oxford things did not go well and Schönberg's health deteriorated to such an extent that he had to leave England after a year. He traveled to Hamburg to see Minna, for the last time, and then to Baden near Vienna. Freud examined him there in June and considered his case hopeless; his larynx was already affected. At this time Schönberg broke off his engagement, not wishing to tie a woman any longer. Freud wrote to Martha about this, saying that they would behave differently in a similar situation; nothing but death itself would part them.[12]

Schönberg died early in February, 1886. As we saw, he had stood firmly by Freud in one of the most difficult times of Freud's relationship to Martha Bernays, and his help then had been invaluable;[f] Freud felt the loss keenly. This death was not the first one in Freud's circle. In the summer of 1883 he was shocked one day to hear that his friend, Dr. Nathan Weiss, a hospital colleague, had hanged himself in a public bath only ten days after returning from his honeymoon. He was an eccentric character and Freud was perhaps the only one drawn to him. After recovering from the shock of the news Freud wrote two letters giving a detailed and very penetrating analysis of his friend's character with a discerning diagnosis of the complex motives that drove him to his end;[13] it would rank as a good psychological study. It was the death of Weiss, a promising neurologist, that emboldened Freud to decide on a neurological career in his place.

Eli Bernays (February 6, 1860-October 14, 1923) was even more closely connected with Freud's future wife than was Schönberg, being her only surviving brother. Freud had long been a friend of his, and he admitted later that had it not been for the quarrel between them he could have become very fond of him. It constantly happens in life that when a man falls in love with a friend's sister, the former friendship is replaced by hostility, and that is what happened here. The part the antagonism to Eli played in the relationship of the engaged couple has already been described.[g]

Intermediate in age between these *Bund* friends and the real seniors may be mentioned those rather older than Freud and belonging to his growing medical circle. Such were Heitler, the editor of the *Centralblatt für Therapie*; Herzig, a lifelong friend and one whose influence was indirectly helpful in Freud's escape from the Nazis so many years later; Pollak, who was the senior *Sekundararzt* when Freud worked in the *Nervenabteilung*; Schwab; the ophthalmologist Königstein, a lifelong friend; Holländer, with whom he worked at the anatomy of the brain; and Josef Paneth, who died prematurely of tuberculosis in 1890.

Of the four real seniors Breuer, the only Jew among them, was the most sympathetic personality. He was the only one whom a psychologist would regard as very nearly "normal," a rare compliment. Freud's letters are full of the warm regard between the two men and of his high appreciation of Breuer's sterling qualities. His intelligence, his wide range of knowledge, his practical sense, his wisdom, and, above all, his delicate understanding, are qualities that again

[f] See p. 12.
[g] See Chap. VII.

and again shine out. Freud was at times given to subjective judgment of people, but in the present case the numerous examples he gives convince the present reader of the letters that it was a just one. If I may use the colloquialism, I should say that Breuer "comes out best" of all the people mentioned in them. He also has the distinction of being, with the other exception of Hammerschlag, the only one for whom Freud has no word whatever of adverse criticism, and Freud was not sparing in this.

Freud was a constant visitor to Breuer's home, and he speaks of how happy and comfortable he felt in the peace there; they are such "dear good understanding people." He was very fond of Breuer's young and pretty wife, and he named his own (eldest) daughter Mathilde after her. To talk with Breuer was "like sitting in the sun"; "he radiates light and warmth." "He is such a sunny person, and I don't know what he sees in me to be so kind." "He is a man who always understands one." Perhaps the most charming thing he said about him was during the worst time with Fleischl. "Breuer has again behaved magnificently in the Fleischl affair. One does not adequately characterize him by only saying good things about him; one has also to emphasize the absence of so much badness." [14]

Breuer hardly ever tried to influence Freud. Freud often sought his advice, for example, about deciding to specialize in neurology, to apply for the traveling grant, to help him in the delicate problems of Schönberg and Minna, and so on. Breuer would always divine Freud's real attitude and encourage him in it, but by actively sharing the problem. When he didn't agree with Freud he had the habit of putting his objection in a word. Thus, when Freud thought of joining the Protestant "Confession" [h] so as to be able to marry without having the complicated Jewish ceremonies he hated so much, Breuer merely murmured, "Too complicated." Before leaving for his month's holiday in Wandsbek in 1884 Freud asked for an extra 50 gulden. "Breuer calmly replied, 'My dear fellow, I'm not going to lend it to you. You would only come back from Wandsbek without a penny, with debts to your tailor and frightfully crapulent after the debauch.' 'My dear friend,' I said, 'please don't disturb my adventurous style of life,' but it didn't help. It was really dear and intimate of Breuer not only to refuse me, but to concern himself with my being sensible, but all the same I am annoyed." However, a few days later Breuer called on him with the money, saying he only

[h] In Austria one had to belong to some sort of "Confession" apart from any real religious views.

wanted to put the brake on a little, but with no intention of restricting him. The only active advice he seems ever to have given Freud was a suggestion for a piece of anatomical research.[15] Since Breuer had first made his name over an important investigation on the acoustic nerve, one wonders if this was not the starting point of Freud's important work on the root fibers of that nerve, the most valuable of all his histological researches. If so, it was a piece of advice worth having.

Breuer often took Freud with him on his rounds. These sometimes covered a considerable distance so that they would have to spend the night away from Vienna. On one such occasion in Baden Breuer entered Freud's name in the *Gasthaus* book as his brother, so that Freud would not have to tip the waiter. But the most unforgettable occasion was when he invited Freud to pass a couple of days in a house he had taken for the summer in Gmunden in the Salzkammergut. Freud had seldom been so far away from Vienna or gazed at such beautiful scenery, and he wrote a long lyrical account of this wonderful experience.

It is well worth bearing all this in mind when one reads in Freud's correspondence of the nineties of the bitter animosity he developed against Breuer; a sentiment, it is true, he never betrayed in any of his published writings, where he always spoke of Breuer in terms of praise and gratitude. One must conclude that Freud had changed more than Breuer,[i] and that the reason for it must have been an internal rather than an external one.

The other seniors had been Freud's superiors in the Institute of Physiology, the men he said he could respect and take as his models.[16] They were Brücke himself and his Assistant Professors, Exner and Fleischl. Of the formidable but friendly Brücke we have already heard, and also of the brilliant and fascinating Fleischl; the dour Exner was to Freud the least attractive, but he maintained a friendly relationship with Freud after the period together at the Institute and at times asked him to dine and pass an evening at his house.

So all in all Freud had a plenitude of friends drawn from very varied circles. The only person we read of as having taken a dislike to him was a certain Dr. Jaksch, an assistant of Nothnagel's who did his best to prejudice the latter against Freud.

Something may now be said about Freud's state of health in these years. He suffered, in the first place, from some physical troubles·

i See p. 145.

two recurring ailments, and an attack of smallpox in April 1885. The latter was a mild attack that left no marks, but the toxic condition accompanying it seems to have been severe.[17] On another occasion, in the autumn of 1882, Nothnagel made the diagnosis of an ambulatory typhoid fever, but that also was of a slight nature.[18] More troublesome were "rheumatic" pains in the back and arms. He spoke from time to time, and also in later years, of having writers' cramp, but he wrote so extensively that this might well have been neuritic, not neurotic. He had had a brachial neuritis earlier, as had his father when a young man. In March 1884 he was confined to bed with a left-sided sciatica, and was away from work for five weeks. After a fortnight in bed, however, he had had enough. "In the morning I was lying in bed with most disagreeable pains when I caught sight of myself in the mirror and was horrified at my wild beard. I decided to have no more sciatica, to give up the luxury of being ill, and to become a human being once more." So he dressed, went round to the barber's, and then called on some friends—to their consternation.

Freud was one of those unhappy victims of severe nasal catarrh, whose extreme discomfort people who get only a mild cold in the head never comprehend, and for years he suffered from sinus complications as well. As he wrote in a letter to his sister-in-law, such ailments differ from serious illnesses only in their better prognosis. When twenty years later Lou Salomé wrote a poem of lyrical optimism, which asserted that she would like to live for a thousand years even if they contained nothing but pain,[19] he drily commented, "One cold in the head would prevent me from having that wish."

In August 1882 he had a very severe angina of the throat that for several days prevented his swallowing or speaking. On recovering from it he was seized with a "gigantic hunger like an animal waking from a winter sleep." In the next sentence he describes how it was accompanied by an intense longing for his beloved: "a frightful yearning—frightful is hardly the right word, better would be uncanny, monstrous, ghastly, gigantic; in short, an indescribable longing for you."

All his life Freud was subject to incapacitating spells of migraine, quite refractory to any treatment. It is still not known whether this complaint is of organic or functional origin. The following remark of his would suggest the former: "It was as if all the pain was external; I was not identified with the disease, and stood above it." That was written when he was too weak to stand but yet felt perfectly clear mentally. It reminded me of a similar remark many years later when I condoled with him over a heavy cold: "It is purely external; the inner man is intact."

These troublesome complaints, however, caused him far less suffering than those of psychological origin, which plagued him for the twenty years of his early manhood. We do not know when what he then called his "neurasthenia" began, nor whether it existed before the date of the letters. It must undoubtedly have been exacerbated by the conflicting emotions that surrounded his love passion, although, curiously enough, it seems to have reached its acme some years after his marriage. The symptoms that chiefly troubled him were intestinal ones (severe indigestion, often with constipation), the functional nature of which he did not then recognize, and moodiness in a pronounced degree. The latter symptom naturally came to expression in his love relationship, as was hinted when describing it. In the neurotic moods he would lose all capacity for enjoyment and have an extraordinary feeling of tiredness. Nor did they improve his temper; in one letter he wrote: "Yesterday I was very grumpy; you should have been here so as to wish you weren't." Milder forms would show themselves in extreme sensitiveness and a tendency to complain; as he wrote once, "I have a great talent for complaining." He even said once that he had spent only three or four happy days in the past fourteen months.[20]

As was customary in those days, Freud attributed his "neurasthenia" to the cares, anxieties, and excitements of the life he was living, and indeed when one reads an account of these in detail it becomes plain enough that he was subject to an inordinate amount of strain. But he notes in the same moment that all his troubles vanish "as with a stroke of magic" as soon as he is in the company of his betrothed. At such a time he felt that he had all that mattered and that his troubles would cease were he only to choose a modest and contented life. So everything would be all right as soon as they got married, a prediction which was not fulfilled. "Although I am endowed with a strong constitution I have not been in a good state for the last two years; life has been so hard that it really needed the joy and happiness of your company to keep me healthy. I am like a watch that has not been repaired for a long time and has got dusty in all its parts. Since my person has become more important even to myself through winning you I give more thought to my health and don't want to wear myself out. I prefer to do without my ambition, make less noise in the world, and have less success rather than injure my nervous system. For the rest of my time in the hospital I will live like the Goys,[j] modestly, learning the ordinary things without striving after discoveries or reaching to the depths. What we shall need for our independence can be attained by honest steady work without gigantic striving." [21]

It is not surprising that the long privation could at times lead to envy. One evening young people were dancing at Breuer's. "You can imagine how furious so much youth, beauty, happiness, and merriment made me, after my painful headache and our long hard separation. I am ashamed to say that on such occasions I am very envious; I have resolved not to join in any company where there are more than two—at all events for the next few years. I am really disagreeable and unable to enjoy anything. The occasion itself was very pleasant: there were mostly girls of from fifteen to eighteen, and some very pretty ones. I fitted in no better than the cholera would have." [22]

But two days after that the reflection that his docentship was now assured gave him confidence enough to go on waiting. "Since I have become a Docent I have noticed that I possess the Horatian 'triple armor on my breast.' Hopes and failures have no more any effect on me. I am quite calm, and very curious about how the dear Lord is going to bring us together again."

Some of these difficulties seem to have been due to a certain sense of inferiority, perhaps with his curious attitude towards medicine.[k] He started with the idea that he was "completely unfit for my difficult profession," [23] though of course this attitude soon changed to some extent. But then came a similar feeling of "not being equal to all the friction of my life."

His moods were certainly labile and when things were going well they could be markedly euphoric. Then he experienced "the precious enjoyment of feeling well." "The work is going splendidly and is most promising. Martha, I am altogether so passionate, everything in me is at present so intense, my thoughts so sharp and clear, that it is wonderful how I manage to keep calm when I am in company." "Since I am enjoying good health life seems to me so sunny." "Life can be so delightful." But the moods could rapidly change. On March 12, 1885, we read, "I never felt so fresh in my life," and on the twenty-first, "I can't stand it much longer."

The bad moods cannot be called true depressions in a psychiatric

[j] Somewhat contemptuous term for "Gentiles."
[k] See Chap. V.

sense. What is remarkable throughout is that there is never any sign of pessimism or hopelessness. On the contrary, over and over again we come across the note of absolute confidence in ultimate success and happiness. "We shall get through all right," [1] is the kind of remark that recurs. "I can see I need not be anxious about the final success of my efforts; it is purely a matter of how long it will take." [24] Freud was altogether more of an optimist than is popularly supposed. When he failed to get the position he sought with Hein,[m] he was highly praised by some of the professors. "So I get that out of it: a good name which will be useful if I apply for anything else. I am a virtuoso in finding the good side of things." At a time when his friend Schönberg was dangerously ill he wrote: "I hope Schönberg will get over it and that we shall all surmount whatever dangers we may experience: neither today nor on any future occasion must we ever give up hope." Then, again, a year later when it looked as if war between Austria and Russia would once more delay their prospect of marriage: "Let us look towards the future to see what will come of it all. Nothing; it is only a caprice of fate to rob us of the years of our youth. Nothing can really touch us; we shall come together at the end and will love each other the more since we have so thoroughly savored privation. No obstruction, no bad luck, can prevent my final success, merely delay it, so long as we stay well and I know that you are cheerful and love me. That is my consolation with which I boldly gaze at the troubled future. Fortunately I was made for such difficult situations; I already overcame a good deal when I had no other motive than a little ambition, so should I be concerned now when your love sustains me?"

We may now turn to more external interests. Freud was a great reader despite his preoccupations, and he did all he could to share the interest with Martha. At first he hoped to arouse her interest in the direction of his work, and he went so far as to write a general introduction to philosophy, which he called a "Philosophical A.B.C.," for her benefit. Then followed Huxley's Introduction to Science, which probably had no greater success. He could not have been surprised to discover that her mind was differently constituted. Nor could he persuade her to master English, although he often pressed her to it at a time when English literature was his chief relaxation; he called it his "favorite wish." On the other hand, Martha

[1]Wir werden es schon zwingen.
[m] See p. 73.

enjoyed discussing good novels with him, and she was of course well acquainted with the usual German classics. They often quoted poetry to each other, mainly from Goethe, Heine, and Uhland, and Martha would at times compose a letter in verse; so did Freud himself on one occasion.[25] Freud often went farther afield in his quotations. Thus, a few weeks after their parting in 1883, one which looked like an indefinite one, he quoted a verse from Burns which he had found in Byron.

> Had we never loved so kindly
> Had we never loved so blindly
> Never met or never parted
> We had ne'er been broken-hearted.

A month later, when the outlook was still dark, he took courage from these lines:

> Let us consult
> What reinforcement we may gain from hope,
> If not, what resolution from despair.[a]

In the same month, in a moment of irritation at some obstacle in his researches, he calmed himself with the motto from Scott's *Bride of Lammermoor*:

> Look thou not on beauty's charming,
> Keep thee still when Kings are arming,
> Speak not where the people listen,
> From the red gold keep thy finger;
> Easy live and happy die,
> Such shall be thy destiny.

To which he adds "Or, as a more recent poet,[o] one evidently lack-ing in practice, has freely and clumsily translated,

> "*Lass Dich nicht nach Schönheit lüsten,*
> *Halt Dich fern, wenn Könige rüsten,*
> *Sprich nicht wo die Volksgunst winket,*
> *Greif Du nicht wo Gold dir blinket;*
> *Stille leb und stirb in Frieden;*
> *Dies werd Dir als Loos beschieden.*"

[a] Milton, *Paradise Lost*, I, 191.
[o] Doubtless himself.

Freud's favorite present was the sending of books, both to Martha and to her sister. Among them may be mentioned Calderon's Works; *David Copperfield*, Freud's favorite Dickens; Homer's *Odyssey*, a book which meant a great deal to both of them; Freytag's *Dr. Luther*; Schiller's *Kabale und Liebe* (Cabal and Love), Ranke's *Geschichte der Päpste* (History of the Popes); and Brandes' *Moderne Geister* (Modern Minds). Of the last named he considered the essay on Flaubert the best, and the one on Mill to be poor. Fielding's *Tom Jones*, although he enjoyed it immensely, he did not think suitable for her chaste mind.

Freud often commented on various books. He called *Hard Times* a cruel book that left him as if he had been rubbed all over by a hard brush. Curiously enough, he did not think so highly of *Bleak House*; it was deliberately hard, like most of Dickens' late work, and there was too much mannerism in it. "You must have noticed that all our writers and artists have a "mannerism," a stereotyped series of motives and arrangements which indicate the limits of their art: that is why it is so easy to parody them, as, for instance, Bret Harte has done so brilliantly with the English authors. To these mannerisms belong, in the case of Dickens, those flawless girls, selfless and good, so good that they are quite colorless; then the fact that all the good people immediately become friends as soon as they meet and work together throughout the whole book; then the sharp distinction between virtue and vice which doesn't exist in life (where should I be, for example?); finally, his easy toleration of feeble mindedness, represented in almost every novel by one or two blockheads or crazy people, who belong to the side of the 'good ones,' and so on. Oh, I had almost forgotten the philanthropist, who has such a frightful lot of money and is available for any noble purpose. *Copperfield* has the least of all this. The characters are individualized; they are sinful without being abominable." [26]

Freud also mentions reading Tasso's *Gerusalemme Liberata*, Gottfried Keller's works, Disraeli's novels, Thackeray's *Vanity Fair*, and George Eliot's *Middlemarch*; this appealed to him very much, and he found it illuminated important aspects of his relations with Martha. Her *Daniel Deronda* amazed him by its knowledge of Jewish intimate ways that "we speak of only among ourselves." [27] Among lighter writings he enjoyed Nestroy, Fritz Reuter, and Mark Twain's *Tom Sawyer*.

The two books that made the deepest impression on him, at least in these years, were *Don Quixote* and *Les Tentations de Saint An-*

toine. He had read the former first in boyhood. Now his friend Herzig gave him a luxurious copy, one he had longed to own, which contained the Doré illustrations. He had always been extraordinarily fond of the stories, and on re-reading them found them the most entertaining and enjoyable of anything he knew. He sent a copy to Martha, and wrote, among other remarks about the book, "Don't you find it very touching to read how a great person, himself an idealist, makes fun of his ideals? Before we were so fortunate as to apprehend the deep truths in our love we were all noble knights passing through the world caught in a dream, misinterpreting the simplest things, magnifying commonplaces into something noble and rare, and thereby cutting a sad figure. Therefore we men always read with respect about what we once were and in part still remain."

The *Tentations* evoked more serious reflections. He read it on the journey to Gmunden in Breuer's company and finished it on the following day. "I was already deeply moved by the splendid panorama, and now on top of it all came this book which in the most condensed fashion and with unsurpassable vividness throws at one's head the whole trashy world: for it calls up not only the great problems of knowledge,ᴾ but the real riddles of life, all the conflicts of feelings and impulses; and it confirms the awareness of our perplexity in the mysteriousness that reigns everywhere. These questions, it is true, are always there, and one should always be thinking of them. What one does, however, is to confine oneself to a narrow aim every hour and every day and gets used to the idea that to concern oneself with these enigmas is the task of a special hour, in the belief that they exist only in those special hours. Then they suddenly assail one in the morning and rob one of one's composure and one's spirits." Then comes a long and lively description of the contents of the book, which he likens to a *Walpurgisnacht* (Witches' Sabbath), and at the end the remark: "What impresses one above everything is the vividness of the hallucinations, the way in which the sense impressions surge up, transform themselves, and suddenly disappear." Then rather an anticlimax: "One understands it better when one knows that Flaubert was an epileptic and given to hallucinations himself." [28]

A discussion about John Stuart Mill gave rise to a revealing account of his views on women. Referring to the translation he had made in 1880 of Mill's last work, he wrote: "I railed at the time at his lifeless style and at not being able to find a sentence or phrase

ᴾ *Erkenntnis*.

that one could commit to memory.[q] But since then I have read a philosophical work of his which was witty, lively, and felicitously epigrammatic. He was perhaps the man of the century who best managed to free himself from the domination of customary prejudices. On the other hand—and that always goes together with it—he lacked in many matters the sense of the absurd; for example, in that of female emancipation and in the woman's question altogether. I recollect that in the essay I translated a prominent argument was that a married woman could earn as much as her husband. We surely agree that the management of a house, the care and bringing up of children, demands the whole of a human being and almost excludes any earning, even if a simplified household relieve her of dusting, cleaning, cooking, etc. He had simply forgotten all that, like everything else concerning the relationship between the sexes. That is altogether a point with Mill where one simply cannot find him human. His autobiography is so prudish or so ethereal that one could never gather from it that human beings consist of men and women and that this distinction is the most significant one that exists. In his whole presentation it never emerges that women are different beings—we will not say lesser, rather the opposite—from men. He finds the suppression of women an analogy to that of negroes. Any girl, even without a suffrage or legal competence, whose hand a man kisses and for whose love he is prepared to dare all, could have set him right. It is really a stillborn thought to send women into the struggle for existence exactly as men. If, for instance, I imagined my gentle sweet girl as a competitor it would only end in my telling her, as I did seventeen months ago, that I am fond of her and that I implore her to withdraw from the strife into the calm uncompetitive activity of my home. It is possible that changes in upbringing may suppress all a woman's tender attributes, needful of protection and yet so victorious, and that she can then earn a livelihood like men. It is also possible that in such an event one would not be justified in mourning the passing away of the most delightful thing the world can offer us—our ideal of womanhood. I believe that all reforming action in law and education would break down in front of the fact that, long before the age at which a man can earn a position in society, Nature has determined woman's destiny through beauty, charm, and sweetness. Law and custom have much to give women that has been withheld from them, but the position of women will

[q] In exculpation of Mill one should mention that his wife is supposed to have been the main author of the book in question.

surely be what it is: in youth an adored darling and in mature years a loved wife." [29]

Much could be overlooked in a woman if she possessed the cardinal virtues. There was an occasion when he met one who talked in a very affected and rather unintelligent fashion. His friend Schönberg was very disdainful of her, but Freud defended her on the ground that she was a good wife and mother. "If a woman feels orthographically, so to speak, it doesn't matter so much whether she writes and speaks orthographically or not."

Freud could not have been a Viennese without frequenting the theater a good deal; in Vienna it often came before food. In the twenties, when he was preoccupied with poverty, work, and cares, such visits became rare. In the letters only half a dozen occasions are mentioned. When he met his half-brothers in Leipzig they accompanied him on his way home as far as Dresden, where they spent a night. In the Residenz Theater they saw Grillparzer's *Esther* and Molière's *Le Malade Imaginaire*; Freud criticized the production unfavorably. In the Paris time there were several visits in spite of the financial stringency. *Oedipus Rex*, with Mounet-Sully in the title role, made a deep impression on him. Then there was Molière's *Tartuffe*, with the brothers Coquelin playing—a wonderful performance. The one-franc seat in the top gallery, however, meant a severe migrainous attack. The next play was Hugo's *Hernani*. All seats were gone except at six francs. Freud walked away, but returned in an extravagant mood, and declared afterwards he had never spent six francs so well, such was the excellence of the performance. With his friend Darkschewitsch he went to see *Figaro*, where he badly missed the melodies of the opera; the latter he had seen in Vienna in Martha's company.

These were all the Comédie Française. But the greatest thrill was seeing Sarah Bernhardt at the Porte St. Martin. He went again with his Russian friend and this time paid four francs. The seat did not give him much room: "one would have more room in a grave and be more comfortable because of being stretched out." Nor was his comfort increased by having to follow the custom of holding his silk hat on his knees throughout the performance. "The piece itself, *Theodora* by Victorien Sardou (who has already written a *Dora* and *Feodora* and is said to be occupied at present with a *Thermidora*, *Ecuadora*, and *Torreadora*) I can't say anything good of." "But how that Sarah plays! After the first words of her vibrant lovely voice I felt I had known her for years. Nothing she could have said would have surprised me; I believed at once everything she said. . . . I have never seen a more comical figure than Sarah in the second act, where she appears in a simple dress, and yet one soon stops laughing, for every inch of that little figure lives and bewitches. Then her flattering and imploring and embracing: it is incredible what postures she can assume and how every limb and every joint acts with her. A curious being: I can imagine that she needn't be any different in life from on the stage."

In Berlin, after Paris, he went only once to the theater, to see Kleist's *Prinz von Homburg* at the Deutsches Theater.

Only three operas are mentioned in these years. Breuer took him once to see *Carmen*. A little later he was shocked to find that his friend Schönberg did not know that *Don Giovanni* was composed by Mozart, so he insisted on taking him to see it; he referred to the irresistible "Lucca" who played Zerlina. Martha and he had seen the opera in their days together in Vienna. Then there was nothing for two years, when he decided to complete his Mozart education by seeing the *Magic Flute*. This proved rather disappointing. "Some of the arias are wonderfully beautiful, but the whole thing rather drags, without any really individual melodies. The action is very stupid, the libretto quite crazy, and it is simply not to be compared with *Don Giovanni*."

His prospects of ever being able to earn a living in Vienna being so uncertain, Freud several times thought of settling elsewhere. The question of how soon he could marry was the most prominent one in his mind, but we know that anyhow he always had a profoundly ambivalent attitude towards Vienna.[r] Consciously he loathed it—there was no beloved "Steffel" for him, only "that abominable steeple of St. Stefan"—and he over and over again expressed that sentiment. But unconsciously something held him in Vienna, and it was the unconscious that won.

The first we hear of such ideas is a couple of months after his engagement. "I am aching for independence, so as to follow my own wishes. The thought of England surges up before me, with its sober industriousness, its generous devotion to the public weal, the stubbornness and sensitive feeling for justice of its inhabitants, the running fire of general interest that can strike sparks in the newspapers; all the ineffaceable impressions of my journey of seven years ago,

r See p. 293.

one that had a decisive influence on my whole life, have been awakened in their full vividness. I am taking up again the history of the island, the works of the men who were my real teachers—all of them English or Scotch; and I am recalling what is for me the most interesting historical period, the reign of the Puritans and Oliver Cromwell with its lofty monument of that time—*Paradise Lost*, where only recently, when I did not feel sure of your love, I found consolation and comfort. Must we stay here, Martha? If we possibly can, let us seek a home where human worth is more respected. A grave in the Centralfriedhof is the most distressing idea I can imagine." [30] And in the end his bones did not repose, after all, in that dreaded Viennese cemetery, but in his beloved England.

When he had his first interview with the great Nothnagel two months later, he informed him of his probable intention of settling in England, so it was certainly not a fleeting idea. And about that time he wrote to Martha: "I hope to become in eighteen months or two years a doctor in whom people can have confidence and will first try my luck in my native town. If I don't get on here quickly enough, which is likely, since a young doctor needs capital and I have none, I will emigrate to England, or perhaps America or Australia."

In the same month as he wrote the lyrical letter about England he asserted that, not being very ambitious, he could quite well live in obscurity and indeed had no pretension to anything else. That was certainly not his true self.

A year later the *Wanderlust* returned. On the one hand he might be able to make a living in Vienna if he became a Docent, but on the other hand this title was thought so highly of abroad that his chances might be better if he emigrated. He was perhaps under an illusion about foreign familiarity with the value of Viennese titles. This time it was America, where many German scientists were finding a home. In November 1883 he became enthusiastic about a project which he laid before Martha for her earnest consideration; he said he was really serious about it. He would finish at the hospital at Easter 1885, borrow enough money from friends to support them for a year, marry Martha in Hamburg, and sail on the spot. She, however, was cool about it all. She was perfectly willing to accompany him on the adventure, but she feared that if it failed he would feel badly at having to let his friends down. Emanuel, whose opinion he asked in the same month, wanted him to come to Manchester. The project was dropped for the time being, but it stayed in his mind. A few months later Martha herself returned to the topic by writing: "I have heard that the Americans have no superfluity of brain anatomists. Shouldn't you rather go there? Let us wait till they offer you a Chair." His only reply was: "So they lived happily ever after, fortunate and highly respected in the United States." Minna made the bright suggestion that he should stay in Austria until his fame reached America, when so many American patients would flock to him that he would be saved the trouble of emigrating. A prediction that came true, even if it took another thirty years to do so.

Intermingled with the doubts about his future prospects came outbursts of optimism. Thus on February 2, 1886, he wrote from Paris: "I feel it in my bones that I have the talent to bring me into the 'upper ten thousand.'"

A month later he was showing Breuer some of his anatomical preparations and remarked, "It is delightful to see how keen on learning he is and how thankful for such opportunities." He took the occasion to lay a new plan before Breuer, who concurred in it. He would apply for the docentship as soon as his anatomical work was finished, and then see if he got any patients and pupils for his courses. If not, which would mean that the auspices were unfavorable, he would take a three months' course in midwifery and children's diseases and settle somewhere in the country in a German-speaking part of Austria (Lower Austria, Moravia, or Silesia). He assured Martha he was quite serious about it. "With you, my pile of books, and my microscope, I should hope to find consolation enough for having missed a town career. One does not suffer from poverty in the country, since there is a shortage of doctors everywhere. And we should not be forever forgotten, since I should go on with my work." But only three days later he wrote: "I feel full of fight and am not thinking of giving up my future in Vienna." Nevertheless, in the next month he consulted Nothnagel about his prospects, where he got a very pessimistic response. Nothnagel advised him, if he wanted to marry, to settle in a provincial town; if not, Nothnagel could give him recommendations in Madrid or Buenos Aires! Since a future in Vienna would depend in large part on Nothnagel's help, this was not very encouraging. Still Freud felt he was friendly to him.

The emigration theme kept cropping up from time to time in the correspondence. Even four months before his marriage he was still uncertain whether it would be possible to make a living in Vienna. On his thirtieth birthday he wrote: "If only you would wake me with a morning kiss I should be quite indifferent to where we were, in America, Australia, or anywhere else."

Through most of his life Freud suffered in varying degrees from *Reisefieber* (anxiety at departing on a journey), which was at its most acute in the nineties. At times he called it a phobia, which it assuredly was not since it never for a moment deterred him. Perhaps it was a counterpart of his very great fondness for traveling. There was more than one source of this: the pleasure in escaping from Vienna, his delight in new scenes and customs, and his search for beauty, whether natural or man-made. He spoke of his "childish delight in being somewhere else," and hoped he would never lose it.[31]

After his first journey as an infant from Leipzig to Vienna he seldom went far away until his visit to England when he was nineteen. Then came the visits to Trieste as a student.[s] His next long journey was to Wandsbek in July 1882. He went there six times in all, the last one being the occasion of his marriage. In June 1883 there was the trip when he escorted Schönberg from Styria to Hungary,[t] and the month afterwards his visit to Gmunden[u] to get his first glimpse of real Alpine scenery. In December was the meeting with his half-brothers in Leipzig and Dresden. There were two trips to the Semmering district, one he would have known from still earlier days. In 1884 he went nowhere except for the post-cocaine visit to Wandsbek, which he also visited twice in 1885. Then came Wandsbek, Cologne, Brussels, and Paris, followed by Berlin, another visit to Wandsbek from there, and in September 1886 the honeymoon tour. In the first years of marriage his holidays were on the Semmering, although his wife went farther afield to stay with her mother in Reichenhall. In 1889 was the well-known visit to Bernheim at Nancy, the second of his three visits to France. After watching Bernheim and Liébault working there, they went on to Paris to attend the International Congress of Hypnotism. He spent ten days in Paris, tiring himself out with sightseeing, and was very bored with the Congress itself. He left Paris for Vienna on the evening of August 9, and then rejoined his family at Reichenau.

Few poor young men of those days could have seen so much of the world, and Freud made the most of his opportunities. He had unusually keen powers of observation and saw all he could in the limited

[s] See pp. 37, 38.
[t] See p. 165.
[u] See p. 168.

time. In his letters there are lively descriptions of various places, notably Gmunden, Teschen, Cologne, Brussels, and of course Paris. There is not the space to detail them here, and I propose to publish them separately.[v] But the one on Brussels may be selected as an example.

"Brussels was wonderfully beautiful, an enormous town with splendid buildings. To judge from their names the people are mostly Flemish and the majority understand a little German. In three and a half hours, without a guide, I discovered the main sights of the town. First of all the rich Exchange and Town Hall; with the latter the Viennese one is not to be compared. One remarks that the town has a history which Vienna lacks. Many statues which really belonged to olden times; inscriptions and images around the houses. I walked through the whole town, passing from the Boulevard du Nord to the Boul. du Sud, and deviating wherever there might be something beautiful. The major discoveries I made only when I came upon a steep hill where there was a building so massive and with such magnificent columns as one images an Assyrian Royal Palace to have had, or as one finds in the Doré illustrations. I really took it for the Royal Palace, especially since a crownlike cupola rose above it. But there was no guard, no life there, and the building was evidently not finished; over the Portal there was a Lion bearing the Ten Commandments. It was the Palace of Justice, and from the edge of the hill one had the grandest view of the town lying below. . . . Going farther up the hill I soon came to the Rue Royale, and then one find followed another; the monument to Egmont and Horn was the finest. Opposite an old church there is an oval *Place* surrounded by a railing of iron work that had the loveliest flowers of iron separated by columns with representations of all the social classes. In the enclosure was a garden, a small pond, and at the broad end stand the two heroes, one of them with his arm embracing the other and pointing to a particular spot; I think that is where they were beheaded. A little farther on I came across a man in a crusader's costume high up on a steed and bearing a flag; when I looked closer it turned out to be Gottfried von Bouillon, the first King of Jerusalem after the First Crusade. I was very pleased to be in such good company, but in the meantime had got very hungry. So I took *déjeuner* in the nearest café, which cost me two francs; it had to last till I got to Paris. After it I discovered the Congress columns and a number of palaces, each of which I took in turn to be the royal one. An advertisement of a farm

[v] International Psycho-Analytical Congress, London, 1953.

to let in Waterloo made a peculiar impression." [32] After this three and a half hours' peregrination he dashed back to the station to catch his overnight train for Paris.

Of life in Paris Freud had so much to say that the task of selection is specially hard. The very word had a magic. Years afterwards Freud wrote: "Paris had been for many years the goal of my longings, and the bliss with which I first set foot on its pavements I took as a guarantee that I should attain the fulfillment of other wishes also." [33]

For the first six weeks he lived at the Hôtel de la Paix, 5 Impasse Royer-Collard, a blind alley from the Rue Gay-Lussac; this was in the Latin Quarter, two minutes from the Panthéon. He gave up his room there when he went to Wandsbek on December 20, and on his return nine days later he took one at the Hôtel de Brésil, Rue de Goff. He paid 55 francs ($11) a month for the former, and 155($30) for the latter, which, however, included board. Noticing that the curtains around his bed were green, he applied chemical tests to make sure they did not contain arsenic. In the earlier period he had two meals a day at 2 francs each. All told it cost him 300 francs a month to live, including books and what he sent to his mother.

He was at first bewildered by the crowds and complex life in Paris, a town that has "two dozen streets like the Ringstrasse, but twice as long." When it rained the streets were so dirty that the Roman name for it seemed well suited—Lutetia, the muddy town. On the first day he felt so lonely in the throng that were it not that he had a long beard, a silk hat, and gloves he could have broken down and cried in the street. The talk of loneliness and longing runs through his Paris letters. "I am here as if marooned on an island in the ocean and long for the hours when the ship is due that re-establishes my communication with the world. For you are my whole world, and the ship sometimes fails to appear." After a time, however, he got better acclimatized, found the town "magnificent and charming," spoke of its "magic," and even began to develop a "local patriotism for Paris." He sent Martha a long account of its geography and sights, illustrated by an excellent sketch. In the Louvre he first visited the Egyptian and Assyrian antiques; he does not mention ever having got to the pictures. But Freud was the sort of man who very soon discovered the Musée Cluny. He was amazed at Père Lachaise, but undoubtedly the building that most impressed him in Paris was Nôtre Dame. It was the first time in his life that he had the feeling of being inside a church. He mentioned climbing the tower on two occasions, Decem-

ber 5 and 11, and in a statement years later said it became his favorite resort.³⁴ He entered into the spirit of Victor Hugo's *Nôtre
Dame*, which previously he had not thought highly of, and even said
he preferred it to neuropathology. His choice of a souvenir of Paris
was a photograph of Nôtre Dame. He spent New Year's Eve in
Paris, but was not edified by the noisy jollifications.

His impression of the French people was less favorable. "Arro-
gant" and "inaccessible" are words that recur in the letters. We may
ascribe much of this judgment to undue sensitiveness on Freud's
part. His spoken French was particularly halting, in spite of the
four lessons he had taken before leaving Vienna—all he could afford
—and he spoke English or Spanish in Paris whenever he could. So it
was natural that the group of hospital doctors, after the first polite-
nesses, would find it easier to talk among themselves, leaving him
rather out of it. Moreover, a German accent was not the best passport to French susceptibilities at that time. General Boulanger had
just been made Minister of War and was about to begin his chau-
vinistic campaign known as Boulangerism. Gilles de la Tourette,
the famous neurologist, dilated to Freud on the fearful revenge
they were going to take on Germany, Freud having announced that
he was a Jew and neither an Austrian nor a German.

The people at large also aroused his suspicion and apprehension.
The tradespeople "cheat one with a cool smiling shamelessness."
"Everyone is polite but hostile. I don't believe there are many decent people here. Anyhow I am one of the few, and that makes me
feel isolated." "The town and the people are uncanny; they seem
to be of another species from us. I believe they are all possessed of a
thousand demons. Instead of 'Monsieur' and 'Voilá l'Echo de Paris,'
I hear them screaming 'A la lanterne' ʷ or 'A bas dieser und jener.' ˣ
They are the people of psychical epidemics, of historical mass convulsions." Even the womenfolk did not redeem them. "The ugliness
of Paris women can hardly be exaggerated: not a decent pretty face."

Freud was greatly concerned with his finances throughout his stay
in Paris, which proved to be more expensive than he expected. He
was driven to buying a finer pen so as to write more on a page and so
save paper and postage.³⁵ And he had to be careful with matches
when he found they cost in Paris a whole penny a box. For the first
couple of months he would have been glad to leave Paris, but then
after making Charcot's closer acquaintance he wished to stay as long

ʷ [Hang them] on the lamp-post.
ˣ Down with this one and that one.

as possible. He certainly would have stayed longer than he did had it been financially possible. His one extravagance in Paris was giving 80 francs ($15) for a complete set of Charcot's Archives, an opportunity he could not resist. He could become a Master himself if he stayed there for three or four years, "but I want what you want, and yourself as well." He felt he could not draw further on the Paneth fund, and wrote to Fleischl for a loan. Fleischl did not reply, probably because of the severe mental condition he was in, so Freud wrote to Breuer. Breuer was eager for him to return to Vienna as soon as possible, partly so as to secure the opening in the Kassowitz Institute, and he sent him only 300 francs. So Freud was after all driven to draw further on Paneth.

But Charcot made up for everything else. Freud uses words of praise very similar to those in the vivid obituary notice he wrote of Charcot seven years later. He could be "tremendously stimulating, almost exciting." "I believe I am changing a great deal. Charcot, who is both one of the greatest of physicians and a man whose common sense is the order of genius,ʸ simply demolishes my views and aims. Many a time after a lecture I go out as from Nôtre Dame, with new impressions to work over. But he engrosses me: when I go away from him I have no more wish to work at my own simple things. My brain is sated as after an evening at the theater. Whether the seed will ever bring forth fruit I do not know; but what I certainly know is that no other human being has ever affected me in such a way." [36] This important passage would alone justify the conclusion that to Charcot must be ascribed the most important influence in turning Freud from a neurologist into a psychopathologist.

There can be no doubt about the impression Charcot made on him. When he came back after being ill he shook hands with Freud and made a friendly remark. Freud's comment was: "Despite my feeling for independence I was very proud of this mark of attention, since he is not only a man to whom I have to be subordinate, but a man to whom I am gladly so."

His description of Charcot's appearance runs thus: "M. Charcot came in at ten o'clock, a tall man of fifty-eight, a silk hat on his head, with dark and curiously mild eyes (one of them is expressionless and has an inward cast), with long hair held back by his ears, clean shaven, with very expressive features and full protruding lips: in short, like a worldly priest, of whom one expects much wit and that

ʸ *Ein genial nüchterner Mensch.*

he understands how to live well." That was Freud's impression the first time he met him, on October 20, 1885.

Charcot was ill for a couple of weeks at the turn of the year, so the total length of time Freud attended his clinic was seventeen weeks.

A passage from Charcot's talk is worth quoting. An unhappy patient had begged him to be like God to him and cure his hands. The answer came: "If I were God I should be eternal, I should have neither beginning nor end and that would ultimately bore me. And I, as the Almighty, when everything had been done, what should I do afterward? I should amuse myself by undoing perhaps."

Mme. Charcot, we learn, was stout, short, lively, agreeable, but with a not very distinguished appearance. Her father was said to be worth untold millions. The daughter, Jeanne, was also short and rather stout. She was about twenty, spoke English and German, and was very natural and sociable. But she bore an almost ridiculous resemblance to her father. "Now if I were not engaged and were a real adventurer, there would be a strong temptation to drop into the situation, since nothing is more dangerous than when a girl bears the features of a man one admires. Then I should be laughed at and thrown out, richer by the experience of a lovely adventure. But it is better as it is."

Freud visited Charcot's palatial residence in the Boulevard St. Germain six times, three being social invitations and the others occasions when they discussed the details of the translation he was making of Charcot's lectures. The first was on January 17 when he fetched the early lectures, and we may quote Freud's description of the study as an example of his quick observation. "It is as large as the whole of our future home, a room worthy of the magic palace he dwells in. It has two sections, the larger one devoted to science, the other to comfort. Two slight projections from the walls mark them off. When you enter you look through a triple window to the garden: the plain panes are separated by pieces of stained glass. Along the side walls of the larger compartment stand bookcases on two levels, each with steps to reach the upper one. On the left of the door is an enormous long table covered with periodicals and odd books; in front of the window are smaller tables with portfolios on them. On the right of the door is a smaller stained-glass window, in front of which is Charcot's writing table, quite flat and covered with manuscripts and books; nearby an armchair and a number of other chairs. The other compartment has a fireplace, a table, and closets containing Indian and Chinese antiques. The walls are covered with Gobelins and pictures." He enclosed an elaborate diagram of the room and its contents.

The high light of the relationship was the first soirée, two days later. Evening dress had to be worn, an unwonted experience. Freud gave up in anger the attempt to tie the white tie he had bought and fell back on a ready-made black one he had brought with him from Hamburg. Later he was delighted to hear that Charcot was unequal to the same ordeal and had to call on his wife's assistance. There was considerable fear beforehand of some *blamage*, but things went off well and Freud was satisfied. Among the guests were Brouardel, the medical jurist; Strauss, who had worked on cholera under Pasteur; Lépine of Lyons, a distinguished clinician; Gilles de la Tourette, the neurologist; Tofano, an Italian painter; Brock, a famous astronomer; and a young son of Daudet.

The next social occasion, on February 2, was an At Home. There were forty or fifty people there, of whom Freud knew hardly any. It was a boring evening. But the third occasion more than made up for it. It was the most enjoyable evening Freud spent in Paris. It was a dinner party. The guests were Richet, Charcot's chief assistant, with his wife; Mendelssohn, a Polish Jew who had been an assistant and who still worked at the Salpêtrière; Arène, an art journalist; Tofano; and a sculptor who had just finished making a statue of Claude Bernard. After dinner other guests arrived. There was Ranvier, the famous French histologist, whom Freud had previously described in a letter to Paneth as a "German University Professor badly translated into French." What was his pleasure at this recollection when Ranvier presently told him he would rather be a Professor at a German University in a small town such as Bonn than anything else. The two men had a good deal in common in their work. Then there was Alphonse Daudet himself and his wife. "A magnificent countenance. A small figure, a narrow head with a mass of black curly hair, a long beard, fine features, a resonant voice, and very lively in his movements."

There was to have been another At Home, but Mme. Charcot had at the last moment to "regret" because of her father's dangerous illness. Six days later Charcot appeared in the hospital with a black band around his hat and a contented smile on his face, from which indications Freud inferred that the end had come.

On February 23 Freud took his leave of Charcot, whom he never saw again. Charcot was away from Paris when Freud was there in

July 1889, and Freud was away on holiday when Charcot was in Vienna on his way back from a consultation in Moscow in August 1891. He asked him to sign a photograph he had bought, but Charcot gave him a better one in addition. He also gave him two introductions for Berlin. He was altogether charming, and they parted on the best of terms.

Ranvier was the only other Frenchman to invite Freud to a dinner party. He met few people outside the hospital. He called on Max Nordau with a letter of introduction, but he found him vain and stupid and did not cultivate his acquaintance. Two cousins of Martha's were in Paris and he saw them a few times. But there were two cronies. One was the Russian nobleman Darkschewitsch, whom he had known in Vienna and with whom he collaborated in his research on the medulla; he was shocked to hear that Freud's debts amounted to 4,000 gulden ($1,600).[37] The other was also an acquaintance from Vienna days, Richetti, an Austrian physician who had a well-to-do practice in Venice; in those days he had excited Freud by offering him his house there for his honeymoon,[38] but nothing was said about it when the time came. He turned up in the middle of November, also to attend Charcot's demonstrations. He knew Charcot, and Freud says he had him to thank both for the invitation to Charcot's house and for the permission to translate the lectures.[39] The Richettis were evidently fond of Freud and since they had no children he was able to indulge in what he calls Schnorrer[z] phantasies about inheriting some of their wealth.[40] They were an amusing couple and Freud tells several stories about them. One was of how the three of them went out to dinner, apparently to a restaurant, and then discovered it was a superior brothel. They were in Paris only ten weeks, from November 13 to January 26.

A more interesting Schnorrer phantasy was one Freud related some fifteen years later. It was of stopping a runaway horse, whereupon a great personage stepped out of the carriage with the words, "You are my savior—I owe my life to you! What can I do for you?" He promptly suppressed the thoughts at the time, but years later recovered them by the curious route of finding he was attributing them in error to a supposed story by Alphonse Daudet. It was an annoying recollection, since by then he had got over his earlier need for patronage and would violently repudiate it. "But the provoking part of it all is the fact that there is scarcely anything to which I am so hostile as the thought of being someone's protégé. What we see of

[z] Beggar.

that sort of thing in our country spoils all desire for it, and my character is little suited to the role of a protected child. I have always entertained a strong desire to be a strong man myself."

Another episode in Paris is worth recording. They had asked him from home to call on the wife of their family doctor who was in Paris, in the Rue Bleu in the Faubourg Poissonière, which he did. "The unhappy woman has a ten-year-old son who after two years in the Vienna Conservatorium won the great prize there and was pronounced highly gifted. Now instead of secretly throttling the infant prodigy the wretched father, who is overworked and has a house full of children, sends the boy with his mother to Paris to study at the Conservatoire and get another prize. Just think of the expense, the separation, the breaking up of the household." The name of the youth who escaped that recommended fate was Fritz Kreisler! A couple of years later he was performing at Steinway Hall in New York.

Freud left Paris on February 28. He was to see it twice again, in 1889 and in 1938.

Of Berlin there was much less to be said. Freud was of course more at home in the town, but he was disappointed in the neurologists there. " '*In meinem Frankreich war's doch schöner.*' [aa] I sighed as a Mary Stuart among neuropathologists." They were far behind Charcot and indeed admitted it themselves. "The comparison brings home to me the greatness of the man." Mendel was the only one he thought anything of, but Mendel regretted that Charcot had turned his attention to such a difficult, fruitless, and unreliable theme as hysteria. "Do you understand why one should regret that the most powerful mind should tackle the most difficult problems? I don't." He established a good relationship with Mendel, however, and undertook to abstract the Viennese neurological literature for his *Neurologisches Centralblatt*. He had already arranged to abstract the neurological literature on children for Baginsky's *Archiv für Kinderheilkunde*. Freud took very much to the children he saw in the Clinic and said he looked forward to the work with children in Vienna.

A visit to the Royal Museum in Berlin evoked nostalgic memories of the Louvre. "The most interesting things there are of course (*sic*) the Pergamene sculptures, fragments representing the battle of the gods and the giants—very alive scenes. But the children I see at the Clinic mean more to me than the stones; I find them, both on ac-

[aa] "*Dans ma France il était mieux*" (In my France it was better): a phrase of Mary, Queen of Scots, which Schiller incorporated in his drama.

count of their format and because they are mostly well washed, more attractive than the large editions of patients."

From time to time Freud made comments in the Letters on outside events, and some of these are of considerable interest. In the summer of 1883 the infamous "ritual murder" trial took place in Hungary, which the Jewish world watched with tension. Freud discussed the psychiatric diagnosis of the principal witness. Naturally he was gratified at the successful outcome of the case, but he had no hope it would do much towards diminishing the prevailing anti-Semitism.

In the same summer an Exhibition of Electricity was held in Vienna, to which Fleischl took Freud several times and explained the latest developments. There was actually a telephone from which one could speak from one room to another, on the occasions when it worked. He thought it was "rather a swindle to maintain that the exhibition was particularly instructive, since most people understand as little about the subject as court ladies do about astronomy. But the total impression that there is such a power remains, and the people need to have more respect than comprehension for science—at least as things are nowadays." Freud also described a visit to the astronomical Observatory in Vienna, which fired his imagination; the internal arrangements reminded him of the scenery of Aida.

Freud had more than once something to say on the subject of the people at large (das Volk). One was a train of thought that occurred to him during the performance of Carmen. "The mob give vent to their impulses (sich ausleben), and we deprive ourselves. We do so in order to maintain our integrity. We economize with our health, our capacity for enjoyment, our forces: we save up for something, not knowing ourselves for what. And this habit of constant suppression of natural instincts gives us the character of refinement. We also feel more deeply and therefore dare not demand much of ourselves. Why do we not get drunk? Because the discomfort and shame of the hangover (Katzenjammer) gives us more 'unpleasure' than the pleasure of getting drunk gives us. Why don't we fall in love over again every month? Because with every parting something of our heart is torn away. Why don't we make a friend of everyone? Because the loss of him or any misfortune happening to him would bitterly affect us. Thus our striving is more concerned with avoiding pain than with creating enjoyment. When the effort succeeds, those who deprive themselves are like us, who have bound ourselves for life and death, who endure privation and yearn for each other so as to keep our troth, and who would assuredly not survive a hard blow of fate that would rob us of our dearest: human beings who like Asra[bb] can love only once. Our whole conduct of life presupposes that we shall be sheltered from the direst poverty, that it is always open to us to free ourselves increasingly from the evils of our social structure. The poor, the common people, could not exist without their thick skin and their easygoing ways. Why should they feel their desires intensely when all the afflictions nature and society have in store is directed against those they love: why should they scorn a momentary pleasure when no other awaits them? The poor are too powerless, too exposed, to do as we do. When I see the people doing themselves well, putting all seriousness aside, it makes me think it is their compensation for being so unprotected against all the imposts, epidemics, diseases, and the evil conditions of our social organization. I will not follow these thoughts further, but one might show how *das Volk* judges, believes, hopes, and works quite otherwise than we do. There is a psychology of the common man which is somewhat different from ours. Such people also have more feeling of community than we do: it is only they who are alive to the way in which one life is the continuation of the next, whereas for each of us the world vanishes with his death." [41]

This whole passage is pregnant with ideas that came to fruition half a century later, particularly in *Civilization and Its Discontents*. It should be borne in mind that the Austrian peasants Freud has in mind in this passsage differed a good deal from any corresponding class in other countries and other times.

Passages of worldly wisdom and psychological acumen abound in the letters. There was a friend of Martha's who after three years of hesitation became engaged, but shortly after found her first doubts confirmed and broke off the engagement. Martha made some derogatory remarks to Freud about the suitor, and this was his comment. "The plucky girl holds her head up high and makes a decision that needs some courage. But, dearest, when you see her you will surely not tell her frankly what a poor opinion we have had of her suitor all along. That for several reasons. In the first place we should look foolish after having warmly congratulated her on her choice. Secondly, she certainly won't listen to you, for I can quite well imagine how she feels. What she most has to keep at bay is the sense of shame at having warmly accepted an unworthy man. A reaction follows the decision to break off in which the effects of her effort to get fond of

[bb] Heine: *Der Asra.*

him becomes manifest in its full strength. Then any derogatory expression on the part of a stranger only evokes a friendly memory of the condemned man, who after all has the outstanding merit in women's eyes of having sincerely and passionately loved. Thirdly, darling, remember Mr. X and how those people look now who at a particular moment abused to his face the woman he had given up and who is now his wife. A good many of those broken engagements are repaired later, and I am paying Cecilie a very great compliment in saying I don't think it likely in her case. So, dearest, use restraint, neutrality, and caution, and learn from me how to be completely open towards a single being, and towards others not insincere but simply reserved."

There are only three remarks about public personages, all three concerning their death. The first was where he expressed the opinion that Bismarck like a nightmare (*Alp*) weighed heavy on the whole continent: his death would bring universal relief. This may well have been a perfectly objective political judgment, but it is perhaps pertinent to recall that Freud's father's birthday was the same as Bismarck's (1815) and that Freud once asked his friend Fliess whether his numerical computations could predict which of the two men would die first. Indeed, the figure of Bismarck seemed, perhaps for the reason just hinted, to have exercised a peculiar fascination for Freud. When the great man visited Vienna in June 1892, Freud made several attempts to see him in the flesh, but the nearest he got to it was a glimpse of his back after waiting two and a half hours in the street—behavior one would have thought very atypical of Freud. A still more interesting feature in the story is that Freud's father had been such an ardent admirer of Bismarck, on the grounds of German unification, that when he had to translate the date of his birthday from the Jewish calendar into the Christian one he chose that of Bismarck's.[cc, 42] So there were many links between Jakob Freud and Bismarck.

The second, oddly enough, was King Alphonso XII of Spain. Freud remarked that his death made a deep impression on him, and then added, which was doubtless the reason, that Alphonso was the first king he had outlived. He commented further, "The complete stupidity of the hereditary system is seen through a whole country being upset by the death of a single person."

The third occasion was the tragic death of King Ludwig II of

[cc] Incidentally, the apparent coincidence between the birthdays of Freud's mother and the Emperor Franz Josef had a similar origin.

Bavaria, which also shocked Freud greatly. In this case, it is true, there was also his regret at the loss of the King's doctor, Gudeler, whom Freud knew as a brain anatomist. But he says that Gudelei was right to risk, and lose, his life in his endeavor to save the King from drowning.

An example of Freud's alertness to public events may be men- tioned from a letter in April 1885. The Bulgarians were agitating to annex Eastern Rumelia and Freud expected that in that event Austria would mobilize to support Serbia, with the consequent pos- sibility of a war with Russia. The Austrian Government must have had similar ideas, for they did in effect declare a partial mobilization at the end of June.cc† The *coup d'état* occurred on September 18, Serbia declared war on Bulgaria in November, but was unexpectedly defeated in the three days' battle of Slivnitza, which Bernard Shaw immortalized in his play, *Arms and the Man*. Austria interposed to save Serbia and dictated a peace in the following March.

An apparent result of all this was that in the following summer, a year earlier than he had expected, Freud had to serve for a month during maneuvers held at Olmütz, a small town in Moravia. He was attached as a senior army surgeon to the Landwehr, to which he had been transferred that February; he was not free of military service until the end of 1887. He ranked as an *Oberarzt* (First Lieutenant), but in the course of the proceedings was promoted to *Regimentsarzt* (Captain).

It was a strenuous performance, and it taxed even Freud's stout frame. Rising at half-past three in the morning, they marched and marched until after noon, after which the medical work itself had to be attended to. Like a true woman, Martha advised him not to do any marching when it was very hot. He was to be very careful and presumably not march too quickly.

Although the phrase "browned off" had not yet been invented, the concept itself was highly developed. That the experience did not increase Freud's admiration for the profession of arms is graphically depicted in a letter he wrote to Breuer towards the end of the time.[43]

"Sept. 1, 1886

"Esteemed Friend,

"I can hardly describe what a pleasant surprise it was to hear that you both visited my little girl and were very 'nice' to her, as the

cc† The Austrian War Office, however, in information they courteously sent me, contradict this statement of the history books.

local expression has it. May you be rewarded by the best holiday, the least annoying weather and a constantly happy mood.

"Here I am tied fast in this filthy hole—I can't think how else to describe it—and am working on black and yellow.[dd] I have been giving lectures on field hygiene: the lectures were pretty well attended and have even been translated into Czech. I have not yet been 'confined to barracks.'

"The only remarkable thing about the town is that it doesn't look so far away as it actually is. It often means marching for three or four hours before one gets there, and there are times when I find myself ever so far from it at an hour when one is not usually awake to anything. Just as Paul Lindau once remarked in a review of a novel that took place in the Middle Ages, 'most of my readers would hardly remember that there had been such a time as the middle of the fourth century,' so I might ask if any decent citizen would think of being busy between three and half past in the early morning. We play at war all the time—once we even carried out the siege of a fortress— and I play at being an army doctor, dealing out chits on which ghastly wounds are noted. While my battalion is attacking I lie down on some stony field with my men. There is fake ammunition as well as fake leadership, but yesterday the General rode past and called out 'Reserves, where would you be if they had used live ammunition? Not one of you would have escaped.'

"The only bearable thing in Olmütz is a first-class café with ice, newspapers, and good confectionery. Like everything else the service there is affected by the military system. When two or three generals —I can't help it, but they always remind me of parakeets, for mammals don't usually dress in such colors (save for the back parts of baboons)—sit down together, the whole troop of waiters surround them and nobody else exists for them. Once in despair I had to have recourse to swank. I grabbed one of them by the coat-tails and shouted, 'Look here, I might be a general sometime, so fetch me a glass of water.' That worked.

"An officer is a miserable creature. Each envies his colleagues, bullies his subordinates, and is afraid of his superiors; the higher up he is, the more he fears them. I detest the idea of having inscribed on my collar how much I am worth, as if I were a sample of some goods. And nevertheless the system has its gaps. The Commanding Officer was here recently from Brünn and went into the swimming

[dd] An allusion to the Austrian colors.

baths, when I was astonished to observe that his trunks carried no marks of distinction!

"But it would be ungrateful not to admit that military life with its inescapable 'must' is very good for neurasthenia. It all disappeared in the very first week.[cc]

"The whole business is coming to an end; in ten days I fly north and forget the crazy four weeks.

"Nothing scientific has occupied me here. The curious case of paralysis agitans I recently related to you has suddenly turned up again, and the man swears he has greatly benefited from the arsenical injections I gave him.

"I apologize for this silly tittle-tattle which has somehow slipped out of my pen, and am looking forward to calling on you in Vienna for the first time with my wife.

"Yours very sincerely,
"Dr. Sigm. Freud"

We may conclude this chapter with some descriptions Freud gave of himself, not forgetting, however, that self-observation is not always the best example of objectivity. Independence he vehemently craved for: it is a word that constantly recurs. Freud repeatedly asserted that he was not ambitious, or only very slightly so. This was doubtless true in the sense of social ambition or even professional rank as such, but he must always have cherished a strong desire to accomplish something worth while in life and, moreover, something that would be recognized as such. He conceived this aim essentially in the form of scientific discovery. When beginning his anatomical researches he wrote: "I am not finding it at all easy to wrest attention from the world, for it is thick-skinned and hard of hearing." But such acknowledgment of his work does not seem ever to have been an inordinate demand for fame. "I have not really been ambitious. I sought in science the satisfaction offered during the research and at the moment of discovery, but I was never one of those who cannot bear the thought of being carried off by death without having left their name carved on a rock." [44] "My ambition will be satisfied in learning to understand something about the world in the course of a long life."

The explanation he gave Martha of his occasional outbursts was doubtless correct. "Since I am violent and passionate with all sorts

[cc] A passage of interest as indicating Breuer's knowledge of Freud's nervous troubles.

of devils pent up that cannot emerge, they rumble about inside or else are released against you, you dear one. Had I only some daring activity where I could venture and win, I should be gentle at home, but I am forced to exercise moderation and self-control, and I even enjoy a reputation for doing so." [45] His work, however, even if it tried his patience, compelled self-discipline. "In medicine one employs the greatest part of one's intellect in avoiding what is impracticable, but it is a very tranquil way of learning to be sensible." [46]

Bourgeois mediocrity and routine dullness were to him abominations. "Our life will hardly be as idyllic as you paint it. Even if I become a Docent, lecturing will not come my way, and my Martha, a born German Frau Professor, will have to do without her fine position. Nor should I have been suited to it. I still have something wild within me, which as yet has not found any proper expression, and I feel quite unequal to the wonderful performance of the Professor of whom Heine sings:

> "Mit seinen Nachtmützen und Schlafrockfetzen,
> Stopft er die Lücken des Weltenbaus." [ff]

> (With his nightcaps and rags of gown
> He stops up the gaps of the universe.)

Freud had the type of mind that was bored by ease and stimulated by difficulties. As he put it himself, "A failure [in research work] makes one inventive, creates a free flow of associations, brings idea after idea, whereas once success is there a certain narrow-mindedness or thick-headedness sets in so that one always keeps coming back to what has been already established and can make no new combinations." [48]

The longest description he gave was a couple of years later, when he had tasted some success. "Do you really think I produce a sympathetic impression at first glance? I really doubt it myself. I believe people notice something strange in me, and that comes ultimately from my not having been young in my youth and now, when maturity begins, I cannot grow older. There was a time when I was onl eager to learn and ambitious and grieved every day that Nature ha not, in one of her gracious moods, imprinted on me the stamp of genius as she sometimes does. Since then I have long known that I am no genius, and I no longer understand how I could have wished to be one. I am not even very talented; my whole capacity for work

[ff] Die Heimkehr. Freud quotes the passage twice in his writings.[47]

probably lies in my character attributes and in the lack of any marked intellectual deficiency. But I know that that admixture is very favorable for slowly winning success, that under favorable conditions I could achieve more than Nothnagel, to whom I feel myself to be superior, and that perhaps I might attain Charcot's level. That doesn't mean that I shall, since I shan't find those favorable conditions and I do not possess the genius or the force to compel them. But how I am running on. I wanted to say something quite different, to explain whence comes my inaccessibility and abruptness towards strangers that you speak of. It is only the result of mistrust, since I have so often experienced how common and bad people treat me badly, and it will gradually disappear as I need to fear them less, as I achieve a more independent position. I always console myself with the thought that those subordinate to me or on the same level have never found me disagreeable, only those above me or who are in some other respect my superiors. I may not look like it, but nevertheless as early as my school days I was always in vehement opposition to my teachers, was always an extremist and usually had to pay for it. Then when I acquired a favored position at the head of my class, when I was accorded general trust, they had nothing more to complain of in me.

"Do you know what Breuer said to me one evening? That he had discovered what an infinitely bold and fearless person I concealed behind my mask of shyness. I have always believed that of myself, but never dared to say it to anyone. I have often felt as if I had inherited all the passion of our ancestors when they defended their Temple, as if I could joyfully cast away my life in a great cause. And with all that I was always so powerless and could not express the flowing passions even by a word or a poem. So I have always suppressed myself, and I believe people must notice that in me." [49]

In his writings Freud referred to his boastfulness and megalomania in youth and to his unseemly behavior with Viktor Adler as a student. In his letters there is an account of how he bravely stood up to a crowd of anti-Semitic opponents on his return journey from Leipzig. So we must conclude that traces of his militaristic childhood lingered on into his early manhood, and that his native pugnacity was only gradually subdued.

X

The Neurologist

(1 8 8 3 – 1 8 9 7)

IN THESE YEARS FALLS ALSO THE BEGINNING OF FREUD'S INTEREST IN
psychopathology, a theme reserved for the following chapter.

When he got engaged he had to instruct Martha, who was probably
rather vague about his activities, to distinguish between what he
called his chemical *Pantscherei* ("messing about") and his histological
Guckerei ("peering"). The former investigations he continued for a
while after he had interrupted the latter ones.

In his first hospital year Freud gave no indications of a wish to
specialize, although his previous researches on the nervous system
must have been still in his mind. He was entirely preoccupied with
adapting himself to the life in a hospital and with the constant problem of how he could—at first surreptitiously—snatch a few minutes'
interview with his betrothed. When he thought of the future it was
more of settling in a provincial town or abroad than of a career in
Vienna.

When, however, in May 1883 he was appointed Junior
Sekundararzt in Meynert's department, he was brought nearer to
disorders of the brain, and towards the middle of the month he obtained Meynert's permission to work in his laboratory.[1] At first it
was a matter of making and studying preparations, but at the beginning of July he proposed to Holländer that they should make together an extensive study of the newborn brain, one that would take
at least a year.[2] Holländer, who was an agreeable person, had a good
knowledge of the anatomy of the brain and held the position of Assistant to Meynert; he used to lecture in place of Meynert in the latter's absence. Freud expected that the research would bring him a
docentship and thus lift him out of the ruck. So his hopes were already pointing in the direction of neurology.

Holländer soon tired of the immense task of examining the thousands of slides, and when it came to his merely dropping in for a chat once a week while his partner was toiling till midnight Freud felt he could gracefully dispense with his cooperation.

Freud was at this time making a study of facial paralysis in mental disorders,[3] but nothing of it was ever published.

It was in the middle of September, just before his period of work under Meynert came to an end, that Freud called on Breuer to elicit his opinion on the possibility of becoming a specialist, but before he could raise the question Breuer himself did so.[4] The occasion was the recent death of Dr. Weiss, who was the coming neurologist. Freud expounded the situation. He considered he had a couple of solid attributes, but little talent and no longer much ambition except to get married. If he confined himself to neurology he would be tied to Vienna and might have to keep his future bride waiting an indefinitely long time, whereas if he had an all-round medical training, could help at childbirth, pull out a tooth, and mend a broken leg he would surely be able to make a living, and would be free to go "to the country, to England, to America, or to the moon." After reflection Breuer gave the sage advice to choose a middle way, to continue as he was doing and keep an eye on both possibilities. So the next day Freud asked the Director of the Hospital to enter his name on the list waiting for a vacancy in the department for diseases of the nervous system and liver (!) and in the meantime to transfer him to the ward for syphilitic patients.

In the fourteen months Freud spent in Dr. Franz Scholz's department, which he entered on January 1, 1884, he had considerable opportunity, although not so much as he wished, of studying organic nervous disease. In a letter of April 1, 1884, he wrote: "I am gradually marking myself off as a neuropathologist to my Chief in the hopes of its furthering my prospects." Freud referred later to Scholz as being at that time "a fossil and feeble-minded." [5] But, although there was little to be learned from him, his senile indolence had at least the advantage that he gave the doctors under him a very free hand. Freud thus had the opportunity of doing some more or less unofficial teaching. This is what he says about it in his usual candid manner: "I gradually became familiar with the ground; I was able to localize the site of a lesion in the medulla oblongata so accurately that the pathological anatomist had no further information to add; I was the first person in Vienna to send a case for autopsy with a diagnosis of polyneuritis acuta. The fame of my diagnoses and of their postmortem confirmation brought me an influx of American physicians, to whom I lectured upon the patients in my department in a sort of pidgin-English.* I understood nothing about the neuroses. On one occasion I introduced to my audience a neurotic suffering from a persistent headache as a case of chronic localized meningitis; they quite rightly rose in revolt against me, and my premature activities as a teacher came to an end. By way of excuse I may add that this happened at a time when greater authorities than myself in Vienna were in the habit of diagnosing neurasthenia as cerebral tumor." [6] The first of these courses, a gratis one on anatomy of the brain, he gave to his hospital colleagues in July 1884. In the next year he earned some money in this way, but usually the courses came to an end for lack of clinical material. They finished in March 1885.

Three clinical publications date from the period spent in the Fourth Division of the hospital. The three cases concerned were all studied in the year 1884. Jelliffe, who has reviewed Freud's neurological writings, speaks of them as "models of good neurological deduction." [7]

The first was the case of a sixteen-year-old cobbler's apprentice who was admitted on January 7, 1884, with bleeding gums, petechiae in the lower limbs, but with no symptom of anything other than scurvy. The next morning, however, he fell into a deep coma and died that evening. During the day, when he was frequently and carefully examined, he showed a number of confusing symptoms, including oculomotor paralyses, vomiting, irregularities in the pupil reactions, and hemiparesis. A diagnosis was made of meningeal hemorrhage, indirectly affecting his basal ganglia (an effect that had been pointed out by Wernicke), and the autopsy, conducted by Professor Kunradt, confirmed this in every detail. Freud added a thorough discussion of the literature, particularly of basal hemorrhages.[8]

The second case was that of a young baker whom Freud observed from October 3, 1884, until his death on December 17 of the same year, and diagnosed as one of endocarditis with pneumonia together with acute multiple neuritis (spinal and cerebral)—all confirmed by Kunradt's autopsy. An account of it was published in February 1886,[9] and Sperling, reviewing it in the *Neurologisches Centralblatt* in the same year, wrote: "This is a very valuable contribution to our knowledge of acute polyneuritis."

The third one was one of muscular atrophy with curious sensory changes, and Freud made the diagnosis of syringomyelia, of which

* The first lecture in English was on February 2, 1885.

at the time very few cases were known. The patient, a weaver, thirty-six years old, was under Freud's observation and treatment for six weeks, from November 10, 1884, onwards, and then left the hospital. The case was reported, like the others, in the *Wiener medizinische Wochenschrift*; it was published in March and April of 1885, and also in the *Neurologisches Centralblatt*.

One reads in his correspondence of other clinical studies, but ones that were never published; for example: "The Distinguishing Features between Anesthesia of Spinal and of Cerebral Origin Respectively," [10] one he entitled, "Crossing Over of Reflexes," [11] and a treatment for trigeminal neuralgia[12] and for sciatica[13]—evidently by cocaine injections.

In the eighties and nineties electricity, both galvanic and faradic, were important in neurology, not only for diagnostic purposes, but still more as the mainstay of therapy. Freud early saw the need to acquire a knowledge of the subject, and in a talk with Fleischl about his chance of obtaining a docentship he expressed the opinion that he would have to publish some investigation on the subject. Fleischl at once offered to help him over the matter, which remained a perennial difficulty, of procuring the expensive apparatus. The other difficulty was of getting the necessary co-worker to attend regularly. For more than a year, from March 1884 to July 1885, Freud attempted various investigations in the hope of making a worth-while discovery, with various colleagues, Bettelheim, Heitler, Plowitz, etc. The only subjects he mentions are an endeavor to ascertain what changes fever produced in the electrical conductivity of the neuromuscular system,[14] and a study together with Königstein on the electrical reaction of the optic nerve.[15] He never published anything, however, in this sphere.

But what is of interest is a remark he made while he was treating his first private patient by electrical measures; it was one he took charge of during Breuer's absence. The remark was that in such cases one treats more with one's personality than with the instruments[16]—an interesting forerunner of his later skepticism concerning electrical therapy.

In 1884 Freud had a bad shock over his choice of profession. It was the news that the great Eulenburg of Berlin had applied for a Chair in Vienna. If he obtained it, no one else could hope for much neurological practice. However, the authorities refused Eulenburg on the score of Austrian doctors not being treated equitably in Germany.

A year later there was a still greater alarm. Nothnagel, the Professor of Medicine on whose support in practice he counted, applied for the corresponding position in Berlin. Not only so, but his probable successor was a neurologist from Prague who was a friend of Jaksch, the man in the hospital who most disliked Freud and did what he could to thwart him.[17] Luckily, however, this danger also passed over. Nothnagel was never transferred.

So much for Freud's training and experience in clinical neurology in the eighteen months preceding his visit to Paris. During this period, however, and also prior to it, his heart was still in his histological researches. In the two years he spent in Meynert's laboratory—from the summer of 1883 to that of 1885—he produced some quite first-class original work.

Two distinguished American neurologists afterwards asserted that they worked with Freud in Meynert's laboratory, but their statements are not easy to substantiate. One of them, Bernard Sachs, mentions "Freud who sat in Meynert's laboratory with the present writer in 1882,"[18] the year Sachs worked there. Since Freud started work there only in the summer of the next year, they could only have sat together there in 1882 to smoke a friendly cigarette. The other, Allen Starr, worked in Meynert's laboratory from October 1881 to March 1882,[19] when Freud was still in Brücke's Institute. In a letter to me of April 28, 1912, Freud wrote: "In the New York *Times* of April 5 there appeared a short article entitled 'Attacks on Freud's Theory,' containing a ferocious assault by Allen Starr on your correspondent, explaining his theory by the immoral character of Vienna and the immoral life I had lived there, professing that he had known me well 'some years ago' and had worked side by side with me for one winter. Now what does this mean? It is remarkable that I have never known the Allen Starr who knew me so well."

Eighteen eighty-three was the year when Freud made a further attempt in experimental physiology in Stricker's laboratory, and after that failure—following the one in the Chemical Institute—he restricted his laboratory work to histology of the nervous system. Like all workers in science he was well aware of the importance of technique—he had distinguished himself in his student studies in this way[b]—and he now made many attempts to discover new methods of examining nervous tissue. Two of them were successful. Both of them were elaborations of hints thrown out by Flechsig, Meynert's great

b See p. 51.

rival, a fact that was perhaps the beginning of Meynert's estrangement from Freud.

He set to work in this direction within a couple of weeks of entering the new laboratory; he was sure of his docentship if he succeeded, but that was not very likely.[20] His first attempt was to direct concentrated sunlight through a thick section of tissue so as to trace the path of the fibers.[21] Nothing came of it. In October, however, he hit upon a new idea that he felt must bring him luck because he had just broken the ring Martha had given him; Freud was always apt to believe in hostages to fortune. He had adopted a hint Flechsig had thrown out in 1876, but never followed up, that it might be possible to stain nervous tissue with some solution of gold chloride. After a few weeks of experimenting with the help of his chemist friend Lustgarten he succeeded, and wrote a most jubilant letter as if all the difficulties in his career had now been overcome. His first act was to assemble some friends, swear them to secrecy, and then grant them permission to use the new wonderful method in their particular fields: thus Holländer was allowed to use it with the brain, Lustgarten with the skin, Ehrmann with the adrenal glands, and Horowitz with the bladder. "So I have allotted the various parts of the body in the manner of a Commander-in-Chief." [22] By the end of the month he was ready to apply it to his sections and start elucidating problems of structure.

In February he heard that Weigert had invented a new method for staining nervous tissue, so he hastened to send a "Preliminary Communication" on his own method to the *Centralblatt für die medizinischen Wissenschaften*, reserving the full account for *Pflüger's Archiv für Anatomie und Physiologie*. He also got his friend Fleischl to send a paper to Ferrier in London for publication in *Brain*, where it turned out to be the first paper of Freud's the present writer came across. He wrote this one in English, but got an American to correct it. Freud was aware of the special difficulty with all such methods, which he pointed out as follows: "Innumerable methods have been devised by histologists which proved themselves useful only in the hands of their inventors; that is why I have decided to publish even the pettiest directions."

Freud was himself highly pleased with the success of his method, which gave him "a wonderfully clear and precise picture" of the cells and fibers. It caused some sensation at the time, and demands at once came in for it to be published in Czech, Italian, and Russian.[23] The results of subsequent trials, however, were more variable; in some hands it produced excellent results,[24] in others more uncertain and therefore unreliable ones.[25] Brücke told him his various new methods alone would bring him fame.[26]

Under Brücke Freud had investigated the cells of the spinal cord, the part of the nervous system that still held his chief interest, but in order to become an all-round neuropathologist it was necessary to proceed higher. So he now began with a piece of research on the next proximate part of the central nervous system, the medulla oblongata. Many years later, in commenting on medical attempts to explain morbid anxiety as a disorder of that organ, he wrote, one might say laughingly: "The medulla oblongata is a very serious and beautiful thing. I remember very well how much time and trouble I devoted to the study of it years ago. Today, however, I must say I do not know of anything that seems to me more irrelevant for the psychological understanding of anxiety than a knowledge of the nervous paths its excitations follow." [27]

Freud concentrated on the medulla for two years, and published three papers on it. The structure of this extremely complicated little organ, into which is condensed a great variety of nervous tracts, was at that time very imperfectly known and a highly controversial topic. To trace the fibers passing through it to their connections elsewhere required great dexterity, patience, and precision. What is especially noteworthy about Freud's researches in this obscure field was the method he adopted. Even as early as November 1883 Freud was dreaming of an entirely different technique for studying the finer structure of the central nervous system. He had already developed Flechsig's hint of staining with gold chloride, and in his hand at least it gave a much clearer picture than any other. He now made use of another and much more important discovery of Flechsig's: namely, that the myelinization of the medullary sheaths of nerve fibers does not proceed simultaneously, but first with one group, then with another. This held out a promise of a further aid to differentiation, and Freud took the fullest advantage of it. He considered, and rightly so, that it was greatly superior to the only other method then current, of studying the slides of a large series of consecutive sections, and was very skeptical of the conclusions reached in this way. The embryological discovery of Flechsig's became a guide for the anatomical interconnections. So he replaced the adult structure by a fetal brain where at first only a few myelinated tracts are visible instead of the "inextricable pictures of cross sections, which permit hardly more than a superficial topographical survey." [28] Then, by comparing the fetal sections of different levels one can directly observe the course and connections of the nerve tracts, which one can only guess at in their mature appearance. One finds that the earliest structures persist and are never buried, though they become increasingly complicated in the course of development. For this purpose he investigated first the brains of kittens and puppies and then those of embryos and infants.

In Freud's earlier histological researches under Brücke it had been the phylogenetic aspect of development that had concerned him. Now it was the ontogenetic aspect. This point of view has some parallel in his later psychological researches. There also he concentrated on the ontogenetic aspect of the data he was investigating, but he had first to find a way of reaching the earliest archaic (phylogenetic) functions, which—though deeply buried—still persisted.

Freud published only a part of his actual researches on the medulla; by the time they were finished he was moving on to more clinical interests. His three papers were all published at the end of his time in Meynert's laboratory or a year after he had left it. The first one was dated "Vienna,[c] in the middle of May, 1885," and it appeared in the following month. In it he traced the roots of the acoustic nerve and discussed the connection of the inter-olivary tract with the crossed trapezoid body. The manuscript of the second is dated "Paris, January 23, 1886," and appeared in the following March. It is co-signed by L. Darkschewitsch, a young Russian neurologist who worked for four years in Berlin, Vienna, and Paris and later founded the neurological school of Kazan, for long the largest and most famous in Russia. Freud met him in Paris in the middle of January—he had known him in Vienna two years before, when Darkschewitsch wrote a report in Russian of Freud's gold chloride method[29]—and he wrote that "independently of each other we had both found confirmation of the Flechsig-Meynert hypothesis. When we noticed the complete agreement in our findings, we decided to report them in a joint publication." [30] Actually the paper was entirely written by Freud, though Darkschewitsch supplied the drawings.[31]

The first of these three papers, all of which are concerned with the roots and connections of the acoustic nerve, appeared in the *Neurologisches Centralblatt* in June 1885. The material was the

[c] Freud retained the habit of noting where his writings were composed as well as when.

medulla of fetuses of five to six months when the acoustic fibers are already myelinated. There are three roots, or groups of fibers, all of which end in nuclei on the side on which they enter: the outer fibers in an anterior nucleus, the middle and a portion of the inner fibers in the inner nucleus, and the remainder of the latter twist so as to reach the outer nucleus. Various bundles of fibers then radiate in the medulla from these nuclei, e.g., to the decussation in the nucleus tegmenti of the cerebellum. Some, issuing from the anterior nucleus, make up the corpus trapezoides and pass through the upper olivary nucleus; after crossing the middle line they turn downward into the inter-olivary tract. The latter tract begins at the level of the decussation of the trapezoid body, and, since no continuation of the fibers could be found, Freud concluded that the two tracts are continuous. But, since the inter-olivary tract was known to pass to the posterior columns of the other side, it must connect them with the acoustic nucleus. This demonstration agreed with a recent observation of Vejas that after artificial extirpation of the posterior column of one side an atrophy was traced as high as the trapezoid body in the inter-olivary tract, but no higher.

The second paper appeared in the same periodical in the following March (1886). Its object was to trace downwards the inferior peduncle of the cerebellum. It has three parts, the destination of two of them being known. Incompatible views were held about the third, and these were fully discussed with the aid of diagrams. The authors' results proved that fibers from the peduncle, i.e., from the cerebellum, enter Wernicke's "nucleus of the restiform body" which is simply the upper portion of the cuneate nucleus, the continuation of the nucleus of Burdach, which in its turn is connected with the nuclei of the posterior columns. Some of these fibers cross the middle line in the so-called sensory decussation. For the first time, therefore, the connection between the posterior column of one side and both sides of the cerebellum was established, a conclusion that was subsequently confirmed by Monakow.

The third paper was published in a special otological periodical in August and September 1886, with several illustrations. It gave a detailed account of the origins and connections of the acoustic nerve, but its chief interest lies in Freud's demonstration that the nuclei of the fifth, eighth, ninth, and tenth (sensory) cranial nerves, with their triple roots, are throughout homologous with the posterior root ganglia of the spinal cord. He even discussed the route taken by these nuclei in their movement (with the fifth nerve, successfully) towards the exterior, one achieved by the spinal ganglia, and he illustrated it in detail in the case of the acoustic nerve. The genetic and evolutionary point is again apparent.

Meynert was still very friendly to Freud; the change in his attitude, which will be considered later, came in 1886. He had passed his prime; he died a few years later, in 1892, in the same year as Brücke. He was finding it hard to keep up with the new methods and ideas in brain anatomy, especially since his own interests had moved over to clinical psychiatry, and perhaps he was envious of the young Freud who easily mastered them and was evidently a coming man. Meynert's reaction to the situation was a gesture of submission. He would confine himself to psychiatry and Freud should replace him in anatomy. "One day Meynert, who had given me access to the laboratory, even during the times when I was not actually working under him, proposed that I should definitely devote myself to the anatomy of the brain, and promised to hand over his lecturing work to me, as he felt he was too old to manage the newer methods. This I declined, in alarm at the magnitude of the task; it is possible, too, that I had guessed already that this great man was by no means so kindly disposed towards me." [32] Perhaps Freud was also alarmed at the suggestion that he should resume a futile academic career, recently abandoned, and wait for the improbable succession to a University Chair; once bit, twice shy.

Then came the visit to the great master Charcot. Freud was in Paris from October 13, 1885, till February 28, 1886, with the exception of a week at Christmas spent at Wandsbek: a total of four and a half months. Charcot was then at the zenith of his fame. No one, before or since, has so dominated the world of neurology, and to have been a pupil of his was a permanent passport to distinction. The Salpêtrière could well be called the Mecca of neurologists. He had stalked through the old wards of that infirmary for chronic cases, marking off and giving names to a number of diseases of the nervous system in a most Adamlike fashion. And he was a great personality: affable, kindly, witty, but dominating by his innate pre-eminence. In an appreciation Freud wrote of him after his death in 1893 he spoke of the magic that radiated from his aspect and his voice, his gracious frankness of manner, the readiness with which he put everything at his pupils' disposal, and his lifelong loyalty to them. "As a teacher Charcot was perfectly fascinating: each of his lectures was a little masterpiece in construction and composition, perfect in style, and so impressive that the words spoken echoed in one's ears, and the subject demonstrated remained before one's eyes for the rest of the day." [33] A simple remark of his remained indelibly engraved on Freud's mind and went far to exorcise his somewhat excessive predilection for theory. When someone interrupted him with the assertion, "that cannot possibly be so; it contradicts the theory of Young-Helmholtz," Charcot tersely replied: "Theory is all very well but it does not prevent [the facts] from existing." [34] He was a true follower of Galileo! This empirical attitude was to stand Freud in good stead in the years of his startling discoveries.

Freud had brought an introduction from Benedikt, the Viennese hypnotist, and perhaps Charcot would have remembered his own name from Darkschewitsch, then a pupil of Freud's, having presented him with a number of Freud's reprints a year before.[35] Charcot received him very politely, but took no further personal notice of him until the following episode occurred. "I became a student at the Salpêtrière, but, as one of the crowd of foreign visitors, I had little attention paid me to begin with. One day in my hearing Charcot expressed his regret that since the war he had heard nothing from the German translator of his lectures; he went on to say that he would be glad if someone would undertake to translate the new volume of his lectures into German. I wrote to him and offered to do so; I can still remember a phrase in the letter to the effect that I suffered only from 'motor aphasia' and not from 'sensory aphasia in French.' Charcot accepted the offer, I was admitted to the circle of his personal acquaintances, and from that time forward I took a full part in all that went on at the Clinic." [36]

The allusion to the war fifteen years earlier seems queer, and perhaps Freud's memory forty years later was not quite exact here. The letters of that time tell the story in a different fashion. Freud, who was not happy there, was on the point of leaving Paris and returning to Vienna, after only two months stay, when "today a stupid idea occurred to me. The third volume of Charcot's Leçons has not yet been translated. How would it be if I were to ask him for permission to do so? But no doubt this has already been given to the translator of the first two volumes, so I had better let the idea drop. But I will try to find out if there is nothing to be done about it." [37] He then despatched the following letter, which a friend, Mme. Richetti, had composed for him.

"My dear Professor,
    "As for the past two months I have been fascinated by your elo

quence and immensely interested by the subject with which you deal in a masterly manner, it has occurred to me to offer you my services for the translation into German of the third volume of your 'Lessons' if you still want a translator and if you agree to avail yourself of my labor. Concerning my capacity for this undertaking it must be said that I only have motor aphasia in French but not sensory aphasia. I have given evidence of my German style in my translation of a volume of essays by John Stuart Mill.

"By translating the first part of the third volume of the 'Lessons' which takes up these new questions which have been raised and elucidated by you, Sir, I am certain of rendering a service to my compatriots to whom this part of your investigations is less accessible than the others and of introducing myself to advantage to the German doctors.

"It remains for me to explain to you, Sir, why I take the liberty of writing to you when I am fortunate enough to be able to speak to you, having permission to be present when you visit the Salpêtrière. It is in order to save you the trouble of giving me a negative answer for which—I frankly admit—I am half prepared, since it is very possible that you have already given the authorization which I allow myself to ask of you or that some other reason decides you to refuse it. In this case you have only not to mention it to me and I hope that you will be willing to excuse this request and to believe me to be, with the most sincere admiration,

"Your completely devoted,
"Dr. Sigm. Freud."

A couple of days later Freud wrote saying he was overjoyed to report that Charcot had consented, and not only to the translation of the lectures that had already appeared in French but also those that had not. Four days later he had arranged for the publication by Deuticke of Vienna, and a month later he had posted part of the translation to him. He was always a very swift translator, and he rapidly finished the present volume. In his Preface to it, dated July 18, 1886, he expressed his satisfaction that the German version should appear several months before the French original. It appeared in 1886 under the title, *Neue Vorlesungen über die Krankheiten des Nervensystems, insbesondere über Hysterie* (New Lectures on the Diseases of the Nervous System, Especially on Hysteria). As he did with the Bernheim translation (1888), he published a long extract from it—a case of hysterical coxalgia in a man following an accident—in the *Wiener medizinische Wochenschrift*.[38] Charcot expressed his thanks by presenting him with a set of his complete works bound in leather with the dedication:

"*A Monsieur le Docteur Freud, excellents souvenirs de la Salpêtrière.*

Charcot"

In his letters Freud gave a vivid description of Charcot's appearance and manner. He contrasted his warm and keen interest in the patients with the "serene superficiality" of the Viennese physicians. Even after a week he could say he had never been anywhere where he could learn so much as with Charcot. In the ward visits through the extraordinary, and indeed unique, wealth of clinical material reposing in the Salpêtrière, illuminated by Charcot's pregnant utterances, Freud must have learnt much neurology. But the abiding impression left on him was Charcot's pronouncements on the subject of hysteria, a theme we shall have presently to consider at length.

Freud brought back from Paris a lithograph in which Charcot is depicted impressively holding forth to his assistants and students. The patient whose case he is demonstrating is languishing in a semiconscious state supported by Babinsky's arm around her graceful waist. Freud's eldest daughter writes about it: "It held a strange attraction for me in my childhood and I often asked my father what was wrong with the patient. The answer I always got was that she was "too tightly laced," with a moral of the foolishness of being so. The look he would give the picture made me feel then even as a very young child that it evoked happy or important memories in him and was dear to his heart." [39]

Of Charcot's assistants Freud was most impressed by Brouardel.[40] Pierre Marie proposed to Freud that they should work together at a clinical study on hysteria, but he soon afterwards withdrew. The only fruit of his clinical studies Freud brought away was the valuable study of hysterical paralyses which he published some years later.

When Freud went to Paris his anatomical researches were still more in his mind than any clinical interests, and he tried at first to continue them in the Salpêtrière laboratory. Charcot and Guinon procured him some infantile brains for the purpose. Then came an investigation he wanted to make on the descending degeneration of his beloved spinal cord. He published nothing on pathology at the time, but in the monograph on cerebral paralyses in children which he wrote five years later he described his study of such a case which

Charcot had entrusted to him.[41] It was the case of a woman who had been an inmate of the Salpêtrière since 1853, suffering from hemiplegia and other symptoms.[d] Freud made a beautifully accurate report of the findings at the autopsy. It was a very detailed account of the sclerosis resulting from an embolism more than thirty years before; he was even able to delineate a tiny area of sclerosis in the temporal lobe corresponding to the part supplied by the sphenoidal branch of the medial cerebral artery.

Freud found the laboratory conditions in the Salpêtrière, which were doubtless very different from what he had been accustomed to, increasingly unsatisfactory, and on December 3 he announced he had decided to abandon them. It was almost the end of his work with the microscope: henceforth he was to become a pure clinician. In the next letter he gave seven convincing reasons for his decision, pleading, however, his intention to resume anatomical researches in Vienna. This multiplicity usually denotes the suppression of the fundamental reason, and it might be assumed that this was a fascination for psychopathology that Charcot had implanted in him. But there was a more personal one besides. Within a year of his engagement he had already felt a certain conflict between being engrossed in his "scientific work," by which he always meant laboratory work, and his love for Martha; he said that at times he felt the former was a dream and the latter a reality.[43] Later he assured her that anatomy of the brain was the only serious rival she had ever had or was likely to have.[44] Then from Paris he wrote: "I have long known that my life cannot be entirely given up to neuropathology, but that one can surrender it altogether for a dear girl has only become clear to me here in Paris"; [45] this was a week before he withdrew from the Salpêtrière laboratory. When announcing this decision he added: "You may be sure that I have overcome my love for science in so far as it came between us." All this had of course its practical aspects as well as the emotional ones. Freud knew very well that a married life could only mean clinical work.

Immediately after giving up the laboratory work in the Salpêtrière Freud started writing a little book entitled *Introduction to Neuropathology*. In six weeks he had finished the first part of it.[46] It was never published. Its place seems to have been taken by another more ambitious book which he also never finished. That was on the anat-

---

[d] A full clinical description of the cause may be found in the *Iconographie de la Salpêtrière*.[42]

omy of the brain, an effort which occupied him during the years 1887 and 1888.[47]

In his last week in Paris Freud achieved a minor triumph. Charcot had just discovered "something very curious"—probably a new syndrome—and Freud suggested both an explanation for it and a suitable name to designate it, which Charcot appears to have accepted.

At the end of February 1886 Freud left Paris, but on his way home he spent a few weeks in Berlin, in order to learn at Adolf Baginsky's Clinic something about the general diseases of children; he knew he would have no further chance to get away once he was back in Vienna. The reason for this study was that he had no prospect, probably for "racial" reasons, of obtaining a position in the University Psychiatric-Neurological Clinic in Vienna, and in fact never did, whereas the pediatrist Max Kassowitz (1842-1913) had offered him before he left for Paris the post of Director of a new neurological department that was being opened in the first public Institute for Children's Diseases. It was an old institution, in the Steindlgasse, founded in 1787 under the Emperor Josef II, but it was just being modernized. Freud held his position for many years, working there for several hours three times a week, and he made there some valuable contributions to neurology.

For the next five years Freud was absorbed in family interests, professional work, and the translation of the Charcot and Bernheim books. The only paper published in that time (1888) was one on an observation of hemianopsia in two children, aged two and three respectively, a hitherto unknown occurrence. Freud discussed the probable localization of the lesion, and grouped the cases among the unilateral cerebral paralyses of children which he was already beginning to investigate. He made the interesting suggestion that the conjugate deviation of the eyes sometimes observed in apoplectic coma may be due to a hemianopsia on the paralyzed side, so that the eyes would look towards the side of the lesion.

From the Fliess correspondence we know that in 1887 and 1888 he was also writing a book on the anatomy of the brain, a topic he was thoroughly versed in. He called it his real "scientific work"; for some years anatomy and histology had this privileged status. The work was never finished, since his interests were already moving towards psychopathology, and the only relics of it are the overcondensed articles in Villaret's *Handwörterbuch*.

The next publication was Freud's first book, *Aphasia*, in 1891. He had already lectured on this subject at the Physiology Club in

Vienna in 1886, and also at the University in 1887: he had furthermore written the article on it in Villaret's *Handwörterbuch der gesamten Medizin* (Encyclopedic Handbook of Medicine) (1888-1891).ᶜ The book was dedicated to Breuer. That he should dedicate his first book to the man who had been his mainstay through his most difficult years, and had also offered him what was to prove the key to all his future work, was assuredly a fitting gesture. Gratitude, however, was not Freud's only motive; he had hoped thereby to win Breuer into a better humor and was disappointed that for some obscure reason it had the opposite effect.⁵⁰

Most students of his works would agree with Freud's own verdict that it was the most valuable of his neurological writings, although it proved not to be the one by which his name was remembered in neurological circles. It is the first authentic glimpse we get of the Freud of later years. It has the close reasoning, the lucidity, the persuasive and thought-provoking argumentation, the candid discussion of objections, and the remarkable capacity for ordering his material that became so characteristic of his writings. Freud, now thirty-five years old, is no longer the modest student, but an experienced neurologist who can speak in a confident tone to his seniors as his equals, and any criticism of their doctrines, however devastating, is expressed in a polite and matter-of-fact manner. In a contemporary letter he wrote of it: "In it I am very '*frech*' (saucy, impudent) and cross swords with your friend Wernicke, with Lichtheim and Grashey, and scratch even the high-throned idol Meynert." ⁵¹

The book has the appropriate subtitle of "A Critical Study," since essentially it consists of a radical and revolutionary criticism of the Wernicke-Lichtheim doctrine of aphasia then almost universally accepted; it was the first to level such criticism. The criticism, however, was far from being simply negative, since Freud put forward views of his own, which, though not so cut and dried as those refuted, are much nearer than these to the modern ones.

After Broca's discovery (1861) of an area in the frontal lobe of the brain, damage to which causes "motor aphasia" (gross disturbance

ᶜ Although the articles there are not signed, those on aphasia and brain anatomy are certainly by Freud, and probably also those on hysteria and on paralyses in children. In a footnote in the book *Aphasia* he states that it was a paper by Exner and Paneth that first aroused his interest in the subject.⁴⁸ In his *Autobiography* (1925), however, he says it was the invitation to write on the subject for Villaret's *Handwörterbuch*, which actually was a couple of years later than his lectures on the topic.⁴⁹ The earlier remark is probably the more authentic of the two.

of the function of speech), and Wernicke's (1874) of one in the temporal lobe, damage to which causes "sensory aphasia" (inability to understand speech), neurologists were faced with the task of explaining the many partial and mixed varieties of such disturbances that could be observed. Bewildering combinations occurred of the inability to speak spontaneously, to repeat words after someone else, to read words while being unable to read letters or vice versa, to understand words in newly acquired languages while still understanding one's mother tongue, and so on. Wernicke, and following him Lichtheim, drew up schemes of the supposed connections of the centers and postulated various sections of these where a lesion would theoretically account for this or that combination of aphasic disturbances. The more of these that were observed, the more complicated became the diagrams, until this Ptolemy-like situation called for a Kepler to simplify it. That Freud undertook to do. A detailed analysis of published cases showed that the schemes had inner contradictions, whereupon Freud was emboldened to throw doubt on the whole basis of the doctrine: namely, that various aphasias could be explained by what had been called subcortical lesions in the associative paths.

His doubts would have been strikingly confirmed had he known what happened to Bastian, the great English authority on aphasia, only a year after this book was published. In a subtle case of aphasia Bastian postulated a minute lesion between the supposed associative fibers below the cortex, but when the autopsy revealed a huge cyst that had destroyed a good part of the left hemisphere of the brain, he was so stunned that he resigned from the hospital.

In place of this minute localizing scheme, Freud introduced a quite different *functional* explanation. Agreeing that destruction of the three main centers, motor, acoustic, and visual, would result in motor aphasia, sensory aphasia, or alexia respectively, he suggested that all the other subvarieties were to be explained by varying degrees of functional derangement radiating from a (slightly or badly) damaged area. In doing so he cited Hughlings Jackson's doctrine of "disinvolution," according to which more recently acquired or less important capacities suffer earlier than more fundamental ones, and he illustrated this by many examples.

The Broca and Wernicke "centers" he deprived of their semimystical meaning of self-acting agencies and pointed out that their significance was purely anatomical, not physiological, and simply due to their neighborhood, in the former case to the motor areas of the brain, and in the latter to the entry of the fibers from the acoustic nuclei. The centers are therefore nothing more than nodal points in the general network.

All this was a stage in Freud's emancipation from the more mechanical aspects of the Helmholtz school in which he had been brought up. He then went further and challenged the notion, based on Meynert's teaching, that ideas and memories are to be pictured as attached to various brain cells. He made a psychological discursus into the development of speech and reading, the acquiring of words and ideas, and protested against the confounding of physiological with psychological data. He called the naming of objects the weakest part of our linguistic equipment and so the one that often suffers first. This defect, Wernicke's transcortical sensory aphasia, he termed asymbolic aphasia, displacing thus Finkelnburg's use of the phrase on the ground that the latter had not distinguished between the naming of objects and the recognizing of them. A defect in the latter capacity Freud now christened "agnosia," a term that has remained, as also the distinction he made. Echolalia in aphasia he regarded merely as a sign of asymboly.

Perhaps the severest criticism was that of his old teacher Meynert's doctrine of the cortex containing a "projection of the various parts of the body." He demonstrated the errors in histological anatomy on which this was based. The fibers entering the cord nuclei are more numerous than those passing on from there to the cortex, so that there can be no continuity between the periphery and the brain. There is only a "projection" of the periphery in the gray matter of the spinal cord itself, though there is probably a "representation" of this on the cortex; one based, however, on functional rather than on topographical groupings.

Freud did not have much luck with this book, in spite of so many of its conclusions ultimately achieving acceptance. The time was not yet ripe for it. Jelliffe remarks that nearly all historical *résumés* on aphasia omit any reference to it (the only exception seems to be Goldstein's *Über die Aphasie*, 1910), and adds: "This comment is particularly pertinent for Head's historical presentation, for here, after devoting many pages to Hughlings Jackson's important genetic conceptions, Head omits entirely the one author who was alive to and who discussed Hughlings Jackson's views and who definitely leveled a strong criticism of the Wernicke-Lichtheim schemes, then much in vogue, in favor of the genetic views that Hughlings Jackson enunciated; particularly on the ideas of the 'dissolution of functions' so ably set forth by Jackson." [52] Freud's name was not even cited in Head's extensive bibliography, nor is it to be found in those by Mingazzini, Brissot, or most of the other writers on aphasia. In spite of all this it still reads like a modern work, even apart from the lively and interesting style.[f]

Of the 850 copies printed, 257 were sold after nine years, when the rest were pulped. There is no copy in any library in Great Britain. Freud was paid 156 gulden ($62) in royalties.

We now come to the last of Freud's neurological investigations, those carried out in the special department of Kassowitz's Children's Institute. Nine papers date from this period, one of which—on hemianopsia in early childhood—has already been noted.

The next, also published in 1891, was a massive monograph of 220 pages, with a bibliography of 180 titles, written in conjunction with his friend, Dr. Oscar Rie, a pediatrist who assisted Freud in his department.[ft] It is a work by which Freud's name was at last— and still is—remembered by the neurologists of the world. The unilateral paralyses of children were dealt with exhaustively from every point of view, and thirty-five personal cases were detailed. First the history and literature of the subject were considered in full. Then followed an analysis of the individual symptoms, the pathological anatomy, differential diagnosis, and treatment. It is a first-class clinical study.

A new syndrome, "choreatiform paresis," was here for the first time identified. It is a condition in which movements like those of chorea replace the unilateral paralysis that would be expected. It is further pointed out that many cases of what is apparently epilepsy in children belong to the group here studied, even if there is no actual paralysis. The authors cast doubt on Strümpell's view that acute poliomyelitis can cause a cerebral hemiplegia, although they expected that a broader conception of the former condition would lead to a common etiology being discovered.[g]

They also published the gist of this study in three papers in the *Wiener medizinische Wochenschrift*, January-February 1891. These

---

[f] The controversy inaugurated by Freud between the dynamic and the static aspects of localization in connection with aphasia still persists, and even sixty years after is far from being settled. See K. Conrad: "Aphasie, Agnosie, Apraxie." [53]

[ft] Klinische Studie über die halbseitige Cerebrallälmung der Kinder.

[g] The modern encephalitis.

contain nothing that is not in the fuller study, but they are a clear presentation useful to non-neurological physicians.

Two years later Freud published a short paper on a mysterious symptom—hypertonia of the lower extremities—found in about a half of the cases of nocturnal enuresis. He was then far from any knowledge of the psychological nature of the condition.

In the same year (1893) he published another monograph of 168 pages on paralyses in children, this time on the central diplegias. Like the former ones, it was published in some archives edited by Kassowitz. It was a pendant to the former one, so that now all forms of paralyses in children had been investigated. Much of it was built on Little's work of thirty years earlier, a copy of which Freud once showed me in his library. Here also a large number, fifty-three, of personally observed cases were described in detail. As in the former monograph the literature was first fully considered, and then the symptomatology, etc., in the same order as before.

Freud divides this group into four: (1) General cerebral spasticity, known as "Little's disease." This comprises two thirds of all the cases. (2) Paraplegic spasticity, due to a bilateral cerebral lesion. This condition had previously, under the name of spastic tabes, been erroneously regarded as a spinal affection. (3) Centralized "chorea" and bilateral athetosis. (4) Bilateral spastic hemiplegia. Freud showed that there is no unitary etiology for a given type of affection and discussed all the causative factors under the headings of (a) congenital, (b) active during birth, and (c) subsequently acquired. There was further no correlation to be found between the clinical types and the pathological findings in the brain. On the other hand, there appeared to be one between the lesion and the preponderance of contracture over paralysis, so common in these cases, the more superficial the lesion the greater the contracture; and also between the site of the lesion and the more intensive affection of the lower limbs, so characteristic of these diplegias. Freud agreed with König-stein that the strabismus which at times accompanies infantile diplegia is due to retinal hemorrhage at birth or soon after.

The hereditary affections of the nervous system were also dealt with, especially from the point of view of diagnosis. About the same time Freud published in the *Neurologisches Centralblatt* (August 1893) an account of two brothers who suffered from an unusual hereditary affection. The symptoms of lateral nystagmus, alternating convergent strabismus, optic atrophy, monotonous and scanning speech, intention tremor of the arms, and spastic weakness of the legs are extraordinarily similar to those of disseminated sclerosis, but Freud considered that the condition was a distinct one, which he termed a spastic counterpart to Friedreich's disease.

Pierre Marie, the leading neurologist in France and in many respects Charcot's successor, in a review of Freud's monograph on the cerebral diplegias in childhood said: "This monograph is unquestionably the most complete, the most accurate and thoughtful which has yet appeared on the confusing problem of cerebral diplegia of infancy about which so little is known." [54] Marie was the editor of the new Revue Neurologique and it was probably at his invitation that Freud wrote, in French, a summarized account of the monograph in question, which appeared in the first volume of the periodical.

In 1895 Freud published a short note on a peculiar and harmless affection of a thigh nerve from which he had himself suffered for a couple of years, and he gave an account of the observations he had made on himself. Bernhardt had recently described the condition to which his name has since been attached, but Freud remarked he had for some years been familiar with it in several patients.

Freud had now become the leading authority on the subject of children's paralyses, so when Nothnagel planned his great encyclopedia of medicine it was only natural that he should commission Freud to write the section on "Infantile Cerebral Paralysis." Probably thinking that he had already said what he had to say on the subject, and having become at that time much more interested in psychopathology, Freud was evidently bored with the request, and it was only with many groans that he brought himself to fulfill it. The most tedious part was the review of the literature and bibliography, and in his correspondence with Fliess (see p. 347) there are many bitter complaints about the task. It was not until the middle of January 1897 that the work got finished, a year late, and it was the last Freud was ever to write on neurological topics.[h]

There was in that interval a certain amount of new knowledge to incorporate, e.g., on encephalitis, and there were a few of the earlier conclusions to modify, but his chief effort was to group the various paralyses into distinct units—a task presenting insuperable

[h] So far as his original writings are concerned. He continued for a few years longer to write reviews and abstracts. For instance, he wrote all those on cerebral paralyses in children for the first three volumes of the Jahresbericht für Neurologie und Psychiatrie (1898–1900), of which he was a co-editor.

difficulties. The whole work, however, 327 pages long, was a comprehensive treatise, one which Bernard Sachs characterized as "masterly and exhaustive." The Swiss neurologist Brun in a recent review says it has still an established place in modern neurology. He writes: "Freud's monograph is the most thorough and complete exposition that has yet been written on the cerebral paralyses of children. . . . One gets an idea of the superb mastery of the enormous clinical material here brought together and critically worked through from the fact that the bibliography alone occupies fourteen and a half pages. It was a superb achievement and alone would suffice to assure Freud's name a permanent place in clinical neurology." [55]

The end of Freud's active neurological period[i] may perhaps be reckoned from his obituary notice of Charcot, which was published in September 1893. It expresses without reserve Freud's great admiration for the man "whose personality and whose work none ever approached without learning from them." [56] His description of Charcot's personality and mode of working is in its vividness an artistic achievement. With his usual generosity Freud accords to Charcot the taking of a step "which gives him for all times the glory of being the first to elucidate hysteria," [57] a phrase which we should nowadays regard as a considerable overestimation. There is no doubt that Charcot's attitude to hysteria afforded very much encouragement—what psychologists call "sanction"—to Freud, and he remained grateful to him for it.

Before we take leave of Freud the neurologist, it would seem fitting to review briefly his achievements in those twenty years. It is impossible to depict the laborious detail which only those who have pursued a similar course can imagine, but we may recall the outstanding discoveries made and conclusions reached in his lengthy investigations of the nervous system.

Beginning appropriately in one of its earliest forms, he established that some mysterious cells in the spinal cord of a lowly fish were the source of the sensory root fibers and were on their way to emerge into the posterior root ganglia so familiar in higher animals. He also demonstrated the continuity between the bipolar cells of the lower organisms and the unipolar ones of the higher. These were solid stones in the edifice of the doctrine of evolution, a remarkable achievement for a young student, and they early illustrate Freud's

[i] With the exception of the long monograph on the paralyses of children he subsequently wrote for Nothnagel's great *Handbuch* (1897).

genetic outlook. Soon after this he showed, in his study of the crayfish, that axis cylinders are always fibrillary in structure, and was the first to recognize that nerve fibers emanate from a netlike substance in the nerve cell. A lecture given a couple of years later revealed the essence of the neurone theory, which, however, he failed to formulate definitely.

Passing upwards from the spinal cord he next made minute studies of the medulla oblongata, making special use of a developmental technique to unravel its complexities. The outstanding results were the demonstrations of connections between the posterior (sensory) columns of the spinal cord, the roots of the acoustic nerve, and the cerebellum; further that the roots of the sensory cranial nerves were homologous with those of the spinal cord, a conclusion again important to the theory of evolution.

Freud made a detailed study of cocaine, with the coca plant from which it is obtained, and foretold that its anesthetic properties would be of clinical use.

The casuistic publications were competent, but, with the exception of those on children's paralyses, of temporary interest only. Freud's comprehensive study of those, however, is a classic of permanent worth.

Last, but not least, comes the book on aphasia. Here Freud shows himself for the first time in his full stature. His revolutionary criticism of the prevailing localization doctrine of aphasia is accompanied by an alternative functional explanation which has important consequences for the general theory of cerebral activity. In it, further, the relation between this and mental functioning is discussed in a stimulating fashion.

Freud had proved himself as a good clinician, a highly skillful histologist, and a thinker. His attempts in experimental physiology were conspicuous failures. With a man of his dynamic type of mind this constitutes a problem, for which some explanation has been suggested.[j]

All this work would have established Freud as a first-class neurologist, a hard worker, a close thinker, but—with the exception perhaps of the book on aphasia—there was little to foretell the existence of a genius. We shall next have to consider the beginnings of his work in psychology and, if possible, trace some threads between it and his investigations of the nervous system.

[j] See pp. 52, 53.

XI

The Breuer Period

(1882 – 1894)

JUST AS THE PREVIOUS CHAPTER OVERLAPPED IN TIME THE PRESENT ONE, so will this one overlap the succeeding one. That overlapping enabled all the neurological work to be considered as a whole, although much of it—and in fact the most important part—was carried out in what is here termed the Breuer period. The beginnings and discoveries of psychoanalysis had better, for certain reasons, also be discussed in two divisions, artificial as this may seem. Freud's development from 1880 to 1900 naturally displays a continuity which schematically could be narrated as a whole, yet it can more comprehensibly be exhibited to the reader if it is grouped in some such way as is here attempted. It is proposed, therefore, to describe in the present chapter the dawn of Freud's interest in psychopathology, his growing interest in the sexual etiology of neuroses, and—most important—the elaboration of his technical method which was the foundation of everything else; and to reserve for subsequent chapters an account of his struggles to formulate a theoretical basis for mental functioning, and also his clinical findings. A paradoxical consequence of this arrangement is that the actual collaborative work between Breuer and Freud, since this was mainly theoretical, will be considered, not in the present chapter entitled "The Breuer Period," but in a later one.

It has not been found easy to estimate Breuer's significance for Freud and his work. Freud certainly overestimated it in the latter connection, though probably not in the former. When at times he would style Breuer the Founder of Psychoanalysis, he was for some reason modestly transferring that title to him from himself, since the essentials of psychoanalysis—both the method and the discoveries —belong entirely to Freud and were made at a time when the two

221

men had already separated for good. Had he said that Breuer's communication to him of the famous case, Frl. Anna O., was one of the starting points that led to psychoanalysis, it would have been much nearer the truth. Freud's attitude has led some writers, on the other hand, to go to the other extreme and to discount Breuer's importance.

Another complication is that what contributions Breuer had to make to the theory of hysteria—apart from that concerning the case in question—were already for the most part common ground between him and Freud, since they were in effect the physiological principles that they had both imbibed and shared in Brücke's Institute. When they discussed together the applications of those principles to the problems of hysteria, each would make suggestions, and it is now not always possible to say from whom a particular idea emanated. Some definite contributions that Breuer made, however, can be distinguished, and they will be noted in due course.

The view that will be taken here is that Breuer was of very considerable significance to Freud personally through the necessary encouragement he supplied at a critical period, but that his intellectual contributions were of less importance.

Dr. Josef Breuer (1842-1925), whose name is known to a wide circle only through his early association with Freud, was not simply a well-known physician in Vienna, as he is sometimes described, but also a man of science of considerable standing. Freud described him as "a man of rich and universal gifts, whose interests extended far beyond his professional activity." In his youth he had done some notable work under Ewald Hering on the physiology of respiration, where he discovered its automatic control by the vagus nerve. Incidentally, the distinguished physiologist Hering, who is chiefly remembered nowadays for his having propounded an alternative to the Young-Helmholtz trichromatic theory of color vision, had once invited Freud to join him in Prague as his assistant;[1] that must have been when Freud was still working in the Institute of Physiology, and it is likely that Breuer had something to do with the invitation. Breuer's subsequent researches into the functions of the semicircular canals were a permanent contribution to scientific knowledge. He became a *Privatdocent* in Vienna in 1868, but withdrew into private practice in 1871 and refused Billroth's offer to propose him for a professorial title.[2] In May 1894 he was elected a Corresponding Member of the Vienna Academy of Sciences; his proposers were Sigmund Exner, Hering, and Ernst Mach, all men with international scientific reputations.[2]†

Breuer was a faithful adherent of the school of Helmholtz, of which we have spoken earlier. The writers he thought most highly of were Goethe and Fechner. He was one of the most highly thought of physicians in Vienna and was the family doctor to Brücke, Exner, Billroth, Chrobak, and others of their standing.

Freud first met Breuer at the Institute of Physiology, in the late seventies, and, sharing the same interests and outlook, they soon became friends. "He became," Freud says, "my friend and helper in my difficult circumstances. We grew accustomed to share all our scientific interests with each other. In this relationship the gain was naturally mine." [3] Mrs. Bernays says he used to visit Freud at his parents' home to discuss scientific topics, and this, though unlikely, is possibly true. In letters to Martha Bernays in 1884 he would refer to Breuer in glowing terms as "the ever-loyal Breuer," and it is certain that in those early years he was on the most intimate and friendly terms with him and also with his wife, for whom he had a special admiration. Later on Freud's and Breuer's families were on very friendly terms. Freud's eldest daughter was named after Breuer's wife and his youngest after a sister of Breuer's son-in-law— incidentally a favorite patient of Freud's.[a] The Hammerschlag and Breuer families, whose flats were in the same building, were intimate friends, and a son of one married a daughter of the other.

From December 1880 to June 1882 Breuer treated what has become recognized as a classical case of hysteria, that of Frl. Anna O.[b] The patient was an unusually intelligent girl of twenty-one, who developed a museum of symptoms in connection with her father's fatal illness. Among them were paralysis of three limbs with contractures and anesthesias, severe and complicated disturbances of sight and speech, inability to take food, and a distressing nervous cough which was the occasion of Breuer being called in. More interesting, however, was the presence of two distinct states of consciousness: one a fairly normal one, the other that of a naughty and troublesome child, rather like that in Morton Prince's famous case of Sally Beauchamp. It was a case of double personality. The transition from one to the other was marked by a phase of autohypnosis from which she would awake clear and mentally normal. This phase happened by luck to be the time when Breuer visited her, and she soon

[a] Anna Hammerschlag, a daughter of Freud's old teacher.
[b] Since she was the real discoverer of the cathartic method, her name, which was actually Bertha Pappenheim (February 27, 1859–May 28, 1936), deserves to be commemorated.

got into the habit of relating to him the disagreeable events of the day, including terrifying hallucinations, after which she felt relief. On one occasion she related the details of the first appearance of a particular symptom and, to Breuer's great astonishment, this resulted in its complete disappearance. Perceiving the value of doing so, the patient continued with one symptom after another, terming the procedure "the talking cure" or "chimney sweeping." Incidentally, at that time she could speak only English, having forgotten her mother tongue, German, and when asked to read aloud from an Italian or French book would do so swiftly and fluently—in English.

After a while Breuer supplemented this evening proceeding by inducing an artificial hypnosis every morning, since the mass of material was becoming overwhelming. In those days, to devote hours every day for more than a year to a single patient, and an hysteric at that, signified very special qualities of patience, interest, and insight. But the psychotherapeutic armamentarium was thereby enriched with the method, associated with his name, which he called "catharsis," and which is still extensively used.

Freud has related to me a fuller account than he described in his writings of the peculiar circumstances surrounding the end of this novel treatment. It would seem that Breuer had developed what we should nowadays call a strong counter-transference to his interesting patient. At all events he was so engrossed that his wife became bored at listening to no other topic, and before long jealous. She did not display this openly, but became unhappy and morose. It was a long time before Breuer, with his thoughts elsewhere, divined the meaning of her state of mind. It provoked a violent reaction in him, perhaps compounded of love and guilt, and he decided to bring the treatment to an end. He announced this to Anna O., who was by now much better, and bade her good-by. But that evening he was fetched back to find her in a greatly excited state, apparently as ill as ever. The patient, who according to him had appeared to be an asexual being and had never made any allusion to such a forbidden topic throughout the treatment, was now in the throes of an hysterical childbirth (pseudocyesis), the logical termination of a phantom pregnancy[c] that had been invisibly developing in response to

[c] In this connection it is of interest that her first social work, beginning in 1890, was to spend twelve years as "Mother" of an orphan institution. Later, however (April 8, 1922), she was to write: "If there is any justice in the next life women will make the laws there and men will bear the children."

Breuer's ministrations. Though profoundly shocked, he managed to calm her down by hypnotizing her, and then fled the house in a cold sweat. The next day he and his wife left for Venice to spend a second honeymoon, which resulted in the conception of a daughter; the girl born in these curious circumstances was nearly sixty years later to commit suicide in New York.

Confirmation of this account may be found in a contemporary letter Freud wrote to Martha, which contains substantially the same story.[4] She at once identified herself with Breuer's wife, and hoped the same thing would not ever happen to her, whereupon Freud reproved her vanity in supposing that other women would fall in love with *her* husband: "for that to happen one has to be a Breuer." [5]

The poor patient did not fare so well as one might gather from Breuer's published account. Relapses took place, and she was removed to an institution in Gross Enzersdorf. A year after discontinuing the treatment, Breuer confided to Freud that she was quite unhinged and that he wished she would die and so be released from her suffering.[6] She improved, however, and gave up morphia. A few years later Martha relates how "Anna O.," who happened to be an old friend of hers and later a connection by marriage, visited her more than once. She was then pretty well in the daytime, but still suffered from her hallucinatory states as evening drew on.[7]

Frl. Bertha (Anna O.) was not only highly intelligent, but extremely attractive in physique and personality; when removed to the sanatorium, she inflamed the heart of the psychiatrist in charge. Her mother, who was somewhat of a dragon, came from Frankfurt and took her daughter back there for good at the end of the eighties. Bertha, who was born and brought up in Vienna, retained her Viennese grace, charm, and humor. Some years before she died she composed five witty obituary notices of herself for different periodicals. A very serious side, however, developed when she was thirty, and she became the first social worker in Germany, one of the first in the world. She founded a periodical and several institutes where she trained students. A major part of her life's work was given to women's causes and emancipation, but work for children also ranked high. Among her exploits were several expeditions to Russia, Poland, and Roumania to rescue children whose parents had perished in pogroms. She never married, and she remained very devoted to God.[d]

[d] I am indebted to Mrs. Ena Lewisohn, a cousin of Bertha's, for access to the source of this information.[8]

Some ten years later, at a time when Breuer and Freud were study-ing cases together, Breuer called him into consultation over an hysterical patient. Before seeing her he described her symptoms, whereupon Freud pointed out that they were typical products of a phantasy of pregnancy. The recurrence of the old situation was too much for Breuer. Without saying a word he took up his hat and stick and hurriedly left the house.

Freud was greatly interested in hearing of the famous case of Anna O., which he did soon after its termination in June 1882; to be exact, on November 18.[9] It was so far outside his experience that it made a deep impression on him, and he would discuss the details of it with Breuer over and over again. When he got to Paris and had an op-portunity of talking with Charcot, he told him about the remarkable discovery, but, as he remarked to me, "Charcot's thoughts seemed to be elsewhere," and he quite failed to arouse his interest. This seems for a time to have damped his own enthusiasm about the dis-covery.

As was mentioned earlier, the most important impression that Charcot's teaching made on Freud was his revolutionary views on the subject of hysteria, which was indeed the topic that was chiefly interesting Charcot at that time. In the first place, that such an emi-nent neurologist should so seriously concern himself with this topic was in itself startling. Before that time hysteria was regarded either as a matter of simulation and at best "imagination" (which seemed to mean much the same) on which no reputable physician would waste his time, or else a peculiar disorder of the womb which could be treated, and sometimes was treated, by extirpation of the clitoris; the wandering womb could also be driven back into its place by valerian, the smell of which it disliked. Now, thanks to Charcot, it be-came, almost overnight, a perfectly respectable disease of the nervous system; one due to congenital degeneration of the brain, it is true, but nevertheless one that could be the subject of serious study. To use a modern colloquialism, Charcot had "put hysteria on the map."

In his obituary notice of Charcot, seven years later, Freud gave great credit to him for this achievement alone. In doing so he cer-tainly exaggerated its importance when he likened it to Pinel's free-ing the insane patients of their chains—also in the Salpêtrière—in the previous century. Charcot's teaching was undoubtedly successful in sanctioning a more scientific attitude towards hysteria in French medical circles, and—most important—with Freud himself. It had little effect elsewhere on the Continent and only a negative one in

Anglo-Saxon countries. There the theatrical nature of Charcot's demonstrations, his obvious credulity concerning the effects of metallotherapy, and, presently, the suspicion that many of the complicated stages he described in hysterical attacks and in the course of hypnosis were artifacts produced by the *dressage* of suggestion, evoked only the skeptical conclusion that he was becoming senile or, put otherwise, that it was another case of a good man gone wrong. And men of science continued to eschew the psychoneuroses with the same wariness they nowadays display towards "psychical research."

Nevertheless, much of what Charcot demonstrated could not be talked away, and constituted a permanent gain in knowledge. He made a systematic and comprehensive study of the manifestations of hysteria, one that made the diagnosis of it more definite, and also showed that many affections otherwise attributed were really of an hysterical nature. He also laid stress on the existence of the complaint in the male sex, which, since it was now classified among nervous diseases, was not to be wondered at. His contribution on traumatic hysteria has since become of importance in legal actions. Above all, and this was his greatest contribution, he demonstrated that in suitable subjects he could by the use of hypnotism elicit hysterical symptoms, paralysis, tremors, anesthesias, etc., that were in the smallest detail identical with those of the spontaneous hysteria as seen in his other patients and as had been described in full in the Middle Ages when they were ascribed to demonic possession.

All this meant that, whatever the unknown neurological basis of hysteria might be, the symptoms themselves could be both treated and abolished by ideas alone. They had a psychogenic origin. This opened the door to a medical motive for investigating the psychology of patients, with all the ramifying results that the past half century has shown. It put psychology itself on a totally different footing from its previous academic one and made possible discoveries concerning the deeper layers of the mind that could not have been made in any other way.

So Freud went back to Vienna agog with all these revelations. Breuer and Charcot looked as if they might be adequate substitutes for Brücke, whom he had lost. His path, however, was to prove more checkered than in that flush of enthusiasm he might have hoped. He finished the publication of his work on the medulla, which has already been described, but, with the exception of two slight papers, he published no researches for the next five years, from 1886 to 1891.

Freud himself attributed this to his preoccupation with his private practice and the necessity of providing for the material existence of a rapidly growing family; not only his own, but numerous relatives as well. This would certainly be an adequate explanation, but it is not hard to see that there were also other factors at work. To begin with, he had embarked on the translation of four large volumes, two of Charcot's and two of Bernheim's. He was not content merely to translate them, however faithfully, but added important prefaces to two of them. The first one was Charcot's *Neue Vorlesungen*,ᵉ 1886, the preface having been written in the previous July; it was a volume of 357 pages. The second one, also a considerable volume of 414 pages, appeared in the following year; it was the first of the Bernheim books.ᶠ There was then an interval of four years, when two books appeared almost simultaneously. One was the second Bernheim book, *Hypnotismus, Suggestion und Psychotherapie* (380 pages). He furnished no preface for this one; by then his interest had moved from direct suggestion in therapy to the deeper matters of psychopathology he had begun to investigate. The last book, Charcot's famous *Leçons du Mardi*, delivered in the session of 1887-1888, appeared in parts during the years 1892-1894 under the title, *Poliklinische Vorträge* (Clinical Lectures); it has 492 closely printed pages. This book Freud did not merely translate; he edited it. He wrote a preface, and added sixty-two footnotes which brought the literary references up to date and contained many of the translator's personal opinions—sometimes in criticism of Charcot's. Some of these footnotes are of great interest in adumbrating Freud's earliest ideas in psychopathology, but he learned later that Charcot had been displeased at what he considered his translator's arbitrary behavior, since no permission had been asked.¹⁰

Besides all this work, Freud wrote in the period in question, besides the two papers he published then, two important books which appeared in 1891.ᵍ They were his chief contributions to clinical neurology and must have necessitated a great deal of work. So his implied apology for not producing any scientific work in those years was quite uncalled for. They were far from idle years.

Moreover, he had to accumulate personal experience of neurotic cases before he could feel in a position to say anything new about them. Material there was in plenty, for like all neurologists he found that his practice would consist largely of psychoneurotics who were

ᵉ See p. 209.
ᶠ See p. 238.
ᵍ See pp. 212, 213, 216.

under the impression that "nerve specialists" could cure "nerves" as well as diseases of the spinal cord. Unlike most neurologists, however, he regarded this state of affairs not as a humiliating nuisance in view of their total ignorance of the subject, but as an opportunity to explore a new and fruitful field.

More important than any of these considerations, however, was probably the inhibiting effect made on him by his reception in Vienna on his return there. In his *Autobiography* Freud says it was his duty to report at the Medical Society on his experiences abroad.[11] Dr. Bernfeld has recently obtained a copy of the application for Freud's traveling grant, which shows he was in error in his previous statement that it contained as a condition the necessity of making such a report.[12] Be that as it may, Freud seems to have had to make what he called a "traveling report," presumably to the Ministry. He spent about ten days over it and posted it on April 22.

Addresses at medical meetings were a different matter, and no doubt Freud was actuated by the youthful enthusiasm that burns to communicate great news. He had so much that was new and exciting to relate. He read a paper on hypnotism before the Physiological Club on May 11 and again before the Psychiatric Society on May 27; they could not have improved his standing with Meynert, to whom hypnotism was anathema. He was down to read a paper before the *Gesellschaft der Ärzte* (Society of Physicians) on June 4 on what he called his "traveling report," but the program was so full that it was postponed to the autumn.

He read his paper entitled "On Male Hysteria" on October 15, 1886, von Bamberger being in the chair. This was the famous occasion that Freud referred to as his "duty to report to the Society," and which caused him so much distress. Freud's was the second of the several papers to be read that evening, at one of the usual weekly meetings. He gave an account of Charcot's grouping of hysterical symptoms into four-stage seizures, the typical visual, sensory, and motor disturbances, and the hysterogenetic zones. It enabled many aberrant cases to be recognized through their varying approximations to the standard type. This definition of positive signs changed the prevailing conception of hysteria as being a vague malingering. According to Charcot, there was no connection between the disease and the genital organs, or any difference between its manifestations in male and female. Freud described a case of traumatic hysteria in a man which had followed a fall from a scaffold, a case he himself had observed at the Salpêtrière. Finally, he mentioned Charcot's suggestion that some cases of "railway spine" after accidents might be hysterical, an American view which was being contested in Germany. This last addition, which was superfluous to the main theme, was not a diplomatic one, since neurologists had rather a vested interest in injuries to the nervous system which often led to court cases.

The neurologist Rosenthal opened the discussion by remarking that male hysteria, though relatively rare, was well recognized, and he described two such cases he had studied twenty years before. Mental shock, even after slight injuries, often produced hysterical symptoms, which he surmised originated in cortical disturbance. Meynert spoke of cases of epileptic seizures following traumatic experiences and labeled them epileptoid. He added, rather ironically, that it would be interesting if Dr. Freud would come to his clinic and demonstrate on such cases the symptomatology he had quoted from Charcot. Bamberger said that, in spite of his admiration for Charcot, he could not find anything new to Viennese physicians in what they had just been told. Male hysteria was well known. He doubted the traumatic etiology. Leidesdorf was sure that many railway cases affected the central nervous system organically. There were patients who suffered from irritability and insomnia after slight accidents, but those symptoms were due to shock rather than to hysteria.

In writing later of this meeting, which seems to have affected him deeply, Freud referred to his "bad reception," and he often indicated how much it had hurt him. (One might gather from his remarks that he ceased attending medical meetings ever after, but that was very far from being so.) The report of the discussion hardly bears this out, although of course it does not depict the coolness of the reception. In fact, there seems to have been nothing very remarkable in the reception, which was very much what might have been expected in the circumstances and would have been the same in most medical circles of the kind. When an enthusiastic, perhaps over-enthusiastic, young man sets out to announce to his seniors (mostly his former teachers) that they have a lot to learn and that he is prepared to enlighten them, the inevitable response is defensive, usually taking the form of minimizing the novelty of the information and damping the exaltation of the speaker. A critical comment on the incident might lay stress on the naiveté of the youthful mentor, and perhaps on his sensitiveness, as much as on the obvious lack of imagination on the part of the seniors.

Meynert, fairly enough, challenged Freud to prove his words by producing for them a case of male hysteria with the typical Charcot symptoms,[h] but whenever he found suitable cases in the General Hospital the senior physicians of the departments refused to allow him to make any such use of their material. One of the surgeons even threw doubts on his classical education by asking if he did not know that the very word "hysteria" came from *Hysteron* (*sic*), the Greek for womb, a fact that by definition excluded the male sex. Before long, however, thanks to the help of Dr. von Beregszászy, a young laryngologist, he succeeded in finding such a patient elsewhere. In his *Autobiography* Freud writes: "At length outside the hospital I came upon a suitable case." [14] The words "at length" are indicative of his indignation and impatience, since actually only a week elapsed before the patient was brought to him, and Königstein made the careful ophthalmological examination on October 24—nine days after the meeting. The case was that of a man of twenty-nine, a metal worker, who after a quarrel with his brother developed a classical hemianesthesia, with typical disturbance in the field of vision and color sense. The case was demonstrated before the Medical Society on November 26, 1886; Dr. Königstein, the ophthalmologist, made a report on the eye symptoms on December 11. Exner was in the chair. This time there was some applause, but there were so many papers that evening that there was no time for any discussion. Still, the *Wiener medizinische Wochenschrift* called it "this very interesting paper." Freud published the case under the title of "Observations of a Pronounced Hemianesthesia in an Hysterical Male," together with Königstein's ophthalmological report, in that periodical on December 4,[15] and 11,[16] 1886, and headed it with the optimistic serial title, "Contributions to the Clinical Study of Hysteria, No. 1." It was, however, the only one of the series, a fact probably to be accounted for by his discouragement at its reception.

Referring to the incident nearly forty years later, Freud still displayed some bitterness. "This time I was applauded, but no further interest was taken in me. The impression that the high authorities had rejected my innovations remained unshaken, and, with my hysteria in men and my production of hysterical paralyses by suggestion, I found myself forced into the opposition. As I was soon after-

[h] Meynert, one of the chief opponents, later confessed to Freud on his death bed that he had himself been a classical case of male hysteria, but had always managed to conceal the fact;[18] incidentally, it is known that he was a very erratic and neurotic person and a heavy drinker. Some consolation for Freud, if only a slight one.

wards excluded from the laboratory of cerebral anatomy and for a whole session had nowhere to deliver my lectures, I withdrew from academic life and ceased to attend the learned societies. It is a whole generation since I have visited the *Gesellschaft der Ärzte*." [17]

The reverberation of the emotions of forty years ago led Freud to give an ambiguous impression in the passage just quoted, from which it might well be assumed that he promptly refrained from attending all medical meetings. We have records of his attending the *Gesellschaft der Ärzte* on May 13, 1887, October 21, 1887, and February 3, 1888,[18] and there may well have been many more. Even if we allow the usual thirty years for a "generation," that would bring us to 1895. In other medical societies he spoke or read papers until about 1904,[19] and his University lectures continued, with few intermissions, until 1917.

We see that Freud was bitterly disappointed at the very outset of his endeavors to convey new ideas to his conservative seniors. Such a strong immediate reaction would argue great expectation of success and praise, an oversanguine view of his former teachers, and perhaps an excessive sensitiveness to any criticism or lack of favorable response.

The conflict with Meynert did not cease. In 1889 Meynert published in the *Wiener klinische Wochenschrift*, in opposition to Charcot's theory of autosuggestion as the cause of hysterical paralyses, an anatomical explanation,[20] which in a footnote to the *Poliklinische Vorträge* Freud tartly stigmatized as "entirely inadequate." [21] According to Meynert, the error underlying Charcot's explanation was that he had overlooked the existence of a small branch of the internal carotid, the choroidal artery! It is plain that much of his antagonism to Freud was connected with the latter's association with Charcot. He sneered at Freud's "liking to instruct him" (Meynert), and added, "I find his defense of the suggestive therapy all the more remarkable inasmuch as he left Vienna (for Paris) a physician with an exact training in physiology." [22] He evidently felt that Charcot had seduced Freud from the strict and narrow path of pure science.

Before we pass by the Charcot episode, however, an aftereffect of it deserves mention. It was a question of making a comparative study of hysterical and organic paralyses so as to ascertain whether their different origins, one mental, the other physical, produced differences in the nature of the paralyses themselves. Freud lectured on the subject in his University course in 1887,[23] wrote the first draft in May 1888,[24] and finished the paper by August.[25] For some strange reason, however, he did not publish it for another five years; it was written in French and appeared in *Archives de Neurologie*, at about the same time as Freud's joint essay with Breuer, seven years after he left Paris. In it Freud made clear the three cardinal differences between the two kinds of paralysis, distinctions now universally accepted. (1) An hysterical paralysis can be complete in one part of the body, e.g., arm, without other parts being affected. Where a cerebral paralysis is intense, it is always extensive in distribution. (2) Sensory changes, especially anesthesia, are more pronounced than the motor (i.e., paralysis) in hysteria; the reverse is true of cerebral paralysis. (3) Most important of all is the fact that the distribution of the latter is explicable by the data of anatomy, whereas hysteria behaves, as Freud piquantly put it, as if there were no such thing as anatomy of the brain; its distribution is purely ideational.

It was a brilliant little study, and a permanent addition to our clinical knowledge. The year Charcot died Freud, in a footnote to his translation of Charcot's lectures, gave him the credit for the ideas. His words were: "When I was leaving the Salpêtrière Charcot suggested to me that I make a comparative study of organic and hysterical paralyses. . . ." [26] In his *Autobiography* nearly forty years later he gave a somewhat different account. "Before leaving Paris I discussed with the great man a plan for a comparative study of hysterical and organic paralyses. I wished to establish the thesis that in hysteria paralyses and anesthesias of the various parts of the body are demarcated according to the popular idea of their limits and not according to anatomical facts. He agreed with this view, but it was easy to see that in reality he took no special interest in penetrating more deeply into the psychology of the neuroses." [27]

There is contemporary evidence for thinking that the second, less modest, version is nearer to the truth, and that in fact the ideas were entirely Freud's own. In a letter of February 21, 1886, he wrote: "I have been carrying about a letter I have written to Charcot in which I speak of two ideas, of which at least one seems to be very important. But I know that in sending such a letter I am risking a good deal, since Charcot does not like people intervening with clever ideas. After hesitating for long over whether to send the letter I have decided to hand it to him tomorrow. I don't want to be cowardly, and after all my Russian friend (Darkschewitsch) likes both the ideas. But I surmise that I shall be sorry." Freud knew that the ideas would be above Charcot's head. However, matters went pretty well. In the next letter, four days later, he told of his great pleasure when Charcot said they were not so bad; that although he could not accept the ideas himself, he would not contradict them and that it would be worth while to work them out; he promised to publish such a paper in his *Archives de Neurologie*, which indeed he did, only a fortnight before his sudden death.

Two years after Freud's paper was published in the *Archives de Neurologie*, one by C. S. Freund of Breslau, a pupil of Wernicke's, appeared in the *Neurologisches Centralblatt* with a similar title ("On Psychical Paralyses").[28] It was directly plagiarized from Freud's, and without any acknowledgment. Freud apparently did not mind this,[29] but he was perturbed at the second half of Freund's paper, which reproduced from a recent book by Heinrich Sachs an account of the "constancy principle." This was a theme that had occupied Freud for some years, and he intended to make it the basis of his new psychology.

Freud foreshortened the story when he wrote in his *Autobiography* that Meynert excluded him from his laboratory on his return from Paris. This could only have happened six months later, after returning from his honeymoon. Actually Meynert greeted him warmly on his return from Paris, and invited him and any pupils he might have to work in his laboratory.[30] And Freud did so throughout that summer.[31] The relationship doubtless became increasingly strained after Freud's lectures on hypnotism in May and his paper on Charcot in October, but we do not know whether the estrangement was a sudden or a gradual one; the indications point to the latter, and after all, Freud relates how he visited Meynert in his last illness. Furthermore, when he spoke of having nowhere to give his lectures for a whole year, that applied only to the clinical demonstrations, and this difficulty cannot be fairly ascribed to Meynert, since his two assistants had a prior claim on the material over Freud. Actually Freud did lecture in the autumn of the year in question, though only on anatomy, and the lectures were well attended.[32]

In the summer of 1886 his life was confined to the work at the Kassowitz Institute three times a week, to his translations and book-reviewing work, and to his private practice. The latter naturally consisted mainly of neurotic patients, so that the question of therapeutics arose with an urgency research students can evade. Freud's first attempts were made by the orthodox electrotherapy as described in Erb's textbook.[33] It seems odd that he should thus bow to authority when he was already acquainted with Breuer's more promising cathartic method; Charcot's derogatory attitude had certainly influenced him in putting it aside in his mind.[34] The phase, it is true, did not last long. "Unluckily I was soon driven to see that following these instructions was of no help whatever and that what I had taken for an epitome of exact observations was merely the construction of phantasy. The realization that the work of the greatest name in German neuropathology had no more relation to reality than some 'Egyptian' dreambook, such as is sold in cheap bookshops, was painful, but it helped to rid me of another shred of the innocent faith in authority from which I was not yet free." [35] Elsewhere he made the caustic remark that the only reason why he could not agree with Moebius in ascribing the results of electrical treatment to suggestion was that he did not find any results to explain.[36]

Nevertheless, he confined himself for twenty months to electrotherapy, accompanied by various adjuvants, such as baths and massage, and indeed he was still using the latter methods in the early nineties. It was in December 1887 that he turned to hypnotic suggestion,[37] with which he persevered for the next eighteen months. This often brought gratifying successes and replaced the feeling of helplessness by the satisfaction of being admired as a magician. While still a student he had attended a public exhibition given by Hansen, the magnetist, and, from noticing that a hypnotized person had been made deathly pale, become convinced that hypnotic phenomena were genuine. Before going to Paris he had seen hypnotism used therapeutically, and perhaps tried his hand himself at Obersteiner's private sanatorium, where he spent a few weeks in the summer of 1885.[38] Since then he had had ample experience of it at Charcot's clinic. And he had occasionally used it from the beginning of his private practice; he mentioned, for instance, treating by hypnotism an Italian patient who was thrown into a convulsive attack every time she heard the word *Apfel* or *poma*.[39] In Germany Moebius and Heidenhaim were taking hypnotism seriously, but most physicians and psychiatrists still regarded it as hocus-pocus or something worse. Denunciations were frequent and did not lack vigor. Meynert himself, for example, wrote in 1889 that hypnotism "degrades a human being to a creature without will or reason and only hastens his nervous and mental degeneration. . . . It induces an artificial form of alienation." [40] It would be a great misfortune were this "psychical epidemic among doctors" [i] to spread. He added contemptuously, "I am not lacking in sympathetic commiseration for those colleagues who perhaps altruistically, believing in their first successes, stoop to the nursemaid's function of boring people through suggestion into sleep." He had on previous occasions made similar remarks, and Freud had the year before answered him rather sharply, as will presently be related.

Freud championed the cause of hypnotism with his characteristic ardor. He sometimes reviewed books for the *Wiener medizinische Wochenschrift*, e.g., Weir Mitchell's book on *The Treatment of Certain Forms of Neurasthenia and Hysteria* [j] and Obersteiner's book on *Neurology*, both of them in 1887, and in 1889 he wrote an extensive review, seven pages long, on Forel's book on hypnotism. It was Forel who had given him an introduction to Bernheim. The review was a thorough and appreciative exposition of the possibilities of hypnotism. One of the first signs of Freud's advance from physiology to psychology may be perceived in the caustic comment that "Forel's remarks have more to do with the problem of hypnosis than with the contrast between cortical and subcortical and speculations about the widening and narrowing of the cerebral vessels." He used the occasion to rebut, in strong terms, a recent sneer of Meynert's to the effect that he was "only a hypnotist"; he maintained that he was a neurologist, prepared to treat all cases by the methods most appropriate to them. As for Meynert's scathing remarks on hypnotism, quoted above, Freud commented thus: "Most people find it difficult to accept that a scientist, who in some fields of neuropathology has gained much experience and shown acute understanding, [k] should be denied acclaim as an authority in other problems of whatever kind. And certainly the respect for greatness, especially intellectual greatness, belongs to the best qualities of human nature. But it should take second place to the respect for facts. One need not be ashamed to admit it when one sets aside reliance on authority in favor of one's own judgment, gained by study of the facts." [42]

When one considers how provoking, and even abusive, the great Meynert's attitude had been towards Freud in these years, one has to admire the dignity of Freud's response. The rebuke, so impersonally and objectively expressed, had every justification. Altogether, in

[i] The identical phrase which Professor Hoche of Freiburg used twenty years later about psychoanalysis.
[j] He approved of, and used, Weir Mitchell's rest cure.
[k] I.e., Meynert.

the Freud-Meynert case, the animosity would appear to have been much greater on the side of the senior, which was probably not so in the not altogether dissimilar Freud-Breuer relationship.

It is not quite easy to explain the change that had taken place. Earlier Meynert had been friendly enough. He had allowed Freud to work in his laboratory for eighteen months after he had left his psychiatric service, until the time Freud left for Paris. Indeed, two months after Freud had moved to another department Meynert gave him the key of the psychiatric wards (*Narrenzimmer*) with free access to any clinical material he might wish to study there—an unwonted gesture.[43] A month later he wrote: "Meynert has just been making me a grand speech about the thanks the Institute owes me for enriching it with so many valuable preparations, for the technical mastery peculiar to me, and for the promise my researches hold. That naturally pleased me a little, but I don't really like him in that extravagant mood. When he is honest he is uncommonly sparing in his praise. Still it probably doesn't signify anything bad." [44] The last sentence sounds like an effort on Freud's part to stifle a dawning doubt.

When Freud tells us he was excluded from the laboratory on his return from Paris,[1] that probably happened in the following autumn, since he worked there for a time after his return.[45] In the meantime his sins in Meynert's eyes had been mounting and by the end of that year they had become unforgivable.

In the previous chapter we noted signs of jealousy on Meynert's part at Freud's growing superiority in the field of histological anatomy of the brain, where he had hitherto been pre-eminent; a superiority which Freud definitely established in his later work on aphasia. And Freud's visible success had been due to the two methods he had elaborated from hints given by Flechsig, Meynert's chief rival in that field. Possibly he resented Freud's refusing his offer to pass to him the teaching in that subject at the time when Meynert's interest was genuinely moving from it to psychiatry. But the unescapable Freud pursued it in that field too. His "disloyal" adherence to Charcot in place of his old Vienna teacher seems to have angered Meynert, if we may judge from his reaction to Freud's report on his Paris experiences. And then came hypnotism, which acted as a red rag to a bull. And Meynert would have associated Freud's fall from grace here with Leidesdorf, the hypnotizing Superintendent of Obersteiner's sanatorium where Freud had worked and whom Mey-

[1] See p. 234.

nert regarded as a mortal enemy. Heavy drinking, as we well know, is often associated with jealousy, suspicion and hostility. By then towards the end of his life (he died in 1892), Meynert had diffi-culty in retaining any self-control.

Freud found, however, that he was not always able to induce hyp-nosis, either at all or deeply enough for his needs. "With the idea of perfecting my hypnotic technique, I made a journey to Nancy in the summer of 1889 and spent several weeks there. I witnessed the moving spectacle of old Liébault working among the poor women and children of the laboring classes, I was a spectator of Bernheim's astonishing experiments upon his hospital patients, and I received the profoundest impression of the possibility that there could be powerful mental processes which nevertheless remained hidden from the consciousness of man. Thinking it would be instructive, I had persuaded one of my patients to follow me to Nancy. She was a very highly gifted hysteric, a woman of good birth, who had been handed over to me because no one knew what to do with her. By hypnotic influence I had made it possible for her to lead a tolerable existence and I was always able to take her out of the misery of her condition. But she always relapsed again after a short time, and in my igno-rance I attributed this to the fact that her hypnosis had never reached the stage of somnambulism with amnesia. Bernheim now attempted several times to bring this about, but he too failed. He frankly ad-mitted to me that his great therapeutic successes by means of sugges-tion were only achieved in his hospital practice and not with his private patients. I had many stimulating conversations with him, and undertook to translate into German his two works upon sugges-tion and its therapeutic effects." [46]

There is a curious mistake here, since Freud had already pub-lished, the year before, the first of the two books in question (*Hyp-notismus, Suggestion und Psychotherapie*), and had furnished it with an extensive preface. He had even published a long extract from it in the *Wiener medizinische Wochenschrift*.[47] It was in Decem-ber 1887, eighteen months before he visited Bernheim, that he had arranged with the publishers to make the translation.[48]

In the preface to the first Bernheim book (1888) he discussed fully the controversy that had recently arisen between the Nancy School (Bernheim, Liébault, etc.) and the Salpêtrière School in Paris (Charcot).[m] On the whole he defended the latter. What stirred

■ An English translation of this has appeared.[49]

him especially was that, if phenomena of hypnosis could be shown to be produced by suggestions on the part of a physician, then the critics might claim the same to be true for the symptomatology of hysteria. (Bernheim himself was rather inclined to do so, as Babinski did emphatically twenty years later.[n]) Then we should lose all sense of the regular psychological laws in that affection to which Freud attached the greatest value. He gave excellent arguments to show that this cannot be so with hysteria: the regularity of the descriptions in different countries and different ages alone prove the point.

As to hypnosis, he considered that most of the phenomena are purely psychological, though some, e.g., neuromuscular hyperexcitability, appear to be physiological. In discussing this anomaly he made the penetrating observation that direct suggestions from the physician are to be distinguished from more indirect ones, which are rather phenomena of autosuggestion and depend on the particular nervous excitability of the individual.

He used the occasion to hit out again rather sharply at Meynert, whose attitude to hypnotism was mentioned earlier. In a private letter of August 29, 1888, he wrote: "In criticizing Meynert, who in his accustomed impudent and malicious manner has been making authoritative pronouncements on a topic of which he knows nothing, I have had to express myself with moderation, since all my friends have urged me to do so. Even so, what I have written seems to them hazardous. I have belled the cat." [50]

The monotony of repeating suggestions began before long to bore Freud. Four years later he trenchantly expressed his dissatisfaction with the method in the following words: "Neither the doctor nor the patient can tolerate indefinitely the contradiction between the decisive denial of the disorder in suggestion and the necessary recognition of it away from suggestion." [51]

He felt sure there were many secrets hidden behind the manifest symptoms, and his restless imagination burned to penetrate them. He wrote later that when using hypnotism he had from the first employed it not only for giving therapeutic suggestions but also for the

[n] Apropos Babinski, Dr. Ludwig Jekels tells me that when he read a paper on psychoanalysis before the Neurological Congress in Warsaw in 1918, Babinski evinced great interest and begged him to come to Paris so that he could learn more about the subject. Jekels consulted Freud on the matter. Freud asked how old Babinski was, and on being told he was of the same age as himself burst out laughing, saying, "As old as I am, and yet you expect him to give up his theory in favor of mine!"

purpose of tracing back the history of the symptom, i.e., Breuer's cathartic method.[52] Some doubt on the accuracy of his memory is perhaps permissible here. The evidence suggests at all events that any such investigations were rather perfunctory in the beginning. In the *Studies in Hysteria* he says that the first case in which he employed the cathartic method was that of Frau Emmy v.N., whose treatment he began on May 1, 1889, eighteen months after he had been using hypnotism. In this first attempt, using deep somnambulism, one would not expect any very penetrating exploration to have taken place, and in fact Freud seems to have relied in the treatment very much on direct therapeutic suggestion, and he combined it, as usual, with massage, baths, and rest. He learned in this case that the reason why so many beneficial effects of hypnotic suggestion are transitory is that they are brought about by the patient in order to please the physician, and hence are apt to fade when contact is withdrawn. One notes further that Freud was still at that time completely under the influence of Charcot's teaching about the importance of traumas in the symptomatology of hysteria. If the patient's brother had thrown a toad at her in childhood, that would apparently suffice to account for the permanent phobia of such creatures. The idea of personal thoughts (wishes) of an unacceptable nature is recorded for the first time three years later.

In 1892 there was a paper by Freud reporting a successful cure by means of hypnotism.[53] The case was that of a woman who, although intensely desirous of feeding her child at the breast, was prevented from doing so by various hysterical symptoms, vomiting, anorexia nervosa, insomnia, and agitation. Two treatments consisting of suggestion during hypnosis sufficed to remove all the obstructive symptoms, and just the same thing happened after the birth of another child a year later. Freud made some rather lengthy comments on the case. They are of great interest as enabling us to gauge the rate of progress in the understanding of the problems of hysteria. From this point of view it must be said that the paper displays little insight compared with the immense advances he was to make in the next two or three years; this was probably the reason why Freud did not include it in his *Sammlung kleiner Schriften* (Collection of Small Papers). It is mainly concerned with the existence of what he called "antithetic ideas" that interfere with conscious intentions. He contrasted interestingly their mode of action in neurasthenia and hysteria respectively. With the former the subject is aware of the conflict, it weakens his will power, but he somehow

Sigmund Freud, age eight, with father, Jakob Freud, in 1864.

*Freud's birthplace in Freiberg, Austria
(now Príbor, Czechoslovakia).*

Martha Bernays and Sigmund Freud in 1885.
The following year they were married.

Sigmund Freud, wife and daughter Anna in
1898.

Martha Bernays in 1883, age twenty-two. Freud became engaged to her the previous year.

Sigmund Freud in 1891, age thirty-five.

Sigmund Freud,
age twelve.

Sigmund Freud, age sixteen, with mother,
Amalie Nathansohn Freud, in 1872.

The lithograph of Charcot in his clinic.
A copy was brought back from Paris by Freud, who studied with Charcot
in 1885 and 1886 (Pages 184 to 188).

Josef Breuer in 1897, age fifty-five.
He was the co-author with Freud of Studies in Hysteria,
published in 1895. Breuer's famous case, Fraulein Anna
O., was one of the starting points that led to
psychoanalysis (Chapter XI).

manages to carry out the intention. Characteristic of hysteria is the subject's unawareness of the opposition, but he finds his will quite thwarted, as in the present case, by some bodily disturbance produced by the antithetic ideas. Freud instituted no inquiry into what these ideas are or why there should exist at all a counterwill interfering with conscious intentions. Assuming their existence, all he had to say was that they manifest themselves strongly or gain the upper hand in moments of excitement or exhaustion. The exhaustion weakens the "primary consciousness" (the ego) much more than it does the antithetic ideas alien and opposed to it, ideas which are often entirely dissociated from it. There is a hint here of Breuer's teaching that neurotic symptoms originate only in a particular mental state (his "hypnoid condition"), which Freud described simply as a state of exhaustion.

We now come to the all-important matter of the transition from the cathartic method to the "free association" method, from which psychoanalysis dates. It was through devising the new method that Freud was enabled to penetrate into the previously unknown realm of the unconscious proper and to make the profound discoveries with which his name is imperishably associated. The devising of this method was one of the two great deeds of Freud's scientific life, the other being his self-analysis through which he learned to explore the child's early sexual life, including the famous Oedipus complex.

The orthodox way for a great genius to make an important discovery or invention is by a lightninglike flash of intuition, and the history of science abounds in dramatic accounts of such happenings. It may be disappointing to those who exult in such chronicles, but we have to record that Freud's story is quite otherwise. Although he had a swift enough intuition, one which functioned freely in his mature years, there is good reason to think that in the years we have so far been considering, particularly between 1875 and 1892, his development was slow and laborious. Hard painful progress seems rather to have been his characteristic way of advance. Increasing insight was won only through arduous work. He had been impressed by Charcot's description of his way of working—to stare at the facts over and over again until they spoke to him;[54] it corresponded with something in Freud's own attitude. The nineties, it is true, once he had got well under way, were otherwise, and one piece of insight after another followed in rapid succession in what was his most creative period. There moods and intuition were added to arduous work and hard thinking, and they became even more important than these. A change in his personality, one of several in his life, seems to have come over him in the early nineties, and in the summer of 1895, three months after the *Studies* were published, we find Breuer writing to their friend Fliess: "Freud's intellect is soaring at its highest. I gaze after him as a hen at a hawk." [55, o]

There can be no exact date for the discovery of the "free association" method. All we can say is that it evolved very gradually between 1892 and 1895, becoming steadily refined and purified from the adjuvants—hypnosis, suggestion, pressing, and questioning—that accompanied it at its inception. But it is possible to discern some of the stages through which this evolution passed, and an attempt will be made to indicate them.

In the *Studies in Hysteria* two cases are recorded from the year 1892. The investigation of them is on quite a different level from that of the Frau Emmy case mentioned above, which had been conducted three years earlier. Freud, of course, had had a considerable experience of the cathartic method in those years. But many of his patients he had been unable to hypnotize, at all events as deeply as he then thought necessary, and so they would be regarded as unsuitable for the cathartic method.

This was one of the motives that made him cast around for some other method where one would not be dependent on the hypnotizability of the patient. The other was his growing insight into the nature of hypnotism itself. He had learned that—as, for example, in the case of Frau Emmy mentioned earlier—the therapeutic improvement was dependent on the personal relationship between patient and physician, and that it often disappeared when this was dissolved. One day a patient suddenly flung her arms around his neck, an unexpected contretemps fortunately remedied by the entrance of a servant.[57] From then on he understood that the peculiar relationship so effective therapeutically had an erotic basis, whether concealed or overt; twenty years later he remarked that transference phenomena had always seemed to him an impregnable proof of the sexual origin of the neuroses.[58] Unlike the scared Breuer on a similar occasion, Freud regarded the problem as one of general

---

o Fliess evidently quoted this to Freud, since only a month later he is explaining to Fliess that he cannot meet him in Oberhof because he will be in Venice just at that time and adds elliptically, "Despite Breuer I am not a bird." [56] Where Breuer had come across Sir Boyle Roche's bull is **not known.**

scientific interest, but he was all the more desirous of freeing himself from the mask of hypnotism. He explained years later how this conceals the important phenomena of resistance and transference, the essential features of psychoanalytical practice and theory.[59] This was assuredly his chief motive for discarding hypnotism, the decisive transition from Breuer's cathartic method to the psychoanalytic one.

In a case refractory to hypnotism, that of Frl. Elisabeth von R. whose treatment he undertook in the autumn of 1892, he was nevertheless determined to proceed. What encouraged him in the apparently hopeless situation was remembering a remark of Bernheim's to the effect that things experienced in hypnosis were only apparently forgotten afterwards and that they could at any time be brought into recollection if only the physician insisted forcibly enough that the patient knew them. Freud divined that this should equally be true for the forgotten memories in hysteria. He therefore tried what he called a "concentration" technique, "one which I later elaborated into a method." [60] The case of Frl. Elisabeth was the first one where he dispensed with hypnotism and used the new technique; it was also, which is of interest, the first one where he felt satisfied with the completeness of what he termed the "psychical analysis."

This was the method. The patient, lying down with closed eyes, was asked to concentrate her attention on a particular symptom and to try to recall any memories that might throw light on its origin. When no progress was being made Freud would press her forehead with his hand and assure her that then some thoughts or memories would indubitably come to her. Sometimes in spite of that nothing would seem to happen even when the pressure of the hand was repeated. Then, perhaps on the fourth attempt, the patient would bring out what had occurred to her mind, but with the comment: "I could have told you that the first time, but I didn't think it was what you wanted." Such experiences confirmed his confidence in the device, which indeed seemed to him infallible. They also made him give the strict injunction to ignore all censorship and to express every thought even if she considered it to be irrelevant, unimportant, or too unpleasant. This was the first step towards the later free association method.

Freud was still given to urging, pressing, and questioning, which he felt to be hard but necessary work. On one historic occasion, however, the patient, Frl. Elisabeth, reproved him for interrupting her flow of thought by his questions.[61] He took the hint, and thus made another step towards free association.[P]

Once started, the procedure went on becoming freer, but only by degrees. Freud would still use hypnotism wherever possible, if only in certain stages of the treatment, and did not finally renounce it as a therapeutic measure until 1896, four years after he had proved the possibility of doing so.[62] Then, the more confidence he acquired in the belief that relaxing conscious censoring would inevitably lead to the important memories, the less need had he to urge, press, or direct the patient's thoughts. Urging was therefore given up; so was pressing on the forehead. Closing the eyes is still advocated in *The Interpretation of Dreams* (1900),[63] though perhaps only for self-analysis; in 1904 he stated that this also is not necessary.[64] The only relic of the old hypnosis period that remained was the patient's reclining on the couch, and this is still found to be desirable in the vast majority of cases. For a long time, however, he continued to use the symptoms as starting points, and this habit was reinforced when it became a question of analyzing dreams, since here one mostly has to start from point after point in the dream.

His chapter on Psychotherapy in the *Studies* (1895) is a sufficient approximation to the future free association method for it to be generally regarded as the inception of the psychoanalytic method. However, there he still called his method "Breuer's cathartic method," though he often talked of the "psychical analysis." It is in this chapter that occurs the unassuming and yet heroic phrase: "Much is won if we succeed in transforming hysterical misery into common unhappiness." [65]

The term "psychoanalysis" was first employed in a paper published in French on March 30, 1896;[66] it occurs in German for the first time on May 15, 1896;[67] both papers had been sent off on the same day (February 5).[68] On July 7, 1897, he observed to Fliess that his technique was beginning to follow a certain path of its own as if that was the natural one. This autonomous course of a psychoanalysis, without the former starting-points, became one of its striking features. A year later (1898) he spoke of the improvements in the method that give him full confidence in it.[69] By then I think one may say that the free association method had become really free, though subsequent improvements in it were continuous.

[P] One of the countless examples of a patient's furthering the physician's work; the "chimney sweeping" in her autohypnosis (i.e., Breuer's cathartic method) was really a discovery of Frl. Anna O.

At first sight the step might seem a curious one to have taken; it meant displacing a systematic and purposeful search with a known aim in view by an apparently blind and uncontrolled meandering.

Since this was a most decisive step in Freud's scientific life, the one from which all his discoveries emanated, one is naturally interested in how it came to be made and what motives were impelling him. Four considerations would appear to be germane here. We have insisted that it was a gradual process, not at all a decision of the moment. Some patients on being asked to revive their memories of the circumstances in which their symptoms began would, especially when in a relaxed mental state, let their thoughts wander on in a diffuse fashion. Freud had learned not to interrupt the flow, as most doctors would have done, and in this attitude was aided by an unusual capacity for patience and by something passive in his nature which was glad to renounce vehement checking or interfering with the patient's thoughts. It was a decided change from the early pressing and urging.

Then Freud was deeply imbued with the principles of causality and determinism,[q] so pronounced in the Helmholtz school that had dominated his early scientific discipline. Instead of dismissing the wandering associations as accidental, unconnected, and meaningless, as others might have done, he felt intuitively that there must be some definite agency, even if not evident, guiding and determining the course of those thoughts. He would be confirmed in this by noting that every now and then a thought or memory would emerge that would reveal the meaning of the preceding train.

Early in his practice he had detected an unmistakable unwillingness on the part of his patients to disclose memories that were painful or unwelcome to them. This opposition he termed "resistance," and he soon connected it with the "repression" that had led to certain memories being replaced by symptoms. It could not have been very difficult to surmise that the roundabout meanderings were an expression of this resistance, an attempt to postpone the emergence of the significant memory, and yet they followed a route ultimately connected with it. This would justify his patience in following the trains of thought with the closest attention and in the greatest detail.

More recondite, and perhaps more instructive, than the foregoing considerations is the following one. When Freud put his trust in the validity of free associations he said he was "following an obscure in-

[q] He himself attached great importance to these factors.[70]

tuition." [71, r] We have now a clue to the source of this interesting intuition. It happens that an author, Ludwig Börne by name, had in 1823 written an essay with the arresting title, "The Art of Becoming an Original Writer in Three Days." It concludes with the words: "Here follows the practical prescription I promised. Take a few sheets of paper and for three days in succession write down, without any falsification or hypocrisy, everything that comes into your head. Write what you think of yourself, of your women, of the Turkish war, of Goethe, of the Fonk criminal case, of the Last Judgment, of those senior to you in authority—and when the three days are over you will be amazed at what novel and startling thoughts have welled up in you. That is the art of becoming an original writer in three days." [s]

Freud relates that Börne had been a favorite author of his, the first one he had been absorbed in. When he was fourteen years old he had been given a present of his collected works,[72] and they were the only books he preserved from his adolescent years. He recollected half a century later many passages from the volume in which the essay in question is to be found, though not the actual lines quoted above.[73] Still we may be sure that Börne's startling proposal had sunk into Freud's mind and played its part twenty years later in stimulating him to give his patients' thoughts free play.

It is comprehensible that Börne should have meant so much to the adolescent Freud. He was a very remarkable man, with an outlook on life that must have been very sympathetic to Freud, and not only in his youth. Ludwig Börne (1786-1837), who had in 1818 adopted this name in place of his own (Baruch Löb), was an idealist, a fighter for freedom, honesty, justice, and sincerity, and always opposed to oppression. He played a part in Germany's *Freiheitskrieg* (War of Liberation) against Napoleon, but attacked the reactionary regimes that followed. He lived for a time in Paris where he knew the young Heine, whose flippant cynicism he found little to his liking. The graves of Börne and Heine were the only two Freud looked for when he visited Père Lachaise.

The following passages from his writings may give some idea of

---

r His more expressive phrase *"einer dunklen Ahnung folgend"* loses in translation.
s Schiller, Garth Wilkinson, and probably others have prescribed a similar plan, also for the purpose of obtaining ideas for literary application, but Freud had not read any of these passages which have subsequently been unearthed. So did Sir Francis Galton.[71†]

the man. "Out of a million men a thousand do some thinking, and of the thousand one thinks originally." "To be creative one must be alone, away from people, from books, and as far as possible from memories. The true act of self-education lies in making oneself unwitting." "The heart is the source at which to drink a fresh draught; the mind is only a stream." "Sincerity is the source of all genius, and man would be more intelligent were he only better. And here follows . . ." (the quotation on free association given earlier).[74]

It is the rarest event—if it ever happens at all—for an "original" idea to be purely spontaneous in origin, with no precursors of any kind. One reason why the present book is being written is in the hope of elucidating something of the processes in Freud's mind, and the experiences in his life, that culminated in his discoveries. The two examples of sexual factors in the neuroses, presently to be narrated, and that of "free association" are striking examples of the combination of influences that precede the emergence of significant ideas. On the other hand, the ideas of "repression" and "resistance" were simple theoretical inferences drawn from innumerable direct observations. As Freud said: "If anyone should seek to regard the theory of repression and of resistance as assumptions instead of as results following from psychoanalysis, I should oppose him most emphatically." [75] He also stated: "The doctrine of repression quite certainly came to me independently of any other source; I know of no outside impression which might have suggested it to me." [76] This is doubtless true, but it has been shown that ideas not entirely dissimilar to that of "defense" and "repression" are to be found in the field of science with which Freud had been deeply concerned, and he was a voracious reader.[t]

The first thing Freud observed in his endeavor to trace back the patient's memories was that they did not stop at the starting point of the symptom, or even at the unpleasant "traumatic event" which would seem to be its cause, but instead insisted on going further back in a continuous series. Freud's scientific upbringing made him regard this causative chain as a legitimate connection even if the effectiveness of the apparent factors was at first not plain. The memories kept going back and back, into childhood itself, and Freud soon saw that here was some explanation of the old controversy concerning the importance of inherited disposition on the one hand and of acquired (traumatic) factors on the other. This was a matter over which his own opinion had wavered a good deal. In dis-

[t] See p. 174.

cussing the Frau Emmy case (1889) he stated that no hysteria is possible without a hereditary predisposition,[77] whereas three years later, in discussing that of Katherina, and also in a footnote to his translation of Charcot's *Poliklinische Vorträge*,[78] he gave his opinion that there is an acquired hysteria with no such predisposition.[79] Now he was realizing that early experiences, with or without heredity combined, constitute the predisposition.

A traumatic event unmistakably concerned in the genesis of a symptom, but seemingly quite banal in itself, was found to produce its effects only if it had become associated with some such earlier mental experience (or attitude) which was neither traumatic nor pathogenic: this was the "predisposition" necessary for the later traumatic event to become pathogenic. This manner of reacting to a later event according to the early associations he termed "regression," and it was at once clear to him that it was a noteworthy discovery.

He also gradually noticed that a remarkable number of the significant memories concerned sexual experiences, though he was not at first in a position to draw any general conclusions from this fact. It was one for which he was not prepared and which astonished him. His attention being once aroused in this direction, however, he began to make deliberate inquiries into the sexual life of his patients, a habit which, as he soon found, had a deleterious effect on his practice.

Increasing accumulation of evidence about the significant part that sexual factors play in the neuroses strengthened some intuition in Freud that he had lighted on an important theme. At first he preened himself on a purely spontaneous discovery of his own, but, much later, reflection reminded him of three curious experiences which had doubtless influenced and guided his thoughts without his being at all aware of the process. In 1914 he gave a vivid description of the experiences in question, from which the essential points may be abstracted here.[80] The first one must be dated very early in his career as a "young hospital doctor," because he says that the second, Charcot, one occurred "some years later"; that would make the former between 1881 and 1883. It was Breuer who remarked to him concerning some neurotic behavior of a patient that such matters were always connected with secrets of the marriage bed. The next was an explanation he heard Charcot deliver very emphatically to his assistant Brouardel to the effect that certain nervous disorders are always a question of *"la chose génitale."* The third experience, in 1886, concerned the gynecologist Chrobak, whom Freud considered to be "perhaps the most distinguished of the Viennese physicians." Wittels relates of him that he had a large signboard erected in the lecture room bearing the words *"Primum est non nocere."* [81, u] On asking Freud to take charge of a patient with a severe anxiety, whose husband was quite impotent, he added that the only cure for it could not be prescribed: repeated doses of a normal penis.[v]

Freud relates that two of these physicians subsequently denied having made those remarks, and he surmises that probably the third one, Charcot, would have also if an opportunity had occurred for asking him. He added, very truly, that there is a vast difference between a casual flash of intuition, often subsequently forgotten, and taking an idea seriously, working through all the complexities surrounding it, and winning for it general acceptance— the difference between a superficial flirtation and a regular marriage with all its obligations and difficulties.

Freud himself was somewhat shocked by these apparently cynical remarks, did not take them seriously, and dismissed the thought of them from his mind. How thoroughly he blotted out the memory of them for many years is illustrated by the following passage from an important paper written in 1896; "I will only remark that in my case at least there was no preconceived opinion which led me to single out the sexual factor in the etiology of hysteria. The two investigators as whose pupil I began my work on the subject, Charcot and Breuer, emphatically had no such presupposition; in fact they had a personal disinclination to it which I originally shared." [83]

Freud was now finding himself in increasing opposition to his "respectable" colleagues and seniors. There was the male hysteria and the importance of trauma in 1886, the serious way in which he regarded hysteria, followed by the growing interest in the still more suspect topic of hypnotism, and before long his appreciation of sexual factors in the neuroses; the extensive experience of the latter which he quotes in his paper on anxiety neurosis (1895) shows that this appreciation must have begun several years earlier. His response to the situation was rather a defiant one. He felt he was leading a crusade of revolution against the accepted conventions of medicine, or at all events his seniors in Vienna, and he accepted his mission wholeheartedly. His master Brücke had done the same in

[u] "The supreme commandment is: Do not harm."
[v] This was in May, 1886.[82]

helping his colleagues of the Helmholtz school to overthrow *Natur-philosophie*, and he had shown the same tenacious adherence to new ideas as Freud was to.

Side by side with this, however, there was still enough left of the youthful need of support and dependence to make him welcome the possibility of joining forces with some other colleague in a more stable position than his own. The first man to be thought of was naturally Breuer; he who had first introduced him to the field of hysteria, had made important discoveries in it, and who had not hesitated to use hypnotism at a time when to do so was looked at decidedly askance. It was therefore inevitable that he should turn to him for collaboration and support.

In the late eighties, and still more in the early nineties, Freud kept trying to revive Breuer's interest in the problems of hysteria or to induce him at least to give to the world the discovery his patient, Frl. Anna O., had made. In this endeavor he met with strong resistance, the reason for which he could not at first understand. Although Breuer was much his senior in rank, and fourteen years older, it was the younger man who—for the first time—was entirely taking the leading part. It gradually dawned on Freud that Breuer's reluctance was connected with his disturbing experience with Frl. Anna O. related earlier in this chapter. So Freud told him of his own experience of a female patient suddenly flinging her arms round his neck in a transport of affection, and he explained to him his reasons for regarding such untoward occurrences as part of the transference phenomena characteristic of certain types of hysteria. This seems to have had a calming effect on Breuer, who evidently had taken his own experience of the kind more personally and perhaps even reproached himself for indiscretion in the handling of his patient. At all events Freud ultimately secured Breuer's cooperation, it being understood that the theme of sexuality was to be kept in the background. Freud's remark had evidently made a deep impression, since when they were preparing the *Studies* together, Breuer said apropos of the transference phenomenon, "I believe that is the most important thing we both have to make known to the world." [84]

They first published together in the *Neurologisches Centralblatt*, in January 1893, a paper entitled "The Psychical Mechanism of Hysterical Phenomena," one which had historical significance.[w] We shall return to it later. It was the year after both Brücke and Mey-

[w] Only three months later F. W. H. Myers gave an account of it in London which was published in June 1893! [85]

nert had died; Freud had already acquired a more contemporary supporter. Breuer had at last consented to cooperate, in June 1892, and in a letter to Fliess dated December 18, 1892, Freud mentions that to get him to do so "had cost struggles enough." [86] The two men often cooperated in the treatment of hysterical patients. Recently there had been a specially interesting case of the kind, that of Frau Cäcilie; it was this circumstance that won Breuer's final consent to their writing their joint paper.[87] Incidentally, Freud, who gives a few abstracts from it, says it was his most instructive case, but that motives of professional discretion prevented his publishing it; we have doubtless lost a great deal thereby.

Two preliminary drafts of that paper have been published.[88] Breuer had preserved them, and in 1909 he presented them to Freud as a memento. The first is a sketched outline Freud had sent him in June 1892.[89] The second is a fuller draft composed by both, but in Freud's handwriting; it is dated "end of November 1892." A week or so after the paper was published Freud lectured on it before the *Wiener medizinische Verein* (Vienna Medical Society).[90]

The authors remarked that the nearest approach to their ideas they had found was in some writings by Benedikt.[91] One supposes the remark came from Breuer, since it was only he who subsequently referred to him.[92] Benedikt did not return the compliment. His opinion about the "Preliminary Communication" was that the authors had been very lucky to find cases where the traumatic experiences were recalled during hypnosis, a chance that might not recur.[93]

Nevertheless Benedikt was a man of parts, about whom the following anecdotes are perhaps worth recording. He had been a pupil of the famous Skoda, long, long before. When his turn came to teach, his first pupil was Ernst Brücke (!), whom he instructed in Cauchy's wave theory. With Heidenhain and a few others, he was one of the early defenders of hypnotism, but when he tried to apply it in the Vienna General Hospital, Oppolzer's Assistant warned him against what was then called "animal magnetism." That Assistant was Josef Breuer! Then when Hansen, the "magnetist" who first aroused Freud's interest in hypnotism, was giving his public performances, Benedikt interviewed him and asked him if he had ever found a hypnotized subject using a language unknown to him. "Yes, in South Africa an English officer once sang songs in a language that neither he (the officer) nor anyone else understood." Whereupon Benedikt pontifically announced, "Those songs were in Welsh." The astonished Hansen asked how he knew that and was still more astonished at Benedikt's reply: "I have the gift of communication at great distances, and I can easily reach South Africa."

The joint paper was followed two years later by the well-known book, the *Studies on Hysteria* (1895), from which it is customary to date the beginnings of psychoanalysis. It consists first of a reprint of the joint paper just mentioned, then five case histories, a theoretical essay by Breuer, and a concluding chapter on psychotherapy by Freud. From Freud's correspondence one gathers that a great deal of the book was written by the middle of 1894—in a letter of May 21, 1894, he mentioned that he was just writing the last of the case histories—but he wrote the important final chapter hurriedly only in March 1895, a month before the date of the preface. The book duly appeared in the middle of May.

The first case history, by Breuer, is that of Frl. Anna O., the patient who invented the cathartic method. The remaining four are by Freud. The first and last of these, those of Frau Emmy and Frl. Elisabeth respectively, have already been mentioned. The second was that of an English governess in Vienna, Miss Lucy, whose symptoms turned out to depend on the repression of a forbidden attachment to her employer. It was in the discussion of this case (1892) that he first clearly described how the active process of repressing[x] an incompatible idea results in the substitution of a somatic innervation (conversion).[94] This was quite a different matter from passively suffering a trauma, a misfortune inflicted on one. The remaining case history described a pathetic story of a girl of eighteen, Katherina, whom Freud encountered in an inn in the High Alps. Learning he was a doctor, she appealed to him to aid her, since she suffered severely from anxiety symptoms. In a single interview he was able to discover the genesis of her troubles, and in all probability to relieve her.

The book was not well received in the medical world.[y] A very antagonistic review by the famous German neurologist, Strümpell, seems to have specially discouraged Breuer, when Freud says he himself was able to laugh at the lack of comprehension it displayed.

[x] He uses here already the word *Verdrängung*.
[y] One exception was a full and favorable review by Mitchell Clarke in *Brain*,[95] which, incidentally, gave the present writer a few years later the first inkling of Freud's psychopathological work; his neurological work had been previously familiar to him.

Two years later another English writer, no less a person than Havelock Ellis, gave in a paper on hysteria an appreciative account of the Breuer and Freud book and also of Freud's other writings on the subject.[96]

"Breuer's self-confidence and powers of resistance were not developed as fully as the rest of his mental organization." [97]

In view of Bleuler's later (temporary) association with psychoanalysis, it is interesting to remark how he treats the *Studies* in a review he wrote for the *Münchner medizinische Wochenschrift*. His characteristic ambivalency is displayed at once. After stating his suspicion that the therapeutic results were due to suggestion rather than to catharsis, he goes on to say, "Be that as it may, the factual account the book gives opens a quite new vista into the mechanism of the mind and makes one of the most important contributions of the past years to the field of normal (*sic*) or pathological psychology." [98]

A good deal of notice was taken of the book in various quarters, and not only in medical ones. One of the reviews was so remarkable in its perspicacity and foresight that it deserves remembrance. It appeared in the *Neue Freie Presse*, the leading daily newspaper of Vienna, on December 2, 1895, and was entitled "Surgery of the Soul" (*Seelenchirurgie*). Its author was Alfred von Bergner, Professor of the History of Literature in the University and Director of the Imperial Theater in Vienna, who was a poet, literary historian, and dramatic critic. He followed the case histories with admiration and understanding, and then added the significant prediction: "We dimly conceive the idea that it may one day become possible to approach the innermost secret of human personality. . . . The theory itself," he continued, "is in fact nothing but the kind of psychology used by poets." He went on to illustrate this thesis from the writings of Shakespeare and to describe Lady Macbeth's distress in terms of a "defense neurosis."

Eight hundred copies of the *Studies* were printed, and at the end of thirteen years 626 of them had been sold. The authors received 425 gulden between them ($85 each).

There had been scientific divergencies in the theory of hysteria between the two co-workers, but it was neither they nor the discouraging reception of their work that led to their separation at that point, the cooperation came to an end in the summer of 1894. This was brought about by Breuer's unwillingness to follow Freud in his investigation of his patients' sexual life, or rather, in the far-reaching conclusions Freud was drawing from it. That disturbances in the sexual life were the *essential* factor in the etiology of both neuroses and psychoneuroses was a doctrine Breuer could not easily stomach. Nor was he alone in that!

Oddly enough, however, he wavered from one side to the other. He never, it is true, subscribed to the view that sexual disturbances were the invariable and specific causes of neurotic affections, but he went a very long way in this direction. In the chapter on "Theory," for example, which he contributed to the *Studies in Hysteria*, the following passages occur: "The sexual instinct is certainly the most powerful source of lasting increases in excitation (and, as such, of the neuroses). . . ." [99] "That such conflict between incompatible ideas has a pathogenic effect is a matter of daily experience. It is mostly a matter of ideas and processes belonging to the sexual life." [100] "This conclusion (about the disposition to hysteria) implies in itself that sexuality is one of the great components of hysteria. We shall see, however, that the part it plays is still greater by far, and that it cooperates in the most diverse ways in constituting the disease. . . ." [101] "The greater number and the most important of the repressed ideas that lead to (hysterical) conversion have a sexual content." [102] The month that the *Studies* appeared Freud wrote to his friend Fliess: "You would hardly recognize Breuer. Once again one cannot help liking him without reservation. . . . He is entirely converted to my sexuality theory. That is quite a different fellow from what we have been used to." [103] Again, only a few months later at a meeting of the *Doktorenkollegium* (College of Physicians) he spoke warmly in favor of Freud's work and expressed himself in agreement with his views on sexual etiology.[104] When Freud thanked him for this afterwards, however, he turned away with the words: "I don't believe a word of it." The relationship naturally cooled, further cooperation was not possible, and the personal friendship of twenty years became a distant one.

Freud seems to have felt that fundamentally Breuer agreed with him, despite the timid ambivalence he displayed, since, in a paper published in 1896, he wrote: "Breuer and I have in earlier communications maintained that the psychical traumas (in hysteria) are concerned with the sexual life." [105] I would make the purely personal guess that Breuer's acceptance referred rather to the later ages, and what he baulked at was Freud's views concerning the incestuous seduction of children; but I have no authority for this suggestion.

The scientific differences alone cannot account for the bitterness with which Freud wrote about Breuer in the unpublished Fliess correspondence of the nineties. When one recollects what Breuer had meant to him in the eighties, his generosity to Freud, his understanding sympathy, and the combination of cheerfulness and intellectual stimulation that radiated from him, the change later is indeed startling. Where previously no word of criticism for the perfect Breuer could be found, now one hears no more of his good qualities, only of the irritating effect his presence had on Freud. The change had not, of course, been a sudden one. Although he complained later of the trouble it had cost him to induce Breuer to collaborate in publication, he was still on friendly enough terms with him in April 1894 to consult him about his health. But after that summer they never collaborated again. The main reversal in Freud's feeling came in the spring of 1896, a date which coincides with the onset of the more passionate phase of his relations with Fliess. In February he wrote to the latter that it was impossible to get on any longer with Breuer,[106] though only a week later he admitted that it was painful to think that Breuer was so entirely out of his life.[107] A year later he was glad he saw no more of him; the very sight would make him inclined to emigrate.[108] These are strong words, and there are stronger ones which need not be reproduced. They go much beyond the actual complaints Freud formulates. Breuer, so it would appear, had certain characteristics which were particularly antipathetic to Freud's nature. One was a weakness in his personality that made it hard for him ever to take a definite stand on any question. The other was a pettifogging kind of censoriousness which would induce him to mar any appreciation or praise by searching out a small point open to criticism—an attitude very alien to Freud's open-hearted and generous spirit.

In just these years Freud was in his most revolutionary stage, both intellectually and emotionally. The boycotting to which he was subjected induced in him a response of defiant rebelliousness. And when he was most in need of a companion with whom to share this, the one man who had the intellectual knowledge for the purpose and who had been the one to start him on his path only damped his ardor and withdrew from the fight.

The matter, however, was still more personal. It is plain that Freud now resented the burden of the old debt of gratitude he owed Breuer, one that could in part be estimated in the concrete terms of money. Early in 1898 he made the first attempt to repay an installment of this. Breuer, who was probably loath to accept what he must long have regarded as a gift, wanted to set off against it an amount he considered Freud should be paid for medical atten tion on a relative of his. Freud seems to have interpreted this as an endeavor to retain the old tutelage,[yt] and bitterly resented Breuer's response. Two years later he announced to Fliess that he would love to break altogether with Breuer, but was unable to because of the old money debt.[109]

And in all this sad story one has to remember Freud's confessed need for periodic experiences of intense love and hate, one which his self-analysis had not yet softened.

The sexual investigations which caused so much trouble were of two kinds. They began through observing the frequency with which analysis of hysterical symptoms (and subsequently of obsessional ones) led back to painful sexual experiences, many of which could be called traumatic. Impressed by the importance of this factor in the classical types of psychoneurosis, Freud wondered what part it might play in the other forms of neurotic trouble—forms which were then loosely grouped under the term of "neurasthenia."

The concept of the latter condition, introduced by Beard thirty years previously,[110] had been a very wide one indeed, and Freud considered that he could effect a nosological clarification by studying, not only the symptomatology of various cases, but also their specific etiological factors. He gave a full description of the symptoms characteristic of what he proposed to call "anxiety neurosis," [z] together with the features distinguishing it from neurasthenia on the one hand and hysterical phobias on the other. His conclusions on this topic were reached by 1893 or earlier; in a private letter late in 1892 he stated: "No neurasthenia or analogous neurosis exists without a disturbance in the sexual function," [112] and in one of February 1893 he gave a full description of the anxiety neurosis. They were formulated early in 1894[113] and published in a paper that appeared in January 1895, a few months before the *Studies in Hysteria*. It was his first independent entry into the field of psychopathology.

What Freud maintained as the result of his observations was that, whenever a thorough investigation of the patient could be carried out, sexual etiological factors would be found which were different in the two conditions; this was his justification for separating them. With neurasthenia there was always an inadequate relief of sexual tension, mostly by some form of autoerotic functioning; as early

[yt] See p. 145.
[z] A couple of years later he remarked that the designation did not altogether please him.

as 1892 he had asserted that "sexual disturbances constitute the sole indispensable cause of neurasthenia." [114] With the anxiety neurosis,[aa] on the other hand, there was no relief of an unbearable amount of sexual excitation, the commonest examples of which were the frustration accompanying the practice of coitus interruptus and that involved in the engagement of a chaste, but passionate couple.

Loewenfeld of Munich, who had written extensive works in the field of the psychoneuroses, published at once an attack on these conclusions, criticizing the interpretation Freud had drawn from the clinical observations. It was easy to answer the objections raised, and Freud promptly did so in a courteous but decisive fashion by citing the principles of etiology accepted elsewhere in medicine. For instance, with tuberculosis we have: (1) predisposition, hereditary or otherwise; (2) Koch's bacillus, the *specific* factor in the absence of which the disease cannot occur, but which might be present without the disease if the dose were a small one; and (3) auxiliary factors such as influenza, etc. With the anxiety neurosis there is a similar series, the outbreak of the complaint depending on a due summation of the factors, provided that the specific sexual one is operative.

This second paper is noteworthy in being the only direct polemical reply Freud ever made to critics in his life. He was constitutionally very averse to "scientific" polemics. This went so far as disliking even discussions in a scientific meeting, doubting their value, and later he always urged that psychoanalytical congresses should be confined to the reading of papers—followed by reflection, testing, and perhaps private discussion. The motive for writing he gave in his reply to Loewenfeld was his unwillingness to let pass the suggestion that his years of patient investigation should be dismissed by a cursory ipse dixit. Years later he told me that another reason—which perhaps fits in with the first—was that Loewenfeld was a friend whom he respected. Evidently his resentment was aroused by being treated so cavalierly by such a person. The friendship, however, only deepened, and nine years later Loewenfeld got him to write a chapter on the psychoanalytic method for a book he was composing (*Psychische Zwangserscheinungen*—Psychic Compulsion Phenomena); a year later Freud also wrote a chapter expounding his views

[aa] It should be remembered that the mild English word "anxiety," by which we translate the German *Angst*, is used in a wide sense in psychoanalysis, where it comprehends many forms and degrees of fear, apprehensiveness, dread or even panic.

on sexuality as an etiological factor in the neuroses for Loewenfeld's *Sexualleben und Nervenleiden* (Sexual Life and Nervous Diseases). Loewenfeld was one of the few who attended the first International Psychoanalytical Congress in 1908.

The explanation Freud offered of his clinical findings is of great interest in connection with his personal development. He had always been greatly puzzled by the old problem of the relation between body and mind, and to begin with had with his strongly held Helmholtzian principles cherished the hope of establishing a physiological basis for mental functioning. As we shall see later, during the years 1888-1898 he passed through a severe struggle before he decided to relinquish the idea of correlating somatic and psychical activity. The dawn of the conflict in his mind on this matter may be perceived in his theory of the anxiety neurosis. It was an appropriate sphere, since there are few problems so fundamental to the question of body and mind as that of anxiety.

Essentially his explanation was this: when sexual tension arising within the body attains a certain degree, it leads in the mind to sexual desire, libido,[bb] with various accompanying ideas and emotions; but when for any reason this natural process is checked, the tension is "transformed" into anxiety. In 1892 he had already formulated the sentence: "Anxiety neurosis in part results from inhibition of the sexual function." [117] The following is an italicized statement in his first paper. "*The mechanism of anxiety-neurosis is to be sought in the deflection of somatic sexual excitation from the psychical field, and in an abnormal use of it, due to this deflection.*" [118] In his second paper it runs: "Anxiety-neurosis is produced by anything which withholds somatic sexual tension from the psychical and interferes with its elaboration within the psychical field." [119] He insisted that the anxiety is a *physical* effect of this state of affairs,[120] and that neither the anxiety itself nor any of its somatic accompaniments (palpitation, sweating, etc.) are susceptible of psychological analysis.

Discussing the question of why just anxiety should result from this blocking, Freud pointed out that the somatic accompaniments of anxiety (accelerated breathing, palpitation, sweating, congestion, and so on) are phenomena accompanying normal coitus. In a letter of a year later he also remarked that anxiety, being the response

[bb] A word he first used, so far as the records go, in June 1894.[115] Oddly enough, in 1922 he credited Moll with the term, in a book Moll published in 1898! [116]

to obstruction in breathing—an activity that has no psychical elaboration—could become the expression of *any* accumulation of physical tension.[121]

In all this the bias of Freud's early training is evident. He was on the brink of deserting physiology and of enunciating the findings and theories of his clinical observations in purely psychological language. But with what he called the actual neuroses,[cc] he saw a chance of saving at least a section of psychopathology for a physiological explanation. A little later he told his friend Fliess that he was "quite entranced" with the latter's suggestion about a "sexual chemistry," [122] and he evidently regarded in chemical terms (*chemische Stoffe*) the action of tension within the seminal vesicles affecting the central nervous system—possibly a premonition of the future discovery of hormones! It has therefore sometimes been referred to as Freud's toxicological theory of the neuroses.

As late as 1925 Freud still wrote: "From a clinical standpoint the (actual) neuroses must necessarily be put alongside the intoxications and such disorders as Graves' disease.[dd] These are conditions arising from an excess or a relative lack of certain highly active substances, whether produced inside the body or introduced into it from outside—in short, they are disturbances of the chemistry of the body, toxic conditions. If someone were to succeed in isolating and demonstrating the hypothetical substances concerned in neuroses, he would have no need to concern himself with opposition from the medical profession. For the present, however, no such avenue of approach to the problem is open." [124]

A remark he made to me years later dates from this attitude. It was a half-serious prediction that in time to come it should be possible to cure hysteria (*sic*) by administering a chemical drug without any psychological treatment. On the other hand, he used to insist that one should first explore psychology to its limits, while waiting patiently for the suitable advance in biochemistry, and would warn his pupils against what he called "flirting with endocrinology." Incidentally, in his *Three Essays on the Theory of Sexuality*, he pointed out the risk of the gonads themselves being overestimated, and that the chemical

cc The German word *aktual* means current, and the causes of these neuroses are current factors.

dd In a footnote to his translation of the *Poliklinische Vorträge*, 1892,[123] Freud comments on Charcot's ignorance of the thyroid origin of this affection; the new discovery of internal secretions, being in harmony with his own train of thought, had undoubtedly interested him.

mechanism concerned is probably more diffuse and complex than consideration of them alone would make one suppose.[125]

Freud drew an interesting comparison between anxiety neurosis and hysteria which explains why the two so often occur together. He called the former the somatic counterpart of the latter. "In each of them there occurs a deflection of excitation to the somatic field instead of psychical assimilation of it; the difference is merely this, that in anxiety-neurosis the excitation (in the displacement of which the neurosis expresses itself) is purely somatic (the somatic sexual excitation), whereas in hysteria it is purely psychical (evoked by conflict)." [126] Again: "There is a kind of conversion in the anxiety neurosis, as there is in hysteria; only in hysteria it is a psychical excitation that proceeds on a false path, exclusively into the somatic field, whereas with the other it is a *physical* tension that cannot enter the psychical field and so remains in a physical path." [127]

Since the theme of "actual neurosis" does not come again into this history, it may be appropriate to add something here about its subsequent fate. Kris says that until 1926 Freud's toxicological anxiety theory dominated psychoanalytical thinking.[128] This extreme statement requires much modification. It is true that Freud's nosological account of the two neuroses, his description of the specific etiological factors (which have never been challenged), and his theoretical explanation all found regular entry into psychoanalytical literature and expositions. But there was a good deal of lip service about this, since no clinical application was made of it all, the reason being that no one seemed to come across just the type of case that Freud had described. When I myself once remarked on this to Freud, he replied that neither did he see any such cases nowadays, but that he used to in the beginning of his practice! In his *Autobiography* (1925) he wrote: "Since that time I have had no opportunity of returning to the investigation of the 'actual' neuroses; nor has this part of my work been continued by anyone else. If I look back today on my early findings, they strike me as being the first rough outlines of what is probably a far more complicated subject. But on the whole they seem to me still to hold good." [129]

The explanation of the paradox lies simply in the word "pure." Freud had artificially isolated a "pure" condition because at that time he saw no reason for delving deeper. Yet at the very beginning he gave a hint which, if followed up, would lead to a more comprehensive conception. In a private communication (early in 1894) he said that the reason why the sexual tension did not follow its natural course in such cases was that the "psychical conditions" were lacking,[130] and in various places he specifies this lack of the proper conditions (which we may simply define by the word "freedom of access") by the use of such phrases as "suppression," "defense," "rejection," etc. So, after all, what prevents the tension leading to conscious desire is the fact that a *psychical* act had with a defensive aim obstructed it. This then raises the whole question of the *previous* repression, and one must reach the conclusion that the sexual etiology correctly described by Freud is valid only with persons with a predisposition proceeding not simply from heredity but from previous mental conflicts and repressions. All of which explains the difficulty of finding the "pure" cases of Freud's early career.

Nevertheless, what did remain—and permanently so—from Freud's observations on the anxiety neurosis was his establishing of an inherent relationship between thwarted sexuality and morbid anxiety (i.e., fear in excess of an actual danger). The precise nature of the relationship might be in doubt, but the empirical observation stood.

Furthermore, so long ago as 1911 the present writer ventured to question the biological validity of the idea of physical sexual tension being "transformed" into anxiety, which is the emotion appropriate to a particular instinct, and had suggested it would be more proper to speak of that defensive instinct having been aroused, or stimulated, by the endogenous pressure. Had Freud gone no further than to state that anxiety occurs when sexual desire might logically be expected, that it occurs in place of the latter, then he would not have trespassed beyond his observations. In 1926 in his invaluable book, *Hemmung, Symptom und Angst* (Inhibitions, Symptoms and Anxiety), he made the necessary rectification and reinstated anxiety as an independent defense agency. Yet it is fascinating to find that in his very first paper on the anxiety neurosis (1895), there is a hint of the exposition of over thirty years later. It is this: "The psyche develops the affect of anxiety when it feels itself incapable of dealing (by an adequate reaction) with a task (danger) approaching it externally; it develops the neurosis of anxiety when it feels itself unequal to the task of mastering (sexual) excitation arising endogenously. That is to say, it acts *as if it had projected this excitation into the outer world*." [131], [ee] Thus the psyche comes into the story at the beginning, despite all endeavors to replace it by physiology.

In the next twenty years a great many plagiarisms of Freud's work

[ee] Italics Freud's.

on the anxiety neurosis appeared without any acknowledgement.[132] Selected symptoms, especially the cardiac ones (the D.A.H. of the first World War!) which he had fully described were singled out and proclaimed as newly discovered syndromes; stress was often laid on their sexual origin!

To return to the psychoneuroses, the field in which Freud first acquired a sense of the importance of sexual disturbances, we may be sure that this was being steadily strengthened by his experience in the four or five years before he gave public expression to it. On the first occasion when he did so it was in a paper entitled "The Defense Neuropsychoses," which appeared May 15 and June 1, 1894, before the one on the anxiety neurosis. In it he put forward his suggestions modestly enough. He remarked that in hysteria it is chiefly sexual ideas (in women) that have proved unacceptable to the personality. As to the obsessional neurosis the pathogenic idea was always, in his experience, a sexual one, but there might well be dissimilar cases which he had not encountered. With neither type of psychoneurosis are the sexual ideas specified, although they are illus trated. Then came a paper published in French in 1895 (*Obsessions and Phobias*); by phobias here he meant simply the ramification of the fears that occur in the anxiety neurosis, the specific etiology of which he had previously announced. In this paper he is more positive and states that in the obsessional neurosis the "replaced ideas" relate to painful experiences which the person is striving to forget.

Later that year he addressed the *Doktorenkollegium* of Vienna on the subject of hysteria, taking up three evenings for the purpose (October 14, 21, and 28). The paper, entitled *"Uber Hysterie,"* appeared in full in the *Wiener klinische Rundschau*.[133] but Freud never included it in his collected works. In letters to Fliess (October 20 and 31) he says it was well received and that he delivered it in a "very saucy" mood. It was certainly outspoken. For instance: "With previously healthy men an anxiety neurosis is rooted in abstinence; with women it occurs mostly through coitus interruptus." The second lecture, devoted mainly to the topic of "repression," proclaimed that "every hysteria is founded in repression, always with a sexual content." He also announced that in his treatment hypnosis could be dispensed with.

In the next year (1896) there is some further development of these ideas. In March the fourth of his papers to be written in French appeared in the *Revue Neurologique*. It is mainly taken up with challenging the prevailing French view that heredity is the essential cause of all neurosis, but he maintains categorically that the *specific* cause of all neuroses is some disturbance in the sexual life of the patient: a current one with the "actual neurosis" and one in the past life with the psychoneuroses. More precisely, the cause in hysteria is a passive sexual experience before puberty, i.e., a traumatic seduction; this conclusion was based on thirteen fully analyzed cases. The age of predilection for the experience was three or four, and Freud surmises that one occurring after the age of eight or ten would not lead to a neurosis. The experience has been undergone with indifference, or perhaps some degree of disgust or fright. With the obsessional neurosis, of which he cites six fully analyzed cases, we have also to do with a sexual experience before puberty, but there are two important differences between it and the hysterical one: it was pleasurable and it was actively aggressive. Furthermore, the obsessional experience of active desire seems to have been preceded by a still earlier passive experience of seduction; this explains the frequent coexistence of these two psychoneuroses. Freud had communicated all these conclusions in full to Fliess in a letter dated October 8, 1895,[134] but in a letter two years earlier (May 30, 1893) there is already a mention of these early seductions.

On May 2, 1896, Freud gave an address to the Society of Psychiatry and Neurology in Vienna entitled "The Etiology of Hysteria"; it was published in amplified form later in the year. According to Freud, the paper met with an icy reception. Krafft-Ebing, who was in the chair, contented himself with saying: "It sounds like a scientific fairy tale." It was almost the last paper Freud was ever to read in Vienna; the only other one was eight years later.

It is a valuable and comprehensive paper, and, although it adds little to the conclusions just mentioned, the arguments are so well marshaled, and the objections so skillfully forestalled, that it may well be called a literary *tour de force*. Incidentally, he cites eighteen fully analyzed cases in place of the earlier thirteen, and writes of them: "You may of course object that the nineteenth and twentieth analyses would perhaps show that hysterical symptoms can be derived from other sources also, and that thus the validity of the sexual etiology would not be universal but would be reduced to 80 per cent. By all means, let us wait and see, but since those eighteen cases are at the same time *all* those which I was able to analyze, and since nobody picked them out to please me, you will understand that I do not share any such expectation, but am prepared to let my belief outrun the evidential force of my discoveries up to the present time." [135] He was evidently full of confidence on this occasion. Referring to the proposition that at the bottom of every case of hysteria will be found one or more premature sexual experiences, belonging to the first years of childhood, experiences which may be reproduced by analytic work though whole decades have intervened, he adds: "I believe this to be a momentous revelation, the discovery of a *caput Nili* of neuropathology." [136]

Naturally he has to deal with the doubt about the real occurrence of the seduction scenes his patients reproduce, and he gives several reasons for his conviction of their truth. One of them displays less psychological insight than we are accustomed to from the skeptical Freud. Referring to the patients' extreme reluctance to reproduce the picture of the scenes, and their attempt to withhold belief by stressing the fact that they have no feeling of recollecting them as they do with other forgotten material, he adds: "Now this last attitude on their part seems absolutely decisive. Why should patients assure me so emphatically of their unbelief, if from any motive they had invented the very things that they wish to discredit?" [137] It was not long before Freud found it easy to answer just this question.

The other paper of the same year published in the *Neurologisches Centralblatt* in May adds a few points to those already mentioned. The childhood experiences of seduction must consist in actual excitation of the genital organs themselves (coituslike processes): active masturbation on the part of the child alone will not lead to subsequent hysteria. When both types of experience have occurred (active and passive), the decision whether hysteria or an obsessional neurosis will develop later depends on *temporal* factors in the development of the libido. He expresses the opinion that "sexual maturity" in a psychological sense antedates puberty and belongs to the period between the eighth and tenth year. But the main theme of the paper concerns the psychological structure of the neuroses, one which will be dealt with in the following chapter.

At the beginning of 1898 he published a paper on "Sexuality in the Etiology of the Neuroses," which he had read before the *Doktorenkollegium* in Vienna. It is mainly a strong plea for the justification of investigating the sexual life of neurotic patients, and the vast importance of doing so. It also contains a well-reasoned defense of the psychoanalytic method, in which he defines its indications and its limitations.

But the paper contains two special features, one positive, the other negative. The former is *the first pronouncement on the theme of in-*

fantile sexuality. Freud writes: "We do wrong entirely to ignore the sexual life of children; in my experience children are capable of all the mental and many of the physical activities. Just as the whole sexual apparatus of man is not comprised in the external genital organs and the two reproductive glands, so his sexual life does not begin only with the onset of puberty, as to casual observation it may appear to do." [138] One might hastily infer from this isolated passage, which is modified by some neighboring ones, that Freud had by now apprehended the full conception of infantile sexuality, but, as will be pointed out in Chapter XIV, this was far from being so.

The second feature is that, while there is no retraction of it, there is no mention at all of the seduction theory of hysteria—the theme which in the past three years had chiefly preoccupied Freud, and which not long before had signified a *caput Nili* of neuropathology. Something very important must have happened.

We come here to one of the great dividing lines in the story. Freud had just recognized something of the significance of phantasies.[ff]

Two years previously he had expressed the opinion that the tales of outrage often related by *adult* hysterics were fictions that arose from the memory traces of the trauma they had suffered in childhood.[140] But up to the spring of 1897 he still held firmly to his conviction of the reality of these childhood traumas, so strong was Charcot's teaching on traumatic experiences and so surely did the analysis of the patients' associations reproduce them. At that time doubts began to creep in, although he made no mention of them in the records of his progress he was regularly sending to his friend Fliess. Then, quite suddenly, he decided to confide to him "the great secret of something that in the past few months has gradually dawned on me." [141] It was the awful truth that most—not all—of the seductions in childhood which his patients had revealed, and about which he had built his whole theory of hysteria, had never occurred. It was a turning point in his scientific career, and it tested his integrity, courage, and psychological insight to the full. Now he had to prove whether his psychological method on which he had founded everything was trustworthy or not. It was at this moment that Freud rose to his full stature.

The letter of September 21, 1897, in which he made this announcement to Fliess is perhaps the most valuable of that valuable

[ff] I think Kris here tends to confound phantasies *about* childhood with phantasies *in* childhood.[139]

series which was so fortunately preserved. In it he gave four reasons for his growing doubts. First his numerous disappointments in not being able to bring his analyses to a proper completion; the results were imperfect, both scientifically and therapeutically. Secondly, his astonishment at being asked to believe that all his patients' fathers were given to sexual perversions; indeed such behavior would have to be much more common than the incidence of hysteria, since several adjuvant factors are needed to culminate in this complaint. Thirdly, his clear perception that in the unconscious there is no criterion of reality, so that truth cannot be distinguished from emotional fiction. Fourthly, the consideration that such memories never emerge in the deliria of even the most severe psychoses.

Although Freud had in the previous months been intensively investigating sexual phantasies concerning childhood, he had simultaneously held fast to his belief in the real occurrence of the seductions. To renounce this belief must have been a great wrench, and it is very possible that the decisive factor had been his own self-analysis, which he had undertaken in the June of that fateful year. Little wonder that he had to rush to Berlin, if only for twenty-four hours, to commune with his mentor.

As the letter proceeds his excitement maintains a hearty note, although he ruefully reflects that, now that he has to renounce his key to the secrets of hysteria, his hopes of becoming a famous and successful physician are dashed to the ground. "I will vary Hamlet's words, 'To be in readiness,' etc., to 'To be cheerful is everything.' I might, it is true, feel very dissatisfied. The expectation of lasting fame, the certainty of wealth and complete independence, the thought of travel, of sparing my children the heavy cares that robbed me of my own youth: it was such a fair prospect. All that depended on the problems of hysteria being resolved. Now I can once more resign myself modestly to daily cares and economies."

In 1914 Freud described his situation at this discovery as follows: "When this etiology broke down under its own improbability and under contradiction in definitely ascertainable circumstances, the result at first was helpless bewilderment. Analysis had led by the right paths back to these sexual traumas, and yet they were not true. Reality was lost from under one's feet. At that time I would gladly have given up the whole thing, just as my esteemed predecessor Breuer had done when he made his unwelcome discovery. Perhaps I persevered only because I had no choice and could not then begin again at anything else. At last came the reflection that, after all, one has no right to despair because one has been deceived in one's expectations; one must revise them. If hysterics trace back their symptoms to fictitious traumas, this new fact signifies that they create such scenes in phantasy, and psychical reality requires to be taken into account alongside actual reality." [142]

Interestingly enough, this dramatic account does not quite tally with the picture of himself drawn in the contemporaneous letter just cited. There, it is true, he admits: "I do not know where I am, since I have not achieved the theoretical comprehension of repression." But only that seems to have disturbed him. Discussing his bewilderment concerning the theoretical mechanism of repression he comments: "If I were depressed or tired such doubts might be regarded as signs of weakness. But since I am in the very opposite mood I must view them as the result of honest and energetic intellectual work and be proud of my critical powers in the face of all that concentration. Perhaps, after all, the doubts are only an episode in the progress towards further knowledge."

As for the recognition of his far-reaching blunder, he confesses with surprise that he is not at all ashamed, although—he adds—he might well be. Then comes an enchanting passage: "Tell it not in Gath, publish it not in the streets of Askalon, in the land of the Philistines,gg but between you and me I have the feeling of a victory rather than of a defeat."

Well might he be elated, for with the insight he had now gained he was on the verge of exploring the whole range of infantile sexuality and of completing his theory of dream psychology—his two mightiest achievements. Eighteen ninety-seven was the acme of Freud's life.

gg Lest the daughters of the Philistines rejoice!

XII

Early Psychopathology

(1 8 9 0 – 1 8 9 7)

BY 1890 FREUD HAD HAD FOR SOME YEARS TO RENOUNCE ALL FURTHER laboratory work in neurohistology, and, although he had become a competent neurologist, he does not appear ever to have been seriously interested in clinical neurology. Fortunately the private practice in it, on which he had to depend for a living, brought, as it usually does, mostly neurotic patients. The problems they provided soon aroused his attention, and his interest in them rapidly grew. His official position at the head of the neurological department of the Kassowitz Institute, it is true, made it incumbent on him to produce some research work in that field, and his publications in it between 1891 and 1897, on the paralyses of children, were valuable contributions to our knowledge of that subject. But his heart was never in such work, and as time went on it irked him more and more. Somehow he never regarded clinical neurology as "scientific," and he longed to get back to "scientific" work. What he meant by the word in that connection is not always evident, but the anatomy of the brain ranked high. It was not simply "original research" he meant, but something more fundamental—probably any investigation that would throw light on the nature of man, on the relationship between body and mind, of how man came to be a self-conscious animal.

The only work of his in neurology of which he thought well was that on aphasia, and since speech is the only function where there is any pretension to linking the mind with the brain (dating from Broca's discovery of the localization of it in the frontal lobe), one can well understand Freud's special interest in it.

His attitude on these matters was expressed in a letter to Fliess, dated May 21, 1894: "Here I am pretty much alone in the elucida-

268

tion of the neuroses. Colleagues look on me as somewhat of a monomaniac, and I have the definite feeling of having touched on one of the great secrets of nature. There is something odd in the disproportion between one's own estimate of one's intellectual work and other people's. Take the book on the diplegias, which I patched up with the minimum of interest and effort, almost in a mischievous mood. It has had an enormous success. The reviewers praise it very highly, and the French in particular are full of high appreciation. Only today I got a book by Raymond, Charcot's successor, which in the section on the subject simply transcribes my work—with, of course, a laudatory reference. And as for the really good things, such as the book on aphasia, the paper on obsessions which is about to appear, and such as the essay on "Etiology and Theory of the Neuroses" will be, I can expect nothing better than a respectable failure. I find it all very perplexing and somewhat embittering."

In contrast to clinical neurology Freud was deeply interested in clinical psychopathology. The observations and findings he made in this field constituted fascinating intellectual problems in themselves, but even that interest was subordinate to the more grandiose plan of establishing a comprehensive theory of neurotic manifestations. And it becomes plain that this in its turn absorbed Freud in the way it did because of the light he hoped it would throw on the structure and functioning of the mind in general.

In this there was true genius. Whereas other people regarded, and still regard, neuroses as mere abnormalities, as diseases that are deviations from the normal, Freud must very early have divined not only that they represent simply a variety of mental functioning but also that they provide access to deep layers of "the mind," i.e., of all minds. Psychopathology, he perceived, would become an avenue of approach to psychology in general, and perhaps the best available one. In one of his 1896 papers he actually uses the expression "the future *Neurosis-Psychology*" to designate the psychology "for which philosophers have done little to prepare the way." [1] Sixteen years later Wilhelm Specht took up an equivalent word and founded the —unfortunately short-lived—*Zeitschrift für Pathopsychologie*; it was to deal not with psychopathology, the study of morbid manifestations for their own sake, but a psychology based on the knowledge gained from that study. Psychoanalysis, which Bleuler later called "depth psychology," was in its theoretical aspects destined, as we shall see in a subsequent chapter (XVII), to attempt this ambitious task.

Over and again in later years opponents of Freud's work were to cite the source of his knowledge as invalidating his generalizations. How could one deduce anything of value to healthy-minded people from abnormal and "diseased" states? Apart from the difficulty of finding these normal and healthy-minded people—since everyone displays either neurotic reactions to life or else scars suffered in the endeavor to check them—what these critics find hard to appreciate is that neurotic reactions are found, when analyzed, to be much closer to the early basis of mental development than are the far greater deviations of the so-called "normal."

Freud himself had disposed of this objection quite early on in the *Studies in Hysteria:* "One has in such work of course to be free of any theoretical prejudice about having to do with abnormal brains of degenerates and *déséquilibrés* whose stigma, peculiar to them, is the freedom to discard the common psychological laws of the association between ideas, or in whom any kind of idea may without any motive acquire an undue intensity and another one may without any psychological reason remain indestructible. Experience shows the contrary to be true in hysteria; as soon as one has uncovered the hidden motives—which have often remained unconscious—and taken them into account, there remains nothing in the connection between the thoughts of hysterics that is enigmatical or lawless." [2]

In *The Interpretation of Dreams* he presented another convincing argument based on the far-reaching similarity in the essential structure of dreams and neuroses: "We see that the psychical mechanism employed by neuroses is not created through there having first been a morbid disturbance affecting the mind, but is already present in the normal structure of the mental apparatus. The two psychical systems, the transitional censorship between them, the way in which one activity inhibits and becomes superimposed on the other, the connection of both to consciousness: all that belongs to the normal structure of our mental instrument, and dreams show us one of the ways leading to knowledge of that structure." [3]

Freud's attitude to sexuality throws another light on his fundamental interests and the motives that urged him forward in his researches, a light which also further illuminates the considerations advanced above. On the one hand there is no doubt that he was greatly excited over his discovery that sexual factors play an *essential* part in the causation of neuroses—I repeat "essential," for they had often been admitted to be occasional factors—and that he made it one of his chief aims to carry through in minute detail his Libido theory of the neuroses. On the other hand, his descriptions of sexual activities are so matter-of-fact that many readers have found them almost dry and totally lacking in warmth. From all I know of him I should say that he displayed less than the average *personal* interest in what is often an absorbing topic. There was never any gusto or even savor in mentioning a sexual topic. He would have been out of place in the usual club room, for he seldom related sexual jokes and then only when they had a special point illustrating a general theme. He always gave the impression of being an unusually chaste person— the word "puritanical" would not be out of place—and all we know of his early development confirms this conception.

Indeed, this must be the explanation of his almost naive surprise when his announcement of discoveries in this field met with such a cold reception. "I did not at first perceive the peculiar nature of what I had discovered. Without thinking, I sacrificed at its inception my popularity as a physician, and the growth of a large consulting practice among nervous patients, by enquiries relating to the sexual factors involved in the causation of their neuroses; this brought me a great many new facts which definitely confirmed my conviction of the practical importance of the sexual factor. Unsuspectingly, I spoke before the Vienna Neurological Society, then under the presidency of Krafft-Ebing, expecting to be compensated by the interest and recognition of my colleagues for the material losses I had willingly undergone. I treated my discoveries as ordinary contributions to science and hoped to be met in the same spirit. But the silence with which my addresses were received, the void which formed itself about me, the insinuations that found their way to me, caused me gradually to realize that one cannot count upon views about the part played by sexuality in the etiology of the neuroses meeting with the same reception as other communications. I understood that from now onwards I belonged to those who have 'troubled the sleep of the world,' as Hebbel says, and that I could not reckon upon objectivity and tolerance. Since, however, my conviction of the general accuracy of my observations and conclusions grew and grew, and as my confidence in my own judgment was by no means slight, any more than my moral courage, there could be no doubt about the outcome of the situation. I made up my mind that it had been my fortune to discover particularly important connections, and was prepared to accept the fate that sometimes accompanies such discoveries." [4]

How is this antinomy to be resolved? The suggestion may be ventured that Freud's interest in sexual activities, like that in the aphasic disturbances of speech, came from the fact that sexuality has so obviously both physical and mental components. Is Libido a mental or physical concept in its origin? So here again might be found a clue to the riddle of the relation of body to mind, of transforming psychology into a biological or even physiological discipline. And it was this aspect of his discovery that really interested Freud.

Even in his first year or two of practice, through which he was beginning to make contact with the problems of neurosis, Freud was taking a serious interest in the subject. In 1887 he talked of a monograph he was planning, entitled "The General Characteristics of Hysterical Affections," an ambitious aim for a novice.[5] In the following February he mentioned that the first draft of it was ready,[6] but the book never appeared in print and unfortunately he did not preserve the manuscript;[a] probably he realized how premature the plan was.

On the other hand Fliess preserved one long essay and fourteen manuscripts which Freud had sent him from time to time to inform him of the progress he was making in psychopathology, and these have now all been published.[7] They are a valuable addition to Freud's published papers, and give us insight into the gradual unfolding of his ideas.

As early as 1893, in the paper on hysterical paralyses, there are, in addition to the more technical diagnostic ones, two general ideas in the realm of psychopathology. When the expression "functional affection of the cortex" is used, as indeed it still is by some neurologists, a pathologist would understand by it a temporary localized lesion, even if one not visible after death. There are many such, produced for example by edema or anemia, so that an hysterical paralysis of the arm would be due to some affection of the arm center near the fissure of Rolando. Freud vigorously and lucidly combated this idea. Having just demonstrated that an hysterical paralysis differs sharply from an organic one in being distributed not according to the anatomical facts but according to the mental concept "arm," he argued that the only possible explanation must be that the concept "arm" is dissociated from the rest of consciousness. It is a question of a break in the mental associations. The reason for this is considered in his other contributions that soon follow, but he hinted that it has to do with an excessive affective saturation of some idea con-

[a] It was hardly ever Freud's custom to keep his manuscripts.

nected with that of the arm which so occupies its "associative affinity" as to make it inaccessible to general conscious associations and volition. The whole argument was really a continuation of his "antilocalization" one in the book on aphasia.

Earlier in the same year there had appeared the joint "Preliminary Communication" by himself and Breuer. This is where their well-known dictum occurs that "hysterical patients suffer mainly from reminiscences." The idea—an extension of Charcot's—of a mental trauma being the cause of hysterical symptoms is upheld, but it is explained that not the trauma itself, but the *memory* of it, is the operative agent. The trauma is not an evoking or precipitating factor, but rather—in its memory trace—resembles a foreign body that continues to irritate the mind. In the *Studies in Hysteria*[8] Freud corrects this medical analogy: "The pathogenic organization does not really behave like a foreign body, but much more like an infiltration. In this comparison the resistance should be regarded as the infiltrating material. The therapy, indeed, does not consist in extirpating something—it cannot do that at present—but in dissolving the resistance and thus opening a way for the circulation into a hitherto closed territory." Later on he gives a number of apt surgical analogies to the action of psychotherapy.[9]

All this is linked with Freud's and Breuer's practical experiences of catharsis. Binet had remarked that suggestive therapy is more effective when a patient's attention is brought back to the moment when the symptom first appeared, but no one before Breuer had connected this tracing back with the fact of abreaction. In the *Studies in Hysteria* the authors insisted that mere recollection without *affective* abreaction is of little therapeutic value, and they went on to discuss the nature and significance of that abreaction. If there is no impediment, then the mental disturbance of the trauma can be dissipated either through a general absorption into the whole complex of mental associations or else through the well-known ways of "working off" emotions (anger, weeping, etc.).

This diffusion of the affect may be prevented in two circumstances. (1) Social situations may make the expression of the emotion impossible, or the trauma may have concerned something so personally painful that the patient may have volitionally "repressed" it. This is the first occasion on which this term (*verdrängt*) occurs in Freud's writings;[10] it presently acquired a more technical meaning. The trauma itself is specified as fright, shame, or psychical pain. (2) The trauma may have taken place in one of the states of mental abstraction for which Breuer coined the generic term "hypnoid." The characteristic of them was, according to him, an intensive daydreaming, connected with either sorrow or sexual thoughts.[11] Although Freud half-heartedly subscribed in the joint paper to the statement that "the existence of hypnoid states forms the foundation and condition of hysteria," [12] he became more and more dubious on the point, and in his chapter on psychotherapy in the *Studies* (written two years later) expressed the opinion that a defensive (repressing) act *precedes* any such state.[13] A year later he definitely repudiated the conception;[14] by 1900 it had become "that unfortunate idea that had been forced on me," [15] and in the next year a "superfluous and misleading idea." [16] It became entirely replaced by his doctrine of "defense" (repression). Breuer's concept of hypnoid states was evidently derived from the French psychiatry, where so much work had been done on hypnosis, and where it was becoming customary to explain hysteria altogether by a congenital tendency to a splitting of consciousness. Breuer seems to have favored this latter idea at first, but he vigorously rejected Janet's simplistic account of it.[17]

We may at this point conclude what need be said further about Breuer's contributions to psychopathology. In the paper on "Theory" which he contributed to the *Studies* one notes the fundamental importance he attached to the idea that the basis of hysteria was an abnormal excitability of the nervous system, so that an excess of free energy that could not be disposed of was available for conversion into somatic symptoms. Breuer gave a clear description of the regressive nature of hallucinations, attributing their intensity and peculiarly objective quality to an excitation of the apparatus of perception proceeding from memory traces.[18] This is one of the two senses in which Freud later used the term "regression," the one he particularly developed in connection with dream processes. Breuer did not agree with Moebius that all hysterical symptoms are ideogenic in origin,[19] and he instanced the vasomotor and cutaneous changes as exceptions. It was he who introduced the term *bewusstseinsunfähig*[b] (inadmissible to consciousness), one which has since been extensively employed in psychoanalysis to designate the ideas which, in spite of possessing an intense affect, still are unable to enter consciousness; in fact, this is because of the intense emotion, not in spite of it. He calls such ideas "unconscious," and speaks contemptuously of the dispute over this term as a "haggling with words." His

[b] Invented on the analogy of *"hoffähig"* (having the entrée).

general outlook, however, is plainly a physiological one, and he describes mental functioning very much in terms of a complicated reflex, with none of the stress Freud laid on its voluntaristic and purposeful aspects.

The "Preliminary Communication," as indeed its full title indicates, attempts to describe simply the mechanism of hysterical symptoms, not the inner causes of the affection itself. Yet less than three years later we find Freud claiming, in a letter to Fliess, that he thinks he "can cure not merely the symptoms of hysteria, but the predisposition to it." [20] This gives him a mild pleasure; he has not lived for forty years in vain. Indeed, he had earlier, in a lecture on hysteria delivered before the *Wiener medizinisches Doctorenkollegium* (October 28, 1895), given reasons for thinking this to be possible. He explained that the only repressions occurring after puberty were such as linked onto those of early childhood—no altogether new ones being possible—so that if the early ones were properly released, the neurosis should be finally effaced. He allows himself here the following imaginative allegory: "One gets the impression of a demon striving not to come to the light of day, because he knows that will be his end." [21]

The two drafts of the "Preliminary Communication," written by Freud but more or less in conjunction with Breuer, contain in a more sketchy form its main ideas—those of psychical trauma, the memory of which has the pathogenic effect, and the dissociation from consciousness. Before they were composed, however, Freud had published in a footnote to one of the Charcot books he translated the very *first account* of the new theory of hysterical symptoms. The following passage is especially noteworthy. "I (*sic*) have tried to apprehend the problem of hysterical attacks in some fashion other than the merely descriptive one, and by examining hysterics during hypnosis have reached new results, some of which I may mention here: the kernel of the hysterical attack, in whatever form this takes, is a *memory*, the hallucinatory living through of a scene that was significant for the outbreak of the illness. It is this process that becomes evident in the phase known as the *attitudes passionnelles*, but it is also present where the attack appears to consist of motor phenomena only. The *content of the memory* is usually the psychical *trauma* which was either through its intensity calculated to provoke the hysterical outbreak in the patient or else the event which became a trauma through happening at a particular moment.

"In the cases known as 'traumatic' hysteria this mechanism is evident to the most casual observation, but it can be demonstrated also in hysteria where there has been no single important trauma. Here one finds repeated lesser traumas or else memories, often indifferent in themselves, which the prominence of the dispositional factor has made traumatic. A trauma may be defined as an increase in excitation in the nervous system which the latter has not been able to dispose of by motor reactions.

"The hysterical attack is perhaps to be regarded as an attempt to complete the reaction to the trauma." [22]

We have here already a hint of the emphasis Freud was to place on "summation of excitations," a concept evidently borrowed from physiology. He expressed this also in the phrase, "symptoms are overdetermined." [23]

It is necessary to recognize clearly, not simply that Freud was interested in psychopathology because it promised a new approach to psychology, but that from the very beginning his theories in that field were interwoven with psychological assumptions and principles of a general nature. This is made very evident in "Manuscript D" (Spring 1894) in the Fliess correspondence, where the mechanism of the neuroses is throughout viewed in terms of the "theory of constancy" as applied in both the mind and the brain.[24] It follows that the exposition here of his psychopathological theories will gain in profundity after the discussion in a subsequent chapter (Chapter XVII) of Freud's general psychological principles.

Of the dozen or so contributions Freud published in the years 1893-1898 three are of outstanding importance in the development of his psychopathology, so we may confine our attention to them. They are the two papers on the "Defense Neuro-Psychoses" and the one on the "Etiology of Hysteria."

In the first of these, published the year *before* the *Studies in Hysteria*, Freud still thought there are three forms of hysteria: defense, hypnoid, and retention respectively. The first of these, which was soon to oust the others completely, was the one to which he already attached the most importance. He explained that the aim of the defense against the painful idea—the process he later called "repression"—was to weaken it by divesting it of its affect, and that it does this by diverting the energy of the affect into somatic channels; to denote this he proposed the term "conversion." [25] Even then the "memory trace" of the trauma remains isolated from the rest of the mind and it may in fact form the nucleus of a secondary system. The displaced affect, however, may on occasion revert from the somatic innervation to the idea where it was first attached, and in that event the result is apt to be an hysterical attack.

Freud gave his reasons for rejecting Janet's theory of hysteria, i.e., a congenital mental weakness that makes a splitting of consciousness easy, and approved of Strümpell's dictum that "in hysteria the disturbance lies in the psychophysical sphere, where body and mind have their connection with each other." By explaining hysterical symptoms as a perverted somatic innervation following on the splitting of consciousness, i.e., "conversion" of the affective energy, Freud must have felt very much at home in the relation of physiology to psychology which his theory betokened.

It seems probable that Freud derived the concept of "conversion" from his investigation, seven years earlier, of the nature of hysterical paralyses.c For his main conclusion there was that they represented ideas rather than anatomical lesions, i.e., that the somatic manifestation replaced something psychical.

In subjects not predisposed to this somatic disposal of affect, the defense against the painful idea leads to the affect being displaced from it to some other indirectly associated idea, one more tolerable, which in its turn becomes invested with an inordinate quantity of affect. He also used here the words "dislocated" and "transposed" for "displaced." This is the mechanism of obsessions.

When the painful idea is inextricably bound up with external reality, then the defense against it results in a denial of reality, i.e., an hallucinatory psychosis.

In one of the French papers he called attention to the remarkable fact that in the psychoneuroses the effect of a memory surpasses that of the traumatic event itself.[26] The only psychological conjunction where this is so would appear to be when a prepuberty sexual experience is reawakened after puberty.

The other two papers, both of which appeared two years later (1896), shows a considerable advance in Freud's theoretical exposition. He is now approaching the height of his powers, although his most important discoveries still lie a year or two ahead.

In the "Further Remarks on the Defense Neuro-Psychoses," "defense" is on the first pages stated to be the "nucleus of the psychic mechanism" of the psychoneuroses, and it is beginning to be called "repression." The two terms are used interchangeably, because it

c See p. 233.

was not until some years later that Freud studied, or perhaps even recognized, the several other defenses besides repression.[d]

It was with the obsessional neurosis that we here meet with the most novel conclusions. Freud began with the simple formula: *"Obsessional ideas are invariably self-reproaches which have re-emerged from repression in a transmuted form and which always relate to some sexual act that was performed with pleasure in childhood."* [28] He then traced the course of events in a classical manner. In the first period there are few indications of what has happened. In the second, at the onset of sexual (mental) "maturity," which is often premature (eight to nine), no self-reproach is attached to the memory of the (originally pleasurable) activities, but a *primary defense symptom* develops: general conscientiousness, shamefulness, and self-distrust— what would nowadays be called "character defenses." The third period, of apparent health, may be called that of *successful defense*. The fourth period, that of the illness proper, is distinguished by the *return of the repressed memories*, i.e., by failure of the defense.

The reanimated memories and the self-reproach attaching to them, however, never appear in consciousness unchanged. The obsessional idea and affect replacing them are compromise formations, compounded of material taken from both the repressed and the repressing ideas.

Here we find for the first time mentioned two mental mechanisms that have ever since been important constituents of all psychoanalytical theory: the notions of "compromise formation" and the "return of the repressed." In a manuscript he sent to Fliess a year later (May 25, 1897) Freud used the term "compromise-displacement" and contrasted the form of this mechanism in different conditions. In hysteria the displacement follows any path of contiguous association, in the obsessional neurosis that of association through resemblance of ideas, in paranoia through causal connections.

In the same connection we note two further important statements: (1) that repression proceeds from the ego, and (2) that not only the original memory trace but the self-reproaches themselves, i.e., derivatives of the conscience, can be repressed.[29] For many years little attention was paid to this latter consideration in psychoanalysis, which at first was occupied in investigating the sexual content of repressed ideas. It is not surprising that for long the public believed that the unconscious, according to psychoanalysis, consisted only of

[d] The earliest hint of one of them, that of "denial," dates from the case of Frau Cäcilie (1891).[π]

the latter, was in fact a sink of iniquity. It was only when Freud studied the super-ego, a quarter of a century later, that the balance was re-established, when it could be said that the unconscious contained elements from both the "highest" and the "lowest" in man.

Two primary forms of the obsessional neurosis are distinguished; one in which the self-reproach, displaced from its original idea, becomes attached to another, associated one, which is no longer a sexual idea; and a form where the affect of self-reproach itself has been transformed into some other affect, most often morbid anxiety. Freud gives a list of the latter varieties.

A third form of this neurosis occurs, characterized by *secondary defense* symptoms. These are various protective measures which, when successful, acquire the sense of compulsion, the typical outcome being obsessive, apotropaic, actions.

The paper concluded with an illuminating comparison and contrast between the mechanisms of paranoia and those of the obsessional neurosis. This was Freud's first excursion into the field of the psychoses. After remarking that he had investigated several other cases of the kind, he gave a detailed analysis of a case of chronic paranoia in a married woman of thirty-two.ᵉ The point he most insisted on was that the connection between the symptoms and repressed thoughts was so demonstrable as to justify clarifying such cases under the rubric of "defense neuropsychoses." He used the word "projection" to describe the most characteristic psychological mechanism in paranoia, and he explained why the affection displays no secondary defenses as does the obsessional neurosis. The reason for this is that the ego can no longer protect itself, but has to become itself modified by accepting the symptoms caused by the "return of the repressed," these then constituting the delusions. Furthermore, he suggested that the apparent weakness of memory in such cases is not a destructive process, but a functional one caused by repression.

In a letter to Fliess (November 2, 1896) Freud expressed his amusement at "the first reaction to my intrusion into psychiatry." Rieger of Würzburg, in reviewing the paper in the *Jahrbücher für Psychiatrie*, had commented that "no experienced psychiatrist could read it without really shuddering." As to the section on paranoia, "that sort of thing could lead to nothing else than a simply horrible old-wives' psychiatry." [30]

Freud had also made an attempt, a not very successful one, to ex-

---

ᵉ He later recognized that dementia paranoides would have been a more correct diagnosis of this case.

plain the genesis of melancholia. It was never published, and we know it only from a letter, dated January 1895.[31] He divided it into three groups: the true melancholia of the periodic or circular type, neurasthenic melancholia (connected with masturbation), melancholia combined with severe anxiety; the latter two would nowadays be called simply depression. The relationship to mourning struck him—it is one he developed fruitfully in later years—and so he defined melancholia as grief at some loss—probably of libido. He insisted on a close connection between sexual anesthesia and "melancholia." His explanation was partly physiological. When the libido loses strength, energy is correspondingly withdrawn from associated "neurones," and the pain of melancholia is due to the dissolving of the associations.

At this time he was still not satisfied with the theoretical basis of repression. He raised, for example, the question of how it is that it can operate only with sexual ideas (a somewhat doubtful assumption, as it turned out later). He proffered the tentative explanation that sexual experiences of early childhood have not the affective value that such experiences have after puberty (also very doubtful). It is the subsequent memory of them, reinforced by the stronger emotions that follow puberty, that gets repressed, and he added: "An inverted relation of this kind between real experience and memory appears to be the psychological condition of repression." [32] He was probably right, however, in his statement that: "Repression of the memory of a painful sexual experience in maturer years is possible only for those people in whom this experience can reactivate the memory trace of an infantile trauma." [33]

As was mentioned earlier,[f] Freud undoubtedly originated the concept of "repression" as a simple inference from the observation of effort expended in the patient's "resistance" against the resuscitation of buried memories; one is the obverse of the other. But it may be that Freud's dissatisfaction with the theoretical basis of the concept sprang from his old wish to unite physiological and psychological conceptions. After all, the physiological concept of "inhibition," one he fully expounded years later in psychological terms, is not entirely remote from that of "repression"; the main difference is that with the former the accent is on the checking of function, whereas with the latter it is on its dissociation—its activity being retained. And Meynert himself, Freud's teacher, had made a somewhat bizarre endeavor to translate physiological inhibition into psychological

f See p. 247.

and even moral terminology.[34] He connected consciousness with cortical activities, a function secondary to what he called the "primary reflex movements" (associated with hunger, thirst, etc.) of the subcortical centers. One was above, the other below; and, appropriately enough, the former represented the good and social part of human nature, a secondary growth brought about by the infant's learning to love the persons around it, while the latter represented the primitive egoistic and asocial aspects of humanity. It was the function of the good cortex, which Meynert called the "secondary ego," to inhibit or check the bad subcortical activities, the "primary ego." [35]

Meynert was here putting into physiological (and also moral) terms a psychological conception of Herbart's, whose theories had greatly influenced him. Herbart, who actually used the word *Verdrängung*, had expounded the notion of one idea driving another out of consciousness (without supplying any motive for its doing so) and taught that the expelled idea could then influence the conscious mood.[36]

Years later the famous neurologist Henry Head in England made a similar attempt to physiologize the concept of "repression," correlating it with the "epicritic" control of "protopathic" sensations—before the erroneous basis of this division was exposed by Trotter and Davies.

The other important paper of the three mentioned above, published in the same month as the one last considered, was an exposition of his ripening views which Freud gave before the Society of Psychiatry and Neurology in May 1896. He began by pointing out that the origin of an hysterical symptom can be accepted as such only if it fulfills two conditions: it must possess the required *appropriateness as a determinant* and the necessary *traumatic power*. He illustrated this by the example of hysterical vomiting due to some experience evoking disgust. This is hardly explicable by discovering a history of a railway accident, which might fulfill the second condition but not the first, or of a story of eating a rotten fruit, which might fulfill the first condition but not the second. Most experiences from which the symptoms dated fulfill either one or the other condition, seldom both, and often enough neither. Nor, in those circumstances, is the therapeutic result satisfactory.

Here is yet another of those situations where another man might well have been discouraged or even given up the work. But some intuition, presumably based on his belief in the determinism of mental associations, told him that the predicament might be because the investigation had been incomplete, that the memories he had obtained were what he was later to call "screen memories," behind which more important ones still lay buried. This surmise proved to be correct, and three things were learned from the deeper investigation: (1) That no hysteria arises from a single experience; it is a matter of cooperation in memories (overdetermination); this rule he held to be absolute. (2) That the significant experiences are invariably sexual in nature and took place in early childhood; this is the paper where he first speaks of the sexual life of children. (3) That the chain of associations is almost incredibly complicated; he likened this to a genealogical tree in which there has been much intermarriage.

The so-called exaggeration of hysterical emotions is thus only apparent. When traced to their source they are found to be appropriate and comprehensible.

Freud remarked here that he had grouped hysteria and the other obsessional neuroses together as "defense neuroses" before he knew anything about their common etiology in childhood.

The differentiation of the various psychoneurotic affections, and the distinguishing factors in their causation, was a problem that greatly occupied Freud in these years, and one to which he returned in an important essay in 1912.[37] On January 1, 1896, he sent Fliess a manuscript which was mainly concerned with it. In it he described four types of pathological deviation of normal affects: (1) Conflict (hysteria); (2) Self-reproach (obsessional neurosis); (3) Mortification (paranoia); and (4) Grief (acute hallucinatory amentia—"Meynert's amentia"). The failure to resolve these affects satisfactorily depends on two conditions that have to be present: *sexual* experiences in *childhood*.

The specific etiology of the obsessional neurosis is an unpleasant (passive) experience in early childhood followed later by a pleasant (and usually active) one. He then listed the various manifestations of the three stages of the disorder: the primary defense, the symptoms arising from compromise, and the secondary defenses.

In paranoia there is self-reproach, but the unpleasant affect of the original sexual experience is projected onto another person, thus giving rise to the primary symptom of mistrust. The "return of the repressed" leads to symptoms in the nature of a compromise (distorted), but they overpower the ego and result in what Freud termed "assimilation delusions," where the ego has accepted the foreign material.

In hysteria the ego is overpowered by the unpleasantness of the original experience, whereas in paranoia that is only a final event. So the first stage here may be called "terror hysteria," a striking illustration of the importance of intense anxiety in early childhood. The repression and the construction of defensive symptoms are concerned rather with the memory of the early experience.

In a letter of May 2, 1897, he had learnt that in hysteria it is not so much the memories as such that are repressed, but impulses derived from the primal experiences. Here was a truly dynamic conception, one which is a foreshadowing of his later conception of a primordial "id." He discerned now the following differences among the psychoneuroses in what breaks through into consciousness and constitutes symptoms: in hysteria it is the memories; in the obsessional neurosis the perverse impulses; and in paranoia the defensive phantasies.

In November of that year Freud suggested to Fliess that the selection of neurosis depended on the stage in development when the repression took place. Two years later (December 9, 1899) he admitted that the dependence of this selection on the age of the child was too simple a formula, and that the stage of sexual development was more important, an idea that took more definite form in later years. He was clear that the psychoneuroses proper are concerned with allo-erotic libido, paranoia rather with auto-erotic.

In a letter of November 18, 1897, there is a clear insight into the true significance of the current factors in neuroses, which have given rise to much misunderstanding, e.g., with Jung. Freud stated that the disorder comes about only when the aberrant libido (deflected through the early experiences) gets combined with motives that have a current value. It is the beginning of the conception which he later termed *sekundärer Krankheitsgewinn* (secondary nosological gain).

As to the explanation why early memories are pathogenic with some people and not with others, that has to do with the special process of "repression" and the peculiarities of *unconscious* ideas—matters that belong to the province of psychology rather than to that of pathology.

An endeavor will now be made to summarize the contents of the two last chapters and in this way to review Freud's progress in psychopathology in the years 1889-1897. This will include both the clinical and the theoretical aspects of his work.

Technique. After treating patients for a year or two with the customary neurological measures of rest, massage, hydrotherapy, and electrical stimulation, Freud began to use hypnotism systematically at the end of 1887. Dissatisfied with the purely "suggestive" aspects of this, he revived Breuer's "cathartic method" in the middle of 1889. In the autumn of 1892 he began to dispense with the use of hypnosis, replacing it by a "concentration technique" aided by repeated pressure on the patient's forehead. His aim was to resuscitate buried memories by following in detail the patient's associations to the symptoms. Hypnosis was entirely discarded after 1896, the year in which the term "psychoanalysis" was first used.

The evolution of this technique consisted essentially in divesting the search for memories from the original adjuvants of direction, pressure, suggestion, questioning, and so on. Instead a passive attitude was adopted, the only activity consisting in from time to time calling the patient's attention to connections he was overlooking. Attention was increasingly paid to the nature of the "resistance" rather than the direct search for memories.

With this gradual refinement Freud had forged an instrument with which he could penetrate the unconscious layers of the mind.

Physical Neuroses. Two of these he delineated, in both symptomatology and etiology, in 1892; the conclusions were published in 1895. Neurasthenia proper was found to be associated with an inadequate form of sexual discharge, particularly masturbation; the anxiety neurosis with an undue sexual excitation the effects of which had been prevented from entering consciousness. With the latter Freud considered that the deflected sexual energy was transformed into morbid anxiety, and he pointed to the similarity of the physical manifestations of this (palpitations, etc.) to those accompanying coitus.

Psychoneuroses. Freud began his work in this field with a knowledge of Breuer's and Charcot's contributions. The latter, with its emphasis on trauma, hindered his perception of the dynamic aspects, and the former, with its emphasis on hypnoid states, delayed the full appreciation of the significance of defensive mechanisms.

His own observations of the phenomena of "resistance" and "transference" date from about 1890 and 1892 respectively. In later years he declared these two concepts to be the hallmark of psychoanalysis. Freud's most important and original contribution in this field was his discovery (1894) that psychoneuroses are due to an intolerance of memories concerning sexual experiences in childhood; this led later to the recognition of childhood sexuality (1898).

He found that the experiences in hysteria were characteristically passive, those in the obsessional neurosis active. He thought the former were those of seduction, often by adults, but in the middle of 1897 he discovered that the "memories" in question had most often originated in phantasies.

Freud was able to trace the various stages in the conflict between the ego and the painful memories and to correlate these with corresponding phases in the development of the neuroses.

Psychopathological Theory. The most important contribution Freud made in this field between 1890 and 1896 lay in his appreciating the significance of what he called the "defense" manifested by the conscious ego against ideas too painful to be borne. From this follows on the one hand the whole conception of a dissociated unconscious and the various complicated results of the intrapsychical conflict, and on the other the detailed study of just which ideas were unbearable and why.

In 1892 he was writing about the tendency of the mind to produce "antithetical ideas" that interfered with conscious intentions. But before this he had sensed the effort needed to overcome opposition in his patients' minds to recovering the forgotten memories, opposition to which he gave the name "resistance." He then easily inferred that the resistance keeping the memories from consciousness was simply another name for the force that had pushed them away to start with, one which he first termed "defense" and before long "repression."

This idea of a volitional repression dawned gradually. Before, he had been puzzled over the question of why the affect investing the dissociated idea had not been discharged along the various familiar paths, of why the traumatic experience had not been absorbed. That in these circumstances the affect either flowed along somatic channels (conversion) or is displaced onto other ideas (as in the obsessional neurosis) depended on the repression.

The first idea of a passively suffered "trauma," e.g., a sexual seduction, one adhered to for long because of Charcot's teaching, gave way, after four years of adherence to it, to the insight that the patient was personally concerned in the experience. The static conception was replaced by a dynamic one. There was wishes and impulses for which the patient felt himself responsible, and recognition of this made the process of volitional repression more intelligible.

Altogether, discovering the sexual nature of the forgotten experiences made sooner or later the recognition of childhood sexuality inevitable. In the form this took Freud perceived the "predisposition" to the various psychoneuroses (and, later on, to the formation of character), one that previously had been exclusively ascribed to hereditary factors.

There remained the mysterious problem of why the memory of an experience should years later prove to be more pathogenic than the experience had at the time. Here Freud described the process he called "the return of the repressed" and attempted an explanation in terms of quantitative changes in affect at different ages and in varying situations.

This condensed account can convey very little of the hard thinking Freud was passing through during those years. His brain was never more active than in that period, just because he had no finished theory of the mind but was constantly struggling to emerge from the simplistic conceptions that had been instilled into him—or at least to combine them somehow with the more dynamic view that the life of his patients displayed to him. The passage from physiology to psychology meant far more than a merely intellectual exchange of outlook: it betokened a reaching towards depths of his own being that had for many years been covered over. The struggle must have been titanic.

XIII

The Fliess Period

(1 8 8 7 - 1 9 0 2)

WE COME HERE TO THE ONLY REALLY EXTRAORDINARY EXPERIENCE IN
Freud's life. For the circumstances of his infancy, though doubtless
important psychologically, were in themselves merely unusual, but not
extraordinary. Again, for a man of nearly middle age, happily married and having six children,[a] to cherish a passionate friendship for
someone intellectually his inferior, and for him to subordinate for
several years his judgment and opinions to those of that other man:
this also is unusual, though not entirely unfamiliar. But for that man
to free himself by following a path hitherto untrodden by any human
being, by the heroic task of exploring his own unconscious mind:
that is extraordinary in the highest degree.

The Fliess story is dramatic enough, and so indeed is the minor one
of how the world came to know of it. Freud destroyed the letters Fliess
had written to him, but Fliess preserved Freud's. Some time after
Fliess's death in 1928 his widow sold the packet of 284 extremely
private letters, together with the accompanying scientific notes and
manuscripts Freud had from time to time sent him, to a bookseller
in Berlin, Reinhold Stahl by name. But she sold them under the strict
condition that they were not to pass to Freud himself, knowing that
he would immediately destroy them. Freud and his wife had both
been very fond of Frau Fliess in the early days, but as time passed
she became increasingly jealous of the close relations between the
two men and did her best—spurred on somewhat by Breuer!—to
disrupt them. Ultimately Freud summed her up as a "bad woman,"
but doubtless she had her point of view. At all events, her final
thrust was a shrewd one.

[a] The really passionate relationship of dependence extended from 1895 to
1901.

Stahl fled to France for a while in the Nazi regime and there offered the documents to Mme. Marie Bonaparte, who at once perceived their value and acquired them for £100. She took them with her to Vienna, where she was doing some postgraduate analysis with Freud, and spoke of them to him. He was indignant about the story of the sale and characteristically gave his advice in the form of a Jewish anecdote. It was the one about how to cook a peacock. "You first bury it in the earth for a week and then dig it up again." "And then?" "Then you throw it away!" He offered to recompense Mme. Bonaparte by paying half of her expenses, but fearing this would bestow some right on him in the matter she refused. She read to him a few of the letters to demonstrate their scientific value, but he insisted that they should be destroyed. Fortunately she had the courage to defy her analyst and teacher, and deposited them in the Rothschild Bank in Vienna during the winter of 1937-1938 with the intention of studying them further on her return the next summer.

When Hitler invaded Austria in March there was the danger of a Jewish bank being rifled, and Mme. Bonaparte went at once to Vienna where, being a princess of Greece and of Denmark, she was permitted to withdraw the contents of her safe-deposit box in the presence of the Gestapo; they would assuredly have destroyed the correspondence had they detected it on either that occasion or earlier in Berlin. When she had to leave Paris for Greece, which was about to be invaded, in February, 1941, she deposited the precious documents with the Danish Legation in Paris. It was not the safest place, but thanks to General von Cholbitz's defiance of Hitler's orders at the war's end Paris, together with the Danish Legation, was spared. After surviving all those perils, the letters braved the fifth and final one of the mines in the English Channel and so reached London in safety; they had been wrapped in waterproof and buoyant material to give them a chance of survival in the event of disaster to the ship.

There they were transcribed and then Anna Freud and Ernst Kris made a suitable selection for publication: Ernst Kris contributed both a comprehensive preface and a number of valuable footnotes, which put any student of Freud deeply in his debt.

The letters and the passages omitted in publication, which the present writer has also read, refer to uninteresting details about arranging meetings, news about the health of various relatives and patients, some details of the efforts Freud made to follow Fliess's "law of periods," and a number of remarks about Breuer which show that Freud

harbored more vigorously critical opinions about him than had gen
erally been supposed; in his writings Freud had always been studiously
"correct" and even generous in any reference to his former friend
and helper.

The correspondence throws important sidelights on Freud's per
sonality in those years, his likes and dislikes, his scientific ambitions
and disappointments, his struggles and difficulties and his need for
the support of a friend during them. Above all, it illuminates the
mode of Freud's intellectual strivings and the empirical—often cir
cuitous—development of his ideas. It enables us not merely to ob
serve the order of this development and to date its various phases,
but to follow in some detail his continuous attempts, often baffled
and often erroneously directed, to get some clear perception of the
laws relating to the mysterious processes operating in the depths of
the mind. With the constant efforts go changing moods, now of ela
tion, now of discouragement, but never of despair. Freud's determi
nation to persist in the face of all difficulties is never for a moment
impaired. And finally he resolves them, and many more personal
difficulties as well, by the remarkable achievement of carrying out,
with the aid of his new technique, a self-analysis, important details
of which are recorded in these letters.

Before we can understand what bound the two men so closely
together, it is necessary to know something about Fleiss himself
(1858-1928). He was the younger of the two by two years. He was
a specialist in affections of the nose and throat who practiced in
Berlin. Of those who knew him, with the exception of the level-
headed Karl Abraham, who was not impressed, everyone speaks of
his "fascinating" personality. He was a brilliant and interesting
talker on a large variety of subjects. Perhaps his outstanding char
acteristics were an unrestrained fondness for speculation and a cor
respondingly self-confident belief in his imaginative ideas with a
dogmatic refusal to consider any criticism of them—a feature that
ultimately led to the break in his friendship with Freud.

His scientific interests ranged far beyond his own special field, par
ticularly in medicine and biology. It was this extension that inter
ested Freud and at first seemed to fit in with his own. Fliess began
with two simple facts on which he then built an enormous superstruc
ture of hypotheses. They were (1) that menstruation occurs once a
month, and (2) that there is a relationship between the mucous
membrane of the nose and genital activities; it often swells with
genital excitement or during menstruation.

Fliess's first publication, in 1897, announced a new syndrome which he termed the "nasal reflex neurosis." It comprised headache, neuralgic pains widely distributed—from the cardiac to the lumbar region, from the arms to the stomach—and, thirdly, disturbances of the internal organs, of the circulation, respiration, and digestion—a very wide net. The point about the syndrome was that all the manifestations could be relieved by applying cocaine to the nose. Its cause was either organic (after-results of infection, etc.) or functional—vasomotor disturbances of sexual origin. This last feature linked with Freud's investigations, more especially since the Fliess syndrome bore the plainest resemblance to neurasthenia, one of Freud's "actual neuroses."

The specificity of this syndrome has never been established, nor has the idea that nasal irritation differs in its nervous effects from any other. Fliess also failed to convince his colleagues that dysmenorrhea has a nasal origin. Nevertheless, the phenomenon of menstruation itself started him off on a far-reaching flight of ideas. It was the expression of a wider process in both sexes throughout life, a tendency towards periodicity in all vital activities. He thought he had found the key to this periodicity by the use of two numbers, 28 and 23; the first was evidently derived from menstruation, the second probably from the interval between the close of one menstrual period and the onset of the next. Fliess laid great stress on the bisexuality of all human beings, and on the whole the number 28 referred to the feminine component, 23 to the masculine one; there was the closest connection between them and sexual processes.

These sexual "periods" determined the stages in our growth, the dates of our illnesses, and the date of our death. The mother's periods determined the sex of the infant and the date of its birth. They operated not only in human beings, but throughout the animal kingdom and probably in all organic beings. Indeed the remarkable extent to which these numbers explained biological phenomena pointed to a deeper connection between astronomical movements and the creation of living organisms. From the nose to the stars, as with Cyrano de Bergerac!

There is much obscure evidence indicating some periodicity in life—the most obvious being the fluctuations in sexual desire—but the difficulty has always been to discover any regularity in it. Needless to say, Fliess was mistaken in thinking he had solved the problem. The mystical features in his writing, and the fantastic arbitrariness with which he juggled with numbers—he was a numerologist par excellence—have led later critics to consign most of his work to the realm of psychopathology.

His magnum opus, *Der Ablauf des Lebens* (The Rhythm of Life), appeared in 1906 and created a little stir in Berlin and Vienna. I read it myself soon after, and a couple of years later discussed it with Freud. I knew that he was acquainted with Fliess, but not of course that there had been a close connection. I asked him how Fliess managed when one attack of appendicitis occurred an irregular number of days after a previous one. Freud looked at me half quizzically and said: "That wouldn't have bothered Fliess. He was an expert mathematician, and by multiplying 23 and 28 by the difference between them and adding or subtracting the results, or by even more complicated arithmetic, he would always arrive at the number he wanted." That was very different from his attitude in the nineties.

Such was the curious personality with whom Freud was to be concerned. Fliess had come to Vienna in 1887 to do some postgraduate study. There he encountered the ubiquitous Breuer, who advised him to attend some lectures Freud was giving on the anatomy and mode of functioning of the nervous system. So for the second time Breuer acted as a catalytic agent in Freud's life. In the scientific discussions that followed, a mutual attraction arose, and the first letter between them (November 24, 1887), written in connection with a patient, begins thus:

"Esteemed Friend and Colleague:

"This letter is occasioned by professional matters. I must however confess, to begin with, that I have hopes of continuing the intercourse with you, and that you have left a deep impression on me which could easily tempt me to say outright in what category of men I would place you."

Fliess responded cordially and even sent a present as a token. A few months later (August 29) Freud sent him his photograph which Fliess had requested. The friendship thus auspiciously begun gradually ripened and became a close one, with a regular correspondence from 1893 onward. The original mode of address, "Esteemed Friend," gave way to "Dearest Friend" within a couple of years, by 1892 the formal *Sie* (you) was replaced by the intimate *Du* (thou), and two years later they were Wilhelm and Sigmund to each other. Freud would have named either of his two youngest children Wilhelm, but fortunately they were both girls.

Of the undeniable personal attraction something will be said presently, but it is important to remember that there were many more objective bonds of serious interest linking the two men. To begin with, their situation in life had much in common. Young medical specialists, emerging from the Jewish middle class, they were both concerned with establishing a practice and maintaining a family. Here Fliess had much the easier time, both through marrying a wealthy wife and being more successful in practice in the freer Berlin. He married a patient of Breuer's, Ida Bondy by name, in October 1892, and had three children by the time Freud had six. His wife being Viennese gave him occasion to visit Vienna and thus to meet Freud there.

They were both educated in the humanities and so could make allusions to both classical and modern literature. Freud constantly quoted Shakespeare to his friend, and we read of his recommending Kipling (particularly *The Light that Failed* and *The Phantom Rickshaw*), while Fliess responded by recommending the stories of Conrad Ferdinand Meyer, the famous Swiss writer. Freud was very taken with these and even supplied a psychoanalysis of two of them as well as making analytic comments on the author. We learn also of Freud's reading in archeology and prehistory and of his excitement at learning of Sir Arthur Evans's discovery of the buried Cretan civilization at Knossos. Freud's beginning to collect antiquities— his only extravagance—did not meet with Fliess's approval; Freud's interest in the past was evidently greater than his friend's.

The scientific background of the two men was very similar, almost identical. The teachings of the Helmholtz school of physics and physiology, which extended to Vienna from Berlin, were those in which Fliess also was brought up. The Christmas present he sent Freud in 1898 consisted of two volumes of Helmholtz's lectures. The bearing this common education had on the scientific outlook and aims of the two men will presently be considered.

On the other hand there were considerable differences in the milieu of the two, and Fliess enjoyed the advantage in this respect. The tired and narrow-minded atmosphere of Vienna contrasted sadly with the lively and progressive spirit that animated Germany, and particularly Berlin, in the era of Kaiser Wilhelm II. Berlin was on the upgrade, whereas Vienna was subject to constant economic crises which had a marked effect on medical practice. Again, the relative liberalism of Berlin aroused the envy of Freud, who had to live in a city ruled by the anti-Semitic Bürgermeister Lueger, and where anti-Semitism prevailed in professional, academic, and governmental circles. The friends anxiously followed together the changing features of the Dreyfus case in France, with keen admiration for Zola's memorable fight for justice, but such things must have mattered much more to someone living in a country where a Jew had practically no chance of advancement than to his friend where such troubles lay forty years in the future.

Presumably this illiberal and anti-Semitic atmosphere, combined with the memory of his early poverty-stricken years that followed the wrenching away from his beloved Freiberg, was one explanation of Freud's intense and permanent dislike of Vienna. At times he uses very strong language indeed about that lovely city: it "disgusts" him, it is "physically repulsive" to him, and so on. In one letter (September 22, 1898) he writes: "I have hardly been back (from the holiday) for three days and already I am overcome by the bad mood of the Vienna surroundings. It is a misery to live here; this is no atmosphere in which to maintain the hope of achieving anything difficult." From Berlin, where he spent a few weeks after leaving Paris in 1886, he wrote: "I believe I should have died on the journey if I had had to travel direct from Paris to Vienna." [1]

Such intensity of feeling must have had deeper roots than the rational ones of consciousness, and perhaps we get a clue to them in the phrase I have italicized in the following passage (letter of March 11, 1900). "I hate Vienna almost personally, and in contrast to the giant Antaeus I gather fresh strength as soon as I remove my foot from the soil of my *urbs patriae* (*vom vaterstädtischen Boden*)[b]." After all, it was his father's misfortunes and lack of success in life that were responsible for what the young Freud had had to endure.

In the early years of my acquaintanceship with Freud, before I knew of that dislike, I innocently remarked on how interesting it must be to live in a town so full of new ideas. To my surprise he started up and barked at me; "I have lived here for fifty years and have never come across a new idea here." [c]

Yet he could never bring himself to leave Vienna. There were at least four occasions when the question arose in a serious fashion. Throughout his long engagement he was uncertain of the chances of success in Vienna and repeatedly suggested emigration to England

[b] Father's city.
[c] I followed this up by another *faux pas*, namely, of praising Moebius, at which Freud also vigorously dissented. Yet in a letter of August 29, 1894, he had described Moebius as having "the best head of any neurologist."

or America.[d] Then, fifteen years later, weary of the hostile attitude of his Viennese colleagues toward his new discoveries, he again toyed with the idea of moving to a more liberal environment. In a letter to Fliess of February 6, 1896, he says he has definitely decided to change his profession (!) and to move elsewhere (presumably to Berlin). This sounds strange, just when he was halfway through *The Interpretation of Dreams*, and of course nothing came of it. Again, after the first World War, when he had lost all his savings in the inflation and Vienna was in a state of hopeless ruin, a friend and former patient offered him a house in Holland with the means to start life again; he refused. Piety once more triumphed. Finally, late in the 1930's he had assured his family he would leave if the Nazis entered Vienna, but not before. Nevertheless, when I got there in March 1939, the day after Hitler's triumphant entry, he was still adamant, saying: "This is my post and I can never leave it." The image of a captain not leaving his ship gave me the idea of telling him the story of the officer who had been blown to the surface by the boiler explosion when the *Titanic* went down. On being sternly interrogated: "At which moment did you leave the ship?" he proudly answered: "I never left the ship, Sir; she left me." Freud saw that this was his case, that Austria had ceased to exist, and so consented to depart for England, the land of his early dreams.

After this digression let us return to the more serious matter of the scientific interests in common between him and Fliess. These are so interwoven with Freud's personal aims and needs that to give a coldly detached account of them alone would leave a misleading impression. What is more significant is the way in which they are connected with Freud's inner development.

To comprehend this connection we must recapitulate a little. We have seen that Freud was endowed with a divine passion for knowledge, though precisely what knowledge he burned to acquire is another matter: let us say for the moment "the origin and nature of humanity: how did human beings come to be what they are; and what in effect are they?" Two passages, both from 1896, bear on this: "Far beyond these considerations (on psychopathology) lurks my ideal and problem child, metapsychology." (December 12.) "I see that you are reaching, by the circuitous path of medicine, your first ideal, that of understanding human beings as a physiologist, just as I cherish the hope of arriving, by the same route, at my original

[d] See pp. 179, 180.

goal of philosophy. For that was my earliest aim, when I did not know what I was in the world for." (January 1.)

Philosophic theorizing and speculation, to which he ventured to give some expression in later life, was something he distrusted—probably on some personal grounds as well as intellectual ones. Perhaps we may even speak of a fear of it. At all events it needed to be sternly checked, and for that purpose he chose the most effective agency—scientific discipline. Until this could be fully incorporated into his being, however, he needed someone to enforce it. There is no doubt that Brücke was by far the most successful of the series he chose, which is the reason why the years in Brücke's laboratory, the place he was so loath to leave, were among the happiest and most carefree of his life. In his later language he would have said here was a guardian of his super-ego who functioned with entire efficiency. Little wonder that he felt somewhat adrift when that support was withdrawn.

I believe we have here an important key to the strange "dependence" he showed at times for so many years. The extreme dependence he displayed towards Fliess, though in diminishing degree, up to the age of forty-five has almost the appearance of a delayed adolescence. And yet it is the complete opposite of the more familiar type of dependence where a weak empty nature clings to a strong one for reinforcement. The self-depreciation of his capacities and his achievements he so often voiced in the correspondence with Fliess sprang not from an inner weakness, but from a terrifying strength, one he felt unable to cope with alone. So he had to endow Fliess with all sorts of imaginary qualities, keen judgment and restraint, overpowering intellectual vigor, which were essential to a protective mentor.

From this point of view it is profitable to ask what there was in Fliess's personality or outlook that rendered him so suitable an object for the formidable role Freud assigned to him. There was, it is true, an urgent vacancy. Freud had had to leave Brücke. Then Meynert, from whom there were at first high hopes, had sadly disappointed him as soon as Freud began to take in interest in the dubious topic of hysteria and hypnotism. Krafft-Ebing, Meynert's successor, was indifferent. Freud could hold out in the field of neurology itself, but this had taken him into that of the neuroses where the safe basis of cerebral pathology was left for the mysteriously unknown realm of the mind, one in which speculation was so inviting and yet held such insidious dangers: the field of the neuroses where one also encountered sexuality and thus relinquished the security of abstinence and "respectability." The *daemon* of curiosity, previously controlled by devotion to the microscope, was awake and would never sleep again. But public opinion, in the form of professional disapproval, was also beginning to voice itself.

In this situation, towards the end of the eighties, Freud naturally turned to Breuer for support. As we know, he got very little. After immense labor he induced Breuer to cooperate in publication. By the spring of 1894 he had induced him to write his chapter on theory for the *Studies in Hysteria*, which appeared a year later. But that was the end. Even in that summer (June 22, 1894) he was complaining of the loneliness he felt "since the scientific intercourse with Breuer has ceased." He hoped to learn from Fliess, since he had been "for years without a teacher." [2]

Now Fliess, like Breuer, had a basis in physiological medicine. Furthermore, as a similar adherent of the famous Helmholtz school, he believed that biological and medical science should strive towards the goal of being able to describe their findings in terms of physics, and ultimately of mathematics. Actually his most important book bears the subtitle, "Foundation of an Exact Biology." That sounded safe enough. He was interested in neuroses, and had even described a neurotic syndrome of his own—moreover, explaining it on a "scientific" organic basis. So far it looked as if he could make a good successor to Breuer. But he had two inestimable advantages over the worthy Breuer, advantages so tremendous that he could perhaps be called Freud's idealization of Breuer, with all the qualities he could wish Breuer to have possessed.

The more obvious advantage was that Fliess, far from balking at sexual problems, had made them the center of his whole work. Not merely was his syndrome, when functional, due to sexual disturbances, but it was his "sexual periods," one male, the other female, that were to explain all the phenomena of life and death. Freud was making his libido theory into an ever-widening explanation of both normal and pathological mental processes, so that—although the two theories were destined for a head-on collision—it looked for some time as if they were exploring the forbidden territory hand in hand. Here was just the combination of collaborator and scientific mentor of whom Freud was greatly in need.

But Freud was here much closer to the ground than Fliess, as he always was. By sexuality he really meant sexuality, in all its strange details; whereas it seemed to mean little more to Fliess than magic numbers. Fliess's critics objected to his numerology, not—as they well might have—to his "pansexualism." So to the world outside Fliess might have appeared crazed, but it was Freud who was really maligned.

The second advantage Fliess possessed over Breuer was more temperamental. Breuer was in his work reserved, cautious, averse to any generalization, realistic, and above all vacillating in his ambivalence. Fliess, on the other hand, was extremely self-confident, outspoken, unhesitatingly gave the most daring sweep to his generalizations, and swam in the empyrean of his ideas with ease, grace, and infectious felicity.

So, after all, it was safe to set the *daemon* free, when he was guided by someone who believed in physics and operated in mathematical symbols. And that was the creative side of Freud: the original love of mastery that had got so completely transformed into the passionate desire to discover the secrets of human life, one so urgent at times that it treacherously beckoned to the short cuts of philosophical speculation.

He seems to have accorded Fliess the right to such speculation, one he diffidently denied himself. Thus: "For your revelations in sexual physiology I can only bring breathless attention and critical admiration. I am too circumscribed in my knowledge to be able to discuss them. But I surmise the finest and most important things and hope you will not refrain from publishing even conjectures. One cannot do without people who have the courage to think new things before they are in a position to demonstrate them." (December 8, 1895.) The assumption evidently was that it was a safe proceeding for someone in the image he pictured Fliess: a man of supreme intellect, of impeccable critical judgment, and thoroughly schooled in the physical and mathematical principles of science. But for himself, drained of the self-confidence he had transferred to his overpowering partner, he had better keep to the empirical observations he was steadily accumulating and allow himself only such theorizing over them as would meet the critical approval of his mentor.

How different from the later Freud when his imaginative powers had been set free. Only a very few years after this, in the Dora analysis, he confidently wrote: "I take no pride in having avoided speculation, but the material for my hypotheses has been collected by the most extensive and laborious series of observations."

This was the first, and chief, demand he made on Fliess: that he should listen to Freud's latest account of his findings and theoretical explanations of them, and pass judgment on them. This Fliess faithfully did. It is not likely that his comments on the subject matter were of any great value, but he made various suggestions for Freud's writings, concerning questions of arrangement, style and discretion, most of which were gratefully accepted. He acted, in short, as a censor. And a censor, besides his obvious activity in eliminating the objectionable, performs an even more important function in silently sanctioning what he has allowed to pass. This sanction is what Freud at that time needed, not the independent-minded, inflexible Freud we knew in later years, but the very different man he was in the nineties. Fliess bestowed this sanction freely. He admired Freud and had no reason (at first!) to doubt the correctness of Freud's work, so the praise he gladly gave must have been highly encouraging. One example alone of its effect will suffice: "Your praise is nectar and ambrosia to me." (July 14, 1894.)

The success of such encouraging sanction in fortifying inner mistrust is exactly proportionate to the value one sets on the bestower, which is why any child in need of such help from his father must first portray him as the most wonderful and powerful man—before the father's inevitable failure to live up to that image makes the child turn to God. That Freud's need was great may therefore be measured by his inordinate overestimation of Fliess, one which to our subsequent appraisal of the two men must have a tragi-comic flavor. The correspondence is replete with the evidence of this, so that again one example will suffice. As late as August 26, 1898, when the end was only two years away, he wrote: "Yesterday the glad news reached me that the enigmas of the world and of life were beginning to yield an answer, news of a successful result of thought such as no dream could excel. Whether the path to the final goal, to which your decision to use mathematics points, will prove to be short or long, I feel sure it is open to you."

Freud was throughout aware of his deep indebtedness and he frequently expressed his gratitude to Fliess. In a letter of January 1, 1896, for example, he wrote: "People like you should not die out, my dear friend; we others need the like of you too much. How much have I to thank you for in consolation, understanding, stimulation in my loneliness, in the meaning of life you have given me, and lastly in health which no one else could have brought back to me. It is essentially your example that has enabled me to gain the intellectual strength to trust my own judgment . . . and to face with deliberate resignation, as you do, all the hardships the future may have in store. For all that accept my simple thanks."

Fliess did whatever anyone could do in meeting the demand just described, but he was able to give a less satisfactory response to the other three demands Freud made on him. After discovering the importance of sexual factors in the causation of the neuroses, with the social implications of this, and noting the more than cool reception which his announcement of them had met, Freud felt impelled to lead a crusade in the matter against the highly respectable leaders of his profession. It was an attitude of revolution and he never shrank from the part he had to play in it. The address he gave in 1898 before the College of Physicians in Vienna was a forcible plea for the necessity of investigating the sexual life of patients. But he would dearly have loved a collaborator and supporter in the campaign, and Fliess's frank views on the significance of sexuality raised the reasonable hope that he had found one. Fliess, however, was a dictator rather than a fighter, and moreover his apparent interest in sexuality turned out to be much more ethereal than Freud's. So the woeful disappointment with Breuer was in this respect only slightly remedied.

Another important demand was that Fliess, with his extensive familiarity with general medicine and biology, would keep Freud's feet on the ground by supplying necessary information concerning any organic basis for neurotic manifestations. It is plain that there was for Freud a security in knowledge of the anatomy and physiology of the nervous system. At the height of his anxious heart illness, which will presently be described, he wrote: "In the summer I hope to return to my old pursuit and do a little anatomy; after all, that is the only satisfying thing." (May 6, 1894.) It was "scientific," assured, and a necessary check on "speculation." This was needed more than ever when he found himself studying mental processes, and for years he cherished the hope of amalgamating the two fields. Here surely Fliess could help him. For instance: "With the theory of repression I have run into doubts, which a word from you—perhaps on male and female menstruation in the same individual—could resolve. Anxiety, chemical ideas, and the like: perhaps I shall find in you the foundation on which I can begin to build a physiological support and cease to explain things psychologically." (June 30, 1896.) It was a long time before Freud brought himself to dispense with the physiological principles of his youth. In a sense he never did entirely, for we shall see that a good deal of his later psychology was modeled on them.

It does not appear that Fliess was of much use to him here either, nor in the nature of the things could he have been. The nearest approach was perhaps his suggestion of a sexual chemistry. This for a time raised Freud's hopes, since he was sure that sexual stimulation must be of a chemical nature (March 4, 1895)—a foreshadowing of the modern gonadic hormones! Both men appear to have hit at the same time on what they called a chemical neurone theory, but of course nothing came of it. Then two years later (March 1, 1897) Freud postulated two kinds of chemical sexual material (male and female), but he remarked that they cannot be identical with the one Fliess is "investigating," although they all obey the 23-28 law. On the whole, any stress Fliess laid on somatic processes must have been a drag on Freud's painful progress from physiology to psychology.

The most complete disappointment, however, was with Freud's last demand. Being convinced of the harmful effects of all the known anticonceptional methods, he dreamed of a satisfactory one that would free sexual enjoyment from all complications. Now if conception, like all vital processes, was determined by Fliess's periodic law, then surely it should be possible to discover the dates in the menstrual cycle when intercourse was safe from that risk. Early (July 10, 1893) he set his hopes on Fliess's solving the problem "as on the Messiah," and a little later (December 11) he promised him a statue in the Tiergarten in Berlin when he succeeded. Two years later (May 25, 1895) it looked as if success were in sight, and he wrote: "I could have shouted with joy at your news. If you have really solved the problem of conception I will ask you what sort of marble would best please you."

So much for Freud's needs and expectations. For these purposes he wrote to Fliess regularly, often more than once a week, sending reports of his findings, details of his patients and—most valuable of all from our point of view—periodical manuscripts containing his ideas of the moment put into a more or less schematic form. They give us, as nothing else can, some notion of his gradual progress and development in psychopathology.

The two men met fairly often in Vienna, and occasionally in Berlin, but whenever possible they would meet for two or three days elsewhere away from their work, when they could concentrate on the development of their ideas. These special meetings Freud half jocu-

larly, half sadly, called "Congresses." Fliess was, as he put it in an allusion to a well-known quotation from Nestroy, his sole public. And
this literally so. There was no one else, no one at all, with whom he
could discuss the problems that so preoccupied him. We know of
several of these meeting places, but the list is probably incomplete.
The first one certainly took place in Salzburg in August 1890. Then
there were "Congresses" in Munich (August 1894), Dresden (April
1896), probably Salzburg (August 1896),e Nuremberg (April
1897), Breslau (December 1897), in or near Aussee (July 1898),
Innsbruck (April 1899), and the final one, when the break took
place, in Achensee, Tyrol (September 1900). They never met again.
In later years an International Psychoanalytical Congress was held
in four out of those six towns; the one arranged to take place in the
fifth town was prevented by the outbreak of the first World War.

It is understandable that such meetings played a central part in
Freud's otherwise isolated intellectual life. They were oases in the
desert of loneliness. As he said in one letter: "When there are two
people of whom one can say what life is, the other (almost) what the
soul f is, it is only right that they should see each other and talk together often." (December 22, 1897.) But there was certainly more
than intellectual stimulation in the matter. Self-confidence depended on it.

As early as August 1, 1890, he wrote, regretting not being able to
come to Berlin: "For I am very isolated, blunted as to science, lazy
and resigned. When I talked with you and remarked what you think
of me, I could even have a good opinion of myself, and the picture
of confident energy you displayed could not fail to impress me. I
should also have profited much from you in medical knowledge, and
perhaps from the Berlin atmosphere, since I have been for years
without a teacher." This mild statement is far surpassed a few years
later. By June 30, 1896, he was looking forward to a "Congress" "as
for the satisfying of hunger and thirst." Following the meeting in
Nuremberg, for which he had "panted," he is "in a state of continuous euphoria and working like a youth" (May 4, 1897), and yet
only three months later the hope of another meeting soon seemed
like "a proper wish-fulfillment, a beautiful dream that will become
real." (August 8.) His freshness for work is a function of the distance from a "Congress." (March 15, 1898.) This was the year when
the need reached its height; curiously enough, since his self-analysis

e For one day only.
f *Seele.*

had already begun the year before. Possibly the early stages of it heightened the dependence before the later ones could dissolve it. The next month, when they could not meet, he wrote: "After each of our Congresses I have been newly fortified for weeks, new ideas pressed forward, pleasure in hard work was restored, and the flickering hope of finding one's way through the jungle burned for a while steadily and brilliantly. This time of abstinence teaches me nothing, since I have always known what our meetings meant to me." (April 3.) "I can write nothing if I have no public at all, but I am perfectly content to write only for you." (May 18, 1898.) Even as late as May 7, 1900, he wrote: "No one can replace the intercourse with a friend that a particular—perhaps feminine—side of me demands."

In spite of all that, Freud retained his self-control even more than the strong desire to meet Fliess. For instance, he had the opportunity of a medical consultation in Berlin but, seeing no real need for it from the patient's point of view, his professional pride would not allow him to take advantage of it. (September 22, 1898.) On another occasion he declined an opportunity because it would impose a specially tiring journey on his friend. (August 14, 1897.)

Loyalty was always a prominent attitude of Freud's. When the *Wiener klinische Rundschau* published what he regarded as an overharsh review of a book of Fliess's, he protested and, since they refused to retract, he severed his editorial connection with the periodical.[8]

There came at last a time, however, when he recognized that his depression was no longer to be lifted by the old cure, and that only courageous painful inner work would help. He decided to stand alone and fight it out. In a very moving letter of March 23, 1900, this is how he described his situation. "There has never been a six months' period where I have longed more to be united with you and your family than in the one just passed. You know I have been through a profound inner crisis, and you would see how old it has made me. So your suggestion of a meeting at Easter greatly stirred me. If one did not know how to resolve contradictions one would find it incomprehensible that I do not immediately assent to your proposal. Actually it is more likely that I shall avoid you. It is not merely my almost childlike yearning for the spring and for more beautiful scenery; that I would willingly sacrifice for the satisfaction of having you near me for three days. But there are other internal reasons, a collection of imponderables, that count heavily with me. (Caviling, perhaps you will say.) I feel greatly impoverished, I have had to demolish all my castles in Spain, and I have only just gathered courage to build them up again. During the catastrophe of that demolishing you would have been of inestimable value to me, but in my present state I could scarcely get you to understand. At that time I mastered my depression with the help of a special diet in intellectual matters; now with that distraction it is slowly healing. Were I with you I should inevitably try to grasp everything in conscious terms so as to describe it to you; we should talk reasonably and scientifically, and your beautiful and sure biological discoveries would awaken my deepest—though impersonal—envy. The end of it all would be that I should keep complaining for five days and should come back all stirred up and dissatisfied with the summer work in front of me when I shall probably need all my self-possession. What oppresses me can hardly be helped. It is my cross and I must bear it, but God knows my back has become distinctly bent from the effort."

The picture we get here is very different from the common one of Freud as that of a clever man who sat down comfortably and calmly and made one discovery after another. They cost him much suffering. And what courage to cast aside the only staff he had to cling to, with only a dim hope of reaching the inner resources of self-confidence that could replace it! Fortunately for himself and for us, that hope was realized within the next couple of years.

Whatever help the meetings with Fliess gave to Freud, it must have been essentially that of psychological encouragement; the purely intellectual assistance could only have been minimal. He had little or nothing to offer in the field of Freud's psychological investigations, and Freud was in a similar position with Fliess's mathematical conjectures, a subject where Freud was rather specially deficient. So the talks were duologues rather than dialogues. As is more than once described in the letters, each would in turn record his latest findings and expound his latest ideas to the other. The chief response would be the gratifying mutual admiration, and the comfort that each could appreciate properly the value of the other, even if no one else did. As might be expected, Freud overestimated Fliess's capacity here at the expense of his own: "In one respect I am better off than you. What I relate to you from my end of the world, the soul, finds in you an understanding critic, whereas what you tell me of your end, the stars, arouses in me only barren astonishment." (October 15, 1897.)

There was at first (1894) some idea of their cooperating in writing a book together, the significance of sexual processes being its main theme, but it was soon dropped.

Although Fliess could have had no deep understanding of Freud's work, he appears to have accepted it and praised it. Freud's acceptance of Fliess's work was of the same order. One cannot doubt that he did accept it for many years, strange as that must appear; the evidence is decisive. He tried to explain in terms of the fatal 23 and 28 the difference between the two "actual neuroses" he had separated, and he also suggested that it was the release of a male 23 material (in both sexes) that evoked pleasure, that of a female 28 material, "unpleasure." (December 6, 1896.) When Fliess's calculations of the sexual periods later extended to the cosmos, Freud went so far as to bestow on him the title of "the Kepler of biology." (July 30, 1898.)

What furthered Freud's attitude would be his own firm belief in strict determinism, that events were invariably brought about by preceding ones. And if the flow of events had a periodic rhythm, why should not a genius like Fliess be able to detect it? All the same, the overpowering motive for his acceptance of the numerology must have been the intimate personal relationship between the two men. Fliess's convictions were too infectious, and Freud's need to believe in his greatness too compelling.

However unpalatable the idea may be to hero-worshipers, the truth has to be stated that Freud did not always possess the serenity and inner sureness so characteristic of him in the years when he was well known. The point has to be put more forcibly. There is ample evidence that for ten years or so—roughly comprising the nineties —he suffered from a very considerable psychoneurosis. An admirer might be tempted to paint this in the darkest colors so as to emphasize by way of relief Freud's achievement of self-mastery by the help of the unique instrument he himself forged. But there is no need to exaggerate; the greatness of the achievement stands by itself. After all, in the worst times Freud never ceased to function. He continued with his daily work and with his scientific investigations, his care and love for his wife and children remained unimpaired, and in all probability he gave little sign of neurotic manifestations to his surroundings (with the sole exception of Fliess). Nevertheless, his sufferings were at times very intense, and for those ten years there could have been only occasional intervals when life seemed much worth living.

He paid very heavily for the gifts he bestowed on the world, and the world was not very generous in its rewards.

Yet it was just in the years when the neurosis was at its height, 1897-1900, that Freud did his most original work. There is an unmistakable connection between these two facts. The neurotic symptoms must have been one of the ways in which the unconscious material was indirectly trying to emerge, and without this pressure it is doubtful if Freud would have made the progress he did. It is a costly way of reaching that hidden realm, but it is still the only way.

That Freud dimly perceived this connection even at the time is shown by several allusions to his mode of working. He did not work well when he felt fit and happy, nor when he was too depressed and inhibited; he needed something in between. He expressed this neatly in a letter of April 16, 1896; "I have come back with a lordly feeling of independence and feel too well; since returning I have been very lazy, because the *moderate misery necessary for intensive work* refuses to appear." [g]

Freud of course recognized the existence of his neurosis, and several times in the correspondence uses that word to describe his condition. There seem to have been no "conversion" physical symptoms, and he would later doubtless have classified it as an anxiety hysteria. It consisted essentially in extreme changes of mood, and the only respects in which the anxiety got localized were occasional attacks of dread of dying (*Todesangst*) and anxiety about traveling by rail (*Reisefieber*). He refers to Fliess's having witnessed one of the worst attacks of the latter on the station in Berchtesgaden at the time of their first "Congress" in 1890—probably as they were parting. He nowhere mentions any connection between the two types of anxiety attack, one which most analysts would now at once suspect, and one cannot help feeling that his analysis of them was never quite complete. Thus he speaks of a patient having indirectly found the solution of his traveling phobia (December 21, 1899)[h] two years after he had himself overcome it (December 3, 1897), which seems strange. Furthermore, he retained in later life relics of it in being so anxious not to miss a train that he would arrive at a station a long while—even an hour—beforehand.

The alternations of mood were between periods of elation, excite-

[g] Italicized here.
[h] See pp. 13, 181. Strictly speaking, the condition cannot be called a phobia, since the anxiety was bearable and so needed no secondary protective measures, e.g., avoidance of traveling.

ment, and self-confidence on the one hand and periods of severe depression, doubt, and inhibition on the other. In the depressed moods he could neither write nor concentrate his thoughts (except during his professional work). He would spend leisure hours of extreme boredom, turning from one thing to another, cutting open books, looking at maps of ancient Pompeii, playing patience or chess, but being unable to continue at anything for long—a state of restless paralysis. Sometimes there were spells where consciousness would be greatly narrowed: states, difficult to describe, with a veil that produced almost a twilight condition of mind. (December 6, 1897.)

He was evidently very given to complaining to Fliess about his distressing moods. It is very surprising to learn this, since it is so alien to the real Freud. Freud had much to endure later on: misfortune, grief, and severe physical suffering. But he faced it all with the utmost stoicism. How often have I seen him in agony from the cancer that was eating away his life, and on only one single occasion did a word of complaint escape him. To be precise, it was two words: "Most uncalled-for" (höchst überflüssig).

Now undue complaining to one person often means that unconsciously—whether rationally or not—the sufferer is ascribing his troubles to that other person's agency, and is in fact begging him to desist. Friendships so intense, and in some respect neurotic, as the one between Freud and Fliess are seldom, if ever, without an undercurrent of latent hostility, and it is not far-fetched to surmise that the unconscious conflict this betokens must have played an important part in Freud's temporary outbreak of neurosis. It is certainly noteworthy that both his suffering and his dependence reached their acme between 1897 and 1900 just when his persistent endeavor to explore his own depths by means of self-analysis was most active. There is, indeed, in a letter of July 7, 1897 (the month he began his own analysis), a broad hint of the connection here suggested: it came after a spell of complete inhibition of writing, so that it starts with an apology for the break. "What has been going on inside me I still do not know. Something from the deepest depths of my own neurosis has been obstructing any progress in the understanding of neuroses, and you were somehow involved in it all. For the paralysis of writing seems to me to have been designed to hinder the intercourse of our correspondence. I have no guarantee for this idea; it is a matter of feeling—of an exceedingly obscure nature." It was already too late to cry absit omen!

There is not much to be said about the meaning of Freud's psychoneurosis. We have, of course, learned from him that the kernel of any neurosis is the Oedipus complex, but that general statement is not very enlightening if one is interested in its specific course and development. The traveling phobia presumably antedated this period, a bad attack having been recorded in 1890. The severe stage of the neurosis was undoubtedly in the second half of the nineties, and it was dispersed within a couple of years after the quarrel with Fliess in 1900.

One may ask what in Freud's life did it coincide with chronologically, and there the answer is not uncertain. There were only two things of high importance to Freud at this time: his approaching exploration of the unconscious, and his remarkable dependence on Fliess. They must be connected. Evidently there was something in leaving the safe, if rather tedious, field of neurology for the unexplored one of psychology which had some supreme inner meaning for Freud. It certainly signified satisfying the deepest wish in his nature, the one that drove him ever farther onward. But it must also have been accompanied by some profound sense of forbiddenness which evoked anxiety and the other distressing and paralyzing moods. It is as if he divined all along that the path he was treading would sooner or later lead to terrible secrets, the revealing of which he dreaded but on which he was nevertheless as determined as Oedipus himself.

Ultimately, as we know, the path ended in the unexpected discovery of his deeply buried hostility to his father. And what more inviting protection against the dark terror can there be than to find a father-substitute to whom one can display the utmost affection, admiration, and even subservience, doubtless a repetition of an early attitude to his own father! Only, unfortunately, such false cures never succeed for long. Always the latent hostility gets transferred also, and the relationship ends, as here, in dissension and estrangement.

The unpublished passages of the Fliess correspondence provide a broad hint of how that inner conflict over psychological investigation was closely connected with a more personal one concerning his relationship to Breuer. We know that it cost Freud a deal of effort, unpleasantness, and what he actually calls "suffering" to induce Breuer to publish his contribution to the psychology of hysteria, a subject which the medical profession of those days regarded as not quite reputable and which Freud's pronouncements on its sexual etiology soon invested with opprobrium. Rightly or wrongly, Freud thought that Breuer never forgave him for having drawn him, or pushed him, into this unpleasant association. At all events he felt that Breuer's behavior towards him in the following years had become very disagreeable.

All that may or may not be so, but what is certain is that Freud conceived a violent antipathy to him, which he conveyed to no one but Fliess. The reasons he gave for his irritation with Breuer are not very convincing, and the expressions he used are so strong as to make one conclude that his reaction had something neurotic in it, i.e., was strengthened by subjective contributions from his unconscious in the nature of a transference from earlier figures in his life —ultimately his father. Now Breuer had always stood in a father relation to Freud, had helped, supported, and encouraged him. More than that, he had lent him—Freud says in his "student years"— a considerable sum of money which so far he had not been able to repay, and Freud's independent nature did not easily tolerate that kind of indebtedness; he even said that it was this matter of the debt that made it impossible to gratify his intense desire to break off all relations with Breuer.

Breuer was failing in his role as father-protector by repudiating Freud's researches and rejecting his conclusions. Yet how could one with an easy conscience turn against a person who for fifteen years had done so much to help and support one? In early life Freud had found it impossible to hate his father, and had concealed his hostility by love. The same solution was the only feasible one now, but the outer reality forbade it except by the device of "decomposing" [i] the father-person into two, one "good," the other "bad." So hatred was directed against Breuer, and love towards Fliess—both in an excessive degree out of proportion to the merits or demerits of the persons themselves. We know that with Freud intense love and hate were specially apt to go hand in hand.

There was also the matter of physical ill-health to add to Freud's troubles in these eventful years. He had by nature a very sound constitution, and the illnesses he suffered from in later life were inflictions rather than innate. He was, it is true, a martyr to migraine throughout his life, although the attacks became much less frequent in later years. Curiously enough, Fliess also suffered from migraine, and the two men conjured up various theories, none of them very fruitful, to account for this distressing disorder. Then, as was fitting

[i] A technical term used by mythologists to describe the same process.

in his relation to a rhinologist, Freud suffered badly from nasal infection in those years. In fact, they both did, and an inordinate amount of interest was taken on both sides in the state of each other's nose—an organ which, after all, had first aroused Fliess's interest in sexual processes. Fliess twice operated on Freud, probably cauterization of the turbinate bones; the second time was in the summer of 1895. Cocaine, in which Fliess was a great believer, was also constantly prescribed. But for a long time Freud also suffered from a recurrent empyema of the antrums, first one side and then the other. Naturally, desperate attempts were made to explain the various attacks and exacerbations in terms of the periodic laws.

In the spring of 1894 there was a more serious affection. An attack of influenza in 1889 had left Freud with an irregular disturbance of the heart's action (arhythmia), and five years later this became somewhat alarming. It followed on a spell of abstinence from smoking, and since it was attributed to nicotine poisoning, something may be said here about Freud's smoking habits. He was always a heavy smoker—20 cigars a day were his usual allowance—and he tolerated abstinence from it with the greatest difficulty. In the correspondence there are many references to this attempt to diminish or even abolish the habit, mainly on Fliess's advice. But it was one respect in which even Fliess's influence was ineffective. Freud soon flatly refused to take his advice: ʲ "I am not following your interdict from smoking; do you think then it is so very lucky to have a long miserable life?" (November 17, 1893.)

But then came the attack, which is better described in his own words. "Soon after giving up smoking there were tolerable days when I even began to write for you a description of the neurotic problem. Then there came suddenly a severe affection of the heart, worse than I ever had when smoking. The maddest racing and irregularity, constant cardiac tension, oppression, burning, hot pain down the left arm, some dyspnea of a suspiciously organic degree—all that in two or three attacks a day and continuing. And with it an oppression of mood in which images of dying and farewell scenes replaced the more usual phantasies about one's occupation. The organic disturbances have lessened in the last couple of days; the hypomanic mood continues, but has been good enough to relax suddenly and to leave me a man who trusts he will have a long life with undiminished pleasure in smoking.

"It is annoying for a doctor who has to be concerned all day long

ʲ This had been given as early as 1890.

with neurosis not to know whether he is suffering from a justifiable or a hypochondriacal depression. He needs help. So I consulted Breuer and told him that in my opinion the cardiac disturbances did not fit in with nicotine poisoning, but that I had a myocarditis that did not tolerate smoking. . . . I do not know whether one can really differentiate the two, but suppose it should be possible from the subjective symptoms and course. But I am rather suspicious of you yourself, since this trouble is the only occasion when I have heard contradictory utterances from you. The previous time you declared it to be of nasal origin and said that the findings of a nicotine heart on percussion are absent. Today you show great concern about me and forbid me to smoke. I can understand that only by assuming that you want to conceal from me the real state of affairs and I beg you not to do that.[k] If you can say anything definite, pray do so. I have no exaggerated opinion either of my responsibilities or of my indispensability, and shall quite well resign myself to the uncertainty of life, and its shortening, that goes with the diagnosis of myocarditis.[l] Perhaps, on the contrary, I might even profit in the managing of my life and enjoy all the more what is left to me." (April 19, 1894.)

A week later digitalis had controlled the irregular action of the heart, but general depression and other symptoms were worse. Breuer doubted Fliess's diagnosis of nicotine poisoning, but he found there was no dilatation of the heart. The diagnosis was still uncertain. Ten days later the patient was feeling better, but was by now convinced he was suffering from a rheumatic myocarditis; he had for some years been troubled by nodules in the muscles and elsewhere (presumably rheumatoid). He was of the same opinion two months after the onset of the attack and proved it was not nicotine poisoning by feeling much better from smoking a couple of cigars a day after seven weeks' complete abstinence. He distrusted both Breuer and Fliess, suspecting that they were keeping something grim from him. He doubted if he would live to fifty-one[m]—the age the periodic law had predestined—and thought it more likely he would die in the forties from rupture of the heart. "If it is not too near forty it won't be so bad." But "one would rather not die too soon nor

---

[k] This situation arose on a graver occasion in his later life. See Vol. III.
[l] Freud always faced with complete courage any real danger to his life, which proves that the neurotic dread of dying must have had some other meaning than the literal one.
[m] An allusion to this may be found in *The Interpretation of Dreams.*[4] See also pp. 348, 357.

altogether!" [5] Fliess, however, persisted in advocating abstinence, so Freud "compromised" by smoking only one cigar a week
—every Thursday to celebrate Fliess's weekly interdiction! A couple of weeks later he noted that the weekly cigar was losing its taste,
so he had hopes of doing without it altogether.

He succeeded in this, for it was fourteen months before he
smoked again. Then he resumed, the torture being beyond human
power to bear, and he must "humor the psychical wretch" (*psy-
chischer Kerl*)—otherwise he won't work. Before that, however,
Fliess had changed his mind and thought the heart condition was of
nasal origin. And this appeared to be borne out by a manifest improvement after an operation and the use of cocaine, evidence
which Freud found persuasive. By the following March (1895) his
attitude towards dying was ambivalent: "Today again I wanted to
die (relatively) young." In April he decided against myocarditis and
reverted to the nicotine diagnosis, but he was not sure which
he would prefer. He must have taken to smoking again, since in October he wrote that he had now quite given it up once more because of his bad pulse and so as not to have to contend with the "vice"
after the fourth cigar: "better to have the fight out with the first."
Nevertheless, in the month following he decided that total abstinence was not possible; he kept within bounds, and the only excess
was an expression of his joy the day the Emperor refused to ratify
Lueger's election as *Bürgermeister*.

Looking back one would come to the conclusion that all these
troubles were in the main special aspects of his psychoneurosis, possibly slightly localized by the effect of nicotine. There was assuredly
no myocarditis. Even in those years he was proving it, for a man of
forty-three who can climb the Rax mountain (in the Semmering
neighborhood) in three and a half hours could not have had much
wrong with his heart—even if he complained that the Rax had got at
least five hundred meters higher of late! Subsequent events were to
show that Freud had an exceptionally sound heart, and also that he
could tolerate considerable quantities of nicotine.

And so the years went on with a constant struggle against
the spells of depression, the anxiety with recurrent attacks of
Todesangst, and all the other troubles, internal as well as external.

In the analysis of the *Non vixit* dream,[6] familiar to all analysts,
Freud had expressed the conviction that, after losing so many good
friends through death and otherwise, he had at last, at a time of life

when one does not so easily make new friends, found one "whom I shall forever retain." In this hope he was doomed to be bitterly disappointed, and the time came when Fliess was to prove neither the first nor the last friend whose personality was in the long run incompatible with Freud's.

The break came in the end over a scientific difference, but this, as is mostly so, was connected with more emotional matters. On reading the correspondence during the ten years of intimate friendship one cannot fail to observe many hints of the coming trouble, although for the most part they escaped recognition at the time. Thus Freud's constant excessive anxiety over his friend's minor disturbances of health, and his sinister fears of what might have happened when he was kept waiting for a letter, cannot be altogether explained by the natural fear of losing someone so important psychologically to him. It is too familiar a manifestation of ill-disposed wishes in the unconscious. And when his friend was on a journey, Freud's anxiety about railway accidents in general got personally applied to an unnecessary extent he was evidently ashamed of.[7] Several dreams he records reveal the same ambivalence. The foundations of the friendship must have been crumbling several years before the final breach.

In a letter of March 1, 1896, he complained of Breuer's attitude, which casts a shadow over his life. Then comes a pregnant passage: "I believe he has never forgiven me for having lured him into writing the *Studies* with me and so committed him to something definite, when he always knows of three candidates for *one* truth and abominates every generalization as a piece of arrogance. It is decidedly not a good arrangement that one has to pay so dearly for everything one has enjoyed in life. Will the same thing happen between us?" His half-meant premonition was only too true. Two years later (March 24, 1898), after reading Fliess's comments on some of the manuscript of *The Interpretation of Dreams*, he contrasted him with Breuer, but in a way that suggests there is an underlying comparison. At all events one man followed the other into the darkness.

Not having the same need of psychological dependence and reassurance as Freud, Fliess was less deeply engaged in the mutual relationship; the difference in the frequency of letters on the two sides is alone an index of that. He had concentrated his emotional needs onto the person of his wife and had developed an extraordinary possessiveness for her; so much so that he grudged her company to her friends and even her own family. All this did not make matters easier.

The fundamental scientific difference can be shortly described. If all the changes in neurotic manifestations—their onset and cessation, their improvements and exacerbations—were strictly determined, as Fliess held, by the critical dates in life revealed by his periodic laws, then all Freud's dynamic and etiological findings were. *de facto* irrelevant and meaningless, even if correct. This is so plain that it is really astounding how the two men managed for ten whole years to interchange their ideas at length in such apparent harmony. Neither could have had much real understanding of the other's work; all they demanded was mutual admiration of it.

Fliess's convictions had a pathological basis alien to Freud's and this made him all the more sensitive to the slightest doubt cast on them. There were in the period in question two little episodes of the kind which could already have been serious had not Freud's tact succeeded in smoothing them over. The first had to do with Loewenfeld's criticism of Freud's paper on the anxiety neurosis in which he said that Freud's theory did not account for the irregularity of the attacks. In his reply Freud pointed to the multiplicity of factors concerned and their varying strength. Fliess thought, on the other hand, that he should have laid more stress on the periodic laws as an explanation and he wrote a separate reply to Loewenfeld on that basis. Freud meekly accepted this filling of the gap in his argument.[f] The other occasion, a year or two later, was when Freud ventured to keep an open mind on a hypothesis Fliess was developing on the theory of left-handedness. He mistook Freud's hesitancy for a sign of doubt about the great theory of bisexuality, with which it was in Fliess's mind connected, and which, as we shall see, was a very sacred topic. He even falsely accused Freud of being left-handed, to which Freud jocularly replied that so far as he could remember in his childhood he had two left hands, but the one on the right side had always had the preference. However, on the main point, that of bisexuality, he pledged his adherence, which, indeed, was permanent.

Naturally, the surer Freud became of the truth of his findings, both through more experience and through his personal analysis, the less attention would he devote to arithmetic, although even in the year of the break itself he still professed belief in Fliess's ideas.

The inevitable clash took place during the last "Congress" at Achensee in the summer of 1900, or perhaps in Munich where Freud was probably seeing his friend off on his return to Berlin. It is possible that the date of the clash was partly determined by one of the rare visits that his half-brother Emanuel, and his son, paid to Vienna at Whitsun a couple of months before; his permanently unclouded affection for Emanuel must have contrasted with the increasingly ambivalent attitude towards Fliess. How the clash itself came about we do not know exactly. Fliess's subsequent (published) version was that Freud made a violent and unexpected attack on him, which sounds very unlikely. What is certain is that he responded, perhaps to some criticism of the periodic laws by Freud, by saying Freud was only a "thought-reader" and—more—that he read his own thoughts into his patients'.

One would have thought that that would have been the end, and, indeed, Fliess said, probably truly, that he thereupon decided gradually to withdraw from the relationship, which he actually did. They never met again. Freud, on the other hand, could not believe that such a valuable friendship had really finished. For another two years he continued his endeavor to mend matters, although he had to recognize that the old "scientific" intercourse could never be resumed. He even proposed a year later that they should write a book together on the subject of bisexuality, Fliess's favorite theme; he would write the clinical part, and Fliess the anatomical and biological. But Fliess was not to be enticed; on the contrary, he suspected this was a trick of Freud's to wrest for himself some of his precious priority in the matter. Nor did he respond to Freud's appeal in January 1902 for a reunion. The remaining correspondence is still friendly, and even warm, but is chiefly taken up with personal and family news. It ends with a card Freud sent from Italy in September 1902.

When it looked as if all was finished there was an aftermath. In the Christmas (Congress) at Breslau, 1897, Fliess had expressed to Freud his conviction that all human beings had a bisexual constitution; indeed, his periodic laws of 28 and 23 were founded on that doctrine. At the last meeting in Achensee in the summer of 1900,[n] Freud announced it to his friend as a new idea, whereupon the astonished Fliess replied, "But I told you about that on our evening walk in Breslau, and then you refused to accept the idea." Freud

[n] In his published account of the incident[e] Freud was subject to another lapse in memory. Two and a half years after Breslau could only have been 1900, whereas he gives the date of this conversation as 1901—a time when he no longer met Fliess, but still wanted to.

had completely forgotten the talk and denied all knowledge of it; it was only a week later that the memory of it came back to him.[o]

The sequel to the incident we know from a short correspondence Fliess published in 1906, in a book entitled *In eigener Sache*, which is a contention about priority. On July 20, 1904, he had written to Freud saying that Otto Weininger, a brilliant Viennese youth, had published a book in which the idea of bisexuality played a prominent part.[p] He had heard that Weininger was intimate with a pupil of Freud's, a young psychologist called Swoboda, and was sure that the great secret had leaked through by this route. What had Freud to say about it?

Freud replied that Swoboda was not a pupil, but a patient to whom he had mentioned in the analysis[q] that a bisexual constitution was universal and who had then casually made the same remark to Weininger. Anyhow Weininger might easily have got the same idea elsewhere, since there are many allusions to it in the medical literature. "That's all I know about the matter." It was perhaps the only occasion in Freud's life when he was for a moment not completely straightforward. He must have been very anxious to placate Fliess.

Fliess then retorted that Freud had previously called Swoboda his pupil; that Weininger had evidently not got the idea from reading, since he claimed it to be entirely new; that any literary allusions were casual and did not refer to the bisexual nature of each living cell, which was the essence of Fliess's doctrine and which Weininger had proclaimed as his own discovery; and could it be true, as he had since heard, that Weininger had actually interviewed Freud and given him his manuscript to read?

Freud was then hard put to it, but he faced the situation manfully. He frankly confessed he must have been influenced by his wish to rob Fliess of his originality, a wish presumably compounded of envy and hostility. He was optimistic if he thought this psychological explanation would mollify or even interest Fliess. He concluded his

[o] A very severe case of amnesia! Only a year before he had written: "You are certainly right about bisexuality. I am also getting used to regarding every sexual act as one between four individuals." (August 1, 1899.) And the year previous to that he had expressed his enthusiasm in the words: "I have taken to emphasizing the concept of bisexuality and I regard youı idea of it as the most significant for my work since that of 'defense'." (January 4, 1898.) (Edith Buxbaum has, in my opinion, wrongly con ceived this passage as indicating a "slip of the pen." [10])

[p] *Geschlecht und Charakter* (Sex and Character) (1903).

[q] In 1900.

letter with the fatal remark of regretting that Fliess had no time to write to him except over such a *trivial* (*sic*) matter as this was. No doubt it should have been, but it certainly was not so to Fliess. He never wrote again, and two years later published what was really a very private correspondence.

The very end of all was really unpleasant. At the close of 1905 Fliess got a friend of his to publish a pamphlet attacking Weininger, Swoboda, and Freud.[11] Freud instantly responded. In January 1906 he wrote a letter to Karl Krauss, editor of *Die Fackel*, of which the following is an extract. "Dr. Fliess of Berlin has brought about the publication of a pamphlet aimed against O. Weininger and H. Swoboda in which both young authors are accused of the grossest plagiarism and are mishandled in a most cruel fashion. The credibility of the wretched publication may be judged by the fact that I myself, a friend of Fliess for many years, am accused as being the one who gave the information to Weininger and Swoboda that served as a basis for their alleged illegality. . . . I hope, dear sir, that you will regard this letter as nothing but a token of my esteem and as an assumption of your being interested in a cultural matter. What we are here concerned with is a defense against the overbearing presumption of a brutal personality and the banning of petty personal ambition from the temple of science."

He also wrote to Magnus Hirschfeld of Berlin, editor of the *Jahrbuch für sexuelle Zwischenstufen* (Yearbook for Sexual Borderline Cases): "May I direct your attention to a pamphlet entitled *Wilhelm Fliess und seine Nachentdecker*. . . . It is a disgusting scribble, which amongst other things casts absurd aspersions on me. . . . Actually we have to do with the fantasy of an ambitious man who in his loneliness has lost the capacity to judge what is right and what is permissible. . . . It is not pleasant for me to utter harsh words in public about someone with whom I have for twelve years been associated in the most intimate friendship and thereby provoke him to further insults."

Independently of Freud, Swoboda also made a vigorous rejoinder and wrote a scathing book exposing Fliess's pretensions.[12] He even instituted legal proceedings against him. The persecutory ideas Fliess may have developed about Freud do not concern us here; they would come as no surprise to the informed reader.

Another aftermath appeared some eight years later. Freud asked five of us to meet him in Munich, on November 24, 1912. He wished to consult us about his editorial difficulties with Stekel and to secure our support for a proposal he had in mind. That matter was quickly and amicably settled, but as we were finishing luncheon (in the Park Hotel) he began reproaching the two Swiss, Jung and Riklin, for writing articles expounding psychoanalysis in Swiss periodicals without mentioning his name. Jung replied that they had thought it unnecessary to do so, it being so well known, but Freud had sensed already the first signs of the dissension that was to follow a year later. He persisted, and I remember thinking he was taking the matter rather personally. Suddenly, to our consternation, he fell on the floor in a dead faint. The sturdy Jung swiftly carried him to a couch in the lounge, where he soon revived. His first words as he was coming to were strange: "How sweet it must be to die"—another indication that the idea of dying had some esoteric meaning for him.

Not long afterwards he confided to me the explanation of his attack. It was a repetition. In a letter of December 8 he wrote to me: "I cannot forget that six and four years ago I suffered from very similar though not such intense symptoms in the *same* room of the Park Hotel. I saw Munich first when I visited Fliess during his illness and this town seems to have acquired a strong connection with my relation to that man. There is some piece of unruly homosexual feeling at the root of the matter. When Jung in his last letter again hinted at my 'neurosis,' I could find no better expedient than proposing that every analyst should attend to his own neurosis more than to the other's. After all I think we have to be kind and patient with Jung and, as old Oliver said, keep our powder dry."

I visited Freud in Vienna a month after this and my memory is that on that occasion he told me that the final quarrel with Fliess took place in the same room. But I cannot completely vouch for this point, since it is possible he only said that the room was associated with Fliess, which it certainly was.

Freud mentioned Fliess a number of times in his subsequent writings. He states that it was from him that he adopted the terms "latency period" and "sublimation." [13]

He was more generous to Fliess in the recognition he accorded to the concept of periodicity, one of which he could make little use, than to that of bisexuality, which proved to be important in his own teaching. He probably continued to believe that there was some periodicity in life, but of an order more complex than Fliess's formulae pretended to discern. In *Beyond the Pleasure Principle* he refers to Fliess's "grandiose conception" of all vital phenomena—and also death—being bound up with the completion of definite terms of time; but he added that there was much evidence to impugn the fixity of Fliess's formulae and to justify doubt of the dominating position he claimed for his laws.[14]

It is open to question whether the stress Fliess laid on periodicity did not influence Freud in his later conception of a "repetition compulsion," and perhaps there may be an opportunity of discussing this when we consider the latest developments of his theories. In a very suggestive passage written in 1924 he explained that the pleasure-unpleasure principle could not depend solely on the quantitative factor of the amount of excitation, as he had earlier supposed. "It seems as if it does not depend on this quantitative factor, but on some peculiarity in it which we can only describe as qualitative. We should be much further on with psychology if we knew what this qualitative peculiarity was. Perhaps it is something rhythmic, the periodical duration of the changes, the risings and fallings of the volume of stimuli." [15]

As to bisexuality, in *Three Essays* he has a footnote enumerating eight authors asserting its universality.[16] Fliess is among them, but since he allots to him the date of his principal book (1906) instead of the actually much earlier date of his "discovery," the five predecessors he gives him should be reduced to two only. Then he adds that these quotations prove what little right Weininger (!) has to priority in the conception. It was perhaps a retort to the ado Fliess had made in the matter.

As for his own indebtedness, all he says is that he had himself observed instances of bisexuality *in the psychoneuroses*, and that a private communication from Fliess had called his attention to this being a general characteristic *of them*.[17, r] The theme of bisexuality evidently remained a sore subject for both men.

The separation left a scar, but it slowly faded. Freud's admiration for Fliess remained, although of course in a modified form, and the resentment gradually died.

r This had happened at Nuremberg in April, 1897, but it applied only to women.

XIV

Self-Analysis

(1 8 9 7 -   )

IN THE SUMMER OF 1897 THE SPELL BEGAN TO BREAK, AND FREUD UNDER-
took his most heroic feat—a psychoanalysis of his own unconscious.
It is hard for us nowadays to imagine how momentous this achievement was, that difficulty being the fate of most pioneering exploits.
Yet the uniqueness of the feat remains. Once done it is done forever. For no one again can be the first to explore those depths.[a]

In the long history of humanity the task had often been attempted. Philosophers and writers, from Solon to Montaigne, from
Juvenal to Schopenhauer, had essayed to follow the advice of the
Delphic oracle,[b] but all had succumbed to the effort. Inner resistances had barred advance. There had from time to time been flashes
of intuition to point the way, but they had always flickered out. The
realm of the unconscious, whose existence was so often postulated,
remained dark, and the words of Heraclitus still stood: "The soul of
man is a far country, which cannot be approached or explored."

Freud had no help, no one to assist the undertaking in the slightest degree. Worse than this: the very thing that drove him onward
he must have dimly divined (however much he tried to conceal it
from himself), could only result in profoundly affecting his relations—perhaps even severing them—with the one being to whom
he was so closely bound and who had steadied his mental equilibrium. It was daring much, and risking much. What indomitable

[a] Kurt Eissler has vividly illustrated the imagination needed adequately to
apprehend the significance of this event in "An Unknown Autobiographical Letter by Freud and a Short Comment." [1]
[b] The first authentic record of the injunction "Know thyself" would appear to emanate from Chilon of Sparta, about 600 B.C.

courage, both intellectual and moral, must have been needed! But it was forthcoming.

It is only from a distance, however, that the dramatic aspect is to be perceived. At the time it was a long and painful groping struggle of Herculean labor, and he must often have thought of "all the lost adventurers, my peers." The decision itself to undertake the task was hardly one of conscious will or deliberate motive. There was no sudden flash of genius, but a growing intuition of its necessity. An overpowering need to come at the truth at all costs was probably the deepest and strongest motive force in Freud's personality, one to which everything else—ease, success, happiness—must be sacrificed. And, in the profound words of his beloved Goethe, "The first and last thing required of genius is love of truth."

In such circumstances Freud could have looked for no reward beyond the satisfying of the imperious need. And it was long before such was forthcoming save for an "indescribable sense of intellectual beauty" which the revelations occasionally yielded. For three or four years the neurotic suffering and dependence actually increased in intensity. But there came a time when he learned that

> To bear all naked truths
> And to envisage circumstance all calm,
> That is the top of sovereignty.

The end of all that labor and suffering was the last and final phase in the evolution of Freud's personality. There emerged the serene and benign Freud, henceforth free to pursue his work in imperturbable composure.

More must now be said about the details of this progress and also about Freud's changing views on sexuality in childhood that preceded and accompanied it. Before doing so, however, it is worth while quoting a sentence he had written no less than fifteen years before this time. "I always find it uncanny when I can't understand someone in terms of myself." [2] He had evidently taken to heart Terence's saying: *"Humani nihil a me alienum puto."* [c] It was one more reason for wishing to know himself completely.

Two important parts of Freud's researches are intimately connected with his self-analysis: the interpretation of dreams, and his growing appreciation of infantile sexuality.

The interpretation of dreams played a triple role. It was observing and investigating his own dreams, the most readily available mate-

[c] Nothing human is alien to me.

rial for the purpose of study and the one most used in his book, that gave him the idea, in conscious terms, of pursuing his self-analysis to its logical end. And it was the method he mainly used in carrying it out. He held later to the opinion that someone who was honest, fairly normal, and a *good dreamer* could go a long way in self-analysis, but then everyone is not a Freud. His self-analysis proceeded simultaneously with the composition of his magnum opus. *The Interpretation of Dreams*, in which he records many of the details. Lastly, it was in the interpreting of dreams that he felt most secure; it was the part of his work in which he felt the greatest confidence.

If we review the development of Freud's views on sexuality and childhood up to the time of the self-analysis, on the basis of both his publications and the Fliess correspondence, we must come to the following conclusions. His insight was much more gradually gained than is often supposed. Things that are now so clear were obscure enough then. He necessarily started with the conventional view of childhood innocence, and on coming across the outrageous stories of seduction by adults he took the similarly conventional view that this constituted *precocious* stimulation. He did not at first consider that it aroused sexual feelings in the child at the time; it was only later, about puberty, that the memory of the incidents became exciting. This idea is in accord with the one expressed in 1895, that memories become traumatic *years after* the experience itself.[3] By 1896 he was surmising that perhaps "even the age of childhood may not be without delicate sexual excitations," but it is plain that these are regarded as purely autoerotic, there being no connection between them and other persons. A year later he was interested in the organic basis of such excitations, and was localizing them in the regions of the mouth and anus, though suggesting that they might concern the whole surface of the body;[4] he used the term *erotogenic zones* in a letter of December 6, 1896, and in one of January 3, 1897, he called the mouth the "oral sexual organ."

The allo-erotic aspects of childhood sexuality he discovered in a curiously inverse way, not through the child but through the parent concerned. From May 1893, when he made the first announcement of it to Fliess, to September 1897, when he admitted his error, he held the opinion that the essential cause of hysteria was a sexual seduction of an innocent child on the part of some adult, most often the father; the evidence of the analytical material appeared irrefragable. For more than four years he maintained this conviction, though being increasingly surprised at the frequency of the supposed occurrence. It began to look as if a large proportion of fathers carried out these incestuous assaults. Worse still, they were usually of a perverse kind, the mouth or anus being the regions chosen. He inferred, from the existence of some hysterical symptoms in his brother and several sisters (not himself: *nota bene*), that even his own father had to be thus incriminated (February 11, 1897); though he immediately added that the frequency of such occurrences often raised his suspicions. Towards the end of this period doubts began to crowd into his mind, but they were repeatedly rebutted by some fresh evidence. When, finally, he had a dream about his American niece Hella, which he had to interpret as covering a sexual wish towards his eldest daughter, he felt he had personal first-hand evidence of the correctness of his theory (May 13, 1897).

Four months after this, however, Freud had discovered the truth of the matter: that irrespective of incest wishes of parents towards their children, and even of occasional acts of the kind, what he had to concern himself with was the general occurrence of incest wishes of children towards their parents, characteristically towards the parent of the opposite sex. This other side of the picture had been quite concealed from him. The first two months of his self-analysis had disclosed it. He was learning the truth of Nietzsche's maxim: "One's own self is well hidden from oneself: of all mines of treasure one's own is the last to be dug up."

Before this, it is true, he had sent Fliess some notes in which he recognized the regular occurrence *in neuroses* of hostility and death wishes directed by the son against his father and the daughter against her mother.[5] This implies the motive of jealousy, which might, however, be thought of in terms of love rather than of sexual wishes. But in the same notes he discusses the cultural significance of incest prohibitions, so the idea of incest (though, again, possibly on the side of the parent) was already in his mind. The decision to discover whether such ideas were present in his own unconscious could not be long postponed.

Even then Freud had not really arrived at the conception of infantile sexuality as it was later to be understood. The incest wishes and phantasies were later products, probably between the ages of eight and twelve, which were thrown back onto the screen of early childhood. They did not originate there. The most he would admit was that young children, even infants of six to seven months old (!), had the capacity to register and in some imperfect way to apprehend the meaning of sexual acts between the parents that had been seen or overheard (May 2, 1897). Such experiences would become significant only when the memory of them was reanimated by sexual phantasies, desires, or acts in later years. Extensive subsequent investigations have proved this concept of "regression" to be both valid and important, but one may wonder whether, at the time we are considering, the exaggeration of it did not impede Freud's vision of the earlier years of childhood.

The first forms of sexual excitation in early childhood that Freud recognized were what are now called "pregenital" ones and concerned the two alimentary orifices, mouth and anus (1896-1897). These could still be regarded as autoerotic. It was much harder to admit that the young child might have genital wishes concerning a parent which could in many respects be comparable with adult ones. And to recognize the full richness of the child's sexual life in terms of active impulses was a still further step that Freud took only later with his usual caution. It is probable that it was achieved at the turn of the century, though we possess no full statement of it before the essay he wrote for Loewenfeld's book in 1905,[d] about the time of the *Three Essays on the Theory of Sexuality.*

Even in *The Interpretation of Dreams* (1900), in which the Oedipus complex is described, one finds what might be called an encapsuled fossil from earlier times in which it is assumed that children are free from sexual desires;[7] the footnote correcting it was added only in the third edition of the book (1911).

There is therefore no doubt that over a period of some five years Freud regarded children as innocent objects of incestuous desires, and only very slowly—no doubt against considerable inner resistance—came to recognize what ever since has been known as infantile sexuality. As long as possible he restricted it to a later age, the phantasies being believed to be projected backwards onto the earlier one, and to the end of his life he chose to regard the first year of infancy as a dark mystery enshrouding dimly apprehensible excitations rather than active impulses and phantasies.

In the light of these considerations we may now return to the self-analysis itself. The earliest inception might well be referred to that historic occasion in July 1895, when he first fully analyzed one of his dreams. In the years following this he several times communicated to Fliess the analyses of dreams of his own. From that correspondence we can also give the date when those casual analyses became a regular procedure with a definite purpose. It was in July 1897.

[d] *My Views on the Rôle of Sexuality in the Etiology of the Neuroses.*

One naturally asks why the decision was taken just at that time. Here again, however, we probably have to do with a gradually increasing pressure of unconscious forces rather than a sudden dramatic stroke of genius. We have noted all along that Freud's genius was that of an unrelenting forward march through difficulties rather than of swift flashes of intuition. In the present instance there were deep and irresistible motives at work.

It was in the previous October that Freud's father had died. In thanking Fliess for his condolence he wrote: "By one of the dark ways behind the official consciousness my father's death has affected me profoundly. I had treasured him highly and had understood him exactly. With his peculiar mixture of deep wisdom and fantastic lightness he had meant very much in my life. He had passed his time when he died, but inside me the occasion of his death has reawakened all my early feelings. Now I feel quite uprooted."

Freud has told us that it was this experience that led him to write *The Interpretation of Dreams* (1898), and the writing of this work went hand in hand with the first year or two of his self-analysis; one may legitimately bracket the two together. In the Preface to the Second Edition, written in 1908, he said he only recognized the connection with his father's death after finishing the book. "It revealed itself to me as a piece of my self-analysis, as my reaction to my father's death; that is, to the most important event, the most poignant loss, in a man's life."

From that moment, therefore, he was destined sooner or later to transform the scientific interest in the mechanisms of his dreams into a regular and unsparing self-analysis. His father's death was the stimulus for this as much as for composing the book.

There are hints, too, that the swelling undercurrent of hostility towards Fliess was connected with the unconscious identification of him with his father.

In the February after his father's death Freud mentioned the incriminating of him in acts of seduction, and three months later his own incest dream which he said put an end to his doubts about the seduction story (May 31, 1897). Accompanying this latter, however, was the manuscript that announced the hostility of the children who later became neurotic towards the parent of their own sex—the very first hint of the Oedipus complex. Apparently both views were held simultaneously.

In the middle of April Freud met Fliess in Nuremberg, and ten days later (April 28) he sent him an account of a dream with an analysis that revealed an unconscious resentment and hostility against him. He was evidently aware of some emotional turmoil, since in a passage (unpublished) of a letter four days later he wrote: "My recovery can only come about through work in the unconscious; I cannot manage with conscious efforts alone." (May 2, 1897.) This is probably the first hint of Freud's perception that he had to pursue a personal psychoanalysis, although it took him another couple of months to bring himself to that decision.

There followed a period of apathy and "an intellectual paralysis such as I have never imagined." (June 12.) He described how he was passing through a neurotic phase: "Curious state of mind which one's consciousness cannot apprehend: twilight thoughts, a veil over one's mind, scarcely a ray of light here and there." Every line he wrote was a torment, and a week later he said his inhibition about writing was really pathological (June 18); he soon discovered, however, that the motive for it was to hinder his intercourse with Fliess. Then comes the poignant passage previously quoted from the letter of July 7, where he speaks of resistances in the very depths of his neurosis in which Fliess is somehow involved.ᵉ But, more cheerfully, something is preparing to emerge. "I believe I am in a cocoon, and God knows what kind of beast will creep out of it." (June 12, 1897.)

Soon after this Freud joined his family in Aussee, and on August 14 he wrote definitely about his own analysis, which, he said, is "harder than any other." "But it will have to be carried through; and moreover, it is a necessary counterpart to my [therapeutic] work." A part of his hysteria is already resolved. He had clearly recognized that his own resistances had been hampering him in that work.

In another fortnight he and his wife had left for a tour in North Italy, and we do not know how much this interrupted the analysis. He got back to Vienna on September 20, and on the next day reported the fateful news to Fliess that the seduction stories he had believed in were not literally true. It is highly probable that this conclusion was reached as a result of recognizing his own phantasies, which would speak in favor of the analysis having continued through the holiday.

In letters of October 3, 4, and 15, Freud reported details from the progress of his analysis. They have been taken into account elsewhere in the story. He had now recognized that his father was inno-

ᵉ See p. 306.

cent, and that he had projected onto him ideas of his own. Memories had come back of sexual wishes about his mother on the occasion of seeing her naked. We get an account of his childhood jealousy and quarrels, and of the rediscovery of his old nurse, to whom he attributes most of his trouble; the recovered memory of her washing him in *red* water in which she had previously washed was a particularly convincing detail.

In the last of these letters Freud related how he inquired of his mother about his early childhood. He in this way got objective confirmation about the truth of his analytic findings, and was also given information, for instance about the nurse, that cleared up some of his bewilderment. He remarked that his self-analysis promised to be of the greatest value to him if it were carried through to the end. He had discovered in himself the passion for his mother and jealousy of his father; he felt sure that this was a general human characteristic and that from it one could understand the powerful effect of the Oedipus legend. He even added a corresponding interpretation of the Hamlet tragedy. Evidently his mind was now working at full speed, and we may even speak of swift intuitions.

A letter of the twenty-seventh gives a very vivid, and almost poetical, account of the varying phases of the analysis. The overcoming of his own resistances gave him a much clearer insight into those of his patients, and he could now understand their changes of mood far better. "Everything that I experience with patients I find here: days when I slink about oppressed because I have not been able to understand anything of my dreams, my phantasies, and the moods of the day, and then again days in which a flash[f] illuminates the connections and enables one to comprehend what has gone before as a preparation for today's vision."

In a letter of November 14 there is a curious passage which one can only interpret as another instance of a lapse in memory. He relates that "before the holidays I told you I was the most important patient at the moment; after them my self-analysis, of which there was at the time no trace, suddenly got under way." This is definitely contradicted by the facts of the previous letters, although it may well be that the analysis speeded up immediately after returning to Vienna.

Naturally Freud's analysis, like all others, produced no magical results at once. In the later letters there are characteristic accounts of variations in the progress: optimism alternating with pessimism, ex-

f *Ein Blitz.*

acerbations of symptoms, and the like. The neurosis itself, and the corresponding dependence on Fliess, seemed to have been more intense, or more manifest, in the next year or two, but Freud's determination to win through never faltered and ultimately conquered. And in a letter of March 2, 1899, we read that the analysis has done him a great deal of good and that he is obviously much more normal than he was four or five years ago.

When the letters changed their tone after the quarrel in 1900 there is, as one would expect, little more heard about the analysis, which was certainly still proceeding. The wish for reconciliation, as we have heard, persisted until the final break over the Weininger episode. Then comes an interesting detail about the dissolution of the old bond. Freud related a dream that occurred while he was occupied with a particular scientific problem.[8] It has been supposed that the theme of this was bisexuality, and the date would therefore be 1904, when he was writing the *Three Essays on the Theory of Sexuality*. The disagreeable Weininger episode had taken place in the summer of that year. The dream, which Freud stigmatizes as a hypocritical one, contains the idea of reconciliation with Fliess, but the analysis revealed the deeper wish to break forever with him. And that was really the end.

Inasmuch as few, if any, psychoanalyses are ever complete—absolute perfection being denied to mortals—it would be unreasonable to expect that Freud's self-analysis, deprived of the assistance of an objective analyst and without the invaluable aid afforded by the study of transference manifestations, was so either. Perhaps we shall have occasion to suggest how the incompleteness may have influenced some of his conclusions.

At the head of this chapter only the initial date is given. The reason is that Freud told me he never ceased to analyze himself, devoting the last half hour of his day to that purpose. One more example of his flawless integrity.

XV

Personal Life

(1 8 9 0 - 1 9 0 0)

THE FLIESS CORRESPONDENCE ADDS MUCH TO WHAT IS KNOWN FROM other sources concerning Freud's mode of life, habits, and general circumstances during this period. Even trivial details get mentioned incidentally, such as that he paid a daily visit to his barber[1]—indicating, for a fully bearded man, an unusual care of his person; that he loathed the apparently harmless dishes of fowl and cauliflower so much that he avoided taking a meal with a family where they were apt to be provided; and that he had a telephone installed as early as 1895.[2]

The roomier flat in the Berggasse, to which the Freuds had moved in the late summer of 1891, was not equal to the increasing number of children, so in 1892 Freud rented another flat. This was on the ground floor in the same house, and gave on to a small but pleasant garden in the back. It had three rooms, used as patients' waiting room, consulting room, and study respectively, so that Freud had every opportunity for quiet concentration. This arrangement lasted until 1907. Frau Fliess celebrated the occasion by sending him an example of her own handiwork.

Freud remarked in one letter that his life was spent in either his consulting room or the nursery upstairs. He was evidently a fond father, and his letters to Fliess are full of details of the children's remarkable sayings and deeds. They all grew up to be sturdy, healthy people, but in childhood they seem to have caught every imaginable infectious disease. This was a source of constant anxiety, since it must be remembered that many of those diseases, such as scarlet fever, diphtheria, tonsillar angina, etc. were much more dangerous then than now, and nursing was the only form of treatment available.

328

Despite his other preoccupations Freud was very much a family man, interested in all that concerned his many relatives. Moreover, in addition to maintaining his own full household, he had to contribute to the support of his parents and sisters. His brother Alexander assisted in this as best he could, though even he had to borrow money occasionally (from Fliess). Freud mentions the great pleasure he got from his English half-brother Emanuel's visits to Vienna, e.g., in 1896 and 1900.

Freud had one important hobby, but few relaxations apart from holidays. He played a certain amount of chess, but gave it up entirely before he was fifty since it demanded so much concentration which he preferred to devote elsewhere. When alone he would sometimes play patience, but there was a card game he became really fond of. That was an old Viennese four-handed game called tarock. He was playing this in the nineties, and probably earlier; later on it became an institution, and every Saturday evening was religiously set aside for it. The initiator was Professor Königstein,[a] the ophthalmologist who was one of the first to use cocaine in his practice. The games took place in his house until his death in 1924. Another partner was Oscar Rie, the children's physician, who was Freud's assistant at the Kassowitz Institute, where he had cooperated with him in the work on infantile paralyses; he was now the family doctor.[b] The fourth was Dr. Ludwig Rosenstein,[c] also a pediatrist from the Kassowitz Institute, who had married Rie's sister. Later on Alfred Rie, a brother of Oscar's, took a hand, and—many years later—Freud's own children replaced his friends.

Freud paid only very occasional visits to the theater or opera. The operas had to be by Mozart, though an exception was made with *Carmen*. He would also now and then attend a public lecture. Thus he greatly enjoyed listening to one by Mark Twain, an old favorite of his (September 2, 1898). An address by the Danish writer, Georg Brandes (March 23, 1900), was a more serious affair. He recalled the experience and commented: "The whole style must have seemed foreign enough to the Viennese; actually he was very rude to his public. We are not familiar here with such strict conceptions of life; our petty logic and our petty morals are very different indeed from northern ones." [3]

An important relaxation was of a more generally social kind. In

[a] In one letter Freud called him the best friend he had in Vienna.
[b] His daughter is a well-known psychoanalyst.
[c] So is his daughter.

1895, when he was finding his professional ostracism depressing, he sought for congenial company among men to whom he felt still nearer. This he found in the Jewish club or lodge, the B'nai B'rith Society, to which he then belonged for the rest of his life.[d] He would attend their social or cultural gatherings on every alternate Tuesday, and he occasionally gave a lecture there himself; he gave one, for instance, on "Dreams" on December 7 and 14, 1897, and one on Zola's *La Fécondité* on April 27, 1900.

The hobby was, of course, his passion for antiquities. This gratified both his aesthetic needs and his abiding interest in the sources of civilization, as indeed of all human activities. It was certainly his only extravagance, if it can be called such. The first mention of it we have in the Fliess correspondence dates from December 6, 1896, when he was decorating his consulting room with reproductions of some Florentine statues: "I find them a source of extraordinary refreshment." In a letter of August 20, 1898, he tells Fliess he has bought a Roman statue in Innsbruck. Then he is reading with enjoyment Burckhardt's *Griechische Kulturgeschichte* (Cultural History of Greece) and noting parallels to his psychoanalytic findings: "My fondness for the prehistoric in all human manifestations remains the same." (January 30, 1899.) When he made himself a present of Schliemann's *Ilias*, he was especially interested in the account of his childhood the author gives in his Preface, and the early ideas that later resulted in the discovery of the buried Troy. "The man was happy when he found the treasure of Priam, since the only happiness is the satisfaction of a childhood wish." (May 28, 1899.) He had stated this more formally in an earlier letter: "I append a definition of happiness. Happiness is the subsequent fulfillment of a prehistoric wish. That is why wealth brings so little happiness: money was not a wish in childhood." (Jan. 16, 1898.) [e] The stone statue of Janus he acquired had two faces that "gaze at him with a very superior air." (July 17, 1899.) On the same holiday his beloved Salzburg yields him two Egyptian antiquities: "they speak to me of faraway times and countries." (August 6.) Of his excitement two years

---

[d] It was this membership in what the Nazis called an "underground political group" that they used as a pretext to seize the *Internationaler Psychoanalytischer Verlag* in March 1938!

[e] A more bitter, though only half-meant, definition from a later date runs: "One gradually gets familiar with a new insight into the nature of happiness. One may assume happiness to be present when fate has not at once fulfilled all its threats." (March 24, 1901.)

later on reading of Sir Arthur Evans's discoveries in Crete we have already spoken.

For climatic reasons long summer holidays were a regular institution in Vienna. On account of heat even schools closed at the end of June, and it was customary for families to spend two or three months in the country even if the men could join them only at intervals. Freud made every endeavor to adhere to the custom even in his most penurious years. There were, it is true, good reasons why such a habit could be regarded more of a necessity than a luxury. He found early, as all other analysts have since, the strain of the work to be such that without an ample period for recuperation its quality would surely deteriorate. Then, after all, there must be some pure pleasure in one's life, and Freud knew of few pleasures so satisfying as the enjoyment of beautiful scenery, and the sight of new parts of the world. He had in him the dichotomy, not a rare one, between the call of the North and that of the South. The high ideals of duty spoke for the North. There was Berlin, for instance, with its restless activity and unceasing impulse for achievement. But for pleasure, happiness, and pure interest the South was pre-eminent. Its softness and beauty, its warm sun and azure skies, above all its wealth of visible remains of man's early stages in development: to Freud as to so many others all this made an irresistible appeal. I once tried to give him pleasure by showing him some poems in which Browning expressed his transcendent love for Italy:

> O Woman country
> Woo'd, not won,
> Loved all the more by earth's male lands
> Laid to their hearts instead.

But he waved them aside with a smile, saying: "I have no need of that; we have our own enthusiasts." No doubt Goethe and Heine were foremost in his mind.

It was Freud's custom in those days to send his family away in June, or even May, and to continue working alone in Vienna until well into July, with occasional week ends with his family; he would return to work about the middle of September. At first they did not go far: Maria-Schutz (Semmering) in 1890, then Reichenau for four years, and in 1895 only to the Bellevue, in the immediate environs of Vienna: it was here that the first dream analysis was carried out. After that they went for three years to Obertressen, near Alt-Aussee, in the Styrian part of the Salzkammergut, and in 1899 for the first time to near Berchtesgaden. In 1900, money being short, they went once again to the Bellevue.

But from these vantage points, and also from Vienna itself, Freud would often set out on more distant travels, accompanied by his wife, his brother, or, on one occasion, by his sister-in-law. When his wife went with him his sister Rosa, while she was still unmarried, would stay to superintend the children and their nurse. The couple of months as a grass widower in Vienna were always trying, and Freud complained especially about the great heat which is apt to afflict the town in June and July. He had of course his writing as well as his patients to attend to, and almost every evening there was an invitation to spend the evening with friends. He had at this time an astonishingly wide, if not varied, circle of acquaintances, almost all being Jewish doctors. There is no point in giving a list of twenty or thirty names, since none of them were of much importance to Freud. His chief friends were Bloch, Oscar Rie, and Königstein. It was about this time that he was giving up chess for tarock, the card game to which he remained faithful; they would often play this until one or two in the morning. When Freud spoke later of the ten years of isolation one must understand that this referred purely to his scientific, not to his social, life. His heart, however, went entirely to the thoughts of rejoining his family or of traveling to wonderful places. As we shall see, he was a restless traveler, eager to crowd in as many impressions as possible in his limited time. Minna once said of him that his ideal was to sleep in a different place every night.[4]

In August 1890 Freud went to Salzburg where he and Fliess held their first "Congress." In 1891 he got away for two week ends for mountain climbing, in July to climb the Rax with Kassowitz, and in August to explore the Dachstein group near Schladming in Styria, apparently alone. In August 1892 he and his wife spent a week in Hallstatt and then one in Bad Aussee in Styria, afterwards rejoining the children in Reichenau.[5] Eighteen ninety-three was a bleak year, and he could only spend three weeks in Reichenau; he had, however, been able to visit his friend Fliess in Berlin for a couple of days in April. Eighteen ninety-four was better. In the first half of August they went to Munich to visit Fliess and the wife whom he had married two years before. Fliess had gone there for medical treatment and was seriously ill at the time.[6] On the way back to Reichenau they stayed at Ischl to see Minna, and then after a couple of weeks with the children there they all spent the first fortnight in September, at his wife's request, at Lovrano, a small fishing village near Abbazia on the Adriatic.[7] At Easter of the following year Freud dashed again to Abbazia, in Istria, to get another glimpse of the Adriatic, of which he had been fond ever since his happy student days at Trieste; he was there only one day. But in August of that year he got his first sight of the promised land of Italy, when he took his brother Alexander for a wonderful week in Venice. He saw a great deal in the time and managed also to visit Murano and Chioggia as well as enjoying bathing on the Lido. From here he took Alexander to Berlin where they were both consulting Fliess; Freud had a nasal operation there.

Eighteen ninety-six must have been a more opulent year, since the holiday plans were much more ambitious. It was the first time that the family could be taken as far afield as Aussee, in Styria, to spend the summer. That was beyond the easy reach of week ends, so by way of compensation Freud planned an extensive tour. Although he had already had a three days' "Congress" with Fliess in April in Dresden he held another one with him in Salzburg in the last week of August, after he had spent a month with the family. After that he joined his brother Alexander at Steinach and traveled with him via Bologna to Venice. They were there only two days and then, after a break of a few hours at Padua, where he put in four hours of "hard work," got to Bologna. This was a town that took Freud's fancy, and he spent three nights there. On the last day he made excursions to Ravenna and Faenza; he was less impressed by the former than one might have expected. Then came a whole gorgeous week in Florence where he was carried away by the "delirious magic" of its wonders. Freud had an extraordinary power of rapid assimilation, and that week must have given him what it usually takes a month to acquire. Among other discoveries was the Galileo museum in the Torre del Gallo outside the town. There he persuaded the owner, Count Galetti, who occupied the upper story, to rent them three rooms for the rest of their stay, and there they spent four days surrounded by priceless treasures, and with a glorious outlook over Florence. This must have been the longest holiday Freud had yet taken; he was away from Vienna for two months. In October his wife was away from the whole family for the first time since her marriage. She spent a couple of weeks with her mother at Hamburg, staying with the Fliess ménage in Berlin on her way and on her return.

In the next year, 1897, he covered more ground still, though the holiday was shorter. At Easter he was in Nuremberg with Fliess, and in June he climbed the Schneeberg, in the Semmering, with his brother. In the middle of July he met his sister-in-law Minna in Salzburg and they made a short walking tour together to Untersberg and Heilbrunn. Then after a visit to her mother in Reichenhall he returned to Vienna where he had to make the arrangements for his father's gravestone. This was just when he was beginning his self-analysis. It was near the end of July before he could join the family at Aussee. He left there at the beginning of September and in a little over a fortnight made the following astonishing tour. He was accompanied by his brother Alexander and a Dr. Gattl whom Fliess had sent to him from Berlin and who was both his student and his patient. First there were two days in Venice, with the usual bathing at the Lido. It was his third visit there and he was getting to know it. Then across to Pisa, which he did not like; he did not omit to climb the leaning tower, but having done that he spent the day in Leghorn, a seaport which reminded him of Trieste. The next day he was in Siena. On the evening of the third day he got to San Gimignano. On the following day he made an excursion to Poggibonsi and also to Chiusi and that evening was in Orvieto. The next day he was at Bolsena, where he specially enjoyed the Signorelli pictures, and the day after in Spoleto to visit the waterfall of Terni. Next came Assisi, where to his surprise he encountered Eleonora Duse, who was spending a holiday there. Perugia occupied three days, followed by Arezzo and three days once more in Florence. He had intended to return via Ancona, sailing from there to Trieste,[8] but the time did not allow this and he went straight back to Vienna.

This tour seems to have been instigated by a suggestion Fliess had made that he should familiarize himself with the masterpieces of Italian art.[9] In the enjoyment of this, however, he was handicapped by disliking the monotony of sacred, especially Christian, themes in the paintings; but he certainly saw a great deal. Of his appreciation we shall have occasion to speak later.

Eighteen ninety-eight was also a year of movement. At Easter he and his brother had three days in the South, but in that time they investigated Aquileia in Istria, where Freud was fascinated by the remains of the once famous Roman city, and also the limestone caves near Gorizia. In June there was a week end with the family at Aussee, with two overnight journeys. There were also two distant consultations that summer, one near Königgrätz in Bohemia, which brought in 300 gulden, and one to Pörtschach in Carinthia, with a fee of 500 gulden. In the middle of June he also made a week-end trip to Salzburg where he met Minna and took her to see her mother in Reichenhall. Freud worked late that year. The children had been ill and his wife was in need of rest. So, instead of joining them and infecting them with a cold he had just contracted, he went early in August to Munich and probably met Fliess there. Then Minna joined him and they traveled together to Kufstein and Innsbruck, where he engaged a carriage and hurriedly visited the sights between trains. Then off to Landeck, Trafoi, up the Stelvio Pass, and over to Bormio in Italy. One night in a bad hotel there was enough, so they took a train to Tirano, and then undertook a long tramp up the valley to a little village called Le Prese on the shore of Lake Poschiavo, which Freud thought a "magically idyllic spot." Then up the Bernina Pass to Pontresina in the Engadine, where they had a five hours' walk on a glacier—a new experience. From there they drove to Maloja and back—a place of "incomparable beauty." [f] They then worked their way back to Aussee to join the rest of the family. After spending a fortnight there he took his wife off to Dalmatia. It was a long journey and he must have debated the cost, but he reminded himself of the "apparently eccentric but very wise saying that 'one should sell one's last shirt and become a rich man.'" She was not such a good traveler and found his pace too fast. Leaving her at Ragusa where she had some gastric disturbance, he made a trip to Cattaro with a stranger; Freud mentioned it in connection with the Signorelli analysis.[10] They then moved on to Spalato (now Split) and then back to Trieste. While his wife went to Merano to recuperate, Freud pushed on to Brescia and Milan. Leonardo's "Last Supper" is one of the very few paintings he singled out for special praise. From Milan he visited Pavia, Monza, and Bergamo, returning to Milan and then to Vienna, which he reached in the third week in September.

Eighteen ninety-nine was the first of many summers the family spent in a large farmhouse called Riemerlehen, near Berchtesgaden in Bavaria. It was the summer when most of *The Interpretation of Dreams* was written, the final, difficult part being composed in an arbor in the garden of the house there. He had been working hard at it in Vienna, and also had to write his first report for the new *Jahresbericht für Neurologie* at the same time, but he had managed to put in four days at Berchtesgaden at the end of June. His last pleasant "Congress" with Fliess had taken place in April in Inns-

[f] For the collector of coincidences! His future biographer was there in the same week and possibly traveled in the same stagecoach.

bruck, and no doubt had been a stimulus to get on with the great work which had been rather hanging fire. Having finished the book, he returned to Vienna in the third week of September after a round-about journey of thirty-two hours through flooded country.

In the summer of 1900 the family were at the Bellevue, within easy reach of his work. But after the fateful last "Congress" at Achensee in the first days of August, Freud embarked on an elaborate tour.[11] With his wife he went first to Trafoi at the foot of the Stelvio Pass; they went up and down it several times and Freud found it beautiful—an opinion not always shared. Then to Sulden, where they had a walk over the glacier. After that they followed the Adige down to Merano and then on to the La Mendola Pass, where they met Lust-garten[g] and other Viennese friends. His wife now returned home via Bolzano. She insisted on his following Lustgarten to Venice to show him around. He did so and was surprised to find there his sister Rosa (his favorite one) and her husband. They took him off, after a couple of days in Venice, to Berghof on the Ossiacher See in Carinthia. There they found the American sister Anna with her children, and his brother Alexander also turned up unexpectedly. The party then broke up and Freud, accompanied by his sister-in-law, slowly wended his way through the Pusterthal to Trient, from which they visited the "dreamlike" Castello Toblino. Then, for a change, they traveled up an "uncannily beautiful" mountain road to Lavarone, but found it rather cold there. So back to Lake Garda, where they stayed for five days in Riva, and of course examined the ruins of the "Villa Catullus." They had several trips on the lake there, to Baveno, Arco, and so on, and were greatly taken with the scenery, which he described as "beautiful as paradise." They sailed from Pallanza to Stresa, where they spent a night, and the next day Freud took Minna to Merano where she was to pass some time in the hope of recovering from her tuberculosis. Freud himself dashed off alone to Milan and Genoa, and then returned to Vienna after a six weeks' tour which must have been very refreshing after the unpleasant time with Fliess.

Whenever Freud was away from his wife he maintained constant contact with daily postcards or telegrams, interspersed with a long letter every few days. He gave short descriptions of what he had seen and every now and then added pointed comments of his own. The moodiness to which he was subject at other times seemed to disappear altogether in holiday time. Freud certainly displayed then

[g] An old medical friend who had emigrated to New York.

high powers of enjoyment and an extraordinary gusto more often found in those of a younger age. As a matter of incidental interest it may be added that of all the places he visited in Italy his favorites, after of course Venice and Florence, were Bergamo, Bologna, and Brescia.

Although these journeys were no doubt undertaken in a modest fashion, inns and stagecoaches playing a considerable part, nevertheless they must have cost something. When we reflect that in those years Freud had to support a dozen people, apart from domestic servants, we can understand why finance was a constant anxiety. Freud's attitude towards money was always realistic: it was there to be spent, but still it had to be taken seriously.

There is in the Fliess correspondence hardly any reference to his earnings in practice before 1896. Then he was beginning to feel the effects of the isolation from professional colleagues that his startling views on sexuality had brought about. His practice, like that of many other physicians, varied greatly, as the following examples show. In May 1896 his consulting room remained empty for the first time, and he had seen no new patient for weeks. In November things were bad, but in December he was working for ten hours and earning 100 gulden ($40) a day, just what he needed for his well-being; so he was "dead tired and mentally fresh." This continued for a while. He was getting known in the world. Wernicke had sent him a patient, he had one from Budapest, and another from Breslau (February 1899). But in the evening, after working for twelve and a half hours, he "falls over as if he had been sawing wood." Last week he earned 700 gulden, but "you don't get that for nothing. Getting rich must be very hard."

In the famous letter (September 21, 1897) in which he announced that he had been deceived in his seduction theory, one of the disturbing features was that, his etiological theory being wrong, he could no longer feel sure of being able to cure neuroses, on which his livelihood depended. His theory of dreams, however, is quite unaffected: "What a pity one cannot live from interpreting dreams." The very next month his foreboding came true. He had only two gratis patients besides himself: "that makes three, but they bring in nothing." For a year things went badly; he could not leave Vienna, since he could not afford to miss a single day's work. In the following October (1898), however, he was again hard at it with eleven hours of psychoanalysis a day. After paying two professional visits, he started at nine and, after an interval of an hour and a half in the middle of the day, finished at nine in the evening. Then came writing *The Interpretation of Dreams*, correspondence, and the self-analysis. Two months later, his earnings had dropped to 70 gulden daily, but the month after he was again earning 100 gulden from twelve hours' work. By May this had gone down to two and a half hours a day, and in the following October he wrote that his earnings for the past six months had not been enough to cover his expenses. So he looked round for some other source of income, and tried to get a post at a sanatorium for the summer months; in this he was unsuccessful.

In January 1900 he reported that he had had only one new case in the past eight months: "how he is going to get through he does not yet know." And in May four patients had finished and he had only three and a half hours' work daily. That was the year when the family could not go farther than a suburb.

When Freud wrote about his "dread of poverty," he knew what he was talking about. In a letter of September 1899, he tells how in his youth he had got to know what "helpless poverty" was like, and how he fears it: "You will see that my style will improve and my ideas become more correct when this town gives me plenty to live on." It is interesting that this passage is not written in the subjunctive mood; his hopes were for once gratified.

When the Czar issued his famous Peace Manifesto (August 1898), Freud made an amusing comment. He had years ago concluded that the Czar suffered from an obsessional neurosis, which accounted for his being "overgood" and squeamish "like Koko in *The Mikado*." Then he relates his own phantasy. "Two people could be helped if we were brought together. I go for a year to Russia, take from him so much (neurosis) that he no longer suffers, but leave just enough so that he doesn't start any war.[h] After that we can hold three 'Congresses' a year, *exclusively* in Italy, and from then on I shall treat all my patients gratis."

Freud had only scientific ambitions—to discover. The nearest to a worldly one was the wish to be well enough off to travel. Social and professional advancement meant nothing except perhaps the chance of greater independence; he complained that his livelihood depended on people (colleagues) whom he despised. Now in Vienna the whole community was permeated by a kind of snobbishness not equaled anywhere else. Questions of reputation and capacity

[h] Russia was Austria's only potential enemy; the thought of war with her was never far away.

were quite subordinate to the simple matter of title, and the hierarchy of titles was manifold in complexity. This was especially pronounced in medical matters. It would be socially lowering to engage a practitioner, however skillful, if one could afford the fees of a *Privatdozent*. And the cream of medical practice went to those doctors with the envied title of Professor. Freud must have heartily despised all this, but he could not fail to recognize its important economic aspects. For that reason he would have welcomed the title, but for no other. The story of his advancement to it throws a vivid light on the Vienna of those days.

In January 1897, after he had been a *Privatdozent* for the unusually long period of twelve years, he wrote that the rumor of his once more being passed over in favor of younger colleagues left him quite cold, but it might hasten his final break with the University. In the next month, however, he reported an interview with Nothnagel, who told him that he (together with Krafft-Ebing and Frankl-Hochwart) was proposing him for the position of Associate Professor, and if the Council of the Faculty did not agree, they were determined to forward the recommendations themselves to the Ministry.[i] He added, however: "You know the further difficulties; perhaps we should achieve nothing more than 'putting you on the carpet'." What gratified Freud was that he was able to retain his opinion of them as "decent men." He then had to prepare for the purpose a dossier of his published work, one which has since been published.[12]

Nothing came of it. The anti-Semitic attitude in official quarters would have been decisive in itself, but Freud's reputation in sexual matters did not further his chances. Against these considerations the splendid work he had done in neurology and his European standing as a neurologist counted as nothing. In the annual ratification in September, he and his group were ignored in 1897, 1898, and 1899. In 1900 all the names proposed were ratified with the sole exception of Freud's. But he was pleased that his friend Königstein had at last been accepted.

Four years passed during which Freud took no steps. Then came the great visit to Rome, after which he says his pleasure in life had increased and his pleasure in martyrdom diminished. Dignified aloofness, no doubt, gave a satisfying feeling of superiority, but he was paying dearly for it. He decided to "become like other men" and descend from his pedestal onto the lower levels. So he took it on

[i] The University being a Government Institution, all posts had to be officially ratified.

himself to call on his old teacher Exner. Exner behaved very rudely to him, but finally disclosed the fact that the Minister[j] was being personally influenced against him by someone and advised him to seek some counter-influence. Freud suggested the name of a former patient, Elise Gomperz, the wife of the man for whom twenty years ago Freud had translated the John Stuart Mill Essays; Gomperz had been Co-Professor of Philology with von Härtel, now the Minister of Public Instruction. The lady was most helpful, but the Minister pretended to know nothing of the old recommendation, so that a new one was necessary. Freud wrote to Nothnagel and Krafft-Ebing, who promptly renewed it. But again nothing happened.

After this, one of Freud's patients, a Frau Marie Ferstel, wife of a diplomat, got to hear of the situation and at once entered into competition with Frau Gomperz. She did not rest till she had got to know the Minister personally and struck a bargain with him. He was eager to get hold of a certain picture by Böcklin (*Die Burgruine*) for the newly established Modern Gallery, and it was her aunt, Frau Ernestine Thorsch, who owned it. It took three months to get it out of the possession of the old lady, but at the end the Minister graciously announced to Frau Ferstel at a dinner party that she was the first to hear he had sent the necessary document to the Emperor to sign. The next day she burst into Freud's room with the cry: "*Ich hab's gemacht* (I've done it)." [k]

Freud's sentiments about the whole affair can easily be guessed, but he wrote to Fliess that he was the biggest donkey of all concerned, in that he should have wangled things years before—knowing the way of the world in Vienna. (March 11, 1902.) At all events he got some amusement out of it, and wrote to Fliess—in the last letter of their correspondence: "The population is participating extensively. Congratulations and bouquets are just now raining on me as if His Majesty had officially recognized the role of sexuality, the Council of Ministers had confirmed the importance of dreams, and the necessity of a psychoanalytic treatment of hysteria had been passed in Parliament with a two-thirds majority." (March 11, 1902.)

This absurd story had the expected results. Acquaintances who had looked over their shoulder when passing him now bowed even from a distance, his children's school friends voiced their envy, and —the only thing that mattered—his practice took a permanent turn

[j] Freiherr von Härtel.
[k] Personal communication. The version given here is more authentic than that given by Hanns Sachs,[14] whose memory is occasionally at fault.

for the better. He had become, if not respectable, at least respected. The incident happened to coincide with another turning point in Freud's life, his emergence from the years of intellectual isolation. Followers began to gather around him, to whom he would always be known simply as "Herr Professor," and before long the outer world would be taking serious notice of his psychological work.

It was Freud's duty to appear personally before the Emperor to thank him for sanctioning the honor bestowed on him, and for this purpose it was incumbent to wear his military service medal—which of course had long been lost. So his friend Herzig lent him his, but warned him that the moment he entered the Audience Chamber the keen-eyed Emperor would at once call out, "Isn't that Herzig's medal?"

The change in title made no intrinsic difference in Freud's academic position. As before, when he was a *Privatdocent*, he was allowed to give lectures at the University, but was not obliged to. Only a full Professor (Professor Ordinarius) who was a member of the Faculty had that responsibility. In 1920 he was at last given the higher title, but, being in independent private practice, he was not made a member of the Faculty or given charge of a Department. So, strictly speaking, Freud was never a regular academic teacher.

Freud availed himself freely of his right to give courses of lectures and continued to do so, though not every year, up to the time of the first World War; they were given twice a week, on Thursday and Saturday. There must be others besides myself who remember the privilege of attending them. He was a fascinating lecturer. The lectures were always enlightened by his peculiar ironic humor, of the kind illustrated by many of the passages that have been quoted. He always used a low voice, perhaps because it could become rather harsh if strained, but spoke with the utmost distinctness. He never used any notes,[1] and seldom made much preparation for a lecture; it was mostly left to the inspiration of the moment. I remember once while accompanying him to a lecture asking him what the subject was going to be that evening and his answer was, "If I only knew! I must leave it to my unconscious."

[1] The only occasion in his life when he is known to have *read* a paper was at the Budapest Congress in late September 1918, just before the end of World War I, when he was in an unhappy mood. His daughter chided him severely for "breaking the family tradition," to which she herself has loyally adhered.

The series of *Introductory Lectures*, delivered in the middle of the war, was also written beforehand, but then committed to memory.

He never used oratory, but talked intimately and conversation-ally, liking, therefore, to gather his audience close to him. One felt he was addressing himself to us personally, and something of this per-sonal manner is reflected in those of his later lectures that have been published. There was no flicker of condescension in it, not even a hint of a teacher. The audience was assumed to consist of highly in-telligent people to whom he wished to communicate some of his re-cent experiences, although there was of course no discussion except privately afterwards. He was not averse to paying occasional compli-ments to his audience. Thus, on one occasion when Abraham, Fer-enczi, Rank, Sachs, and myself were seated in the front row, he made a graceful little bow, waved his hand towards us, and mur-mured: *"Un parterre des rois."* ᵐ

As his work became better known there was a risk of this pleasant intimacy being disturbed by numbers. On one occasion, at the be-ginning of a session, a large new batch of students flocked in. Freud was evidently annoyed and, divining their motives, announced, "If, ladies and gentlemen, you have come here in such numbers ex-pecting to hear something sensational or even lewd, rest assured I will see to it that your efforts were not worth the trouble." On the following occasion the audience had dwindled to a third.¹⁵ In later years Freud controlled the situation by admitting no one without a card which he granted only after a personal interview.

Freud does not appear to have ever given any lectures elsewhere than in the University with the exception of a few in his Jewish circle. He tells an amusing story of one he nearly gave before the *Philosophische Gesellschaft* (Philosophical Society). He expressed doubts about its suitability, but his manuscript was approved be-forehand, so he accepted. At the last moment an urgent message came asking him to give only drawing-room examples in the first half, after which there would be an interval for the ladies to leave and he could then continue with the rest! Naturally he refused. (February 15, 1901.)

There is a general impression that, because of the bad reception of his ideas, Freud early decided to boycott scientific meetings in Vienna. This is very far indeed from the truth, as may be ascertained from his remarks made in the discussion of various medical societies. In addition there are records of nine or ten papers between 1892 and 1896 (to be listed in Mr. Strachey's final bibliography) which

ᵐ (A row of kings.) An allusion to Napoleon's comment in the theater at Erfurt.

Freud himself read before the *Medizinische Club,* the *Verein für Psychiatrie und Neurologie,* and the *Wiener medizinisches Doktorenkollegium.* It was only the *Gesellschaft der Ärzte* that fell under his displeasure, and that not for a few years. Thus, although he complained bitterly of his isolation inasmuch as he had no one to understand his views sympathetically, he was never barred from putting them forward to his colleagues. On one occasion, for instance, a paper of his on hysteria, read before the *Doktorenkollegium,* occupied three whole evenings, and even then two more were devoted to discussing it. Any ostracism, if one may use such a strong word, was passive rather than active. But it undoubtedly increased after 1896, the last year in which Freud ever read a paper before any medical society.[n]

There is no definite record of Freud ever having attended any international scientific meeting after the Paris one on hypnotism in 1889, except of course the International Psychoanalytical Congresses in later life. He had, it is true, on three occasions announced to Fliess his intention of attending one, but there is no subsequent confirmation of his having carried it out: He was chosen as Secretary of the Section of Neurology in the 66th *Versammlung Deutscher Naturforscher und Ärzte* (Congress of German Natural Scientists), which took place in Vienna from September 24 to 28, 1894. As it happened, no such section was constituted, though perhaps Freud, since he had got back to Vienna a week before it began, attended the meeting. Then he thought of attending the First International Congress of Psychology, which was held in Munich in August 1896, but, although he could easily have done so from Salzburg where he was that month, there is not the subsequent mention of it that one might expect. In the following month the 68th *Versammlung Deutscher Naturforscher und Ärzte* took place in Frankfurt, and Freud had accepted an invitation to act as co-rapporteur on the subject of Little's Disease, one on which he was the greatest living authority. Yet for some unknown reason no such symposium was ever held. In any event, Freud had decided not to attend.[17]

Of how far removed Freud's mode of working was from purely intellectual activity such as takes place in much of mathematics and physics one gets a vivid impression from his own descriptions. They make it plain that, especially in those formative years, he was being

[n] A sole exception was an address on psychotherapy in 1904 before the *Doktorenkollegium.*[16]

moved forward almost entirely by unconscious forces and was very much at the mercy of them. He oscillated greatly between moods in which ideas came readily into his mind, when there would be a clear view of the conceptions he was building up, and on the other hand moods when he was evidently inhibited, with no flow of ideas, and when his mind was quite sluggish and dull. He wrote, for example: "The new ideas that came to me during my state of euphoria have gone; they no longer please me, and I am waiting for them to be born afresh. Thoughts throng my mind that promise to lead to something definite, that seem to unify the normal and the pathological, the sexual and the psychological problems, and then they vanish. I do not try to hold on to them, since I know that both their appearance and their disappearance in consciousness is not a real expression of their destiny. On days like yesterday and today everything is quiet inside me, and I feel terribly lonely. . . . I must wait till something stirs in me and I can feel it. So I often dream whole days away." (December 3, 1897.) On another occasion when he was very depressed over his clinical work he said: "I soon found it is impossible to continue this really difficult work when I am in a bad mood, and assailed by doubts. Every single patient is a torturing spirit when I am not myself and cheerful. I really believed I should have to succumb. I helped myself by renouncing all conscious mental effort so as to grope my way into the riddles. Since then I have been doing the work perhaps more skillfully than ever, but I hardly know what I am really doing." (March 11, 1900.)

In a letter of February 2, 1899, he shared with Fliess the sense of being engrossed in excessive work "to which every effort of thought has to be given and which gradually absorbs all other capacities and the ability to receive impressions—a sort of neoplastic substance that infiltrates into one's humanity and then replaces it. With me it is even more so. Work and earning are identical with me, so that I have become wholly carcinoma. Today I have to go to the theater; it is ridiculous, as if one could transplant anything onto a carcinoma. Nothing else could stick to it, and my existence is from now on that of the neoplasm." This was when he was engaged on *The Interpretation of Dreams*. The tyrant of his unconscious had him in its toils, and he was so much its slave that he could barely protest. He had made a rather similar remark three years before: "I hope to be provided with scientific interests to the end of my life. For I am no longer a human being apart from them." (February 13, 1896.)

"I can quite clearly distinguish two different intellectual states in myself: one in which I take very good note of everything my patients say and even make discoveries during the [therapeutic] work, but apart from it cannot reflect or do any other work; the other in which I draw conclusions, write down notes, and am even free to take an interest in other things, but in which I am actually farther away from the business in hand and do not pay close attention to what is going on with the patients." (March 2, 1899.) This corresponds somewhat with his analogy of the tides which he depicted a little later when he was wrestling with a particular problem and which shows also that his self-confidence varied with the moods: "There is a curious alternation of flood and ebb. Sometimes I am carried up to a state in which I feel certain, and then everything flows back and I am left high and dry. But I believe the tide is gaining on the land." (December 24, 1899.)

There was in later years a change in his mode of working. Thus in a letter to Abraham (dated December 11, 1914), he wrote: "My way of working was different years ago. I used to wait until an idea came to me. Now I go halfway to meet it, though I don't know whether I find it any the quicker."

The changes in mood were hardly at all under his conscious control. As he put it: "I have never been able to guide the working of my intellect, so my leisure time is quite wasted." (May 1, 1898.)

His moods were no doubt mainly brought about by unknown shiftings in the unconscious processes. They were also influenced by certain conscious factors; the amount of work in his practice, and the varying anxiety over his economic situation. There is, it is true, an obvious connection between the two, but they are by no means identical. Freud needed the stimulation of his work, and could do little if he had too much leisure, as happened from time to time. Thus when he had ten patients a day he remarked that it was perhaps one too many, but, "I get on best when there is a great deal of work." (February 2, 1897.) The significant point is, however, that happiness and well-being were not conducive to the best work. That depended on an internal, and rather unpleasant, disturbance, a rumbling from below the surface. As he remarked himself: "I have been very idle because the moderate amount of discomfort° necessary for intensive work has not set in." (April 16, 1896.)

The moods had similar effects on Freud's actual writing powers. In spite of his fluency and distinction in style his confidence in the capacity to write well often wavered, and apparently Fliess was a

° *Mittelelend.*

fairly severe critic in this respect. Just as the power to work well needed a certain measure of unhappiness—not too much, not too little—so did his capacity for writing. An amusing passage that refers to a section of *The Interpretation of Dreams* runs: "My style in it was bad, because I was feeling too well physically; I have to be somewhat miserable in order to write well." (September 16, 1899.)

His style was pithy and incisive, often ironic and occasionally caustic. Here are a few examples, although they inevitably lose in translation. Announcing the death of Billroth, the leading European surgeon of his time: "Enviable not to have outlived himself." (February 7, 1894.) "I live in such isolation as if I had discovered the greatest truths." (March 16, 1896.) "That shows once more how hard it is to see except for the seer himself." (May 4, 1896.) "I am too sensible to complain; I know that I have everything, and how little according to the statistics of human misery one has a right to." (May 7, 1900.)

In those years Freud read enormously, as his library testified. He had of course long been steeped in the German classics and frequently quotes them. In the correspondence there are occasional references to books he is reading, but they can represent only a fraction of what he got through. Among those mentioned are Gottfried Keller, Jacobsen,ᴾ Multatuli, Guy de Maupassant, Kleinpaul, Dante, Vasari (*Lives of the Painters*), G. F. Meyer, Friedjung (*Der Kampf um die Vorherrschaft in Deutschland, 1859-1866*), Laistner (*Das Rätsel der Sphinx*), Schliemann's *Ilias*. When he read Schnitzler's *Paracelsus* he commented: "I was astonished to see what such a writer knows about these things." (March 19, 1898.)

When one recalls how extensively Freud had read both classical and modern literature, one must regard Thomas Mann's remark as gratuitous when he deplored the hard work Freud had had in his investigations, labor which a knowledge of literature would have spared him.[18] Freud himself often contrasted the intuition of creative writers with the effort it costs a scientific investigator to examine the same ideas in a systematic manner.

His observation, already made by French workers, that all the classical symptoms of hysteria as enumerated by Charcot had already been fully described hundreds of years before by writers on demoniac possession led Freud to read extensively the literature on that

ᴾ In a letter of October 16, 1895, he said that Jacobsen's *Niels Lyhne* had moved him more deeply than anything he had read in the past nine years; the final chapters were classic.

subject in the sixteenth and seventeenth centuries; it was a final proof that the symptoms could not be the result of suggestion proceeding from any current medical theory. One annoyance of having to work on his monograph for Nothnagel was that it held him up when he was eager to study the *Malleus Maleficarum*. Freud was particularly struck by the fact of the sexual perversions the Devil practiced on his worshipers being identical with the stories his patients related from their childhood, and he threw out the suggestion that such perversions are an inherited relic of an ancient Semitic semi-religious sexual cult. (January 24, 1897.) We see here that Freud early cherished the Lamarckian belief to which he adhered throughout his life.

Something more may be said about Freud's aims in life, immediate and remote, in this decade. Apart from the mundane wish to be well enough off to be independent and to travel, Freud had constantly in mind the ambition of incorporating his discoveries about repression, etc., into the body of psychopathology, and then of working through this into a normal psychology which by that means would be transformed into a new science, to be called Metapsychology.

The nature of this ambition was clear enough to Freud. As early as a month before even the *Studies in Hysteria* appeared, he wrote: "A man like myself cannot live without a hobby-horse, without a dominating passion: in fact, without a tyrant, to use Schiller's expression, and that is what it has become. For in its service I know no moderation. It is psychology which has been the goal beckoning me from afar, and now that I have come into contact with the neuroses the goal has drawn much nearer. Two aims plague me: to see how the theory of mental functions would shape itself if one introduced quantitative considerations, a sort of economics of nervous energy; and, secondly, to extract what psychopathology has to yield for normal psychology." (May 25, 1895.) There were occasions, however, when he revolted against the tyrant, such as in his dissatisfaction with his first attempt (the *Entwurf*), and then he would cast everything aside for a time. (November 8, 1895.)

A few months later he wrote to Fliess: "If we both are granted a few years of tranquil work we shall surely leave behind us something that may justify our existence. In this thought I feel myself strong to bear up against all the daily troubles and labors. As a young man I longed for nothing else than philosophical knowledge, and I am now on the way to satisfy that longing by passing over from medicine to psychology. It was against my will that I had to concern myself with therapy." (April 2, 1896.) ᵠ

In these years Freud would appear to have had no great hopes of a long life. Fliess's prediction that he would die at fifty-one, and his doubts about the condition of his heart, seem to have influenced him. But perhaps the task could be accomplished: "Give me ten years and I shall finish the matter of the neuroses and the new psychology." (January 3, 1897.) A year or two later, however, reflection on the size of the task makes him feel "like an old man. If establishing so few points as are needed to solve the problem of neurosis necessitates so much work, energy, and mistakes, how dare I hope to get a glimpse, as I once fondly expected, into the totality of mental functioning?" (October 23, 1898.)

A half-serious, but very interesting, description of himself may be quoted in this context: "You often estimate me too highly. For I am not really a man of science, not an observer, not an experimenter, and not a thinker. I am nothing but by temperament a *conquistador* —an adventurer, if you want to translate the word—with the curiosity, the boldness, and the tenacity that belongs to that type of being. Such people are apt to be treasured if they succeed, if they have really discovered something; otherwise they are thrown aside. And that is not altogether unjust." (February 1, 1900.)

He often voiced the opinion that any recognition of his labors would be unlikely in his lifetime, or perhaps ever. "No critic, not even the stupid Loewenfeld, the Burckhardt of Neuropathology,ʳ can see more keenly than I do the disproportion between the problems and the solutions, and I shall suffer the just punishment that none of the undiscovered provinces of mental life which I was the first mortal to enter will bear my name or follow the laws I have formulated." (May 7, 1900.)

What would happen would be that in perhaps fifty years some later investigator would make the same discoveries, and then his name might be recollected as an early pioneer. It is a thought that does not seem to have at all depressed him. What mattered was the opportunity of achieving his goal, for his own satisfaction.

The concrete terms in which Freud visualized the fulfillment of his ambition naturally varied from one time to another. At first (March 16, 1896) there were to be two books: (1) *Lectures on the Major*

ᵠ See also p. 53.
ʳ For this allusion see p. 360.

Neuroses and (2), a better work,* *The Psychology and Psychotherapy of the Defense Neuroses,* into which he will pour his soul. Three years later (July 17, 1899) these had changed into *The Psychopathology of Daily Life* (which he had actually begun) and *Repression and Wish-Fulfillment—A Psychological Theory of the Neuropsychoses.* In the same month, when referring to *The Interpretation of Dreams,* he designates it "a part of the first third of the Great Task—to range the neuroses and psychoses among the sciences by means of the theory of repression and wish-fulfillment: (1) The Organic-Sexual, (2) The Factual-Clinical, (3) The Metapsychological Aspects."

Freud's ambition to transform psychology by means of psychopathology was in a large sense fulfilled in the course of time. But the task proved to be far more complex and elaborate than it seemed at the outset, and he discovered later on that all his labors could result only in a scaffolding for the final building.

Beyond this ambition, grandiose enough in itself, beckoned the still more distant goal of a philosophy of life which would end all his restless curiosity and uncertainties.

* *Schöneres* is really untranslatable.

XVI

The Interpretation of Dreams

(1 8 9 5 – 1 8 9 9)

BY GENERAL CONSENSUS "THE INTERPRETATION OF DREAMS" WAS FREUD'S major work, the one by which his name will probably be longest remembered. Freud's own opinion would seem to have agreed with this judgment. As he wrote in his preface to the third English edition, "Insight such as this falls to one's lot but once in a lifetime." It was a perfect example of serendipity, for the discovery of what dreams mean was made quite incidentally—one might almost say accidentally—when Freud was engaged in exploring the meaning of the psychoneuroses.

I asked him once which were his favorites among his writings, and he fetched from the shelves *The Interpretation of Dreams* and the *Three Essays on the Theory of Sexuality*,[a] saying: "I hope this one will soon be out of date through being generally accepted, but that one should last longer." Then, with a quiet smile, he added: "It seems to be my fate to discover only the obvious: that children have sexual feelings, which every nursemaid knows; and that night dreams are just as much a wish-fulfillment as day dreams." Shall we call this a catachrestic meiosis?

The reasons for this general judgment of the book are not far to seek. It is Freud's most original work. The main conclusions in it were entirely novel and unexpected. This applies both to the theme proper, that of dream structure, and to many that appear incidentally. The most important of the latter is the description of the now familiar "Oedipus complex"; the erotic and the hostile relations of child to parent are frankly exposed. Together with this goes the ap-

[a] It is interesting to observe that these were the only books that Freud systematically kept "up to date" in the various editions.

350

preciation of infantile life and its overwhelming importance for all the innumerable developments that make up the adult human being. Above all, it affords not only a secure basis for the theory of the unconscious in man, but provides one of the best modes of approach to this dark region, so much more important in man's actual behavior than his consciousness. Freud very justly termed the interpretation of dreams the *via regia* to the unconscious. The book, moreover, contains a host of suggestions in the fields of literature, mythology, and education—the famous footnote on Hamlet is a striking example—which have since provided the inspiration for a great number of special studies.

The book is especially comprehensive. The main topic, the investigation of dream life, was carried out with such detailed thoroughness that the conclusions have experienced only a minimum of modification or addition in the half century since the book was published. Of very few important scientific works can this be said.

This is not the place to give any account of the contents of such a wide-embracing book, of which so many abstracts have been made. It is the best known and most widely read of all Freud's works, and one cannot imagine anyone who is not familiar with it wishing to read a biography of him.

Looking back on this unhurried rate of publication in earlier days, Freud wrote: "*The Interpretation of Dreams*, for instance, was finished in all essentials at the beginning of 1896 but was not written down until the summer of 1899." [1] Some years later, in 1925, he also wrote: "My *Interpretation of Dreams* and my *Fragment of an Analysis of a Case of Hysteria* were suppressed by me—if not for the nine years enjoined by Horace—at all events for four or five years before I allowed them to be published." [2] The contemporary evidence now available enables us to amplify these simple statements and in certain respects to correct them.

Freud's interest in dreams went back very far, probably to his boyhood: he was always a good dreamer and even in early life not only observed but also recorded them. Only a fortnight after getting engaged he wrote to Martha: "I have such unruly dreams. I never dream about matters that have occupied me during the day, only of such themes as were touched on once in the course of the day and then broken off." [3] This became later a familiar constituent of his dream theory. A year later he mentioned a blissful dream of a landscape, "which according to the private notebook on dreams which I have composed from my experience indicates traveling." [4]

That precious book of his dreams doubtless perished in the holocaust described in the Preface to this volume.

On the last day of 1883 he wrote to his betrothed: "Last night I dreamed again about traveling, this time in Spain. I saw the 'harbor' of Madrid and was surprised that the Manzares carried so much water. I believe the Manzares was really the Elbe. I am a little superstitious about such dreams, since hitherto every traveling dream has soon been followed by a journey. Where will it be this time, and how long will it last?"

At other times his remarks were more conventional, such as in his allusions to "those disagreeable dreams that one has only when one's stomach is upset." [5] He related a good number of his dreams, but mostly without comment. There is one, however, especially worth recording on account of its exceedingly unusual structure. It was what he called a "sharp" dream, quite different from the usual confused ones. He had just taken some ecgonin to compare its action with that of cocaine. "I dreamt that after taking this drug I walked and walked and kept on walking through the most beautiful scenery which was very vivid, and finally came to a harbor with pretty gardens around and the Holsteinthor, whereupon I called out 'Lübeck'! [b] Coming into the town I suddenly met Fleischl and Exner who were very astonished and asked me how I had got there. When they heard of my great walk they insisted on my going to bed. Once there it occurred to me that the whole thing might be a dream, but then I laughed at the idea and was quite convinced it was reality—after which I woke up." [6] This seems an improvement on the more familiar "dream within a dream."

Another one is worth mentioning because of its being a recurrent one. "Last night I dreamt I was fighting someone for your sake and had the disagreeable feeling of being paralyzed just when I wanted to strike a blow. I often dream that and it comes at the place of the dream where I still have to pass my doctor's examination, a task which had tormented me for years." [7]

The first evidence in his published writings of Freud's interest in dreams occurs in the course of a long footnote in the first of his case histories (that of Frau Emmy von N.) under the date of May 15, 1889, in the Studies in Hysteria. He is discussing the fact that neurotic patients seem to be under a necessity to bring into association with one another any ideas that happen to be simultaneously present in their minds. He goes on: "Not long ago I was able to convince

[b] A town much associated with Martha.

myself of the strength of this compulsion towards association from some observations made in a different field. For several weeks I found myself obliged to exchange my usual bed for a harder one, in which I had more numerous or more vivid dreams, or in which, it may be, I was unable to reach the normal depth of sleep. In the first quarter of an hour after waking I remembered all the dreams I had had during the night; and I took the trouble to write them down and try to solve them. I succeeded in tracing all these dreams back to two factors: (1) to the necessity for working out any ideas which I had only dwelt upon cursorily during the day—which had only been touched upon and not finally dealt with; and (2) to the compulsion to link together any ideas that might be present in the same state of consciousness. The senseless and contradictory character of the dreams could be traced back to the uncontrolled ascendancy of this latter factor."

The account of the case was written in 1894, doubtless from the notes made at the time, and the footnote in question must have been added either then or, at latest, by the spring of 1895. His description of the "association by contiguity" shows that he was still in the stage of the old non-dynamic Association Psychology.

There would appear to have been two starting points of Freud's interest in the interpretation of dreams, both of which he mentioned himself. One was the simple fact that in following his patients' associations, which were gradually allowed to become freer and freer, he observed that they often interpolated in them an account of a dream, to which of course they would in turn produce associations. The other was his psychiatric experience of hallucinatory states in psychotics, where the feature of wish-fulfillment is often evident. This had been pointed out by Meynert in connection with the condition he described under the name of Amentia (now known as acute hallucinatory psychosis). Freud himself repeatedly refers[8] to a sentence of Griesinger's which called attention to the wish-fulfillment feature common to dreams and psychoses, a remarkable piece of insight.[9]

In the first dream analysis of which we have any published record (March 4, 1895, i.e., before the publication of the *Studies*), that of Breuer's nephew Emil Kaufmann, Freud draws the analogy between the obvious wish-fulfillment in it and the dream psychosis of an ex-patient of Fliess's whom he had been treating.[c] It is the first indica-

---

[c] The dream, incorporated in *The Interpretation of Dreams*, is that of a lazy medical student who, to save himself the trouble of getting up, dreamed he was already at work in the hospital.

tion of the wish-fulfillment theory of dreams. He relates, however, that before his collaboration with Breuer ceased, which we know was in the spring of 1894,[10] he had reported to him that he had learned how to interpret dreams.[11]

That the fulfillment of a hidden wish is the essence of a dream, an idea Freud had already suspected, was confirmed by the first complete analysis he made of one of his own dreams on Wednesday, July 24, 1895, an historic moment; it was the dream known by the name of "Irma's injection." Years later Fliess queried the exact date of this, but Freud verified it by referring to his diary of the time. (Letter of June 18, 1900.) Freud once took me to the Bellevue Restaurant, and we occupied the table at the (northeast) corner of the terrace where the great event had taken place. When I made the obvious remark about a tablet I did not know that years ago Freud had half-jokingly asked Fliess in a letter if he thought there would ever be a marble tablet on the spot bearing the inscription: "Here the secret of dreams was revealed to Dr. Sigm. Freud on July 24, 1895." (June 12, 1900.) That may still happen.

Four months later Freud was confidently referring to the confirmations of his conclusion that the fulfillment of a wish is the motive of dreams. (September 23, 1895.) On his return from visiting Fliess in Berlin Freud feverishly wrote the "Project," which will be considered in the next chapter. The first part, which was written by the middle of September, contains three sections on dreams. This was the first time that Freud came to close quarters with the problem as a whole. But he did so by an inductive route connected with the general theoretical assumptions in psychology he was trying to develop at that moment rather than by a close study of the actual characteristics of dream processes, origin and content. The result is naturally somewhat meager; it may be compared to *The Interpretation of Dreams* of only four years later as a cottage to a mansion. Nevertheless, it contains a few important elements of the future theory.[12]

Freud had already made the momentous distinction between two fundamentally different mental processes, which he called primary and secondary respectively. He notes that the primary process dominates dream life, and he explains this by the relative quiescence in the activity of the ego (which at other times inhibits the primary process) and the almost total muscular immobility; if the cathexis of the ego were reduced to nothing, then sleep would be dreamless.

He deals with these other aspects. The hallucinatory character of dreams, which is accepted by the dream consciousness so that the dreamer believes in what is happening, is a "regression" back to the processes of perception which he relates to the motor block in the usual direction of discharge.

The mechanisms found during the analysis of a dream display a striking resemblance to those with which he had become familiar in analyzing psychoneurotic symptoms. He appears to have forgotten this later, since in a letter of February 19, 1899, he spoke of it as if it were a fresh discovery.

He is throughout clear that every dream represents a wishfulfillment, but his attempt to explain why this appears in a disguised form does not take him far. In tracing the train of associations he notices that some links do not appear in consciousness (during the dream), so that the dream often appears to be quite senseless. His explanation of this is on the lines of physiological economics, concerning the relative strength of cathexis of various ideas, but he is plainly dissatisfied with it. It is remarkable that he makes here no use of the process of "repression," already familiar to him in the field of psychopathology.

On May 2, 1896, he lectured on the subject before a young audience in the *Jüdisch-Akademische Lesehalle* (Jewish Academic Reading Hall). He appears to have written a sketch of the topic, for in a letter to Fliess of March 7 he had promised to bring it to a "Congress." Most unfortunately no trace of it is extant; it would have been very interesting to know how far Freud had got in the theory by then. The year after he gave a more extended account before his Jewish society, the *Verein B'nai B'rith*, which took up two evenings (December 7 and 14, 1897). On May 14, 1900, when he was now fully master of the subject, he began a course of lectures on dreams at the University. The audience on this very interesting occasion consisted of three people! They were Hans Königstein, the son of his great friend, Frl. Dora Teleky, and a Dr. Marcuse of Breslau.

In a letter of July 7, 1897, the month in which he began his self-analysis, he spoke of his insight into the problems of dreams, including the laws of their genesis, as the best established of any, whereas all around masses of riddles stare at him. He had already perceived the similarity in the structure of dreams and neuroses. "Dreams contain the psychology of the neuroses in a nutshell," a sentence which recalls the earlier pronouncement by the great Hughlings

Jackson: "Find out about dreams, and you will find out about insanity." On October 15, 1897, in the letter which related important details of his self-analysis, Freud announced the two elements of the Oedipus complex, love for one parent and jealousy hostility towards the other; this discovery was more than incidental to the theory of dreams, since it vividly illustrates the infantile roots of the unconscious wishes animating all dreams. He went on to explain in this way the moving effect of the Oedipus legend and also suggested that it underlies Hamlet's dilemma. Fliess in his reply did not refer to these matters, whereupon Freud became anxious lest he had made another blunder and begged for reassurance. (November 5.)

The first allusion to the idea of writing a book on dreams occurs in a letter of May 16, 1897, i.e., a couple of months before the self-analysis actually began but while Freud was certainly under the influence of the motives that led him to undertake it. Altogether the two projects were carried out so much hand in hand that they may be regarded almost as one; *The Interpretation of Dreams* is, among other things, a selection from the self-analysis. The after-effects of his father's death had been slowly working in those months between it and the decisive reaction to the event.[d] On November 5, when the self-analysis was getting under way, he said he intended to force himself to write the book as a means of getting out of a bad mood.

On the failure of his important seduction theory in September 1897, he reflects on what is saved. "In the collapse of all values[c] only the psychological theory has remained unimpaired. The theory of dreams stands as sure as ever."

By February 9, 1898, the next reference to the matter, Freud was already writing hard, and probably had been doing so for a couple of months. He had already looked up some of the literature before the first letter in May 1897 and had been gratified to find that no one had had a notion of dreams being a wish-fulfillment, or indeed other than nonsense. The book was finished by September 1899, so that we may say it took Freud the best part of two years to write it.

The Fliess correspondence throws light not only on the composition of the book but also on many details that have puzzled readers. For instance, the mysterious number 1851 in the "Absurd dream of the dead father," [13] which has been supposed to refer to the date of

[d] It was in the preface, written in 1908, to the second edition of *The Interpretation of Dreams* that Freud announced that he had after writing the book recognized it as a reaction to his father's death (October 1896).
[c] A paraphrase from Nietzsche.

his father's marriage[f] is almost certainly derived from the age which Fliess had from his calculations predicted Freud would reach (51).

The progress of the writing can be followed in some detail. By February 23, 1898, some chapters are already written, and "it looks promising. It takes me deeper into psychology than I intended. All my additions belong to the philosophical side of the work; from the organic-sexual there has been nothing." By March 5 a whole section is finished, "no doubt the best composed part." On March 10 there is an interesting preview of an important part of the future book as it appeared at that time. "It seems to me that the theory of wish-fulfillment gives us only the psychological solution, not the biological—or, better, metapsychical one. (I would ask you seriously whether I may use the term metapsychology for my psychology that takes one beyond consciousness.) It seems to me that biologically the dream life proceeds altogether from the relics of the prehistoric period (age one to three), the same period that is the source of the unconscious, and the sole one that contains the etiology of the psychoneuroses; the period for which there is normally an amnesia analogous to that of hysteria. I surmise the formula: what was *seen* in that prehistoric period gives rise to dreams; what was *heard* to phantasies; what was *sexually experienced*, to psychoneuroses. The repeating of what had been experienced in that period is in itself the fulfillment of a wish. A recent wish can bring about a dream only when it can become connected with material from the prehistoric period, when it is itself a derivative of a prehistoric wish or gets assimilated to one." This passage shows well the restless penetration of Freud's mind. Like a true man of science he found that the solution, however brilliant, of one problem leads only to cogitation of others which the solution had exposed. And so on and on without end.

The letter of March 15 gives some chapter headings, which were later altered. At that time Freud intended to write one on "Dreams and Neuroses," a plan he abandoned; the nearest to its fulfillment was the Dora analysis which will be mentioned presently. By April 3 the second section, dealing with typical dreams, is nearly finished, but is much less satisfying than the first. On May 24 he reports that the third section, on the construction of dreams, is finished, but after that Freud gets held up by the impulse to sketch out the essay on general psychology, where he finds—rather strangely—that ideas from psychopathology are more helpful than those from dreams. Evi-

[f] Actually this was 1855.

dently the final chapter is giving a great deal of trouble. He had been held up by it for some time, and partly because of his dissatisfaction with it, partly because of the intimate allusions in the book, felt disinclined to publish it at all. (October 23, 1898.)

In a letter of February 19, 1899, he tries to distinguish between the nature of dreams and that of hysterical symptoms, both of which are the disguised expression of fulfilled wishes. He concludes that in dreams there is only a repressed wish, while in symptoms there is a compromise between the repressed wish and the repressing agency; he uses, for the first time, "self-punishment" as an example of the latter. It was only a good deal later that he detected the same state of affairs in the so-called "punishment dreams."

By May 28, 1899, there was a sudden burst of activity over the dream book "for no particular reason," and a final decision to proceed with the publishing; it should be ready for press by the end of July, before the holidays, "I have reflected that all the disguises won't do, nor the omissions, since I am not rich enough to keep to myself the finest discovery I have made, probably the only one that will survive me." On June 9 he thinks less of it. "The whole matter resolves itself into a platitude. Dreams all seek to fulfill *one* wish, which has got transformed into many others. It is the wish to sleep. One dreams so as not to have to wake, because one wants to sleep. *Tant de bruit.*" [g] In the next letter he finds that the last chapter of the book keeps on getting longer, and is neither good nor fruitful. It is his duty to write it, but it does not make him fonder of the theme. (June 27.) On the following day, however, the first chapter (not the literature) is sent to press.

The dream book proper went pretty well, but the two additional chapters that were necessary gave Freud a good deal of trouble. The first of them that he wrote was the review of the previous literature on the subject. He began to tackle this thankless task in December 1898, and found it "frightfully tedious." He seems to have dropped it then, but had to take it up again six months later so as to get the book ready. This time, on going through the literature more thoroughly, he found several productions, particularly Spitta's book, *Die Schlaf- und Traumzustände der menschlichen Seele* (Sleep and

[g] Freud got this piece of insight from Liébault's *Du Sommeil provoqué.*[14] Since he must almost certainly have read this book when it appeared (in the same year, 1889, as his visit to Liébault), it is strange that he should announce it in this fashion, and so late, to Fliess; but there are several examples of his forgetting and subsequently recapturing a piece of insight.

Dream States of the Human Soul), which for the first time makes him wish he had never touched the subject. (June 9, 1899.) By July 27 the task is completed, but he is very displeased with the way he has done it. Actually his review is a masterpiece in itself. It is not only comprehensive, and not only did he turn the "tedious" material into something charged with interest, but above all he selected from diverse sources all that has positive value and wove the whole into a narrative that is an excellent introduction to his own contributions. His capacity for mastering and giving order to a mass of heterogeneous material was never better displayed.

Most of the literature—Spitta's book being an example—he had found repellently superficial. Scherner's remarks on symbolism were perhaps the only thing of value. As regards his main ideas he had come across no precursors. Many years later, however, his attention was directed to a book by a physicist, Josef Popper-Lynkeus, *Die Phantasien eines Realisten* (Phantasies of a Realist) published in 1899. In a chapter of it entitled "Dreaming like Waking" the suggestion is made that the distortion in dreams is due to a censorship of unwelcome thoughts, which could be called a casual anticipation of a central part of Freud's theory.[15]

Freud has an amusing passage about this chapter in a letter of August 6: "Aren't you always right? You say outright what I have quietly thought to myself, that this first chapter will keep back a number of readers from going any further. But there is not much to be done about it. You didn't want the literature scattered through the book itself, and you were right: nor at the beginning; and you were again right. The secret seems to be that neither of us likes having it at all, anywhere. Yet if we don't want to give the 'scientists' a birch to trounce us with, we shall have to put up with it somewhere. The whole thing is now arranged on the analogy with a stroll in the forest. At the outset the dark wood of authors (who can't see the trees), without any outlook, and full of blind alleys. Then a concealed path along which I conduct the reader—my collection of dreams with their peculiarities, details, indiscretions, bad jokes—and then suddenly the heights, the prospect, and the inquiry: Where should you like to go from here?" And for the first time Freud seemed to be rather pleased with the book.

The good opinion now persisted. After sending it to the printers he felt very much the parting with what had been such a private part of himself, and that also seemed to soften his judgment of the book. Six months later he wrote that in many unhappy hours it had been a consolation to think that he would leave this book behind him. (March 23, 1900.)

The other great trouble was the formidable final chapter on the psychology of dream processes, one which we shall have to consider in some detail in the following chapter of the biography. It is the most difficult and abstract of all Freud's writings. He himself dreaded it beforehand, but when it came to the point he wrote it rapidly "as in a dream" [st] and finished it in a couple of weeks, in the first half of September. Freud expressed vividly his fears of what psychologists would have to say about it, and of course he made his usual derogatory criticism of it.

The same remark applied to the writing itself. Referring to the descriptions of the dreams, for instance, he said: "What I don't like about them is the style. I was quite unable to find any simple or distinguished expression and degenerated into jocular circumlocutions with a straining after pictorial imagery. I know that, but the part of me that knows it, and knows how to estimate such matters, unfortunately doesn't produce anything." (September 11, 1899.)

The last manuscript was dispatched by that date and a copy of the book itself was sent off to Fliess before October 27. It was actually published on November 4, 1899, but the publisher chose to put the date 1900 on the title page.

The motto on the title page from Vergil's *Aeneid*, *"Flectere, si nequeo Superos, Acheronta movebo,"* with its obvious reference to the fate of the repressed, Freud had three years previously intended to use as a heading for the chapter on "The Formation of Symptoms" in a projected book on the psychology of hysteria.

Six hundred copies of the book were printed, and it took eight years to sell them. In the first six weeks 123 copies were sold, and then 228 in the next two years. Freud was paid 522.40 gulden for it ($209).

Writing eighteen months later Freud said that no scientific periodical, and only a few others, had mentioned the book.[16] It was simply ignored. The Vienna *"Zeit"* had published a most stupid and contemptuous review written by Burckhardt, the former Director of the Burgtheater, six weeks after it appeared, and this put an end to any sales there. Short articles on it appeared in the *Umschau* (March

[st] Letter of June 20, 1898. Ernst remembers how his father used to come into meals, from the arbor where he had been writing, "as if he were sleepwalking," and altogether gave this impression of "being in a dream."

3, 1900) and the *Wiener Fremdenblatt* (March 10). Six months later a favorable one appeared in the *Berliner Tageblatt*, and again nine months after that a less favorable one in *Der Tag*. And that was all. Even Fliess's influence in Berlin failed to procure a review in any weekly.

As an example of its reception in Vienna Freud mentions the incident of an Assistant at the Psychiatric Clinic writing a book to disprove Freud's theories[17] without reading *The Interpretation of Dreams*; his colleagues at the Clinic had assured him it was not worth the trouble.[18] That was the late Professor Raimann. Not long afterwards Raimann gave a lecture on hysteria before an audience of four hundred students, and concluded with the words: "You see that these sick people have the inclination to unburden their minds. A colleague in this town has used this circumstance to construct a theory about this simple fact so that he can fill his pockets adequately." [19]

The book was, however, not entirely ignored in the psychological periodicals, although the reviews were almost as annihilating as complete silence would have been. Thus Wilhelm Stern, the psychologist, proclaimed the danger that "uncritical minds would be delighted to join in this play with ideas and would end up in complete mysticism and chaotic arbitrariness," [20] while Professor Liepmann, also of Berlin, could only observe that "the imaginative thoughts of an artist had triumphed over the scientific investigator." [21]

As late as 1927 Professor Hoche of Freiburg, in his book, *Das träumende Ich* (The Dreaming Ego), grouped Freud's theory of dreams in a late chapter on "Dream Mysticism" together with prophetic dreams and "the well-known dream books, printed on bad paper, which may be found in cooks' drawers."

For some years there was no sale at all for *The Interpretation of Dreams*. Seldom has an important book produced no echo whatever. It was ten years later, when Freud's work was coming to be recognized, that a second edition was called for. In all there were eight in Freud's lifetime, the last being in 1929. No fundamental change was ever made, nor was one necessary. The various editions merely incorporated more illustrations, fuller discussions here and there, and a more adequate account of the important theme of symbolism, one which Freud admitted he was late in properly appreciating.

The first translations of the book were into English and Russian both in 1913. Then followed one into Spanish (1922), French (1926), Swedish (1927), Japanese (1930), Hungarian (1934), and Czech (1938).

On February 1, 1900, Freud wrote that he had promised a condensed version of *The Interpretation of Dreams* for Loewenfeld's series entitled *Grenzfragen des Nerven- und Seelenlebens* (Borderline Problems of Nervous and Mental Life). He began in October and he must have written it with his usual facility, since it was published in the following year while he was simultaneously engaged in writing two other monographs. It was not to be the only time that Freud wrote a more popular version of his great work, and each time he accomplished this far from easy task with an astonishing freshness, so that even those familiar with the subject read the new version with the sense of reading something new to them.

The first translation of this smaller work was again into Russian (1909). The others are, in order: Dutch (1913), English (1914), Hungarian (1915), Italian (1919), Danish (1920), Polish (1923), Spanish (1924), French (1925), and Japanese (1929).

In a letter of October 14, 1900, Freud reported to Fliess that he had a new patient, a girl of eighteen. She was destined to figure five years later as "Dora" in the first of Freud's great series of case histories.[h]

The treatment lasted only eleven weeks, for the patient broke it off on the last day of the year. Freud finished writing an account of the case on January 24, 1901, but for motives of professional discretion did not publish it until April 1905.[i] Two months after he wrote down his notes of the case he showed them to his friend Oscar Rie, but the reception was such that "I thereupon determined to make no further effort to break down my state of isolation."

He told Fliess it was to be called *Dreams and Hysteria*, and was a *Fragment of an Analysis of a Case of Hysteria*. The second of these was ultimately chosen as the title; in the description of the case Freud mentions he had at first intended to give it the former.

---

[h] She was the sister of another Socialist leader, but I cannot disclose her name.

[i] On May 8, 1901, he expressed his hesitation about publishing it, but on June 7 he sent it to Ziehen (one of the editors of the *Monatsschrift für Psychiatrie und Neurologie* where it ultimately appeared).[22] Shortly after, however, he again changed his mind and retrieved the manuscript, to keep it in his desk for another four years.

Freud says that the patient subsequently visited him a year and a quarter later, on April 1, 1902, a fortnight after reading in the newspapers that he had been given the title of Professor.[23]

Contemporary evidence is therefore conclusive about the date of the analysis. Yet in 1914[24] and again in 1923[25] Freud three times gives a wrong date, placing it a year earlier than it actually was. It is permissible to suggest that his lapse of memory came from the connection in his mind between the essay and *The Interpretation of Dreams* (which the publisher also misdated by a year), since it had closely corresponded with the chapter of the same title he had intended to insert in that book. Dora had in fact arrived a year or two after this time, so the "omnipotence of thoughts" antedated her.

Freud had been for two reasons preoccupied with the relations between dreams and psychoneurotic symptoms, and he had evidently had considerable difficulty in arranging the material derived from the two sources. The first reason was the remarkable resemblance in the essential mechanism of the two processes, as also in their infantile origins: a resemblance which in its turn gave rise to further interesting problems, e.g., of the distinctions between them.

Then, secondly, both subjects made important contributions to the general theory of mental structure. This made it hard to know from which point of view to describe the latter. Freud's first intention was to make use of both, after incorporating in the dream book a chapter on the relationship between dreams and psychoneurotic symptoms. Then, either because he had not suitable material for that chapter, or because he thought it inartistic to confuse two themes in the same book, he decided to exclude the psychopathology and confine himself to the dream material. The final chapter of the *Interpretation*, that dealing with general psychology, is thus written from one point of view only. It was not an ideal arrangement, and there are passages in it where Freud has to break off the argument because to carry it further would raise questions that can be answered only by psychopathological material.

One sees, therefore, that the Dora analysis is really a continuation of *The Interpretation of Dreams*. It centers in two main dreams which are analyzed at length in a way that beautifully illustrates the interconnection between them and the patient's sufferings. The essay is especially instructive from the point of view of technique, both in the analytic procedure itself and in the therapeutic handling of the case. In the latter respect Freud considered he had made some mistakes, particularly in not dealing in good time with the signs of transference, and he subsequently expounded them with his usual frankness.

The comparison, or rather the contrast, between Freud's early case histories in the 1895 *Studies in Hysteria* and this beautiful little monograph composed six years later is illuminating. Freud's own comment on it at the time was that it was the most subtle of what he had till then written, and "that it would prove more shocking than usual. Still one does one's duty, and after all one doesn't write for today only." [26] The almost clumsy groping in the one, and the confident penetration in the other, could let one well believe that they proceeded from two different men.

And, indeed, they did. For the self-analysis separated the two, not only in time, but in nature.

XVII

Freud's Theory of the Mind

(1 9 0 0)

IN FREUD'S THEORY OF THE MIND AT ABOUT THE TURN OF THE CENTURY there were permanent elements to which he adhered all his life. There were others which he subsequently modified or added to, and there were still others which were themselves modifications of views he had held at an earlier period.

The reason why the date chosen is the most convenient to discuss the subject is that the fullest exposition Freud ever gave of it was in the well-known seventh chapter of *The Interpretation of Dreams* (1900). Most students have found this the most abstruse and difficult part of any of Freud's writings, which are usually pellucid. Fortunately, in the documents accompanying the Fliess correspondence, we now have material that throws light on the genesis of those later ideas and also helps to explicate the meaning they had in Freud's mind.

It is for philosophers to decide according to their way of thinking what label they would attach to Freud's basic conceptions, but an attempt may be made here at least to describe some of them.

FREE WILL AND DETERMINISM

Freud came from his early training deeply imbued with the belief in the universality of natural law and with a disbelief in the occurrence of miracles or spontaneous or uncaused acts. Scientific investigation would indeed be pointless if the order it strove to ascertain did not exist. He would certainly have subscribed to the closing words his teacher Meynert's address to the 54th *Versammlung Deutsche Naturforscher und Ärzte*: "On the Lawfulness of Human Thought and Behavior": "I should like to say in general that all philosophy, all human acceptance of wisdom so far as history spans, has really brought to light only two conclusions in which the outlook of those who have made use of the thought of all mankind differs from that of the common man. One is that everything in the world is only appearance and the appearance is not identical with the essence of things;[a] the second is that even the freedom we feel in ourselves is only apparent." [1]

The reason Meynert gives for the illusion of free will is that we are not yet able to follow in the finest details the regular processes in the life of the brain. Nevertheless, the apparent freedom is really based on law, therefore on necessity.

Herbart, to whom many of Meynert's and Freud's ideas can be ultimately traced, had also in 1824 protested against "this false doctrine of a free will that has raised its head in recent years," [2]—referring here to his own teacher Fichte, about whose idealistic philosophy he felt equally strongly.

Writing on this subject in 1904, Freud gave the reason for our unshakable conviction of freedom of choice. He remarked that it is far stronger with trivial decisions than with weighty ones; with the latter we commonly feel that our inner nature compels us, that we really have no alternative. With the former, however, for example the arbitrary choice of a number, we discern no motive and therefore feel it is an uncaused act on the part of our ego. If now we subject the example to a psychoanalysis we discover that the choice has after all been determined, but this time the motive is an unconscious one. We actually leave the matter to be decided by our unconscious mind and then claim the credit for the outcome. If unconscious motivation is taken into account, therefore, the rule of determinism is of general validity.[3]

Freud never wavered in this attitude and all his research into the workings of the mind is entirely based on a belief in a regular chain of mental events. He would have endorsed the view of the great anthropologist Tylor that "the history of mankind is part and parcel of the history of Nature, that our thoughts, wills and actions accord with laws as definite as those which govern the motion of the waves." When enumerating the essential elements of psychoanalytical theory, in 1924, he included "the thoroughgoing meaningfulness and determinism of even the apparently most obscure and arbitrary mental phenomena." [4] He does not appear ever to have expressed any opinion on the general theory of causality, but he presumably held the simple nineteenth-century view of invariable antecedents.

[a] Cf. the words of Goethe: *"Alles Vergängliche ist nur ein Gleichnis."*

MIND AND MATTER

In this context it would be possible to place Freud as belonging to the category of idealistic philosophy, materialistic, or even phenomenonalistic,[b] since passages could be quoted from different periods of his life in favor of each view. He never showed any sympathy with either scholastic realism or solipsism.

In his early student days Freud passed through a phase of radical materialism,[c] but this could not have survived his attendance at Brentano's and Meynert's lectures. In his most radical moments, however, it is very unlikely that he would have subscribed to the dictum of Cabanis that the brain secretes thought as the liver secretes bile! Later he adopted the general scientific attitude of empiricism. The mind is evidently the only source of information about the outer world, including the body itself, but this need not give it any position of priority in the universe. Nor need its perceptual data concerning the outer world have any close correspondence with the essential nature of the latter. As to the physical world itself, Meynert, like most scientists of the time, had replaced Kant's *Ding an sich* by the notion of Force, and Freud would doubtless have subscribed to the prevailing view that this, combined with the atomic theory, was the most convenient way of coordinating the data of chemistry and physics. Einstein's amazing formula, $E = MC^2$, by which he united matter and energy, appeared five years after the date we are now contemplating. Freud would also have believed that further knowledge of such laws would make them applicable to the realm of living organisms.

In all this Freud was the child of his time and we have no reason to think that he ever indulged in individual speculations beyond those prevailing in his milieu. He was never attracted by the apparently unknowable, and his interest was aroused only when he could perceive some approach that had a prospect of extending the previously known. Agnosticism was a state of mind that came easily to him.

MIND AND BRAIN

In this narrower field there is more to be said. The first statement on it is to be found in Freud's *Aphasia* (1891). There he proclaimed

[b] Ernst Mach of Vienna published his *Beiträge zur Analyse der Empfindungen* (Contributions to the Analysis of Sensations) in 1886.
[c] See p. 43.

himself an adherent of the doctrine of psychophysical parallelism. "The chain of the physiological processes in the nervous system probably does not stand in any causal relation to the psychical processes. The physiological processes do not cease as soon as the physical ones begin; the physiological chain continues, but from a certain moment onwards there corresponds with each link in it (or several links) a psychical phenomenon. Thus the psychical is a process parallel to the physiological ('a dependent concomitant' d)." He then proceeds to quote the following passage from Hughlings Jackson: "In all our studies of diseases of the nervous system we must be on our guard against the fallacy that what are physical states in lower centers fine away *into* psychical states in higher centers; that, for example, vibrations of sensory nerves *become* sensations, or that somehow or other an idea produces a movement." [6,7]

Two opinions in this context, however, Freud held all his life. One was that there was no evidence of psychical processes occurring apart from physiological ones: that no mind could exist apart from a brain. And since he never had any belief in the immortality of the soul—or indeed in its existence—that would apply equally to the next world as to this. The other was that physical processes must precede psychical ones: information reaching the mind, whether from the outer world through the sense organs or from the body through the chemical stimuli it provides, must begin as a physical excitation. Both opinions would argue a certain priority for physiological processes.

His experience had taught him that the most complicated processes of thought could go on without being accompanied by consciousness, and he habitually referred to these as "unconscious mental processes." Yet how far from dogmatism he was in the matter may be seen from this quotation which follows a passage concerning the displacement of affects: "Perhaps it might be more correct to say: these processes are not of a psychical nature at all, but are physical processes the psychical consequences of which are represented as if what is expressed by the words 'detachment of the idea from its affect and false connection of the latter' had really happened." [8]

Freud held that not only was the essential nature of both mind and matter quite unknown, but they were so intrinsically different in kind as to make it a logical error to translate a description of processes in the one into terms of the other. Nor was there any clue

d A phrase from Hughlings Jackson, "On Affections of Speech from Diseases of the Brain." [5]

for elucidating the direct relationship of one to the other. How an excitation of the retina could be followed by a perception of light or form was an unapproachable mystery. Of course, like all doctors and many other people, Freud would often use loose language incompatible with what has just been expounded: bodily, e.g., sexual, changes would *produce* anxiety, or an emotion would *produce* paralysis of a limb. Clearly, however, these are shorthand expressions not meant to be taken as literal exactitude. Psychosomatic medicine, for example, is replete with phraseology of this kind.

Nevertheless Freud believed, much more strongly in his early years but perhaps to some extent always, that the correlation of mental processes with physiological ones hinted at a similarity in the way both worked. As we shall see presently, he cherished the hope for a time that by applying physical and physiological concepts, such as those of energy, tension, discharge, excitation, etc., to mental processes it would be possible to achieve a better understanding of such processes. He even made a valiant, if somewhat forlorn, endeavor to put this into operation and he wrote a brochure (in 1895)[dt] describing his effort in detail. This he never published, and his reactions to it soon afterwards would indicate his recognition that the endeavor was wildly premature if not altogether vain. From then on he decided to follow the sound example Breuer had given in his chapter in the *Studies in Hysteria* where, after remarking that ideas represent something familiar and cortical excitation only a postulate, so that to translate the former by terms belonging to the latter is only a "pointless masquerade," he laid it down that "psychical processes should be treated in the language of psychology." [9]

Strictly speaking, the language of physiology into which Freud attempted to transcribe the phenomena of psychology was in its turn rather the language of physics which had been grafted on to the data of physiology. Brücke and others of the Helmholtz school had made it their life's task, with varying success, to describe those data in the terminology of chemistry and physics and to apply the laws of those sciences to physiology, as far as they found it possible. There existed the hope, born with Herbart in the 1820's, and later strongly supported by Fechner in particular, that the same extension could be carried out in the field of psychology, and in his earlier years Freud also must certainly have cherished that hope.

In the half century since then that hope seems to have remained fairly dormant, but of late it has revived under the stimulus of the

[dt] See p. 380.

new work being carried out in the field called cybernetics.[10] It would be interesting to attempt a correlation between Freud's early attempt and the modern outlook.

PHYSICS, PHYSIOLOGY, AND PSYCHOLOGY

We know that Freud's main aim in life, certainly in the early productive period and perhaps always, was to formulate a theoretical basis for the new discoveries he was making in psychopathology and, with the help of that, to found a theory of the mind that would take into due account the peculiar features of the unconscious; the outcome of his endeavors is called psychoanalysis. It is therefore pertinent to inquire into what foundation he had to work on apart from his own clinical observations.

Freud himself once wrote that "Psychoanalysis grew on a narrowly restricted basis." [11] It is now possible to define this basis pretty closely. The most evident part of it was that of psychopathology itself. He was well informed in the doctrines and literature of the period, but this field was so limited that it is easy to survey it. There were a few workers in Germany, such as Moebius, Loewenfeld, and Heidenhain, from whom, however, Freud could have derived but very little. The only important sources of stimulation were Breuer, Charcot, and Bernheim, in that order, and their influence has already been fully discussed.ᵉ The French schools were certainly in advance of the contemporary German ones in being more willing to regard psychopathology as a branch of psychology in its own right, the German workers adhering more conservatively to the language of cerebral anatomy. In the Preface to his translation of one of the Charcot books Freud had already commented on this difference. He remarked, "A feature that may be explained by the historical development of German clinical medicine: namely, the tendency to offer a physiological interpretation of disease states and of the connections between symptoms. The clinical observations of the French surely gain in independence through their subordinating the physiological points of view to a secondary place. This may explain why French clinical medicine makes an alien impression on the uninitiated. But really it is not a matter of neglectfulness; it is a deliberate exclusion for practical reasons." [12]

Freud's contact with France, both personally and through reading, must have helped him to emancipate himself from neurology, although he was dilatory in availing himself of it—evidently

ᵉ See Chaps. XI and XII.

from an unwillingness to forsake what he felt to be a secure and "scientific" basis.

Freud was, on the contrary, ill-informed in the field of contemporary psychology and seems to have derived only from hearsay any knowledge he had of it. He often admitted his ignorance of it, and even when he tried to remedy it later did not find anything very useful for his purpose in it, with perhaps two exceptions. Lipps's writings[13] evidently encouraged him to undertake the study of wit and humor, problems that had already engaged his attention. And both Lipps and Jerusalem,[14] of whom Freud also speaks very highly, were stout supporters of the conception of unconscious psychical processes, even if not in Freud's dynamic sense.

We have here one reason why psychologists, not only at that time but also later, found much of Freud's terminology alien to them. Not having been schooled in any psychological discipline, even in the little there was at that period, he was apt to be careless and imprecise in his use of terms, using, for instance, "perception" as interchangeable with "idea," and the like. He came in time to forge his own terminology, largely by the device of taking over concepts from other branches of science and giving them fresh meanings appropriate to their new context. That, again, made it harder for professional psychologists to apprehend his thought.

Although Freud had no occasion ever to progress beyond the elements of chemistry and physics, he was without doubt thoroughly familiar with the basic conceptions of these sciences, since it was just these his teachers were enthusiastically endeavoring to extend into the fields of biology, general physiology, and particularly neurology. It is important, therefore, to examine the connections they had with his own field of work. His first grounding in the principles themselves he obtained in his six years of work in the Institute of Physiology, from the great Brücke and his colleagues. But it was Meynert, whose lectures on psychiatry he attended with special interest, who was trying to apply them in the field of neurology and psychology; so it is to his figure we have to pay particular attention.

Much work has been done in tracing the genealogy of the basic ideas that Freud employed in his psychology. The most painstaking example is a slight volume by Maria Dorer, of Darmstadt, one unfortunately somewhat marred by an undue intentness on establishing a particular thesis.[15] Some of her conclusions will presently be mentioned. It was a Polish psychologist, Luise von Karpinska, who first called attention to the resemblance between some of Freud's fundamental ideas and those promulgated by Herbart seventy years previously.[16] We have mentioned above one on freedom of the will. The one Karpinska especially dwells on is Herbart's conception of the unconscious, which was the only dynamic one before Freud's. According to it, unconscious mental processes are dominated by a constant conflict which Herbart describes in terms of ideas of varying intensity—a notion which Freud later replaced by a conflict of affects; with Herbart ideas are always primary to affects, as in the later James-Lange theory. The conflict Herbart describes is partly intrapsychical but more characteristically between those of one person and of another. The latter are treated as disturbing, or aggressive, elements which evoke "self-preservative" efforts on the part of the subject. Mental life is throughout dualistic, as Freud also always conceived it. Herbart actually describes an idea as *"verdrängt"* when it is unable to reach consciousness because of some opposing idea or when it has been driven out of consciousness by one! He conceives of two thresholds in the mind, which correspond topographically with the position of Freud's two censorships. One, the "static threshold," is where an inhibited idea is robbed of its activity and can enter consciousness only when the inhibition is lifted; it is, therefore, not unlike a "suppressed" idea in the preconscious. At another level is what he calls the "mechanistic threshold" where wholly repressed ideas are still in a state of rebellious activity directed against those in consciousness and succeed in producing indirect effects, e.g., "objectless feelings of oppression (*Beklemmung*)." [17] "Science knows more than what is actually experienced [in consciousness] only because what is experienced is unthinkable without examining what is concealed. One must be able to recognize from what is experienced the traces of what is stirring and acting 'behind the curtains' ! "

All this is very interesting, but there is more. People vary in the way in which the body responds to affects (Freud's somatic compliance), which Herbart calls the "physiological resonance"; this leads to a "condensation of the affects in the nervous system." Mental processes are characterized by a "striving for equilibrium" (Freud's constancy principle).[f] "Ideas" are indestructible and are never lost. Nor do they ever exist alone, only in chains of ideas that are so interwoven with one another as to form networks. Affects arise only when the equilibrium is disturbed through an excessive quantity of intensity being present in the ideas. Consciousness of self (the ego) comes about when active ideas are inhibited (frustrated?).

[f] An idea akin to what Cannon later termed "homeostasis."

Herbart's principal thesis was that mental processes must be capable of being resumed under scientific laws. "Regular order in the human mind is wholly similar to that in the starry sky." [18] The processes must ultimately be measurable in terms of force and quantity. He dreamt of a "mathematical psychology" and drew up a project for one. Some years later Fechner seemed to have made important progress in this direction by generalizing Weber's law into the statement that the strength of our sensations increases proportionally to the logarithm of that of the stimulus.[19] Perhaps these hopes could be traced back to Spinoza's use of geometry in his *Ethics,* but they overlook Pascal's classic remark that "the heart has reasons which the reason knows not of."

It is hardly likely that Freud, who was not very given to reading books on psychology, would have been at that time familiar with William James's detailed criticism of Fechner's work, one which culminated in the following devastating conclusions: "Fechner's book was the starting point of a new department of literature, of which, in the humble opinion of the present writer, the proper psychological outcome is just *nothing*." [20] "It would be terrible if even such a dear old man as this could saddle our science forever with his patient whimsies, and, in a world so full of more nutritious objects of attention, compel all future students to plough through the difficulties, not only of his own works, but of the still drier ones written in his refutation. Those who desire this dreadful literature can find it; it has a 'disciplinary value'; but I will not even enumerate it in a footnote." [21]

Nevertheless, Herbart held that psychology was anterior to physiology and that to let it be dominated by physiological thought would be to reverse their proper relationship, "a mistake frequently committed both in ancient and in more recent times."

Notions such as those just described could have filtered through to Freud from many sources, but those echoes from the past are nonetheless noteworthy. It is not very likely that Freud would ever have had reason to make a study of Herbart's writings, though it is of course possible.[g] We do not even know if Meynert did, but his published works make it certain that he was very familiar with the Herbartian psychology, on which his own was based and of which his was an extension and modification. He must in any case have had access to it through the full exposition of it by Griesinger, of

[g] In his search through the literature on dreams Freud would have examined Herbart's section on the topic.[ss]

whose writings Meynert thought highly and which Freud probably also read.

After this paragraph was written, Dr. and Mrs. Bernfeld, thus increasing my great debt to them, communicated the remarkably interesting fact that in Freud's last year at the Gymnasium the following textbook was in use: Gustaf Adolf Lindner, *Lehrbuch der empirischen Psychologie nach genetischer Methode* (Textbook of Empirical Psychology by Genetic Method) (1858). The author's teacher was Franz Exner, the father of Freud's instructor at the Brücke Institute. Now in the preface to the book the author states categorically that only thinkers of the Herbart school come into consideration, and in fact the book may be described as a compendium of the Herbartian psychology. It contains among other things, this passage: "A result of the fusion of ideas proves that ideas which were once in consciousness and for any reason have been repressed (*verdrängt*) out of it are not lost, but in certain circumstances may return." [23] There is a detailed account of the conflict between stronger and weaker ideas along correct Herbartian lines.

Fechner's psychology is altogether built on Herbart's, whose main principles (except the metaphysical ones) he fully shared; it was strengthened by his endeavor to apply to living organisms the recently discovered principle of the conservation of energy. He went further in maintaining that pleasure-unpleasure phenomena were themselves susceptible of quantitative treatment, and not simply qualitative. The word "threshold" stands at the center of all his writings, and he maintained that whenever certain physiological processes attained a given intensity they would be followed by conscious ones. He did not commit himself on the question of whether unconscious processes could be psychical, but of their importance otherwise he was convinced. "What is below the threshold *carries* the consciousness, since it sustains the physical connection in between." [24] He likened the mind to an iceberg which is nine-tenths under water and whose course is determined not only by the wind that plays over the surface but also by the currents of the deep.

Fechner exercised an important influence on Brücke, who held that "movements in the nervous system give rise to ideas," on Meynert, whom we shall consider presently, and on Breuer, who ranked him next only to Goethe. Freud, who had studied his writings at first hand, also spoke highly of him. He said, "I was always open to the ideas of G. T. Fechner and have followed that thinker upon many important points." [25]

For Meynert mind and brain were so closely connected that they could be spoken of in the same breath, and sometimes interchangeably; the "mechanics of the brain" was a favorite phrase of his. Although he was much influenced by Kant and Schopenhauer—he was altogether well read in philosophy—his psychology was essentially founded on the "association psychology" of Herbart and Fechner. All three repudiated the "faculty psychology" that had such a vogue in England in the early nineteenth century.

A prominent characteristic of Meynert's psychology was his "projection" theory, in which he uses various optical analogies (camera, etc.), as Freud did later. He used this term to indicate the gathering from various sources of impressions that finally reached the cells of the cortex, and then are from there "projected into consciousness." [26] It may be recalled that Freud, in his book on aphasia, had pointed out the errors in Meynert's account of the anatomy of this process.[h] The main function of the brain cells, according to Meynert, is to establish associations, but they do this in a very peculiar fashion. Since the heart cannot regulate the flow of blood in the smaller vessels finely enough, the brain cells assist in the process. They send messages to these vessels by which they dilate or contract as required, and on that flow of blood depends the nutrition and therefore the activity of the cells. When brain cells are impelled to extend their associations, they have first to attract nutriment to themselves in the manner just mentioned.[27] On the degree in which the cells are nourished will depend the strength of the resulting ideas, and—what is specially interesting—whether the ideas can pass beyond the threshold of consciousness; when they are strong they can do so, otherwise they remain below the threshold.[28] This is somewhat reminiscent of the Weir Mitchell feeding therapy, based on the assumption that the "functional" deficiency of the brain cells in hysteria is due to their being undernourished.

Meynert followed Herbart in describing two directions of energy (or of affect) in terms of "attack" and "defense." He accepts the "unpleasure principle," and, again like Freud, speaks of a summation of excitations.[29] However, the latter applies primarily to the intensity of ideas; their accompanying affects are not capable of being dissociated, as Freud held.

The brain (and mind) receive stimuli from two sources: the outer world and the body, and they are treated alike by the mind (as with

[h] See p. 215.

Freud); everything in the body except the brain cells themselves, therefore, belongs to the outer world, not to the self.[30]

The fundamental process in the brain and mind is, according to Meynert, a reflex. The "secondary ego" is a controlling agency. He uses the word "inhibiting"[i] and "pressing back"[j] in place of Herbart's "repressing,"[k] but they evidently have the same meaning. The primary ego is unconscious and belongs to the earliest period of life, which reminds one of Freud's statement that the unconscious is infantile. At this point Meynert develops his moral theory of the superior "good" part of the brain controlling the inferior "bad" part, which has been described earlier.[l]

Despite the materialistic ideas mentioned in the foregoing passages Meynert would nevertheless have counted himself a philosophical idealist. For him consciousness was the only (immediate) reality. The outer world and the body itself are "states of consciousness." "All the scientific orderliness of phenomena proceeds from the atomistic *Weltanschauung*. Inasmuch as we have irrefutably to build matter out of atoms, the reality of matter vanishes, since, as Mach in his *Vorlesungen über Psychophysik* points out, we can attribute no sense qualities to atoms. . . . Thus the atomistic world consists of mathematical points, whence forces which can be quantitatively defined evoke forces in our consciousness." [31]

Finally a few words should be said concerning the views of the famous Berlin psychiatrist, Griesinger, of whose works Meynert was a careful student. Griesinger was throughout a follower of Herbart, although he laid more stress on the volitional aspects of the mind. He had naturally a more pronouncedly medical outlook, so that the connection between ideas and brain cells is more in evidence; he did not hesitate to use expressions like the "cerebral activity of ideas," etc. He fully accepted the idea of unconscious activity and held that the ideas "absent from consciousness" were of greater importance than those present in it; for their absence, however, he gave no explanation beyond vague phrases like "clearness" and "strength." He connected the unconscious particularly with impressions received from bodily organs; these make important contributions to our moods and determine many of our sympathies and antipathies.[32]

[i] *Hemmung.*
[j] *Zurückdrängen.*
[k] *Verdrängen.*
[l] See p. 281.

Like all these writers, Griesinger shrinks with abhorrence from the risk of being called a materialist, and rejects the philosophy of a "trite and shallow materialism." [33] Although it is quite justified to regard the mind as above all the "sum of all the states of the brain," how mental processes arise remains a riddle. "How a material, psychical process in the nerve fibers or ganglion cells can become an idea, an act of consciousness, is wholly incomprehensible." [34]

Breuer, who was deeply and widely versed in philosophical and psychological literature as well, of course, as in physiology and neurology, must, since he stood in a closer relationship to Freud than any of the others, constitute an important link in the chain.

Maria Dorer, who has worked over in great detail the data presented above, is concerned to develop two theses as the result of her labors. One is that Freud's psychology is completely materialistic and mechanistic, and so must be imperfect because of its soulless omission of the sense of values; she repudiates the possibility of the latter being susceptible to objective investigation. Freud's psychology was undoubtedly deterministic: whether the epithets "materialistic" or "mechanistic," often used as terms of abuse, should be applied to it is a question that could be answered only by philosophers.

Her second thesis is that Freud's psychology was in the main derived from earlier sources, and here a biographer has more right to a word. She maintains that Meynert, deriving in turn from the other authors mentioned above, was the main source of his psychological ideas, and goes so far as to state that "Freud's dependence on Meynert's teaching can be demonstrated in detail." [35] She goes on to comment on Freud's never having made any acknowledgment to Meynert, and to his referring to him in his writings (with the exception of the book on aphasia) only in a personal context. We know now that this was not, as Dorer appears to suggest, a sign of ingratitude: it was simply that the main ideas in question had been familiar to Freud since his boyhood.[m]

Two comments would seem to be in place here. When one speaks of someone acquiring an idea from someone else, it usually concerns not only a significant idea but one peculiar to the latter person. When it is a matter of general knowledge, on the other hand, it is comparatively unimportant who one's particular teacher was. If we review the main ideas in question we may fairly assert that they are of that order, and were both familiar and widely accepted

[m] See p. 374.

throughout the educated, and particularly the scientific, world of the nineteenth century; nor are they, indeed, alien to the twentieth century.

A dualistic conception of mental processes has existed throughout the ages. Sometimes it is expressed in moral terms: "animal" versus "spiritual" nature, "higher" versus "lower"; and sometimes more objectively, "simple" versus "complex," "controlled" versus "uncontrolled," and so on. Again, that their activities can similarly be expressed dualistically, as "aggressive" versus "defensive," etc., is also a ready generalization. Furthermore, that both the mind and the brain receive impressions from two sources, the body and the outer world, is sufficiently obvious in itself.

That ideas can be expressed in terms of a network of associations is a notion that does not need much reflection.

As for the unconscious, thinkers, and particularly poets, have for long noticed that novel ideas may appear spontaneously in consciousness, and the fact of their source being unknown has often led to an unconscious one, i.e., one of which the mind is not cognizant, being postulated. The more romantic philosophers of the eighteenth and early nineteenth century greatly favored this conception, one which reached its apogee in Von Hartmann's celebrated work.[36] It was inevitable that medical writers should connect this unknown region with cerebral activity even more closely than they did the conscious mind; in fact, it was in England commonly described by Carpenter's expression "unconscious cerebration."

The second comment is that Miss Dorer apparently failed to perceive the vast difference between the general theoretical statement of the ideas in question and the detailed experiential investigations that in Freud's hands first gave them life and meaning. To take a couple of examples. Wordsworth's line, "The child is father of the man," has become a proverbial saying, but Freud's discovery of the precise way in which the previously unknown instinctual basis of childhood life evolves into the adult personality gave that saying a far profounder significance.

The network of associated ideas described in the Association Psychology of the nineteenth century, with its categories of contiguity, causality, etc. took on a very different appearance when Freud introduced the conception of "purposive ideas" in the unconscious together with the dynamic conception of wish-fulfillments.

That human beings prefer pleasure to pain is an observation that was made the basis of a hedonistic psychology, one, however, that most philosophers refused to regard as comprehensive—there being apparently so many exceptions to the rule. Freud's demonstration of how the pleasure-unpleasure principle evolves into what he later called the reality-principle gave a deeper meaning to the hedonistic view.

The dualistic conception of the mind had been based partly on theology and partly on physiology. As will be recounted presently, Freud showed that there were two fundamentally different types of psychological functioning, which he called "primary process" and "secondary process" respectively, and he described in full detail their widely diverging characteristics. This was bound up with his exploration of the unconscious, its origin, its peculiar features, and its mode of functioning, all of which opened up a new region in a manner completely unlike the previous philosophical postulating. If anyone were to say that he got the idea of the unconscious from someone else, the crass ignorance implied in the remark would not be redeemed by the tiny atom of truth in it.

PROJECT FOR A SCIENTIFIC PSYCHOLOGY

In the days of which we are now writing a great deal was known of both the gross anatomy and the histology of the brain, subjects which Freud had fully mastered, but very little of its physiology. Fritsch and Hitzig in Germany, with Ferrier and Horsley in England, had shown that electrical stimulation of certain areas of the cortex produced movements in the limbs on the opposite side of the body, and it was also known that destruction of certain other areas would lead to aphasia, either motor or sensorial. Beyond this there was very little, and a great deal of the talk about brain physiology and its application to the mind was really little more than using the language of physics—with terms like energy, tension, force, etc.—in another sphere.

Doubtless all psychologists expected, as they still must do, that one day scientific law and order would prevail in the apparent chaos of mental processes as it has in other sections of the universe. The illusion, however, that scientists of those days labored under was that the most promising approach to that desideratum was through brain physiology. In the event brain physiology has turned out to be even more refractory than psychology itself.

Freud seems to have shared this illusion himself for many years, until there was a gradual liberation from it which was complete by

1897. It brought about a very interesting episode in his life, the writing of a long essay which is here called the "Project." We know that his ambition in those years was to advance in knowledge along the avenue signaled by the designations: anatomy of the brain, physiology of the brain, psychopathology, psychology, philosophy. The first two of these proved to be will-o'-the-wisps, and the final goal was only partially attained. But of the advance there is no doubt.

The earlier ambition of proceeding direct from the brain to the mind reached its climax in 1895. On April 27, in the month after he wrote the chapter on psychotherapy for the *Studies in Hysteria,* he wrote to Fliess that "I am so deeply immersed in the 'Psychology for Neurologists' [n] as to be entirely absorbed until I have to break off, really exhausted by overwork. I have never experienced such intense preoccupation. I wonder if anything will come of it? I hope so, but it goes on slowly and with difficulty." A month later (May 25) he described his aims in a passage quoted earlier,[o] and, after giving as one of them the hope of extracting from psychopathology something useful for psychology, he went on: "Actually a satisfactory general understanding of neuropsychotic disturbances is not possible unless one can make a connection with clear presuppositions about normal psychical processes. I have devoted every free minute to this work during the last few weeks, spending the hour from eleven to twelve in phantasy, in translation from one field to the other, and guesswork, and ceasing only when I have reduced some idea to an absurdity or else really and seriously overworked to the extent of losing all interest in my professional activities." (May 25.)

It is not surprising that this obsessive preoccupation found a limit. By August 16 we hear that he was throwing it aside and pretending to himself that it was not interesting. He was on holiday and felt he had been setting himself a crucifying task. "Anyhow, playing at skittles and searching for mushrooms are much healthier occupations." He had found that one topic had led to another, to memory, to sleep, and so on in such an endless fashion as to give the whole project mountainous proportions.

One suspects that an important immediate stimulus to this gigantic undertaking, for which he was assuredly ill-prepared and untrained, had been given by a huge volume that his teacher Exner had published only the year before on the same theme.[37] It was written more diffusely than Freud's "Project," and was eight times as long,

[n] Presumably the title for the intended book.
[o] See p. 294.

but there is a good deal of similarity between the two. Exner held that the degrees in excitation in the nervous system must be subject to quantitative laws.[38] He uses the same phrase as Freud, "summation of excitations," [39] and discusses at length the function of inhibition in the control of simple stimuli.[40] It was he who developed the conception of *Bahnung* (facilitation of the flow of excitation) [41] that plays an important part in Freud's exposition. Like Freud, he covers a wide field, dealing with the topics of perception, judgment, ideation, recognition, thinking processes, and so on. The pleasure-unpleasure principle is a regulating one. His disbelief in free will is based on the same arguments as Freud's, the illusion of it arising from a break in the antecedent ideas in consciousness; where, however, Freud demonstrated the existence in the unconscious of the missing links, Exner could only fall back on a vague remark about the continued activity of the subcortical centers.[42] His fundamental aim was the same as Freud's: to deprive mental processes of their peculiar status among natural phenomena. By way of contrast, however, it must be said that Freud's essay was not only far more concise, but much more closely reasoned than Exner's.

The year before that another of his seniors in the Brücke Institute had published (posthumously) a volume which would provide Freud with any basis he needed for his cerebral physiology.[43]

The respite the holiday gave did not last long, and the tyrannical compulsion to get his ideas set forth was soon again in action. On September 4 Freud went to Berlin to visit Fliess and doubtless to talk over the problems concerned. The result of this was so exciting that Freud could not wait to get home but started composing in the train; ᴾ the first part of his essay was thus written in pencil. The whole essay, which would make a brochure of some hundred pages, was written feverishly in a couple of weeks, with a few necessary intervals. All three parts were dispatched to Fliess on October 8, and fortunately he preserved them; they were published as an Appendix to the letters of the *Aus den Anfängen der Psychoanalyse* (From the Beginnings of Psychoanalysis) (1950).

It is noteworthy that Freud never asked for the return of that interesting manuscript which had cost him so much trouble, nor apparently did he ever want to see it again. He had been relieved of an oppressive burden, and his attitude towards what he had given birth to rapidly changed. In sending it off he said he was keeping

ᴾ In announcing this to Fliess he remarked: "I write so little to you because I am writing so much for you." [44]

back a final section, on the "Psychopathology of Repression," which he was finding extremely difficult; his mood about it was alternately "proud and happy" or "ashamed and miserable."[45] This final section has not come to light; possibly it was never completed. The following sentence, written a week later, probably refers to it: "For two weeks I have been in a fever of writing and believed I had the secret; now I know I haven't and so have put the matter aside." [46] Three weeks later he wrote that he had deposited the manuscript of the "Psychology" (probably again that troublesome section) in a drawer, partly because he ought to begin writing the monograph for Nothnagel[47, q]—for which he had only another six weeks, but which actually plagued him for another whole year[r]—and doubtless also because he could not find a satisfying solution to the problems.

The elation at his recent accomplishment lasted a little while and was accompanied by the following interesting experience. In a letter of October 20, less than a fortnight after finishing what we possess of the "Project," he wrote: "One evening last week when I was hard at work, tormented with just that amount of pain that seems to be the best state to make my brain function, the barriers were suddenly lifted, the veil drawn aside, and I had a clear vision from the details of the neuroses to the conditions that make consciousness possible. Everything seemed to connect up, the whole worked well together, and one had the impression that the Thing[s] was now really a machine and would soon go by itself. The three systems of neurones, the free and bound state of Quantity, the primary and secondary processes, the main tendency and the compromise tendency of the nervous system, the two biological laws of attention and defense, the indications of Quality, Reality, and Thought, the (particular) position of the psychosexual group, the sexual determinant of repression, and finally the necessary conditions for consciousness as a function of perception: all that was perfectly clear, and still is. Naturally I don't know how to contain myself for pleasure." This passage, with its hint of artistic intuitiveness, may mark the transition from Freud the dogged worker to Freud the imaginative thinker.

The mood of elation, however, could not last, and the excitement soon died down. Only ten days later he was telling Fliess that on reflection he saw that what he had sent him had in part lost its value and was meant to be only a preliminary draft, but he hoped it might

q See p. 218.
r Loc. cit.
s I.e., the mind.

come to something.[48] And a month later it was all over: "I no longer understand the state of mind in which I hatched out the "Psychology," [t] and I can't understand how I came to inflict it on you. I consider you are always too polite; to me it seems pure balderdash." [49]

We may now ask what claims this curious document has on our interest. It has many.

In the first place, it is a magnificent *tour de force*. Nowhere in Freud's published writings do we find such a brilliant example of his capacity for abstruse thought and sustained close reasoning. It reveals a brain of the highest order and makes a mockery of his own complaints about his poor intellect. With its elliptical style and somewhat obscure phraseology, almost unrelieved by concrete examples, it imposes more exacting demands on the reader than any of his published work; there must be very few who can apprehend its full meaning without several perusals. Much of this difficulty, of course, is because the essay was couched in language familiar only to its solitary audience.

Then it is of great value to the student of Freud's psychology because it throws light on many of his later conceptions, some of them rather alien, which he seldom defined or even elucidated. The language of physics and cerebral physiology in the "Project" was Freud's natural one, to which he in great part adhered later even when he was dealing with purely psychological problems. It is true that he then gave the terms he used psychological meanings which take them away from their original context, but all the same they are often terms that no psychologist would have employed to start with. It has not been easy to translate some of them into more familiar terminology or to define their precise signification in Freud's mind. For this the study of the "Project" should prove most helpful.

The richness of the ideas contained in the "Project," and the extraordinarily close relationship subsisting among them, provide the student with a wealth of material for research. There is room for several monographs devoted to the elucidation of this little essay.

For the student of Freud's personality the "Project" has several instructive lessons. It shows what a hold the concrete studies of his youth had obtained over him. In the realm of the visual, of definite neural activities that could be seen under the microscope, he had for many years felt entirely at home; he was as safe there as at the

[t] The term by which Freud usually referred to the Project in his letters.

family hearth. To wander away from it and embark on the perilous seas of the world of emotions, where all was unknown and where what was invisible was of far greater consequence than the little that was visible, must have cost him dear. He was called to a high endeavor, which he was now on the brink of undertaking, and we may regard the feverish writing of the "Project" as a last desperate effort to cling to the safety of cerebral anatomy. If only the mind could be described in terms of neurones, their processes and synapses! How fond the thought must have been to him.

Another important consideration is that never again until the last period of his life, and never before so far as we know, did Freud indulge in deductive reasoning as he did here. The great Herbart, it is true, had maintained that in psychology deduction has equal rights with induction, but this metaphysical heresy had been vehemently repudiated by both Griesinger and Meynert, and Freud himself had been drilled in the sacred doctrine that all conclusions were to be founded on experience, and experience alone. Yet in the "Project" there is very little direct reference to any experience. Axioms and assumptions—whether plausible or not is beside the point —are taken as the basis for far-reaching trains of thought and somewhat dogmatic conclusions. It is an essay one would have expected from a philosopher rather than from a pathologist.

The word philosopher is suggestive. Perhaps Freud was here for the first time releasing his early, and so thoroughly checked, tendency to philosophize. The feverish obsessiveness with which he wrote the essay hints at some deep underground activity, one of which his quick subsequent repudiation expressed disapproval. If not checked, this tendency might end in empty speculation, an arid intellectualizing of the underground urges. Fortunately the issue was otherwise. Freud returned to the empirical experience of his clinical observations, but he had taken the crucial step of releasing, even if only for a month or two, something vital in him that was soon to become his scientific imagination—a realm in which both sides of his nature were to find free play in a fertile cooperation.

It is indeed remarkable how closely the "Project" already unites and expresses the two opposite sides of Freud's nature, the conservative and the freely imaginative. It was doubtless that combination, once effected, that gave such a powerful urge to its composition. Its relative sterility is to be explained by its divorce from clinical data. He had yet to find more fruitful outlets, which only the courage to explore emotional experiences could provide.

After such a long preamble it is time to consider what is contained in this "Project." Unfortunately it is not only highly abstruse but is already so condensed that any synopsis of it would be totally unintelligible. I must therefore content myself with some general remarks and with providing a list of the topics dealt with, most of which—though not all—Freud expanded in his later writings.

The essay itself had no title, though Freud had spoken of a monograph to be called "Psychology for Neurologists." The editors of the *Anfänge* decided to label it *"Entwurf einer Psychologie,"* (Project for a Scientific Psychology).

What is available to us is divided into three parts: (1) General Plan; (2) Psychopathology, particularly of hysteria; (3) Attempt to represent normal psychical processes.

The General Plan is introduced by a statement that the aim of the "Project" is to furnish a psychology which shall be a natural science. This Freud defines as one representing psychical processes as quantitatively determinate states of material elements which can be specified. It contains two main ideas: (1) to conceive in terms of Quantity, which is subject to the general laws of motion, whatever distinguishes activity from rest; (2) to regard the neurones[u] as the material elements in question.

Freud's aim was therefore to combine into a single whole two distinct theories. One was the neurone theory derived from his neurohistological studies. The other dated farther back to the Helmholtz-Brücke school, although it must have been powerfully reinforced by Meynert and the other authors discussed above. It was to the effect that neurophysiology—and consequently psychology—was governed by the same laws as those of chemistry and physics.

The key word "Quantity" which is constantly employed in the "Project" may be nearly equated with the physiological expression, "sum of excitations," or the physical one, "energy." It is a concept probably derived from Breuer, and may be likened to the latter's "intracerebral tonic excitation," [50] to Meynert's "energy of nutritive attraction," [51] and also to Exner's "cell-tonus." [52]

Freud distinguished between two sources of Quantity: that derived from the outer world and that from within the body, a distinction he

[u] This word had been coined by Waldeyer only four years previously, but Freud had for several years before been familiar with the conception of a nerve cell, with its processes, as a distinct unit definitely marked off from its neighbors by what he here calls "contact barriers" (for which Sherrington in 1897 introduced the term "synapse"). See pp. 49, 50.

subsequently abandoned. Thus a neurone might either be "empty" or "filled with a given Quantity," a conception he replaced in *The Interpretation of Dreams* by the more psychological one of "cathected ideas." "Nervous excitation" was to be regarded as a Quantity that flowed, and this current might either be resisted or facilitated according to the state of the "contact barriers" between the different neurones.

The functioning of the nervous system, according to the "Project," was subject to two general and closely related principles. One was that of "inertia" (*Trägheit*), which stated that neurones tend to get rid of any Quantity they contained;[53] in later years it became the "pleasure-unpleasure principle." Freud maintained that this idea was born in his clinical observations of the psychoneuroses, from the notions of intensive ideas, of stimulation, substitution, discharge, and so on, and that he felt it legitimate to transfer it to the field of neuronic activity (which in its turn was to explain the working of mental processes). Reflex movement, where a sensory excitation is followed by a motor discharge, is the purest form of this principle in animals. Freud traced the neuronic reaction to an origin in the excitability of the surface layer of protoplasm.

This discharge may be called the primary function of the neuronic system; nothing matters but the discharge in any direction. A secondary function comes into play when paths of discharge are chosen that put an end to the stimulation—"Flight from excitation." But what really causes the mechanism to break down, so that it has to be modified, is its inability to deal with internal stimulation (from the body) in the simple way it can with external stimulation. Here both discharge and flight are impossible, and help can be obtained only by specific changes to be brought about in the outer world, e.g., getting food. For this purpose the neurones have to keep in readiness a certain reserve of Quantity, reducing it to nil being no longer feasible.

The other principle, that of "constancy," was more obviously derived from the domain of physics. It was one used extensively by both Breuer and Freud, although Breuer gave Freud the credit for perceiving its importance in the present connection.[54] They had defined it together in 1892 as follows: "The nervous system endeavors to keep constant something in its functional condition that may be described as the 'sum of excitation'." [55]

On the basis just described Freud was able to construct what James Strachey has truly called "a highly complicated and extraordi-

narily ingenious working model of the mind as a piece of neurological machinery," [56] one which Freud said "nearly worked by itself."

The first problem to arise was that of *memory*. How was it possible for neurones to be permanently altered from receiving an impression, and storing its traces, and yet to receive fresh ones in just
the same manner as before? This riddle Freud solved by postulating two classes of neurones, one for each purpose. One class, to which
he gave the designation ϕ, allowed a current of excitation to pass
through without effecting any change; this was specially concerned
with stimuli from the outer world and could be identified as the
nuclei of afferent nerves. The other, which were labeled ψ, retained
permanent traces of any stimulation affecting them; they were the
nerve cells of the brain proper. These latter are concerned principally with stimuli arising in the body itself, and Freud even specu-
lates—strangely enough—that the brain could have arisen from an
enormous complication of sympathetic ganglia.[v]

The correlation between two classes of neurones, easily permeable
and less permeable, on the one hand, and the phenomena of perception and memory on the other, was a fundamental feature of Freud's
theory, one which was retained later when expressed in psychological
language only. In the present context the variation in permeability
was supposed to reside in the contact barriers of the neurones (synapses), which would be different not only with different cells but
also with the various processes belonging to each neurone. It is a
conception he fully shared with Breuer, who may well have originated it; in his theoretical chapter Breuer had phrased it thus: "This
perceptual apparatus, including the cortical areas for the senses,
must be different from the organ that preserves and reproduces sensorial impressions as memory images. For the fundamental condition for the functioning of the perceptual apparatus is the swiftest
restitutio in statum quo ante; otherwise no further proper perception could occur. The condition for memory, on the contrary, is that
no such restitution takes place, but that every perception produces lasting changes. It is impossible for one and the same organ
to fulfill both of these contradictory conditions; the mirror of a reflective telescope cannot be at the same time a photographic
plate." [58] Breuer also followed Meynert, as did Freud, in ascribing
hallucinations to the reverse process, i.e., a stimulation of the perceptual apparatus emanating from the memory images.

[v] Soon after this Gaskell proved the contrary: namely, that these ganglia
arose in the central nervous system.[57]

Since no support for this distinction between two kinds of cells can be found in histology, Freud threw out the suggestion that permeability and impermeability depended not on the type of cell but on the Quantity emanating from two different sources; with the ϕ neurones from the outer world, with the ψ neurones from the cells of the body (plus perceptual stimuli passed on to them through ϕ). There is every reason to suppose that the strength of the former stimuli is much greater than that of the latter, so much so that Freud presumed that the arrangement of the peripheral nerve endings act as a screen (an idea he was to elaborate later in his psychology proper); nevertheless they easily overcome the resistance at the ϕ contact barriers. He thus associates his distinction with the fundamental biological functions of the nervous system, of dealing with the stimuli of the outer world and of the body respectively.

There was one thing that could dislocate all the machinery—bodily pain; no contact barriers could hold up painful stimuli. Flight from pain is therefore a primordial tendency of the nervous system, and the memory itself of the object that had evoked the pain causes unpleasure (*Unlust*). This conception of the breaking of barriers Freud later linked both with the importance of the part played in psychopathology by trauma and also with the theory of fright and the warning signals of anxiety.

The problem of consciousness naturally gave great difficulty, since in addition to the physical laws governing variations in Quantity a new factor, Quality, enters. Freud therefore introduced a third set of neurones, which he labeled ω, intermediate between ϕ and ψ, the function of which was somehow to transform Quantity into Quality; the other two operated only in terms of the former (ω). Freud saw consciousness neither as a mere appendage of the physiological-psychical processes nor as the subjective aspect of *all* psychical processes, but as the subjective aspect of a *part* of them, namely, the perceptual processes (ω), so that the apparatus is different when consciousness is absent inasmuch as then no contribution is being made from the ω neurones. Nevertheless, the mechanism seemed to creak a little at that point. Freud had to introduce a third dimension into his measurements, that of time: he terms it a "Period."

We meet here the familiar conception that unpleasure (*Unlust*) signifies a heightening of the level of Quantity, pleasure its discharge. It is the basis of the pleasure-unpleasure principle.

It was remarked earlier that the ψ neurones received stimuli from two sources, from ϕ neurones and from the interior of the body.

Freud accordingly postulated two sets of neurones: "mantle" neurones[w] and "nuclear" neurones respectively. It is stimulation of the latter by instinctual processes that manifests itself as the *Will*, and supplies the motive power for the whole machine. This necessitates some action in the outer world. With the infant it means crying for help from another person, a complicated method of getting the inner tension discharged. Here Freud added an illuminating formula: "This path of discharge thus acquires the highly important secondary function of *establishing human contact*, and it is the early helplessness of human beings that provides the *original source of all moral motives*." [60] It anticipates his later account of the part played by human relationships in the transition from the pleasure to the reality principle.

The *ego* is described as an organization of neurones charged with a constant reserve of Quantity, with fairly free communication between themselves. An essential function of it is its capacity to inhibit incoming excitation; this is accomplished through part being diverted to what Freud called "side cathexes," i.e., charged neurones connected through simultaneity with the first neurone stimulated; they are always available.

We come next to a theme of the utmost importance, the distinction Freud established between what he called "primary processes" and "secondary processes." It was perhaps his most fundamental contribution to psychology, one which he defined and extended on several occasions. The only feature he considers in the present context, however, is the difference in the flow of discharge with the two processes. The working of the apparatus can suffer in two ways. With a wish clamoring for satisfaction the excitation may, after stimulating the memory image of the satisfying object, revert to ω, evoking an hallucination that is biologically futile; an indication is needed to distinguish between this and the perception of the real object. A criterion of reality is similarly needed in the second case, that of a "hostile" memory associated with unpleasure; when it is present a defensive flight can occur, whereas otherwise the excitation would evoke the full amount of unpleasure.

The criterion of reality[x] is afforded by the inhibiting powers of the ego. The stimuli proceeding from within the body can stir the qualitative difference characteristically associated with external real-

---

[w] A concept derived from Meynert.[59] "Pallium" was the more usual word.

[x] In his various writings Freud used the word "reality" in several different senses.[61]

ity only if they are strong; when subject to the inhibition exercised by the ego they cannot. ϕ excitation (from external stimuli), on the other hand, can provoke the qualitative difference, however weak it may be. What actually gives the ψ neurones the information that a stimulus from the "real" outer world is operative is an excitation from the (motor) discharging mechanism which always then comes into play to some extent; even with thought there is some slight involuntary action of the muscles concerned with speech.

In a word, therefore, the "primary process" is an uninhibited one, with a freely flowing current; the "secondary process," distinguishing between an external and an internal stimulus, is an inhibiting one, the level of whose Quantity is therefore lower. The distinction between "free mobile" energy and "tonic, bound" energy Freud ascribed to Breuer, and he expressed the opinion that it represents our deepest insight into the nature of nervous energy.[62] Incidentally, it may be remarked that this nomenclature is the reverse of the one used in physics, where kinetic energy is "free" as contrasted with potential energy.[63]

Taking the search for satisfaction, "wish-fulfillment," as the fundamental motive power of the machine, Freud analyzed in physiological terms what may be supposed to happen in and between the various neuronic systems during the processes of *judging, recognizing, distinguishing, remembering, and thinking,* all of which are complicated methods of conducting the search. Freud asserted indeed that the search, when wishes arise, is the biological justification of every process of thought.[64]

The beginnings of the theory of dreams that the "Project" contains have been mentioned in the chapter on that topic. It was perhaps in that field that Freud had found the purest example of the "primary process"; during sleep the diminution of bodily needs makes the secondary function of the ego superfluous.

In the *Second Section,* on psychopathology, Freud distinguished between a "primary defense" against pain, on the one hand, and, on the other, "repression," which is an exclusion from consciousness—or, as he says, more strictly an exclusion from the processes of thought—of an idea which would cause unpleasure in the ego; provided always that the idea in question takes its origin in a sexual impulse. The peculiarity of the latter feature is that so often with it the release of affect occurs in connection with the memory rather than with the sexual event itself. Freud attributed this to the lateness of puberty, an explanation that became inadequate after his discovery of infantile sexuality. The enigma of repression, however, was not fully solved. But the conclusion that affects hinder thought—which can only operate with small "testing" amounts of Quantity—by facilitating the passage of "primary processes" remains valid.

In the *Third Section* Freud applied the general principles mentioned above to the working of the normal mind as a whole. This section is so technical, complicated, and closely thought out that it would need a special treatise adequately to expound it. It is mostly concerned with the changes in cathexis, and the flow of energy from one set of neurones to another that is supposed to take place during different kinds of thinking—observing, recognizing, judging, discriminating, "practical" thinking, reflective thinking; and also with the various kinds of errors in the processes of thought.

A prominent idea is that of *Attention*. Freud described how the ego neurones respond to an external stimulus not simply passively, but by actively directing a charge of energy to the ω neurones. This happens particularly when consciousness is present. He thought it easier to explain biologically than mechanically, though he endeavored to do this also. It is a theme that plays little part in his later writings. Nevertheless he here establishes as one of his two "biological laws"—the other is the primary defense against pain—the cathecting by the ego of any perceptual element that has the indication of reality (*Realitätszeichen*), i.e., one signifying a source in the outer world.

Great importance is attached to *Speech Associations*. They have two special features: they are limited in number, and they are exclusive or peculiar. Their motor aspects are valuable in affording one of the tests of reality, and also in furthering the processes of memory. In his later writings speech is regarded as an attribute distinguishing the preconscious from the unconscious proper.

Speech also plays an important part in the early stages of development in the relations with the human environment. Here the inevitable frustrations are the main stimulus to the sense of reality, of the outer world, and the act of crying is the first attempt to replace the original relief through hallucinatory imagination by the circuitous route of bringing about changes in the outer world.

Freud found the origin of the *ego* the most obscure problem of all. He explained it by a particular interaction between the nuclear neurones (those fed by somatic stimuli) and the process of satisfying a desire. When this occurs associations are forged in the "ego" with the perceptual image of the satisfying object on the one hand and on the other hand the information derived from the motor activity that brought that object within reach. This primitive ego has to learn through experience, however, not to cathect these images of movement before certain conditions are fulfilled in respect of the perception, i.e., before tests of reality have been applied. Nor, moreover, must it allow the wish-idea to be cathected beyond a certain degree, lest it regress to the original hallucinatory fulfillment. If it commits either of these mistakes, no satisfaction of a real kind will be attained, and the situation will become one of unpleasure (*Un-lust*). This is the threat that leads to the growth and development of the ego: "Unpleasure remains the sole means of education." [65]

The list of topics dealt with in the "Project" is as follows. All except the last three were developed further in Freud's later writings, often thirty years later.

Principles of Inertia and Constancy
Primary and Secondary Processes
Unconscious and Preconscious
Urge towards Wish-Fulfillment
Hallucinatory and real fulfillment of Wishes
Criteria of Reality
Inhibitory function of the ego—Mobile and bound energy
Separation of function between perception and memory
Relation of Memory to contact barriers and facilitations
Three conditions for the arising of consciousness
Significance of Speech
Thought as experimental small-scale action
Traumas and pain as excessive stimuli
Protective screen against them and concentration of cathexes to deal with irruptions
No screen against internal stimuli
Signals of unpleasure instead of full doses
Dreams: wishful, hallucinatory, regressive, distorted—No motility during sleep
Parallelism of dreams and neurotic symptoms
Importance of sexuality in neuroses
Hysteria: defense, repression, displacement, distortion
Significance of Attention
Analysis of intellectual processes, including logical errors, etc.
Connection between repression and retardation of puberty

It does not pertain to a biography, but I would throw out the suggestion that an interesting study could be made of a comparison and contrast of Freud's sketch of cerebral physiology sixty years ago, one he discarded as worthless, with the recent electronic theories of cerebral functioning as expounded by Hebb,[66] Lashley,[67] Benfield and Rasmussen,[68] Wisdom,[69] Wiener,[70] Young,[71] and others. Freud's conceptions of "unpleasure" producing neuronic disorder, the order being restored by pleasure, of the significance of varying electrical resistances at the synapses, the nature of memory traces, his views on the association areas, etc., would seem to be of special interest in this connection.

We have told earlier how Freud soon cast aside this remarkable production as a thing of no value, of which he was almost ashamed. It is not the least curious feature of the story. His revulsion in attitude, from elation to depreciation, did not proceed, as one might have supposed, from insight into the inherent incompatibility of the double task he had attempted to perform. On the contrary, he continued for more than a year longer to bring emendations to his theory in the same terms of brain anatomy and physiology. It was not that he had appreciated the impossibility of the task, merely that he was dissatisfied with his endeavor to carry it out.

One cannot, however, be quite sure on this point. As we saw earlier in connection with his seduction theory, Freud had a way of rather obstinately persisting with an idea even when he was uneasily half aware of being on a wrong track. To have to retrace one's steps is never pleasant. So perhaps, after all, the alternative explanation of dawning insight may be the correct one.

However that may be, we have in a letter to Fliess of January 1, 1896, the continuation of the same train of thought in physiological terminology. There he made several emendations to the earlier exposition which to some extent simplified it. Perhaps the most important was the doctrine that the Quantity reaching the neurones is derived from one source only, the internal organs; they are powerless to excite the ω neurones. Stimuli reaching the brain from the sense organs do not increase the Quantity in the neurones; they merely excite them. They convey, however, their qualitative attribute to the ω section of the ψ neurones, and in this way evoke consciousness. This simplification might seem to make the concept of special φ neurones superfluous. Yet it was retained as follows. They receive the stimulation from the sense organs and pass on to the ω neurones the qualitative element; these in their turn stimulate the ψ neurones without passing on to them either Quantity or Quality.

The ψ neurones do not in themselves involve consciousness until they have become connected with speech associations.

The reversal of the excitation in hallucinations is no longer towards the ψ neurones, only to the ω neurones.

He now traced the arising of unpleasure to a conflict between the Quantity in the ψ neurones derived from internal organs (including sexual energy) and the processes of consciousness. In other words, he had perceived that mental conflict and suffering emanate essentially from man's difficulty in coping with his bodily needs and impulses, predominantly the sexual ones.

In a letter of December 6, 1896, Freud showed he had made further progress in some important respects. The most novel feature here was the conception of memory traces not being deposited once and for all, but undergoing several rearrangements as time goes on. He had in his book on Aphasia made a similar suggestion concerning the incoming pathways from the periphery, a point he cites in his letter.

He maintained his view that no memory trace is left in the ω neurones, those associated with consciousness, so that memory and consciousness are "mutually exclusive." The first trace is laid down (evidently in the "primary process") according to the association law of simultaneity. The second transcription, formed in accord with causal connections, is also in the unconscious, like the last one inaccessible to consciousness; it corresponds to conceptual thinking. The third, bound up with verbal imagery, belongs to the preconscious system.ʸ The secondary thinking consciousness probably depends on an hallucinatory reanimation of the verbal images, so that once again one sees that consciousness is bound up with the perceptual ω neurones which themselves contain no memory traces.

Freud added that were he only able to furnish a complete account of the psychological characteristics of perception, and the three sets of memory traces, he would be in a position to construct a new psychology.

He then made the interesting suggestion, one he hardly followed up, that the three sets of traces are laid down in different periods of life.

There is a normal defense against the release of unpleasure (Unlust) in each of these three phases. Pathological repression, however,

ʸ An early exposition of this conception.

is different. That signifies the blocking of the transition of the memory trace from one phase to the next, and this is invariably due to the avoidance of the unpleasure that such a transcription would evoke. It is not, however, a mere question of the *amount* of unpleasure that decides this: it happens only when the awakening of a memory evokes *fresh* unpleasure, not simply the recall of an old one. This state of affairs is peculiar to certain unpleasant sexual experiences, so only sexual impulses are capable of undergoing repression.

One easily sees that, in spite of the neuronic systems being still evoked in the descriptions, Freud was now rapidly moving into the field of pure psychology. It is, in fact, the last we ever hear of brain physiology.

There is a later echo in a letter of September 22, 1898, when he wrote: "I have no inclination at all to keep the domain of the psychological floating, as it were, in the air, without any organic foundation. But I have no knowledge, neither theoretically nor therapeutically, beyond that conviction, so I have to conduct myself as if I had only the psychological before me." He never moved from this position. In 1905, for instance, he wrote: "To avoid any misunderstanding I would add that I am not attempting to proclaim cells and fibers, or the systems of neurones that nowadays have taken their place, as psychical paths, although it should be possible to represent such paths by organic elements of the neurone system in ways that cannot yet be suggested." [72] And, again, in 1917: "Psychoanalysis hopes to discover the common ground on which the coming together of bodily and mental disturbances will become intelligible. To do so it must keep free of any alien preconceptions of an anatomical, chemical or physiological nature, and work throughout with purely psychological auxiliary hypotheses." [73]

We come finally to Freud's published account of his theory of the mind. It is contained in the seventh chapter of *The Interpretation of Dreams*, which served ever after as the basis for subsequent extensions and modifications of his views.

Freud employed here a working model of the mind very similar to the one he had in the "Project" and also a good many of the same fundamental conceptions, but the physiological terminology has almost entirely disappeared. In comparison with the Project it is both simpler and more lucid; one reason for this is that he was writing for a wider and less informed audience.

Freud had of course gathered his knowledge of practical psychology almost entirely from his clinical experience, and it had long been his ambition to make use of it in formulating a theoretical psychology. It must, therefore, have been very hard for him to renounce this cherished plan in favor of one based on his recently acquired knowledge of dream processes, and yet if he was to make his book on dreams complete there were cogent reasons why he should make that decision. For a while he played with the idea of combining the two sources of knowledge, and presumably it was his sense of artistic congruity that impelled him to make *The Interpretation of Dreams* a book on dream life alone. From that point of view he was undoubtedly right, but we have suffered thereby in being offered a less comprehensive statement. He himself insisted that the view of the mind he there presents is necessarily a partial one, which needed amplifying by studies based on other data than those of dreams alone.

In what follows here the general psychological principles will be abstracted from the application of them to the special problems of dream psychology, with which the chapter in Freud's book is primarily concerned.

Of psychological dicta in Freud's writings preceding *The Interpretation of Dreams,* two in particular deserve to be singled out, both dating from 1894. One is the regulating Principle of Constancy,[z] to which he always adhered.[74] It was evidently derived from Helmholtz's principle of the conservation of energy, according to which the sum of forces remains constant in every isolated system. Freud's own definition of it was given earlier in this chapter.[aa] He seems to have felt some proprietary rights in the idea of its being applicable to the nervous system, since he relates in a letter of November 29, 1895, being annoyed at its being appropriated by Heinrich Sachs.[75, bb]

The other is one of his only too rare definitions: "There is to be differentiated in psychical functions something (an amount of affect, a sum of excitations) which has all the attributes of a Quantity—although we possess no means of measuring it—something capable of being increased, diminished, displaced, or discharged, and which extends itself over the memory traces of ideas, rather as an electric charge does over the surface of bodies." [76] The two words in brackets indicate that the property in question can be described either in psychological (*Affektbetrag*) or in physiological (*Erregungssumme*)

[z] See pp. 234, 386.
[aa] See p. 385.
[bb] See p. 234.

terms. The conception that it has a certain autonomy, that it can be "displaced" from one idea to another, was a momentous one and one alien to the psychology of the time; the idea of the affect being independent and detachable differentiated it sharply from the old conception of "affective tone." [77] It was a pure gain from the realm of psychopathology.

It is generally held that Freud's greatest contribution to science, the one usually associated with *The Interpretation of Dreams*, was his conception of an *unconscious mind*. It was certainly one of the two that provoked the strongest opposition; the other was of course his libido theory. Two comments are in place here. It is interesting to remember that the idea of unconscious mental processes was much more widely accepted in the last twenty years of the nineteenth century than in the first twenty of the present one, when it was met with a spate of incredulity and ridicule. A couple of examples may be quoted. In 1885 Sir Samuel Wilkes, a distinguished London physician who was later President of the Royal College of Physicians, in reviewing a book by Hack Tuke, agreed that the author shows "that consciousness is not an essential element in all our mental acts," and added, "It is now generally admitted that the higher centers of the brain (i.e., the mind) may be in full operation without consciousness being called up." [78] The other is from Theodor Lipps, Professor of Psychology in Munich, a man whose writings Freud much admired. The following passage Freud had underlined in his copy of a book of Lipps, which he read in 1898 (August 31): "We maintain not merely the existence of unconscious mental processes besides the conscious ones. We postulate further that unconscious processes are the basis of conscious ones and accompany them. Conscious processes rise out of the unconscious when conditions are favorable, and then sink back again into the unconscious." [79]

One would conclude from this observation that the change after 1900 from easy acceptance to bitter opposition was not so much, as it appeared to be, to the idea itself of an unconscious mind as to its content which Freud had revealed.

In the second place, careful students have perceived that Freud's revolutionary contribution to psychology was not so much his demonstrating the existence of an unconscious, and perhaps not even his exploration of its content, as his proposition that there are two fundamentally different kinds of mental processes, which he termed primary and secondary respectively, together with his description of them. The laws applicable to the two groups are so widely different that any description of the earlier one must call up a picture of the more bizarre types of insanity. There reigns in it a quite uninhibited flow towards the imaginary fulfillment of the wish that stirs it—the only thing that can. It is unchecked by any logical contradiction, any causal associations; it has no sense of either time or of external reality. Its goal is either to discharge the excitation through any motor exit, or, if that fails, to establish a perceptual—if necessary, an hallucinatory—identity with the remembered perception of a previous satisfaction.

In the secondary process there occur extensive inhibitions of that freely flowing energy; it is attached, "bound," and allowed to flow only after processes of thought have found a direction in which it is possible to find a "real" satisfaction of the wish through taking into account the facts of the outer world. "It is from the contrast between Reality and Wish-Fulfillment that our psychical life grows." [80]

This division of the mind has, of course, a physiological counterpart, one with which Freud was very familiar. It is that between the simple reflex on the one hand, where the movement of excitation from the sensory to the motor fibers is immediate and unchecked, and on the other hand the various complex reactions to stimuli which may or may not be followed by a motor response and in the course of which inhibition always plays a part. It is therefore not the division itself that is original, but Freud's detailed exploration and description of the two sets of processes, something that had never before been even attempted.[cc]

There is, it is true, a rough correlation between this differentiation in the nature of mental processes and the distinction between the unconscious and consciousness, but the latter is the broader conception and needs further description which will presently emerge.

A noteworthy remark of Freud's in this connection is that from certain points of view the contrast between "the ego" and "the repressed" is more instructive than that between consciousness and the unconscious.[81]

Many of the ideas expounded in *The Interpretation of Dreams* have already been considered, in another language, in the account given of the "Project." Some of them have simply to be translated. Thus, instead of a system of neurones we have psychical constellations, instead of the physical concept of Quantity we have a hypothetical "cathexis" of psychical energy, and the physical principle of inertia develops into the well-known pleasure-unpleasure (*Lust-Unlust*) principle.

cc For this the reader must be referred to Freud's own writings.

Freud still uses the word "Apparatus" and the model he provides is constructed on lines very similar to those of the physiological model. But here, in terms of psychical processes, the model comes to life.

The concept of reflex action is taken as prefigurate for all mental functioning, and in the model of the mind energy flows from its afferent entry towards its efferent exit. This "progressive" direction is, it is true, in certain circumstances replaced by a "regressive" one towards the entering sensations or perceptions.[dd] The "primary process" itself approximates to a simple reflex; the excitation proceeds unchecked towards the motor outflow.

As was explained when considering the "Project," Freud was always emphatic on the separation of perception and memory. In his plastic model he gave different places for the two. Memory traces are deposited beyond where perceptions enter, and—just as in the physiological description—have several transcriptions according to the type of association which the new idea has forged.[ee] They are all of them in themselves unconscious (or preconscious), although some of them can enter consciousness; so, as Freud somewhat elliptically asserts, "consciousness and memory are mutually exclusive."

Freud starts with what he maintains is the sole motive force for the whole apparatus, a *wish*. This he defines as "a current in the apparatus, issuing from unpleasure (*Unlust*) and arriving at pleasure (*Lust*)." [82] What gives rise to pleasure is the relief of tension achieved by its discharge, the carrying off of the current (of excitation). If we take hunger as a typical wish, then the first effect of the resulting mental excitation is the passage of a current from the sensory to the motor end of the apparatus, manifesting itself in inchoate purposeless movements (kicking, etc.). On its passage, however, it has touched a memory trace of a previous perception associated with satisfaction of the hunger, so when this persists and is not relieved by the movements the current "regresses" back through the memory traces and reanimates the perception itself of the previous satisfying experience. Freud calls this a "hallucinatory wish-fulfillment," an occurrence familiar in the psychoses and also highly characteristic of the processes of dream formation. Sooner or later, for obvious reasons, this in its turn fails to relieve the situation and the unpleasure (*Unlust*) persists. Something else is necessary.

We see now what Freud meant when he said that it is the vital

[dd] Freud seldom distinguishes between these and uses the word *Empfindung* indiscriminately.

[ee] See p. 387.

needs (*die Not des Lebens*) that bring about all mental development.[83] What has to happen is that the excitation must once more proceed in a progressive direction towards the further memory traces which this time have got grouped, no longer by simple associations of simultaneity or contiguity, but according to causal laws. We meet here the beginnings of the processes of thought. In the case chosen, the infant recognizes that it has to bring about a change in the outer world as the only means of really satisfying its needs. So it cries and the mother comes.

The "primary process," with which we began, is so in more senses than one; it is the most fundamental, and also the earliest in time. It is, in fact, infantile.

Freud used the term "regression" in three senses: (1) a *topical* sense, i.e., in reference to the first section of his model, (2), a *temporal*, signifying a casting back to older psychical formations, and (3) a *formal*, when primitive modes of expression replace the customary ones.[84]

The pleasure-unpleasure principle is fundamental in Freud's psychology. It automatically regulates all the processes of cathexis.[85] Freud relates, in a letter of October 9, 1899, when—*after* expounding his theory of mind which we are now considering—he read extensively works on psychology, how he enjoyed discovering a full account of the same principle in the writings of an English author.[86]

We come next to the *Secondary System* of psychical processes. It contains the later memory traces, causally associated, already mentioned. Two special features characterize it. It has the capacity of inhibiting the free uncontrolled flow distinctive of the "primary system," and so of "binding" its energy. Only when this has been achieved can it cathect the ideas concerned, giving them thus a certain "charge of energy." But it cannot fulfill the former function if the amount of unpleasure (*Unlust*) released is excessive. In that case it can only turn away, an action which is the prototype of "repression." Every effort is therefore used to prevent the release of unpleasure and thus ensure a dormant cathexis, probably with a rise in potential. For that purpose it employs signals, ideas that give warning of the neighborhood of unpleasant memories; this conception Freud developed much later in a fruitful manner in his *Hemmung, Symptom und Angst* (Inhibition, Symptom and Anxiety) (1926.)

The mechanical relations governing the flow of energy, therefore, are entirely different in the two systems.[87] Yet the aim, or function, of both is identical: the search for satisfaction of a wish or need.

Whereas, however, the primary system merely worked towards a "perceptual identity," reproduction of the recollected perception of the satisfying experience, the secondary system aims at an "identity in thought," i.e., reproduction of the effective action. The process of thought Freud conceived of as a probing procedure guided by the "purposive ideas" of satisfaction; no thinking is possible without such purposive ideas.[88] Small amounts of energy are sent in various directions until the "identity" is achieved. The amounts have to be small, not only so as to avoid wasteful expenditure, but in order to retain enough for the final purpose of motor discharge once the correct avenue for it has been found; this Freud refers to as the "principle of minimal expenditure of innervation." All thinking is no more than a complicated and circuitous path towards the goal of wishfulfillment.[89]

Evidently, in order to avoid the error of the primary system in confounding a reanimated perception with a real perception, the secondary system has to have some means of testing a perception so as to effect the distinction (*Realitätsprüfung*). This it does on much the same lines as described above in connection with the "Project."

We have mentioned Freud's distinctive idea of the autonomy of *affects*, one which broke away from the old association psychology. The intensity of ideas depends on the amount of affect with which they are invested. There are passages in Freud which are very suggestive of the James-Lange theory of the emotions,[90] giving a primacy to ideas over the secondary motor and secretory manifestations; if so, however, Freud's conception would have been independent of those authors.

The concept of *repression* is central in all Freud's writings, and the significance of it may certainly be counted as one of Freud's most important and original contributions. The facts he had elicited were clear enough. What gave him endless trouble was the theory. The special importance this had to him was its bearing on psychopathology, the possibility of normal repression differing from pathological repression, the choice of neurosis, and so on.

An early statement of Freud's on the matter was to the effect that an idea could be repressed only when it had little intensity.[91] So the ego has first to rob it of its affect, which gets transposed to other ideas or otherwise disposed of. Then, a year later, he says, in a letter of January 1, 1896, that repression occurs when a conflict between the impulses proceeding from the body and the psychical processes stirred by a conscious perception releases unpleasure (*Unlust*). Repression can occur at different levels of the mind, thus not only between the preconscious and the unconscious but within the preconscious itself. (Manuscript accompanying letter of May 25, 1897.)

All along he felt there was a special connection between repression and sexuality. He inferred that in the sexual life there must be an independent (specific) source for the release of unpleasure;[92] perhaps this was because of the characteristic way in which sexual pleasure can be turned into unpleasure (disgust, etc.). He then played a good deal with a comparison between male and female libido in this connection. First (in the manuscript mentioned above) he was inclined to think that what was repressed was the feminine element and that what men repress is the tendency to play a passive part in pederastia. He perhaps got this notion from Fliess, because a few months later he tells him he has not yet had the opportunity of testing either that hypothesis, which he ascribes to Fliess, or his own, which is the exact opposite, namely, that it is the masculine element which is repressed by the feminine. (October 15.) Only a month later, however, he announced that he had given up the latter notion. (November 14.) [These are ideas similar to the one Adler later put forward ("masculine protest") at the time of his seceding from Freud, and then Freud explained how they could not account for the analytical data.] Nevertheless, several years later he proclaimed very firmly that repression was possible only through a "reaction" (i.e., conflict) between two sexual urges. (August 7, 1901.) What remained permanently from this train of thought was the stress Freud always laid on the importance of bisexuality in intrapsychical conflicts.

The explanation Freud gave of the specific part that sexual impulses play in repression was the fact that the memory of unpleasant sexual experiences had the power of evoking *fresh* current unpleasure. (November 14, 1897.) This view, however, was largely based on his old idea that sexual traumas in infancy achieved significance only in puberty, the time when sexual emotions were supposed to arise for the first time.

We therefore have three stages in development. (1) The primary defense against pain or shock; (2) the later repression in which the preconscious ego turns away from whatever tends to evoke (sexual) unpleasure (*Unlust*); and (3) conscious disapproval of an impulse by an act of judgment.

As is well known, Freud divided the mind, in an imaginary topographical fashion, into the unconscious proper, the preconscious, and the conscious. In this one has to bear in mind that the more important dividing line was not between consciousness and the rest but between the unconscious and the other two. Whether a given process was conscious or not was much less important than whether it belonged to the primary system or the secondary; in the latter case it might or might not be conscious.

The "primary process," as defined above, constitutes the kernel of the unconscious proper, that distant province of the mind which Freud might fairly claim to have both discovered and explored. It has the distinctive feature of being inadmissible to consciousness (Breuer's *bewusstseinsunfähig*). So Freud maintained that "in what is psychically real there is more than one form of existence." [93] Further, "that the unconscious is the true psychical reality; in its inner nature it is just as unknown to us as is the reality of the outer world, and it is just as imperfectly communicated to us by the data of consciousness as is the outer world through the information reaching us from our sense organs." [94] Freud took care never to use the term *unterbewusst* (subconscious), which he regarded as misleading;[95] it suggests merely something that is slightly less conscious. On one early occasion, however, he used *subconscient* in French.[96]

The greater part of the mind—if one may use such an expression —is contained in what Freud termed the *preconscious*. This is not accompanied by consciousness and so corresponds with what previous writers had called the Unconscious or Subconscious. It is nearly equivalent to what is also called the ego, although this has "prolongations" into both the unconscious proper and consciousness. The important inhibiting function of the preconscious on the original free flow of energy has already been mentioned; it is the distinguishing mark of the Secondary System. There is therefore a sievelike barrier between the unconscious and the preconscious, and also one between the latter and consciousness; ideas can traverse these barriers only when certain conditions are fulfilled, the pleasure-unpleasure principle being again the regulating one. In a letter of December 22, 1897, Freud likened the barrier to the Russian censorship, an inefficient instrument of the Czarist regime for excluding contaminating ideas from the West, and the word has since been incorporated in psychoanalytical terminology. He had already used it in print the year before.[97]

Freud held that the preconscious possessed no qualitative attributes, only quantitative ones. In that it differed from consciousness, which derives qualities from three sources: (1) the release of either pleasure or unpleasure, (2) from association with speech memories, which have a quality of their own, and (3), more directly, from perceptions. No consciousness can exist without some quality. Freud could therefore define consciousness as "a sense organ for the perception of psychical qualities." [98] There are two ways in which conscious-ness may be brought into being: through a perceptual stimulus emanating from the outer world or through the evocation of pleas-ure or unpleasure from the preconscious. The rest of the mind may be regarded as an outer world from the point of view of conscious-ness; it perceives some of it, and may thus be likened to the primary perceptual process.

What now is the biological function of consciousness, one which seems to distinguish human from other animals? Freud did not, as some philosophers have done, regard consciousness as an epiphe-nomenon, or even as an index that a given mental process has been completed. His parallelism of consciousness and perception gave him a clue to the function of the former.[99] Just as perception at-tracts an act of *attention* which directs its path, and uses its qualita-tive attribute as a means of regulating the quantitative distribution of energy in the psychical apparatus, so does consciousness by the same means (attention plus quality) serve as a fine regulator of the various displacements of cathexis which may even run counter to the grosser automatism of the pleasure-unpleasure system. This sig-nifies the opportunity for a more stable control and guidance of the flow of mental processes, although, it is true, it partakes itself of an automatic nature.

At the point where we leave our subject for the time being, and corresponding with the turn of the century, it may fairly be asserted that Freud had attained full maturity in every sense. His intellec-tual development had been precocious, but the emotional side of his life, itself late in being aroused, had taken longer to achieve stability. After this moment of time, however, we shall encounter a very differ-ent being from the disturbed and distressed man who had had to fight his way through both inner and outer difficulties.

That he was always industrious, and indeed an unusually hard worker, engrossed to the full in his work, must be plain from what he accomplished, although only a small part of that has been recorded. That he was a close thinker will be manifest to any reader of the pres-ent chapter. But he had two far rarer qualities: a creative imagina-tion that, once it was released from the strict discipline of his scholas-tic upbringing, took him to the very confines of thought; and a superb courage which, when combined with his absolute integrity, enabled him to conquer the phantoms that lurk in depths where no human being before had dared venture.

Short Title Index

Anf. Marie Bonaparte, Anna Freud, Ernst Kris (eds.), *Aus den Anfängen der Psychoanalyse.* London: Imago, 1950. (English translation to be published in 1954 by Basic Books, Inc.)

Aph. Freud, *Zur Auffassung der Aphasien.* Vienna: Deuticke, 1891.

Auto. Freud, *An Autobiographical Study.* Translated by James Strachey. London: Hogarth, 1935.

Bf.(1). Siegfried and Suzanne Cassirer Bernfeld, "Freud's Early Childhood," *Bulletin of the Menninger Clinic,* VIII (July 1944), 107-15.

Bf.(2). Siegfried Bernfeld, "Freud's Earliest Theories and the School of Helmholtz," *The Psychoanalytic Quarterly,* XIII (July 1944), 341-62.

Bf.(3). Siegfried Bernfeld, "An Unknown Autobiographical Fragment by Freud," *The American Imago,* IV (Aug. 1946), 3-19.

Bf.(4). Siegfried Bernfeld, "Freud's Scientific Beginnings," *The American Imago,* VI (Sept. 1949), 163-96.

Bf.(5). Suzanne Cassirer Bernfeld, "Freud and Archaeology," *The American Imago,* VIII (June 1951), 107-28.

Bf.(6). Siegfried Bernfeld, "Sigmund Freud, M.D., 1882-1885," *International Journal of Psycho-Analysis,* XXXII (July 1951), 204-17.

Bf.(7). Siegfried and Suzanne Cassirer Bernfeld, "Freud's First Year in Practice, 1886-1887," *Bulletin of the Menninger Clinic,* XVI (March 1952), 37-49.

C.P. Freud, *Collected Papers.* 5 vols. London: Hogarth, 1924-1950.

G.C. Geheime Chronik. Secret Record kept by Sigmund Freud and Martha Bernays during their engagement.

G.S. Freud, *Gesammelte Schriften.* 12 vols. Vienna: Internationaler Psychoanalytischer Verlag, 1925-1934.

G.W. Freud, *Gesammelte Werke.* 18 vols. London: Imago, 1940-1952.

I.J. International Journal of Psycho-Analysis. London: Baillière, Tindall and Cox.

I.Z. Internationale Zeitschrift für Psychoanalyse. Vienna: Internationaler Psychoanalytischer Verlag.

M. Unpublished letters from Freud to Martha Bernays, later Martha Freud.

Studien. Breuer and Freud, *Studien über Hysterie.* Vienna: Deuticke, 1895.

Reference Notes

CHAPTER I

[1] G.W., XIV, 34.
[2] Information from Mrs. Lily Freud-Marlé, daughter of Moritz and Marie Freud.
[3] From the family Bible in the possession of Ernst Freud.
[4] Unpublished Fliess correspondence, Aug. 1, 1898.
[5] Data from Harry Freud, who possesses the marriage certificate.
[5†] Rachel Baker, *Sigmund Freud* (New York: Messner, 1952), p. 1.
[6] M., July 19, 1883.
[7] *Ibid.*, Jan. 1, 1884.
[8] Helen Walker Puner, *Freud: His Life and His Mind* (New York: Crown, 1949), p. 11.
[9] M., April 18, 1885.
[10] G.W., II/III, 143.
[11] M., Feb. 10, 1886.
[12] G.W., II/III, 488n.
[13] *Ibid.*, p. 342n.
[14] *Ibid.*, p. 198.
[15] *Ibid.*, p. 199.
[16] *Ibid.*, XII, 26.
[17] *Ibid.* II/III, 253.
[18] *Ibid.*, p. 201.
[19] *Anf.*, p. 236.
[20] *Ibid.*, p. 39.
[21] G.S., I, 472ff.
[22] Bf.(3).
[23] G.W., X, 172.
[24] *Ibid.*, XII, 307.
[25] *Ibid.*, II/III, 462.
[26] *Ibid.*, p. 221.
[27] *Ibid.*, X, 207.
[28] G.S., III, 164, 279.
[29] G.S., I, 474.
[30] Puner, *op. cit.*, p. 254.
[31] *Anf.*, p. 233.
[32] G.W., XII, 20.
[33] *Ibid.*, II/III, 204.
[34] *Ibid.*, p. 427.
[35] *Ibid.*, p. 487.
[36] *Ibid.*, IV, 245.
[37] *Ibid.*, p. 58.
[38] *Anf.*, pp. 236-37.
[38†] G.W., II/III, 589.
[39] G.W., IV, 58.
[39†] *Anf.*, p. 237.
[40] G.S., IV, 60n.
[41] G.W., II/III, 217; XIII, 167.
[42] *Anf.*, p. 233.
[43] *Ibid.*, p. 252.
[44] G.S., I, 474; *Anf.*, pp. 228, 234, 252, 304, 327.
[45] *Anf.*, p. 233.
[46] G.W., II/III, 447n.

CHAPTER II

[1] G.W., IV, 58.
[2] Anna Freud Bernays, "My Brother, Sigmund Freud," *American Mercury*, Nov. 1940.
[3] G.W., II/III, 178.
[4] *Ibid.*, p. 211.
[5] *Anf.*, p.
[6] F. Wittels, *Sigmund Freud: His Personality, His Teaching and His School* (New York: Dodd, Mead, 1924), p. 100.
[7] G.W., II/III, 221.

[8] *Ibid.*, p. 589.
[9] Bernays, *op. cit.*
[10] G.W., II/III, 203.
[11] M., Sept. 28, 1883.
[12] *Ibid.*, Jan. 25, 1885.
[13] G.W., II/III, 236.
[14] *Ibid.*, p. 178.
[15] Bernays, *op. cit.*
[16] Wittels, *op. cit.*, p. 60.
[17] Letter to Freud from his mother, July 5, 1886.
[18] Records of Sperl Gymnasium (Bernfeld).
[19] I.Z., XXVI (1941), 5.
[20] Bernays, *op. cit.*
[21] *Ibid.*
[22] G.W., II/III, 178.

[23] *Ibid.*, p. 211.
[24] M., Jan. 14, 1884.
[25] *Ibid.*, June 22, 1883.
[26] *Ibid.*
[27] Anf., p. 224.
[28] G.W., II/III, 328.
[29] *Ibid.*, p. 203.
[30] *Ibid.*
[31] *Ibid.*, p. 427.
[32] *Ibid.*, p. 447.
[33] *Ibid.*, p. 523.
[34] *Ibid.*, p. 450.
[35] *Ibid.*, IV, 245.
[36] *Bf.*(3).
[37] Anf., pp. 289, 299.
[38] G.S., I, 465.

CHAPTER III

[1] G.W., II/III, 281.
[2] *Ibid.*, XIV, 34.
[3] *Ibid.*, p. 290.
[4] F. Wittels, *Sigmund Freud: His Personality, His Teaching and His School* (New York: Dodd, Mead, 1924), p. 20.

[5] F. Wittels, *Freud and His Time* (New York: Liveright, 1931), p. 34.
[6] *Bf.*(4), p. 163.
[7] G.W., XIV, 461.
[8] *Ibid.*, II/III, 201.
[9] *Ibid.*, XIV, 290.

CHAPTER IV

[1] *Bf.*(5).
[2] *Bf.*(4), p. 166.
[3] *Bibliographie und Inhaltsangaben der wissenschaftlichen Arbeiten des Privatdozenten Dr. Sigmund Freud* (1897); reprinted, I.Z., XXV (1940), 69.
[4] Auto., p. 15.
[5] *Bf.*(4), p. 169.
[6] G.W., XIV, 290.
[7] *Ibid.*, II/III, 425.
[8] *Ibid.*, XIV, 290.
[9] *Bf.*(2) and (4).
[10] M., Oct. 28, 1883.

[11] G.W., XIV, 301.
[12] G. S. Brett, *A History of Psychology* (New York: Macmillan, 1921), III, 129.
[13] G.W., II/III, 217, 218.
[14] "Sigmund Freud's Leistungen auf dem Gebiet der organischen Neurologie," *Schweizerisches Archiv für Neurologie und Psychiatrie*, XXXVII (1936), 200.
[15] "Sigmund Freud as Neurologist," *Journal of Nervous and Mental Disease*, LXXXV (1937), 696.

[16] *Centralblatt für die mediz. Wissenschaften*, XVII (1879), 468.

[17] *Bf.(4)*, p. 187.

[18] *Anf.*, p. 21n.1.

[19] *Wiener medizinische Presse*, Nov. 2, 1879, p. 1403.*

[20] Carl Koller, *Wiener medizinische Wochenschrift*, 1935, p. 7.

[21] G.W., IV, 271.

[22] M., June 15, 1885.

[23] *Internationale Psychoanalytische Bibliothek*, XX (1926).

[24] G.W., II/III, 453.

CHAPTER V

[1] G.W., II/III, 479.

[2] *Ibid.*, p. 480.

[3] *Auto.*, p. 16.

[4] G.W., XIV, 290.

[5] Letter from Freud to Wittels, 1923.

[6] M., April 6, 1886.

[7] *Bf.(6)*, p. 208.

[9] M., Sept. 9, 1884.

[10] *Ibid.*, Aug. 5, 1882.

[11] *Bf.(6)*, p. 208.

[12] *Bf.(4)*, p. 180.

[13] G.W., II/III, 488.

[14] M., Aug. 15, 1882.

[15] *Ibid.*, Oct. 13, 1882.

[16] *Anf.*, p. 66.

[17] *Bf.(6)*, p. 210.

[18] M., April 17, 1883.

[19] G.W., II/III, 439.

[20] M., July 3 and 6, 1883.

[21] *Bf.(6)*, p. 213.

[22] M., Sept. 29, 1883.

[23] Personal communication from Dr. Alfred Winterstein.

[24] M., Jan. 12, 1885.

[25] *Ibid.*, Dec. 12, 1884.

[26] *Ibid.*, Aug. 12, 1884.

[27] *Ibid.*, Aug. 31, 1884.

[28] *Auto.*, p. 20.

[29] M., Jan. 16, 1885.

[30] *Ibid.*, Jan. 17, 1885.

[31] *Bf.(6)*.

[32] M., June 26, 1885.

[33] *Ibid.*, Feb. 22, 1885.

[34] *Ibid.*, March 7, 1885.

[35] *Ibid.*, March 16, 1885.

[36] *Ibid.*, April 4, 1883.

[37] *Ibid.*, June 8, 1885.

[38] *Ibid.*, June 23, 1885.

CHAPTER VI

[1] *Auto.*, pp. 24, 25.

[2] G.W., II/III, 176.

[3] Letter to Wittels, Dec. 12, 1923.

[4] M., June 19, 1884.

[5] *Ibid.*, June 12, 1885.

[6] *Ibid.*, July 16, 1883.

[7] Theodor Aschenbrandt, "Die physiologische Wirkung und die Bedeutung des Cocains," *Deutsche medizinische Wochenschrift*, Dec. 12, 1883.

[8] M., May 3, 1884.

[9] *Ibid.*, May 7, 1884.

[10] *Ibid.*, May 25, 1884.

[11] G.W., II/III, 181.

[12] Hanns Sachs, *Freud, Master and Friend* (Cambridge, Mass.: Harvard University, 1944), p. 71.

* The report in the *Wiener medizinische Wochenschrift*, 1879, p 1133, does not mention Freud, but has an allusion in another connection to a certain M. Freund which has misled some research students.

[12+] G.W., II/III, 176.
[13] M., April 6, 1885.
[14] G.W., II/III, 176.
[15] C. Koller, "Nachträgliche Bemerkungen über die ersten Anfänge der Lokalanaesthesie," Wiener medizinische Wochenschrift, 1935, p. 7.
[16] M., April 4, 1885.
[17] Ibid., Oct. 10, 1884.
[18] Ibid., Oct. 18, 1884.
[19] Letter to Minna Bernays, Oct. 29, 1884.
[20] M., June 27, 1882.
[21] Ibid., Jan. 27, 1886.
[22] Ibid., Jan. 9 and Feb. 13, 1885.
[23] Ibid., May 19, 1885.
[24] Ibid., July 9, 1885.
[25] Wallé, Deutsche medizinische Zeitung, 1885, No. 3.
[26] Erlenmeyer, "Ueber Cocainsucht," Deutsche medizinische Zeitung, May, 1886; reprinted in Wiener medizinische Presse, July, 1886, pp. 918–21.
[27] Pp. 155–59.
[28] Internationale Klinische Rundschau, III (1888), 23.
[29] G.W., II/III, 116
[30] Freud, "Bemerkungen über Cocainsucht und Cocainfurcht," Wiener medizinische Wochenschrift, July 9, 1887, p. 929.
[31] M., Jan. 7, 1885.
[32] G.W., II/III, 120, 122.
[33] M., May 10, 1886; G.W., II/III, 245.
[34] G.W., II/III, 123.
[35] F. Wittels, Sigmund Freud: Der Mann, d. Lehre, d. Schule. (Vienna: Tal, 1923), p. 21.
[37] Letter to Wittels, Dec. 18, 1923.
[38] Private communication.
[39] G.W., II/III, 116.

CHAPTER VII

[1] Letter to James Putnam, July 8, 1915.
[2] M., Aug. 2, 1882.
[3] G.W., II/III, 651, 662.
[4] M., Aug. 26, 1882.
[5] Ibid., July 8, 1882.
[6] Ibid., June 17, 1883.
[7] Ibid., Aug. 7, 1883; July 5, 1885.
[8] G.C., Jan. 31, 1883.
[9] M., Dec., 1882.
[10] Ibid., Jan. 27, 1886.
[11] Ibid., July 11, 1882.
[12] Ibid., Aug. 18, 1882.
[13] Ibid., Aug. 5, 1883.
[14] Ibid., July 7, 1885.
[15] G.W., X, 317–18
[16] M., Jan. 6, 1886.
[17] Ibid., July 6, 1886.

CHAPTER VIII

[1] M., Oct. 29, 1883.
[2] Ibid., Aug. 4, 1882.
[3] Ibid., Aug. 18, 1882.
[4] Ibid., May 16, 1884.
[5] Ibid., April 19 and 21, 1886.
[6] Letter to Suzanne Bernfeld.
[7] M., May 3, 1886.
[8] Ibid., April 18, 1886.
[9] Letter from Frau Bernays, June 27, 1886.
[10] Private information from Arnold Marlé.

CHAPTER IX

[1] M., July 4, 1882.
[2] Ibid., Dec. 16, 1885.
[3] Ibid., Aug. 10, 1884.
[4] Bf.(5), p. 211.
[5] G.W., II/III, 400.
[6] M., Feb. 25, 1886.
[7] Ibid., Nov. 12, 1884.
[8] Ibid., July 11, 1885.
[9] Unpublished Fliess correspondence, Jan. 16, 1898.
[10] M., April 15, 1884.
[11] Ibid., Jan. 27, 1886.
[12] M., June 25, 1885.
[13] Ibid., Sept. 18 and 19, 1883.
[14] Ibid., June 6, 1883.
[15] Ibid., May 23, 1884.
[16] Auto., p. 15.
[17] M., April 25, 1885.
[18] Ibid., 1882.
[19] Lou Andreas-Salomé, *Lebensrückblick* (1951), p. 213.
[20] M., Aug. 17, 1884.
[21] Ibid., Sept. 4, 1883.
[22] Ibid., March 2, 1885.
[23] Ibid., Aug. 5, 1882.
[24] Ibid., Feb. 29, 1884.
[25] Ibid., Jan. 1, 1884.
[26] Ibid., Oct. 5, 1883.
[27] Ibid., Aug. 26, 1882.
[28] Ibid., July 26, 1883.
[29] Ibid., Nov. 5, 1883.
[30] Ibid., Aug. 16, 1882.
[31] Ibid., Dec. 16, 1883.
[32] Ibid., Oct. 13, 1885.
[33] G.W., II/III, 201.
[34] Ibid., p. 472.
[35] M., Oct. 15, 1885.
[36] Ibid., Oct. 21, 1885.
[37] Ibid., Feb. 23, 1886.
[38] Ibid., Aug. 1, 1885.
[39] Ibid., Jan. 27, 1886.
[40] Ibid., Dec. 5, 1885.
[41] Ibid., Aug. 29, 1883.
[42] Personal communication from Ernst Freud, who was told it by his father.
[43] In possession of Martin Freud.
[44] M., Sept. 9, 1883.
[45] Ibid., Nov. 10, 1883.
[46] Ibid., Oct. 6, 1883.
[47] G.W., II/III, 494; XV, 173.
[48] M., Oct. 31, 1883.
[49] Ibid., Feb. 2, 1886.

CHAPTER X

[1] M., May 7, 1883.
[2] Ibid., July 2, 1883.
[3] Ibid., June 17, 1883.
[4] Ibid., Sept. 19, 1883.
[5] G.W., II/III, 678.
[6] Auto., pp. 19, 20.
[7] S. E. Jelliffe, "Sigmund Freud as Neurologist," *Journal of Nervous and Mental Disease,* LXXXV (1937), 702.
[8] *Wiener medizinische Wochenschrift,* March 1884, Nos. 9 and 10.
[9] Ibid., Feb. 6, 1886, No. 6, pp. 168-72.
[10] M., Feb. 6, 1884.
[11] Ibid., Feb. 15, 1884.
[12] Ibid., Jan. 9, 1885.
[13] Ibid., Jan. 1, 1885.
[14] Ibid., April 29, 1884.
[15] Ibid., May 3, 1884.
[16] Ibid., Aug. 5, 1883.
[17] Ibid., May 16 and 29, 1884, and April 16, 1885.
[18] B. Sachs, "The False Claims of the Psychoanalyst—A Review

and a Protest," *American Journal of Psychiatry*, XII (1933), 728n.

19 F. Peterson, *Bulletin of the New York Academy of Medicine*, Nov., 1932.

20 M., July 2, 1883.

21 *Ibid.*, Aug. 23, 1883.

22 *Ibid.*, Oct. 12, 1883.

23 *Ibid.*, Feb. 10 and 29, 1884.

24 Pollack, *Lehrbuch der Farbentechnik des Nervensystems* (2nd ed., 1898).

25 Upson, *Journal of Nervous and Mental Disease*, XIII (1888), 685.

26 M., Oct. 28, 1883.

27 G.W., XI, 408.

28 *Monatsschrift für Ohrenheilkunde*, XV (1886), 247.

29 M., Jan. 28, 1884.

30 Freud and L. Darkschewitsch, "Ueber die Beziehung des Strickkörpers zum Hinterstrang und Hinterstrangskern nebst Bemerkungen über zwei Felder der Oblongata," *Neurologisches Centralblatt*, V (1886), 123.

31 M., Jan. 17 and 23, 1886.

32 *Auto.*, p. 18.

33 G.W., I, 28.

34 *Auto.*, p. 22.

35 M., Oct. 9 and 11, 1884.

36 *Auto.*, pp. 20, 21.

37 M., Dec. 9, 1885.

38 May, 1886, pp. 711, 755.

39 Personal communication.

40 G.W., X, 453.

41 F. N. Kassowitz, *Beiträge zur Kinderheilkunde* (Vienna: 1891), No. III, 155-57.

42 III (1879-80), 22-30.

43 M., Oct. 9, 1883.

44 *Ibid.*, May 17, 1885.

45 *Ibid.*, Nov. 28, 1885.

46 *Ibid.*, Jan. 27, 1886.

47 *Anf.*, pp. 60, 68.

48 *Aph.*, p. 68.

49 *Auto.*, p. 31.

50 Letter to Minna Bernays, July 13, 1891.

51 *Anf.*, p. 71.

52 Jelliffe, *op. cit.*, pp. 707-8.

53 *Fortschritte der Neurologie, Psychiatrie und ihrer Grenzgebiete*, XIX (July 1951), No. 7.

54 Pierre Marie, *Revue Neurologique*, I (1893), 643.

55 R. Brun, "Sigmund Freud's Leistungen auf dem Gebiet der organischen Neurologie," *Schweizerisches Archiv für Neurologie und Psychiatrie*, XXXVII (1936), 205.

56 G.W., I, 21.

57 *Ibid.*, p. 53.

CHAPTER XI

1 M., May 27, 1884.

2 J. Breuer, *Curriculum Vitae* (Vienna: Academie der Wissenschaften, 1923), p. 23 of reprint.

2+ H. H. Meyer, *Neue Oesterreichische Biographie* (1928), V, 30.

3 *Auto.*, p. 33.

4 M., Oct. 31, 1883.

5 *Ibid.*, Nov. 11, 1883.

6 *Ibid.* Aug. 5, 1883.

7 Letters from Martha Freud to her mother, Jan. 2 and May 31, 1887.

8 Double Memorial Number of the *Blätter des Jüdischen Frauenbundes für Frauenarbeit und Frauenbewegung*, XII (July-Aug. 1936), 1-4.

9 M., Nov. 19, 1882.

10 G.W., IV, 178.

11 *Auto.*, p. 25.

[12] Personal communication.

[13] G.W., II/III, 439.

[14] *Auto.*, p. 25.

[15] Pp. 1635-38.

[16] Pp. 1674-76.

[17] *Auto.*, p. 26.

[18] *Anf.*, p. 63.

[19] *Bf.*(7).

[20] T. Meynert, "Beitrag zum Verständnis der traumatischen Neurose," *Wiener klinische Wochenschrift*, June 14, 20, 27, 1889.

[21] Charcot, *Poliklinische Vorträge* (Vienna: 1892), p. 100.

[22] Meynert, *op. cit.*, p. 501n.

[23] *Anf.*, p. 85.

[24] *Ibid.*, p. 65.

[25] *Ibid.*, p. 68.

[26] Charcot, *op. cit.*, p. 268n.

[27] *Auto.*, p. 22.

[28] *Neurologisches Centralblatt*, 1895, p. 935.

[29] *Anf.*, p. 145.

[30] M., April 19, 1886.

[31] *Ibid.*, May 3, 1886.

[32] Letter from Martha Freud to her mother, Oct. 16, 1886.

[33] W. Erb, *Handbuch der Elektrotherapie* (1882).

[34] *Auto.*, p. 33.

[35] *Ibid.*, pp. 26, 27.

[36] G.W., X, 46.

[37] *Anf.*, p. 61.

[38] M., June 23, 1885.

[39] *Ibid.*, June 5, 1886.

[40] *Wiener medizinische Wochenschrift*, XXXIV (1889), p. 687.

[42] *Wiener medizinische Wochenschrift*, XXXIV (1889), 1098.

[43] M., Nov. 26, 1883.

[44] *Ibid.*, Jan. 2, 1884.

[45] *Ibid.*, May 3, 1886.

[46] *Auto.*, pp. 29, 30.

[47] 1888, p. 898.

[48] *Anf.*, pp. 61, 62.

[49] C.P., V.

[50] *Anf.*, p. 68.

[51] Charcot, *op. cit.*, p. 286n.

[52] *Auto.*, p. 32.

[53] C.P., V, Ch. 3.

[54] G.W., X, 60.

[55] Letter from Breuer to Fliess, July 5, 1895.

[56] Unpublished Fliess correspondence, Aug. 16, 1895.

[57] *Auto.*, p. 48.

[58] G.W., X, 60.

[59] G.S., IV, 421.

[60] *Studien*, p. 119.

[61] *Ibid.*, p. 50n.

[62] G.W., V, 17.

[63] *Ibid.*, II/III, 105.

[64] *Ibid.*, V, 5.

[65] *Studien*, p. 269.

[66] G.S., I, 397.

[67] *Ibid.*, p. 363.

[68] *Anf.*, p. 166.

[69] G.S., I, 460.

[70] G.W., XIII, 214.

[71] *Ibid.*, X, 57.

[71+] I.J., XXXII (1952), 489.

[72] Published in New York: 1858.

[73] *Ibid.*, XII, 312.

[74] L. Borne, *Sämtliche Werke* (1858), pp. 312-14.

[75] G.W., X, 54.

[76] *Ibid.*, p. 53.

[77] *Studien*, p. 87.

[78] Charcot, *op. cit.*, p. 224n.

[79] *Studien*, p. 104.

[80] G.W., X, 50.

[81] Wittels, *American Journal of Psychiatry*, 1944, p. 522.

[82] M., May 13, 1886.

[83] G.S., I, 414.

[84] G.W., XIV, 563.

[85] *Proceedings of the Society for Psychical Research*, June, 1893.

[86] *Anf.*, p. 73.

[87] *Studien*, pp. 57, 63, 155-60.

[88] C.P., V, Ch. 2.

[89] G.W., XVII, 5; *Anf.*, p. 71.

[90] *Wiener medizinische Presse*, Jan. 22 and 29, 1895.

[91] *Studien*, p. 5

[92] *Ibid.*, p. 184.
[93] Benedikt, *Hypnotismus und Suggestion* (Vienna: 1894), pp. 64-65.
[94] *Studien*, pp. 99, 105.
[95] 1896, pp. 401-14.
[96] "Hysteria in Relation to the Sexual Functions," *The Alienist and Neurologist*, XIX (1898), 599.
[97] *Auto.*, p. 40.
[98] *Münchner medizinische Wochenschrift*, June 2, 1896, p. 524.
[99] *Studien*, p. 174.
[100] *Ibid.*, p. 184.
[101] *Ibid.*, p. 215.
[102] *Ibid.*, p. 216.
[103] *Anf.*, p. 130.
[104] *Ibid.*, p. 144.
[105] *G.S.*, I, 364.
[106] Unpublished Fliess correspondence, Feb. 6, 1896.
[107] *Ibid.*, Feb. 13, 1896.
[108] *Ibid.*, March 29, 1897.
[109] *Ibid.*, May 20, 1900.
[110] Henry A. Bunker, "From Beard to Freud: A Brief History of the Concept of Neurasthenia," *Medical Review of Reviews*, XXXVI (1930), 108.
[112] *Anf.*, p. 75.
[113] *Ibid.*, pp. 95, 105.

[114] Charcot, *op. cit.*, p. 399n.
[115] *Anf.*, p. 101.
[116] *G.W.*, XIII, 229.
[117] *Anf.*, p. 75.
[118] *G.S.*, I, 325.
[119] *Ibid.*, p. 344.
[120] *Anf.*, pp. 89, 90.
[121] *Ibid.*, p. 103.
[122] *Ibid.*, p. 144.
[123] P. 237n.
[124] *G.W.*, XIV, 101.
[125] *G.S.*, V, 89-91.
[126] *Ibid.*, I, 332-33.
[127] *Anf.*, p. 104.
[128] *Ibid.*, p. 31.
[129] *Auto.*, p. 45.
[130] *Anf.*, p. 101.
[131] *G.S.*, I, 329.
[132] Ernest Jones, *Papers on Psycho-Analysis* (London: Baillière, Tindall and Cox, 4th ed., 1938), 426-27.
[133] IX, 662, 679, 696.
[134] *Anf.*, p. 136.
[135] *G.S.*, I, 414.
[136] *Ibid.*, p. 418.
[137] *Ibid.*, p. 419.
[138] *Ibid.*, p. 459.
[139] *Anf.*, p. 230n.1.
[140] *G.S.*, I, 365n.
[141] *Anf.*, p. 229.
[142] *G.W.*, X, 56.

CHAPTER XII

[1] *G.S.*, I, 435.
[2] *Studien*, p. 258.
[3] *G.W.*, II/III, 613.
[4] *Ibid.*, X, 60.
[5] *Anf.*, p. 62.
[6] *Ibid.*, p. 63.
[7] *Ibid.*
[8] *Studien*, p. 255.
[9] *Ibid.*, p. 268.
[10] *G.S.*, I, 15.
[11] *Studien*, pp. 190-191.
[12] *G.S.*, I, 17.

[13] *Studien*, p. 251.
[14] *G.S.*, I, 408.
[15] Unpublished Fliess correspondence, April 28, 1900.
[16] *G.W.*, X, 185.
[17] *Studien*, p. 204.
[18] *Ibid.*, p. 164.
[19] P. Moebius, "Über den Begriff der Hysterie," *Centralblatt für Nervenheilkunde und Psychiatrie*, 1888, No. 3.
[20] *Anf.*, p. 138.

[21] *Wiener klinische Rundschau,* IX, 697.

[22] Charcot, *Poliklinische Vorträge* (Vienna: 1892), p. 107n.

[23] *Studien,* pp. 229, 255.

[24] *Anf.,* pp. 97, 98.

[25] *Studien,* pp. 235, 250.

[26] *G.S.,* I. 400.

[27] *Studien,* p. 63.

[28] *G.S.,* I, 370.

[29] *Ibid.,* p. 372.

[30] *Jahrbücher für Psychiatrie,* 1896, p. 251.

[31] *Anf.,* p. 117.

[32] *G.S.,* I. 368.

[33] *Ibid.*

[34] T. Meynert, "Gehirn und Gesittung," *Sammlung von populär-wissenschaftlichen Vorträgen über den Bau und die Leistungen des Gehirns,* 1892, Abschnitt "Gehirn und Gesittung."

[35] *Ibid.,* pp. 117, 144, 169.

[36] J. F. Herbart, "Psychologie als Wissenschaft" (1824), p. 341, and "Lehrbuch zur Psychologie," *Sämtliche Werke,* 1806, Band V, p. 19.

[37] *G.W.,* VIII, 321.

CHAPTER XIII

[1] *M.,* March 19, 1886.

[2] *Anf.,* p. 69.

[3] Unpublished Fliess correspondence, April 27, 1898; *G.W.,* II/III, 441.

[4] *G.W.,* II/III, 452.

[5] Unpublished Fliess correspondence, May 21, 1894.

[6] *G.W.,* II/III, 490.

[7] *Anf.,* p. 228.

[8] *Ibid.,* p. 171.

[9] *G.W.,* IV, 159-160.

[10] "Freud's Dream Interpretation in the Light of His Letters to Fliess," *Bulletin of the Menninger Clinic,* Nov. 1951, p. 206.

[11] Pfenning, *Wilhelm Fliess und seine Nachentdecker* (Berlin: 1906).

[12] H. Swoboda, *Die gemeinnützige Forschung und der eigennützige Forscher* (Vienna: 1906).

[13] *G.W.,* V, 79.

[14] *Ibid.,* XIII, 47.

[15] *Ibid.,* p. 372.

[16] *Ibid.,* V, 42n.

[17] *Ibid.,* p. 65n.1.

CHAPTER XIV

[1] *International Journal of Psycho-Analysis,* XXXII (1951), 319.

[2] *M.,* Oct. 29, 1882.

[3] *Anf.,* p. 435.

[4] *Ibid.,* p. 246.

[5] Manuscript N, May 31, 1897.

[6] Loewenfeld, *Sexualleben und Nervenleiden,* 4th ed. (1906).

[7] *G.W.,* II/III, 136.

[8] *Ibid.,* p. 150n.

CHAPTER XV

[1] *Anf.,* p. 183.

[2] *Ibid.,* p. 436.

[3] *Ibid.,* p. 337.

[4] Letter from Minna Bernays to her sister, Aug. 7, 1898.

[5] Letter to Rosa, Aug. 5, 1892.

[6] G.W., II/III, 202-3.
[7] Unpublished Fliess correspondence, Aug. 29, 1894.
[8] Anf., p. 229.
[9] Ibid., p. 228.
[10] G.W., IV, 7.
[11] Unpublished Fliess correspondence, Sept. 14, 1900.
[12] I.Z., XXV (1940), 69.
[14] Freud, Master and Friend

(Cambridge, Mass.: Harvard University, 1944), p. 78.
[15] Communication from Dr. Ludwig Jekels.
[16] G.W., V, 11.
[17] M., Sept. 16, 1896.
[18] "Die Stellung Freud's in der modernen Geistesgeschichte," Die Psychoanalytische Bewegung, I (1929) 26.

CHAPTER XVI

[1] G.W., X, 60.
[2] Ibid., XIV, 20.
[3] M., June 30, 1882.
[4] Ibid., July 19, 1883.
[5] Ibid., March 29, 1884.
[6] Ibid., Nov. 11, 1884.
[7] Ibid., Jan. 13, 1886.
[8] G.W., II/III, 95, 139, 236; VI, 194.
[9] W. Griesinger, Pathologie und Therapie der psychischen Krankheiten (3rd ed., 1871), p. 111.
[10] Anf., p. 105.
[11] G.W., X, 57-58.
[12] Anf., pp. 419-26.
[13] G.W., II/III, 437, 440, 518.
[14] Ibid., p. 576n.
[15] "Josef Popper-Lynkeus und die Theorie des Traumes," G.W., XIII, 359; "Meine Berührung mit Josef Popper-Lynkeus,"

G.W., XVI, 261; F. Wittels, "Freud's Correlation with Josef Popper-Lynkeus," The Psychological Review, Oct. 1947.
[16] Anf., p. 346.
[17] Raimann, Die hysterische Geistesstörung (Vienna: 1904).
[18] Auto., p. 88; G.W., X, 61.
[19] Communication from Dr. Ludwig Jekels.
[20] Zeitschrift für Psychologie und Physiologie der Sinnesorgane, XXVI (1901), 133.
[21] Monatsschrift für Psychiatrie und Neurologie, 1901, p. 237.
[22] Unpublished Fliess correspondence, June 9, 1901.
[23] G.W., V, 284, 286.
[24] Ibid., X, 48.
[25] Ibid., V, 171.
[26] Anf., p. 349.

CHAPTER XVII

[1] Tageblatt der Versammlung Deutscher Naturforscher und Ärzte, 1881, p. 118.
[2] T. F. Herbart, Sämtliche Werke (Leipzig: 1886 ed.), V, 218.
[3] G.W., IV, 282.
[4] Ibid., XIII, 413.
[5] Brain, Vol. I (1879).

[6] Ibid., p. 306.
[7] Aph., pp. 56, 57.
[8] G.S., I, 298.
[9] Studien, p. 161.
[10] N. Wiener, Cybernetics (New York: Wiley, 1948); Hixon Symposium (L. A. Jeffress, ed.), Cerebral Mechanisms in Be-

havior (New York: Wiley, 1952).

¹¹ G.W., XIII, 405.

¹² Charcot, *Poliklinische Vorträge* (Vienna: 1892).

¹³ T. Lipps, *Grundtatsachen des Seelenlebens* (Munich: 1883); *Komik und Humor* (Munich: 1898).

¹⁴ W. Jerusalem, *Urteilsfunktion* (1895).

¹⁵ M. Dorer, *Historische Grundlagen der Psychoanalyse* (Leipzig: 1932).

¹⁶ "Ueber die psychologischen Grundlagen des Freudismus," *I.Z.*, II (1914), 305.

¹⁷ Herbart, *op. cit.*, II, 19.

¹⁸ *Ibid.*, V, 20.

¹⁹ G. T. Fechner, *Elemente der Psychophysik* (1860).

²⁰ *Principles of Psychology* (London: 1891), I, 334.

²¹ *Ibid.*, p. 549.

²² G.W., II/III, 80.

²³ G. A. Lindner, *Lehrbuch der empirischen Psychologie nach genetischer Methode* (1858), p. 63.

²⁴ Fechner, *op. cit.*, II, 521.

²⁵ G.W., XIV, 86.

²⁶ T. Meynert, *Sammlung von populär-wissenschaftlichen Vorträgen über den Bau und die Leistungen des Gehirns* (Vienna: 1892), "Das Zusammenwirken der Gehirnteile," p. 231; "Zur Mechanik des Gehirnbaus," pp. 11, 24ff.

²⁷ *Ibid.*, p. 223.

²⁸ *Ibid.*, p. 12ff.

²⁹ *Ibid.*, p. 229.

³⁰ *Ibid.*, p. 33.

³¹ *Ibid.*, p. 20.

³² W. Griesinger, *Pathologie und Therapie der psychischen Krankheiten* (2nd ed., 1867), p. 26ff.

³³ *Ibid.*, p. 6.

³⁴ *Ibid.*

³⁵ Dorer, *op. cit.*, p. 149.

³⁶ Ed. von Hartmann, *Philosophie des Unbewussten* (Vienna: 1869).

³⁷ Sigm. Exner, *Entwurf zu einer physiologischen Erklärung der psychischen Erscheinungen* (Vienna: 1894).

³⁸ *Ibid.*, Part I, p. 3.

³⁹ *Ibid.*, p. 50.

⁴⁰ *Ibid.*, p. 79.

⁴¹ *Ibid.*, p. 76.

⁴² *Ibid.*, pp. 366-67.

⁴³ E. von Fleischl-Marxow (O. von Fleischl-Marxow, ed.), *Gesammelte Abhandlungen* (Vienna: 1893).

⁴⁴ *Anf.*, p. 134.

⁴⁵ *Ibid.*, p. 136.

⁴⁶ *Ibid.*, p. 137.

⁴⁷ *Ibid.*, p. 143.

⁴⁸ *Ibid.*, p. 141.

⁴⁹ *Ibid.*, p. 145.

⁵⁰ *Studien*, pp. 167-73.

⁵¹ Meynert, *op. cit.*, p. 223.

⁵² Exner, *op. cit.*, p. 171.

⁵³ *Anf.*, p. 380.

⁵⁴ *Studien*, p. 171.

⁵⁵ C.P., V, 30.

⁵⁶ James Strachey, Introduction to Vol. IV of the Freud Standard Edition (London: Hogarth, 1953).

⁵⁷ W. H. Gaskell, *The Involuntary Nervous System* (1916), pp. 150-60.

⁵⁸ *Studien*, p. 164.

⁵⁹ *Aph.*, p. 47.

⁶⁰ *Anf.*, p. 402.

⁶¹ Hans Loewald, "Ego and Reality," *I.J.*, XXXII (1951), 10; Lajos Székely, "Die Realität in der Auffassung Freud's," *Theoria*, XVII (1951), 240.

⁶² G.W., X, 287.

⁶³ L. S. Penrose, *I.J.*, XII, 92.

⁶⁴ *Anf.*, p. 440.

[65] *Ibid.*, p. 450.
[66] D. O. Hebb, *The Organization of Behaviour* (New York: Wiley, 1949).
[67] K. S. Lashley, *Brain Mechanism and Intelligence* (Chicago: University of Chicago, 1929).
[68] W. Penfield and T. Rasmussen, *The Cerebral Cortex of Man* (New York: Macmillan, 1950).
[69] J. O. Wisdom, "The Hypothesis of Cybernetics," *The British Journal for the Philosophy of Science*, II (1951), 1.
[70] Wiener, *op. cit.*
[71] J. Z. Young, *Doubt and Certainty in Science* (New York: Oxford, 1951).
[72] *G.W.*, VI, 165.
[73] *Ibid.*, XI, 14.
[74] *Anf.*, p. 98.
[75] H. Sachs, *Vorträge über Bau und Tätigkeit des Grosshirns* (1895).
[76] *G.S.*, I, 305.
[77] J. H. Schultz, "Psychoanalyse; die Breuer-Freudschen Lehren, ihre Entwicklung und Aufnahme," *Zeitschrift für ange-wandte Psychologie*, II (1909), 442.
[78] S. Wilks, *Brain*, II (1885), 533.
[79] Lipps, *Grundtatsachen des Seelenlebens* (1883), p. 149.
[80] *Anf.*, p. 296.
[81] *G.W.*, XIII, 244.
[82] *Ibid.*, II/III, 604.
[83] *Ibid.*, p. 570.
[84] *Ibid.*, p. 554.
[85] *Ibid.*, p. 580.
[86] H. R. Marshall, *Pain, Pleasure and Aesthetics* (New York: 1894); *Aesthetic Principles* (New York: 1895).
[87] *G.W.*, II/III, 605.
[88] *Ibid.*, p. 533.
[89] *Ibid.*, p. 607.
[90] *Ibid.*, p. 588.
[91] *Studien*, p. 146.
[92] *Anf.*, p. 158.
[93] *G.W.*, II/III, 625.
[94] *Ibid.*, p. 617.
[95] *Ibid.*, p. 620.
[96] *G.S.*, I, 288.
[97] *Ibid.*, p. 386.
[98] *G.W.*, II/III, 620.
[99] *Ibid.*

Index

To avoid burdening the Index casual references to the main personages, e.g. Breuer, Fliess, etc., are not listed. When a name is not found on the page mentioned it will be found in the corresponding list of Reference Notes.